DATA COMMUNICATIONS: PRINCIPLES AND PROBLEMS

GEORGE J. MOSHOS

NEW JERSEY INSTITUTE OF TECHNOLOGY

DATA COMMUNICATIONS: PRINCIPLES AND PROBLEMS

WEST PUBLISHING COMPANY

ST. PAUL   NEW YORK   LOS ANGELES   SAN FRANCISCO

COPYRIGHT © 1989 by   WEST PUBLISHING CO.
50 W. Kellogg Boulevard
P.O. Box 64526
St. Paul, MN 55164-1003

96   95   94   93   92   91   90   89   8   7   6   5   4   3   2   1   0

Library of Congress Cataloging-in-Publication Data
Moshos, George J.
    Data communications: principles and problems/George J. Moshos. c. cm.
    Includes bibliographies and index.
    ISBN 0-314-48129-X
    1. Data transmission systems.   I. Title.
TK5105.M83   1989
621.38—dc19   88-28262
                                            CIP

INTERIOR DESIGN: Judith Getman
COMPOSITION: The Clarinda Company
COPYEDITOR: Janet Greenblatt
ARTWORK: Rolin Graphics

TO MY FIRST TEACHERS, JOHN AND MARY MOSHOS

PREFACE

One will not find in this book a rigorous theoretical treatment of data communications, for rigor was not my intent. My goal was to lay the foundation of data communications for structuring the communications in distributed systems and computer networks at a level suitable for an upper division undergraduate or first year graduate course. The challenge has been to present the principles through the system models, both mathematical and behavioral, so that the concepts could be intuitively understood and the terms definitively given; although the individual topics could not possibly be treated exhaustively. It is here that I felt persons being introduced into the field can best be served—they can obtain a working knowledge of the field and use the literature with an understanding of where it fits into the total field as well as in their own specialty areas.

Students drawn into this subject come from a wide variety of disciplines. Indeed at my university, as in other schools, computer science graduate students may come from disciplines other than computer science. Nevertheless, a limited proficiency in discrete mathematics, calculus, statistics and basic computer science studies is normally required before they can undertake their advanced studies. So in this academic environment it is not unusual to find the classroom filled with students whose backgrounds are as varied as the field itself.

To accomplish the goal which had been laid out, the wide range of mathematical and systems subjects that have been embodied into the field had to be addressed. It is almost mindboggling to think of the number of abstract sciences from which the field of data communications has developed. Although mathematics is in the mainstream of the engineering sciences, students who are unexposed to these topics find the degree of abstraction disconcerting. I have tried to remove these distractions by tailoring the presentation so as to presume the least amount of requisite mathematics.

ORGANIZATION

The book evolved from the compilation of notes I have used to teach data communications to first year graduate students. The topics have been organized into nine chapters. Other than the introductory chapter where data communications is presented from the point of view of an industrial complex, and introduces the players in the industries that offer and use the products and standards; the sequence of the remaining chapters may be reordered. I use the present sequence in the book to present the topics in my courses, but I intentionally kept these chapters loosely coupled so professors can reorganize the material in the order they prefer, adding whatever transition may be needed to make the subject flow smoothly.

Several appendices have been included from which additional topics may be pulled to supplement the material in the main body of the text. Optionally, the appendices may be left for self study. Exercises have been inserted after each section and at the end of each appendix in order to give the reader the opportunity to review the material just presented and also to append other concepts that are an immediate outgrowth of the material.

From the many excellent articles and books written on data communications, I have selected a few for suggested reading. Some are easier to read, others more difficult, but each gives a different perspective of the topic under discussion. I have not given a separate reference list. The reason for this is that many of the books in the suggested reading lists have a good compilation of reference material. Moreover, since this field is growing unabatedly, it should be continuously tracked through the latest publications (e.g., through the publications of the Computer Society of the IEEE, the Association for Computing Machinery, and the Society of Manufacturing Engineers).

ACKNOWLEDGEMENTS

It is now time to recognize those persons who helped and supported me during the production of this book, First, I would like to single out Dr. Richard W. Hamming and John Pustai with whom I had the pleasure of having personal discussions that have directed me to this field of study, and whose styles of presentation I have admired. Many thanks too, to the many, many students who have taken my course. I want to particularily thank them as well as Michael Slaughter for encouraging me to write this book, they will be pleased to see the exercises worked out. From the many others, my appreciation to the following persons who took time from their busy schedules to give their insights and who made many valuable suggestions to the manuscript:

Peter G. Anderson	*Rochester Institute of Technology*
William Doremus	*IIT Research Institute*
Johnson Hart	*Boston University*
Wayne Mathews	*Army Armament Research Development and Engineering Center*
Eugene Pinsky	*Boston University*
Ravi Sankar	*University of South Florida*
George Sheets	*Oklahoma State*
Evangelos Yfantis	*University of Nevada*
Tony Lui Yu	*California State University, San Bernardino*

Finally to complete this chain of indebtness, I gladly include my family partners; Evangeline, Victoria, and Elizabeth and James Buley, who joined together to make an arduous task pleasurable.

CONTENTS

CHAPTER 4
COMMUNICATION LINES

CHAPTER 5
CODING THEORY

CHAPTER 6
NODAL INTERFACING TECHNOLOGY   **141**

CHAPTER 7
DATA COMMUNICATION NETWORK ARCHITECTURE   **173**

DATA COMMUNICATIONS: PRINCIPLES AND PROBLEMS

CHAPTER 1

COMMUNICATIONS AND COMPUTERS

What we've got here is a failure to
communicate.
DONN PEARCE
COOL HAND LUKE

1

1.1 DATA COMMUNICATIONS IN DISTRIBUTED SYSTEMS

DISTRIBUTED SYSTEMS

From their inception, computing systems and communication systems shared a common technology, often giving the inchoate feeling that they are one and the same. Indeed, the distinction between distributed computer systems and computerized communication systems depends on one's viewpoint. Moreover, even the philosophical differences between these systems are less important now that the major marketing constraints imposed on the computer and communications companies have been removed, so that each can supply products or services in either field. The issues pertaining to these systems do not concern their differences so much as the principles that unify them, principles that allow the decentralization of information facilities.

More and more, the industrial community has shifted from centralized to decentralized information systems. This shift is not just a fluke, but rather a planned strategy put forth by the industrial community under the general umbrella of computer-integrated business (CIB) and computer-integrated manufacturing (CIM). These efforts dictate that system resources fabricated with modern technology serve best when physically distributed. (System resources include the equipment, application programs, program development facilities, data, and data-gathering sources.) More specifically, here are some reasons for distributing the system:

- Most data generated locally have only local significance and need not be transported and maintained in data bases already crowded with other, unrelated data.
- The integrity of the data resides where it is generated.
- Small cohesive processors can be managed directly by the users and do not require the services of in-house specialists or a tightly controlled operating environment.
- When an operational unit fails, it disrupts only the local operations, and the remaining system can continue to function independently.
- The best subsystem that can meet the specific requirements of an application can be selected from a competitive market, rather than a subsystem that conforms to the dictates of a rigidly defined centralized system.
- Obsolete processors can be replaced with more advanced technology without the cost of tailoring the products to an existing system.

Notwithstanding the advantages that can be realized by distributing the resources, the resources often have a utility that transcends their local environments to other remote areas. For example, an enterprise operating a computing facility might want to make the equipment, programs, and/or data accessible to users other than those located at the home site. Because the cost of computing equipment and communications has dramatically decreased in recent years, while programming and data gathering have remained labor intensive and have increased in cost, it is more economically feasible to use computer networks to deliver computer and data services to the users rather than to physically transport the users to the computer site.

The marriage of communications and computing into computer networks offers opportunities for new applications that cannot be realized by localizing all the facilities. Consider, for example, the possibilities that computer networks offer for electronic mail, banking, reservation systems, marketing, computer-aided education, computer-integrated manufacturing, and project management. In addition, computer networks enhance the reliability, availability, and maintainability of the resources by making it possible to test remotely located equipment and making the system configuration less susceptible to local disasters.

MAJOR COMMUNICATION PATHS IN AN ENTERPRISE

Perhaps the most singular prospect for industrial improvement is the opportunity that computer technology offers for automating the information flow in an enterprise. An enterprise may be of any size or complexity, from a single-purpose office to a multiple-plant conglomerate. It exists to accomplish a mission in its environment.

Normally, an enterprise must deal with both material (goods) flow and information flow, but the computer and communication system handle only those transactions associated with information flow. For example, an enterprise orders goods from a vendor and receives a confirmation of the order; eventually, an invoice arrives, which the enterprise pays accordingly, receiving a receipt. The information system must track the data associated with all of these activities. In the meantime, however, the goods arrive, are shelved, and are used; but the physical operations and procedures for handling these activities lie outside the scope of the computer and communication system.

An enterprise's need to communicate with the outside world stems from its very existance. Figure 1.1 depicts an external, macroscopic view of an enterprise as seen by the organizations to whom it provides services. The circle represents the organized functions and facilities that the enterprise uses to provide its services. Once created, an enterprise can be looked on as a data-driven, functional block sitting in a quasi-quiet state until it receives a stimulus in the form of a communication from some outside organization. After receiving a stimulus, the enterprise functions internally until it produces its planned response.

FIGURE 1.1 External view of an enterprise.

Figure 1.2 groups the internal functions of an enterprise, independent of whether they operate manually or by automation, into those that fall under the purview of the facility offices and those provided by the shop floor. The shop floor provides the information needed by the material handlers, production machinery, and their immediate interfaces. The facility offices provide the technical support for the plant; management control of the shop floor through scheduling, monitoring, tracking, and reporting of its operations; and communications with outside organizations. It might appear that this separation is arbitrary, but in fact, the facility offices and shop floor place different demands on the data and communications facilities:

- While all computerized functions might have a critical deadline, the shop floor supports real-time processes. A real-time process is a process that must complete its response within a critical deadline or else the results of its operations become moot. For example, payroll has a critical deadline, but failure to meet this deadline does not negate completing the payroll function. On the other hand, if a controller delays supplying data or responding to a numerical machine by the critical deadline, then the operations performed lose any significance they might have had and serve no purpose at this or any other time.

- The grade of communication services needed by the facility offices and shop floor differ to the extent that they require different forms of communications. The shop floor processes must be able to communicate on demand, while those in the facility offices require communication techniques whose timing is not critical to its operations, such as line switching or contending for the use of the transmission facilities when they are not otherwise in use.

- On the shop floor, one sees the emphasis on material flow. The information associated with material flow directs or follows the material flow so that the physical operations can be coordinated and managed.

- The data support for each application, although it can be quite massive has only temporal use in a local data base. The centralization of data from all the processes into a common data base assumes that all applications can be micromanaged from the same collection of data. Such an organization not only clouds the data base with unnecessary details, but also can deny the local processors immediate access to the information needed for meeting critical deadline obligations.

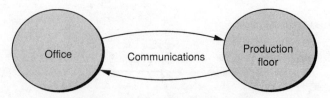

FIGURE 1.2 Internal view of an enterprise.

COMMUNICATION STRUCTURES IN AN ENTERPRISE

Figure 1.3 depicts the total information system of an enterprise as separated segments: the automated procedures of the facility offices, the automated production processes of the shop floor, and the manual operations used for decision making. The communication system integrates these activities by making the data accessible to any application that needs them in a timely and reliable manner, regardless of where the data reside in the industrial behemoth.

Different types of communication structures support the different applications an enterprise needs to perform its mission. For internal communications, one or more privately owned networks, called **local area networks (LANs),** serve to direct the communications between the devices that are distributed over a confined geographical area that does not extend outside the company's premises. LAN construction is characterized as a network typically serving the data devices on part or all of a factory shop floor or office building at data rates of 1 million to 100 million bits per second. One type of LAN serves the office facilities; another type serves the shop floor.

Long-haul, external communications make use of the **wide area networks (WANs)** available to the public from commercial vendors. These facilities reach out of the enterprise's private land base to other remote sites and transmit data at more modest rates, up to a few thousand bits per second.

Although WANs and LANs have different structures, they must be interconnected to integrate the data and processors supporting an enterprise, regardless of how they are distributed. Unless integrated, the operations would create isolated is-

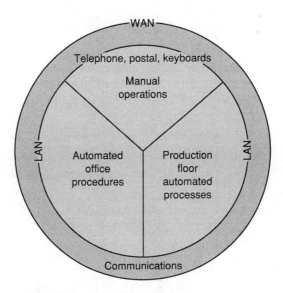

FIGURE 1.3 Communication structures supporting an enterprise.

lands of automation that required manual intervention to coordinate their activities. The history of automation proves that modifications made to existing systems for correcting shortfalls in meeting the operational requirements fragment the islands even more until the advantages of automation are lost in the manual interfaces. Other considerations notwithstanding, modern communications architecture provides the means for integrating the information system of an enterprise.

DATA COMMUNICATIONS

Data communications is the exchange of digital information over communication paths in a reliable and efficient manner. In today's technology, electrical and optical pulses form the bits that represent the digital information. Consider the physical problem of transporting bits between two devices—say, a computer and one of its peripheral devices. Clearly, the two devices must agree on the shape and timing of the pulses and on their interpretation. While close to each other, the communicating devices transmit pulses that arrive in good shape, allowing clear recognition and unambiguous interpretation. But as the peripheral devices move to a more distant user's environment, not only do the pulse shapes degrade during transmission, but other extraneous signals in the communication channel become more pronounced, making the recognition of the pulses difficult, if not impossible. This brings us to the subject of this book: the principles of transporting information from where it is gathered or generated to where it is used in a reliable, recognizable, and interpretative form.

Exercises

1.1 The computer industry has for years delivered software products known to be defective, and yet customers have bought these products and operated them with restrictions in the high hope that later versions would correct the deficiencies. Structured programming techniques have been developed to put engineering specificity into computer programs. These techniques have proved useful not only for computer programs, but also for the analysis and design of other kinds of systems. Some formatting and diagramatic tools used in practice are:

- Data flow diagrams
- Control flow diagrams (flowcharts)
- Data dictionary
- Entity-relationship diagrams
- Decision tables
- Structured English
- Structured charts
- State transition diagrams

Describe each of these tools, giving an example of each.*

1.2 The following diagram shows the external information flows between a mail-order house and its customers. Draw the data flow diagrams that describe the internal operations that the mail-order house performs to respond to its customers (see exercise 1.1).

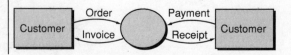

Exercises *(continued)*

1.3 A service request may be confirmed at various times during transmission. For example, the sender may receive confirmation that the request has
(a) been sent
(b) arrived at the receiver
(c) been received and accepted by the receiver
Illustrate each of these forms of confirmation with services offered by the postal services.

1.4 Give one or more physical examples that illustrate each of the reasons for distributing a system.†

1.5 Discuss the mechanics used to exchange information between humans, between machines, and between humans and machines.†

1.6 Using real time as it has been defined in the text, find examples of systems that have real-time constraints.†

---

*Selected questions have been marked with an asterisk to indicate that their solution requires added material found in the suggested reading list at the end of the chapter. While these questions are beyond the scope of the text, they have been included to give the reader a better insight on the science and technology upon which the discussion has been based.
†Class discussion exercise.

1.2   DATA COMMUNICATIONS NETWORKS

DEFINITION

One may be tempted to define a data communications network as a collection of computers and computer devices that operate autonomously and are interconnected to cooperate in providing computing services. This definition is perhaps too generous, allowing the whole gamut of computing systems. It would be better to exclude many computing systems that would sidetrack the discussion from the data communication channels that form the data paths in the network. For example, locally clustered systems whose components communicate under control of a single operating system may be excluded with little loss of generality, although not all tightly coupled systems communicating under control of a master computer should be excluded. By remotely separating the computing resources from each other, the data communication paths become more prominent in the network and still allow the definition to include both tightly and loosely coupled networks. With this minor modification, the definition of a data communications network can be restated as follows:

> A data communications network is a collection of computers and computing devices that operate autonomously, are remotely separated from each other, and are interconnected to cooperate in providing computing services.

NETWORK STRUCTURAL ELEMENTS

Network design and implementation as it is known today is an evolving medley of science, engineering, and folklore. Like other complex structures, the design of a network as a monolithic system would be immediately lost in a myriad of details. It is therefore better, to model the network to identify further functional details in the context of the total organization.

The basic elements used to model a network structure are nodes and communication lines. A **node,** which will be shown as a circle in network diagrams, represents a station that houses the service hardware and software components. The physical equipment at a node might consist of a computer, data terminal, multiplexer, line switch, or process control device that may be of any size or complexity, together with the line interfacing hardware. Communication lines, sometimes called **data links** or **links,** interconnect the nodes into a network structure. Data may flow between nodes through a line in either one or both directions.

Some nodes serve as end nodes that locate the **data sources** for the generated signals or that locate the **data sinks** (i.e., destination points) for the transmitted signals, but often these nodes provide both services. Other nodes in a network serve as intermediate points for establishing a path from the source to the sink and act to separate and/or redirect the incoming or outgoing signals or to re-form and retransmit the signals. Communications from a data source to a data sink, called **end-to-end communications,** may pass through several intermediate nodes before finally arriving at their destination points.

In bidirectional communications, the nodes connected to the path may exchange roles. The direction of flow can be explicitly shown by connecting the nodal points with arrows rather than simple lines, even though the lines may support flow in both directions. By these simple diagrams, the skeletal structure of a network representing the nodes and their interconnections can be organized and scrutinized for further structural detail.

Example 1.1

Enumerate all the end-to-end communication paths from source to sink in the following diagram, assuming no backtracking on any path.

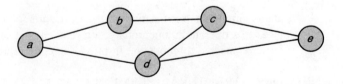

Paths: *abce, abcde, ade, adce.* ◀

NODAL INTERCONNECTIONS

Figure 1.4 shows the interconnections of nodes in a network to allow one-to-one, one-to-many, and many-to-one stations. The direct interconnection of two nodes by a link, called a **point-to-point connection** (Figure 1.4a), allows two stations to communicate one to one. Each node transmits or receives communications from the other node. To allow one-to-many or many-to-one stations to communicate, the nodes may be interconnected either through a central node, representing an **exchange,** or **switching, station** (Figure 1.4b), or through a common line, representing a **multipoint,** or **multidrop line** (Figure 1.4c). Communications on a multipoint line may or may not be controlled by a master station. The nodes connected to a switching station, however, require that the central node contain a multiplexer, switching equipment, broadcast capabilities (as in radio or satellite transmission), or even a communications computer.

To reference the individual nodes connected to a common line or common node, each node is assigned a unique address. By affixing the destination address to the messages transmitted, a node can direct its communications to a particular node; and by recognizing its own address, a node can accept messages destined to itself and bypass communications directed to other nodes that share the facilities. When the network contains a switching station, the addresses serve to select and connect the path between the communicating partners before they start exchanging data.

A node connected to a common line may initiate communications when it finds the line free of other traffic, called **contention,** or it may respond to a request to transmit, called **polling.** Polling may be organized in two ways: by roll-call polling or by hub polling. In roll-call polling, a master station calls the tributary stations in sequence, giving each the right to transmit. After the called station sends any prepared messages it has ready for transmission, it returns control back to the master

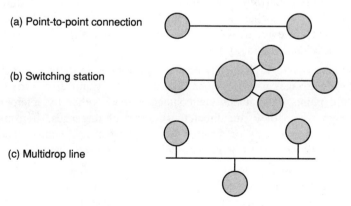

(a) Point-to-point connection

(b) Switching station

(c) Multidrop line

FIGURE 1.4 Nodal interconnections.

station and allows the master station to continue the roll call. Hub polling may or may not involve a master station. In hub polling, the polling station relinquishes the right to transmit directly to the polled station rather than returning the control back to a master station.

BASIC NETWORK STRUCTURES

It would be convenient if operational networks could be used to model the details of design. Normally, the topology of these configurations appears too complex, if not chaotic, for describing the essence of the network. A few simple structures that have some distinguishable features can instead be used for understanding segments of existing networks as well as for designing new configurations.

Figure 1.5 shows several basic network structures. The differences in the interconnections of the nodes affect the roles that the individual nodes play in the network. These differences especially affect the routing of messages through the network; the network's reliability, availability, and maintainability; and the services that the individual nodes provide to the other nodes in the network. The following descriptions highlight some of these differences:

- The **star network** connects a central node to several radial nodes (Figure 1.5a). The central node, containing a computer or a complex switch, controls the communication between nodes. All communications pass through the central node, creating a master-slave relationship between the central node and the remaining nodes. A failure in the central node incapacitates the whole network. However, a failure in any other node leaves the remaining network operational.

- The **tree network** is a hierarchical structure, connecting each node to a node at a higher level (Figure 1.5b). Each node except the terminal nodes contains a network switching component or a computer. The terminal nodes may contain either a computerized workstation or a dumb terminal. A failure in any node removes the branches connected to that node from the network. The severed branches, however, as well as the remaining network, may still function independently until the faulty node is restored.

- The **ring network** physically connects each node to its nearest neighbor (Figure 1.5c). Messages pass from one node to the next until they arrive at their destination points. The nodes are coupled to each other by interconnecting lines through which they can direct the transfer of messages. If a node leaves the network intentionally or through failure, or if a new node enters the network, the total network must be reconnected before communications can be reinitiated.

- The **bus network** connects all nodes to a common line (Figure 1.5d). Each node may independently contend for the right to transmit when the line is free of other traffic. The nodes listen and hear all messages transmitted, but accept only those messages destined to themselves by recognizing their own unique address. A group of nodes may also be assigned a group address to permit messages to be

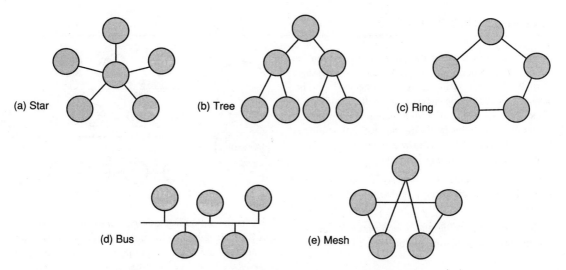

FIGURE 1.5 Basic network structures.

broadcast to all the nodes in the group. Alternatively, by using the unique address assigned to each node, the bus network may be structured into a virtual star or a virtual ring ("virtual" in the sense that the connections are logical rather than physical). A virtual star is formed by designating one node the master in order to provide centralized communication control. The master node passes the right to transmit to each of the remaining nodes by polling them through their addresses. In a virtual ring, no node acts to provide centralized control; instead, each node passes the right to transmit to a designated successor node.

- The **mesh network** provides for alternative paths between the nodes (Figure 1.5e). The network configuration may appear similiar to a ring network, but the ring network passes messages from one node to the next, while in a mesh network, messages may be passed by any connecting path. Different routes can be assigned to achieve end-to-end communications by switching the lines connecting the nodes. This structure enhances the network's reliability, since a failure in any node leaves the remaining network operational.

Exercises

1.7 Consider a telephone system with no switching stations, whereby a separate line connects any two phones in the network. Plot the number of lines versus the number of phones needed to be able to communicate with any subscriber.

1.8 A star network depicts a number of computing devices that can cooperate with each other by exchanging information through the central node. One way the central node acts to direct the traffic is to first establish a physical connection between the nodes that

Exercises *(continued)*

need to cooperate. After the physical connection has been established, the nodes can exchange messages until the connection is finally disconnected. Another way the central node acts to direct the traffic is to route the data to the receiving station on a message-by-message basis by prefixing the destination address to each message. Discuss how messages are delayed in each of these switching strategies.

1.9 Given a number of phones connected to a bus network, discuss the discipline that must be followed in using the network.†

1.10 Enumerate all the end-to-end paths for the following network, assuming no backtracking.

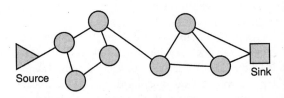

1.11 The first configuration shown below depicts roll-call polling, whereby a master station polls each tributary station in sequence, giving the called station the opportunity to transmit any message it has ready for transmission. After completing the communications, the called station relinquishes control back to the master station. The second configuration shown depicts hub polling, whereby the master station starts the polling sequence with the station farthest away. Each station polled appends any message it has ready for transmission onto a common block containing the messages transmitted by the previous stations, passes the composite block of messages to its nearest neighbor, and then polls its nearest neighbor. The polling cycle is repeated after all the transmitted messages arrive at the master station.

(a) Discuss the delay a message suffers during transmission in each of the two configurations.

(b) Discuss the amount of time each of the two configurations spends in polling.

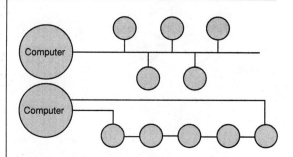

1.12 In the following configurations, each station is constantly listening to the traffic on the common line. A station in the first configuration may transmit when it finds the line free of other traffic. In the second configuration, each station has the right to transmit after it finds its address in a special polling message. When the polled station has no further messages to transmit, it relinquishes control of the line by polling a designated neighbor. The broken line indicates the polling sequence. Define the inherent problems in these configurations, give a possible solution to each problem, and then suggest applications where one would be better suited than the other.

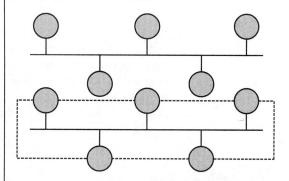

1.13 Track the essential switching stations involved in a long-distance phone call placed from an office phone.

1.14 The primary concern of the nodes in a network

Exercises *(continued)*

is to guard against—and if possible correct—errors during communications. List the possible errors that can arise during a phone call and suggest how they can be detected and corrected.†

1.15 Compare the features that characterize data communications networks, communications net-

works, computer networks, and information networks.*

---

*See footnote, p. 7.
†Class discussion exercise.

1.3   ORGANIZATIONS IN DATA COMMUNICATIONS

RESTRUCTURING THE COMMUNICATIONS INDUSTRY

Date communications, especially in the area of commercially supplied products and public networks, cannot avoid the users, vendors, and assorted groups attempting to arbitrate between interested parties. But who are these players? To understand the role that these various organizations serve in the communications industry, a few will be introduced in this section; but by necessity, this topic will be incomplete and perhaps biased.

In 1974, the federal government filed suit seeking to break up AT&T; and in 1984, AT&T was divested of its operating companies. The plan behind this new arrangement was to place the communications industry in a more favorable position for developing new products and services through competition, especially in the area of data communications.

Prior to this action, AT&T enjoyed a virtual monopoly in the telecommunications business, in spite of some 1500 other companies, mostly small, that provided regional or specialized services. AT&T consisted of Western Electric, its manufacturing arm; Bell Laboratories, its research organization; 22 operating companies (Bell System), providing intrastate communication services (primarily phone services); and the Long Lines Division, providing interstate communications. After the divestiture, the 22 operating companies were reorganized into 7 independent regional operating companies, and AT&T retained its other segments, adding a new company, AT&T Information Systems, to market computers and communications. This change set the stage for today's communications industry.

REGULATORY AGENCIES

Companies offering communication services are known as **common carriers.** Before a common carrier can offer a service, it must file a document called a **tariff,** describing the services and rate schedule for these services, with an appropriate regulatory agency. For intrastate communications, an appropriate state government body serves as the regulatory agency, and for interstate and foreign communications, the Federal Communications Commission (FCC) serves this purpose. Once accepted, the services cannot be removed or the rates changed without further approval from the regulatory agency. So public communications facilities depend on both the common carrier offering the services and the agency regulating the services, with the result that different tariffs exist for essentially the same service, depending on whether the common carrier operates interstate or intrastate.

The FCC was created by the Communications Act of 1934, which empowered it with broad responsibilities to review and set operating practices and rates in the segment of the communications industry falling under the jurisdiction of the federal government. Until the advent of computer technology, the commission's main concern was with the radio and telephone industries, and it adopted a posture that allowed the analog transmission facilities used by these forms of communication to evolve in an orderly fashion. As the needs for data communications facilities became more apparent, the commission gradually reversed its previous positions with several landmark decisions. These decisions have been instrumental in fostering the development of new products and services and, equally important, in modifying the public's expectations of the communications industry.

COMMUNICATION DEVICE MANUFACTURERS

A key FCC decision, made in 1968, is now known as the Carterphone decision. While not directly concerned with data communications facilities, it nevertheless had immediate and long-term implications in the development of data communications products. The case involved the Carterphone Electronics Corporation, which sought to interconnect their base station for a mobile radio system to the dial phone system. The problem was that they wanted to connect a **foreign device**—a device from a vendor other than the one operating the communications facilities, which in this case meant a non–Western Electric device—to the phone system; and the common carrier operating the phone system felt that if this practice went unchecked, it could jeopardize the entire voice communication network. The problem was solved by letting Carterphone connect its base station to the phone system through a protective device provided by the common carrier, but gradually, this ruling was relaxed so that now such devices need only be verified and approved for connection. The implications of this decision to data communications industries were (and are) far-reaching, first, in expanding the market for devices used to interface data equipment to the analog transmission lines operated by the established phone companies, and now, for creating the economic climate for developing a wide variety of data communications devices.

EXPANDED CARRIER SERVICES

In another key FCC decision, Microwave Communications, Inc. (MCI) asked permission to function as a common carrier by offering specialized services between

Chicago and St. Louis using a microwave relay system they proposed to build. In 1968, after many years of litigation and FCC hearings, MCI was given approval. From this beginning, MCI and a number of other companies expanded their facilities, and now they compete with each other offering similar services over the same geographical area.

Meanwhile, ARPANET developed a digital network for the federal government. This effort demonstrated the feasibility and benefits of a network using a digital form of data communications. Initially an experimental network, it has since been upgraded and now forms the digital data network operated on behalf of the federal government to make specialized computer facilities accessible to users located at remote sites.

Following the success of ARPANET, the FCC approved in 1973 the petition from Telenet Corporation and later the petition from the Tymnet Corporation to build public packet-switched networks and operate as common carriers. The idea behind these networks was to use existing communications facilities already offered by other common carriers, and by adding high-speed, computerized interfaces, provide low-cost data transaction services to their subscribers. These companies, called **value-added carriers,** operate by leasing available communications facilities and reselling them with a new type of service.

Exercises

1.16 Study the issues involved in the Carterphone decision. Given the benefits of hindsight, argue either for or against the decision.†

1.17 Compare a similar tariff for long-distance service and the rate schedule for this service offered by AT&T, MCI, and Sprint. List any unique services provided by any of these common carriers.*

1.18 How has the MCI decision benefited or hindered the end user?

1.19 Compare the services and the rate schedules offered by value-added carriers.*

---

*See footnote, page 7.
†Class discussion exercise.

1.4 STANDARDS AND COOPERATIVE GROUPS

VOLUNTARY STANDARDS

The aim of standardization is to balance flexibility and experimentation with conformity and compatibility. The problems are delicate and never really solved, but each attempt identifies the direction of the technology. This ongoing activity has been delegated to a number of concerned government, industrial, and professional organizations.

The success of a standard depends on its acceptance. To arrive at an acceptable compromise, organizations developing standards seek the widest possible consensus before recommending any standard. In this way, vendors' and users' preferences can be integrated into the standards. Although published as a recommendation, a standard has legal status, permitting users to use it in contractual specifications and vendors to advertise its use.

Literally hundreds of organizations have responsibilities in developing and adopting data communications standards. Since none report to the others and each cooperates with all, differences and infringements on each other's scope of activities can be expected. Out of this maze of organizations, voluntary standards emerge that are accepted and widely used. While the role of every organization involved in standardization cannot be included here, the few that are listed play a prominent role and will be referred to again throughout the text.

INTERNATIONAL STANDARDS GROUPS

The international forum for standards is the International Organization for Standardization (ISO). National standards organizations make up the core of its membership, with ANSI (described shortly) representing the United States. Like other standards groups, ISO divides its work among technical committees. Two subcommittees of Technical Committee 97 are delegated responsibility for codifying the standards in data communications networks.

Coupled to ISO is the Comité Consultatif Internationale de Télégraphique et Téléphonique (CCITT). Organized as a committee of the International Telecommunications Union (a specialized agency of the United Nations Organization), it serves as the international body for establishing agreements by consensus or treaties in the field of data communications. Every four years, the results of CCITT's work over this period are acted on and its recommendations published in books whose color identifies the year (e.g., CCITT Yellow Book, 1980). Representing the United States within the structure of CCITT is the Department of State, individual common carriers, and the FCC. In general, ISO and CCITT divide the work of recommending international standards according to the needs of customers and vendors, respectively, although there is some overlap.

The European Computer Manufacturers Association (ECMA), as its name implies, is composed of representatives from the major European producers of computer products. It aims to study and develop methods and procedures for facilitating and standardizing the use of commercial data processing equipment, except for equipment used exclusively for military purposes. The association delegates its work to technical working committees, which in turn refer specific problem areas within their defined scope to task groups. Table 1.1 lists the active technical committees of ECMA working in data communications or related areas together with their designated responsibilities. As is evident from this list, the technical committees of ECMA actively participate in the work of other national and international standards groups, especially with ISO and CCITT.

TABLE 1.1
ECMA TECHNICAL COMMITTEES ON DATA COMMUNICATIONS*

TECHNICAL COMMITTEE DESIGNATION	RESPONSIBILITIES
TC23–Open Systems Interconnections	• Overall responsibility for the reference model for open systems interconnection (OSI) within ECMA.
	• Developing service and protocol standards for those layers above the transport layer.
TC24–Communication Protocols	• Developing service and protocol standards for the physical, link, network, and transport layers of the reference model of OSI
TC25–Data Networks	• Studying physical, link, and network layers services and protocol standards in relation to CCITT or postal telephone and telegraph agencies-defined services.
	• Preparing coordinated viewpoints of common interest to ECMA and its users
	• Standardizing selected facilities within these services for specific applications
TC29–Text Preparation and Interchange	• Developing standards in field of preparation, processing, and interchange of text
TC30–Small-Computer Systems Interface	• Developing standards for device-independent interfaces for interconnecting small computers to each other and with devices (ensuring coherence with ISO model and ECMA standards on local area networks)

*The terms used to specify the areas of responsibilities are defined in the Glossary and are discussed in later sections of the text.

NATIONAL STANDARDS GROUPS

The American National Standards Institute (ANSI) is a nonprofit, privately funded standards organization in the United States whose membership consists of some 240 standards-developing organizations and many individual companies. It coordinates voluntary standards activities, approves standards as American national standards, serves as a national clearing house for national and international voluntary standards, and represents U.S. interests in international standardization activities, such as those of ISO.

ANSI is organized into a hierarchical structure of sectional committees, technical committees, and task groups. While the sectional committees are composed of a balanced membership representing producers, consumers, and the public, membership in the task groups is open to any interested persons. By common practice, companies assign knowledgeable professionals to represent their interests and work on specific standards.

TABLE 1.2
ANSI TECHNICAL COMMITTEE TASK GROUPS ON DATA TRANSMISSION

TASK GROUP DESIGNATION	RESPONSIBILITIES
X3S31–Planning	• Overall planning for all X3S3 groups
X3S32–Glossary	• Developing common vocabulary for data transmission
X3S33–Data Communications Heading and Formats	• Defining control requirements for data systems and bit formats for characters
X3S34–Data Communications Control Procedure	• Developing protocols
X3S35–System Performance	• Studying techniques and criteria for system performance
X3S36–Digital Data Transmission Rates	• Standardizing signaling speeds for use with communication equipment
X3S37–Public Data Networks	• Developing standards for use on public networks

ANSI's Sectional Committee X3 on Computers and Information Processing is responsible for investigating all standards related to the computer industry. The Technical Committee X3S3 on Data Transmission, working under X3, is specifically charged with developing and recommending standards for data communications. Currently, X3S3 has seven task groups assigned specific responsibilities (Table 1.2).

Among the cooperative trade organizations for promulgating standards in the United States, the Electronics Industries Association (EIA) has contributed several important standards. EIA draws its membership from manufacturers of electronic products. In the field of data communications, EIA has a similar relationship to ANSI as ECMA has to CCITT. As with other standards groups, the association delegates its work to technical committees and subcommittees composed of engineering specialists. Table 1.3 lists two important technical committees assigned to develop standards in data communications together with their respective areas of responsibility.

TABLE 1.3
EIA TECHNICAL COMMITTEES ON DATA COMMUNICATIONS

TECHNICAL COMMITTEE DESIGNATION	RESPONSIBILITIES
TR30–Data Transmission	• Developing and maintaining standards for the interface between data communications equipment and data terminal equipment
	• Providing advisory services to ANSI X3S3
	• Engineering specialties are further divided between three subcommittees: TR 30.1–Signal Quality, TR30.2–Digital Interfaces; and TR30.3–Telecommunications Network Interfaces.
TR37–Communications Interfaces	• Developing and maintaining standards for the interface between system and common carrier equipment

GOVERNMENT STANDARDS

Important users and vendors often have designated departments within their organizational structure for tracking standards or defining other standards for internal use. Perhaps the largest single user of standards in the United States is the federal government. The federal government has designated two agencies, the National Bureau of Standards (NBS) and the General Services Administration (GSA), the primary responsibilities for government participation in national and international standards groups and for developing, coordinating, and promulgating standards for government use.

NBS and GSA share the roles of advisory and liaison in data communications standards. The responsibilities of the National Bureau of Standards extend over all automatic data processing (ADP) standards, including standards for teleprocessing. NBS's studies on these standards are documented in the Federal Information Processing Standards (FIPS) publications. While the federal government does not operate the public networks, it does operate several national networks besides the military networks. GSA administers the cooperative program through which standards are adopted for use in these networks. Together, NBS and GSA share the responsibilities for data communications interface standards.

PROFESSIONAL SOCIETIES

Professionals in the engineering fields often have specific concerns for particular areas of standardization and work through their professional societies on standards. In data communications, the work conducted under the auspices of two engineering societies—the Institute of Electrical and Electronics Engineers (IEEE) and the Society for Manufacturing Engineering (SME)—should be singled out.

IEEE has undertaken through their Project 802 the development of LAN standards for office and plant automation. Their standards in this area have drawn national attention and have been submitted for national and international standardization. Details on these standards will be described later in the text.

Members of SME, on the other hand, are more involved in adopting standards than in developing them. They have undertaken the national and international role of coordinating the cooperative industrial effort of selecting suites of LAN standards suitable for integrating communications on the shop floor and in office facilities. These suites of standards, called Manufacturing Automation Protocols (MAP) and Technical and Office Protocols, (TOP), respectively, have also been adopted for government-wide use under the title Government Open System Interconnections Profile, (GOSIP). In a similiar way, both industry and government have designated standards for WAN communications.

Figure 1.6 presents a pictorial view of the communication structures integrating the physically distributed data devices supporting the applications of an enterprise. The plan behind the activities of the professional societies mentioned here is to achieve interoperability among the devices connected to the network independent of

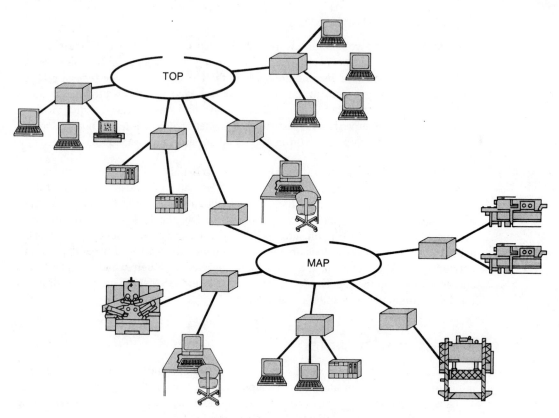

FIGURE 1.6 The communication structures integrating the activities of an enterprise.

the vendor supplying the products or the application they support. Without common standards, the industrial community would be forced to use products offered by a single vendor (or clones of these products) or else pay the penalty of tailoring the hardware or software to conform to the standards arbitrarily adopted for the network. With common standards, interoperability between communication products can be achieved in a cost-effective way using plug-to-plug compatible components independent of the supplier.

Exercises

1.20 ANSI has some 240 members involved in developing standards. Many of these members submit standards for approval as American national standards. Briefly report on some of these organizational members that have been involved in developing data communications standards and the particular

Exercises *(continued)*

standards they have submitted for national approval.*

1.21 The identification of published standards are prefixed by symbols to indicate the source of the standard. For example, ISO standards and IEEE standards are prefixed by the symbols ISO and IEEE, respectively. The prefixes designating the source of other standards are not as obvious. Through the literature, identify the source of standards prefixed by X., V., RS-, MIL-STD, and FED-STD. Explain why standards from different sources may contain equivalent specifications.

1.22 Describe how product manufacturers can restrain competition by adopting their own standards rather than nonproprietary standards, and explain how industrial users can frustrate these efforts.†

_____

*See footnote, p. 7.
†Class discussion exercise.

SUMMARY

Data communications is the exchange of digital information over a communication path in a reliable and timely manner. The present study relates the data communication facilities to the data needed to support the various activities of an enterprise. To avoid creating isolated islands of automation, users must have access to the information they need, regardless of where the data reside in the industrial complex. The communications substructure can integrate these distributed islands of automation by making the data accessible to the users.

By definition, a data communications network is a collection of computers and computer-like devices that operate autonomously, are remotely separated from each other, and are interconnected to cooperate in providing computing services. A network consists of nodes that house the equipment, computing services and data, and the paths through which the activities can exchange data. Some paths connect nodes that lie entirely within the enterprise's premises; others lead to nodes outside of this restricted area. To form network structures, the nodes may be interconnected to the data paths in a variety of ways: by point-to-point connections, through a common-node switching station, or through common-line multipoint connections.

For internal communications, an enterprise must construct one or more privately owned LAN facilities. External communications, on the other hand, make use of WAN facilities, which commercial vendors have constructed for public use. The restructuring of the computer and communications industries has resulted in an expansion of the options of products and services available to the users for meeting their specialized requirements. For example, foreign devices can now be attached to public networks without penalty, common carriers can offer competing tariffs, and most important, new data services have been made available.

To realize the advantages that data communications networks offer, we must develop and adopt standards. Voluntary standards emerge from many national, international, industrial, and professional groups that cooperate with each other and seek the widest possible consensus before publishing their recommendations. These recommendations can be viewed as lists of features from which users can select specific standards. Government and industrial users have long taken the posture of using standards. They have now joined together in adopting suites of data communications standards for achieving interoperability between plug-to-plug compatibility products independent of the supplier.

KEY TERMS

Local area network (LAN)
Wide area network (WAN)
Node
Data link
Data source
Data sink
End-to-end communications
Point-to-point connection
Exchange station
Switching station
Multipoint line
Multidrop line

Contention
Polling
Star network
Tree network
Ring network
Bus network
Mesh network
Common carriers
Tariff
Foreign devices
Value-added carrier

SUGGESTED READINGS

DeMarco, T. *Controlling Software Projects*. Englewood Cliffs, N.J.: Yourdon Press, 1982.

DeMarco, T. *Structured Analysis and System Specification*. Englewood Cliffs, N.J.: Yourdon Press, 1978.

Enslow, P. H., Jr. "Non-Technical Issues in Network Design—Economic, Legal, Social, and Other Considerations." *Computer Networks*, 1975.

Government Open System Interconnections Profile (GOSIP). Washington, D.C.: U.S. Government Printing Office, 1988.

Manufacturing Automation Protocol Specifications. MAP Version 1.0, 23 October 1982; MAP Version 2.0, 7 February 1985; MAP Version 2.1, 31 March 1985; MAP Version 2.2, 1986; MAP Version 3.0, 1987. Society of Manufacturing Engineering.

Mathison, S. L., and Walker, P. M. *Communications and Telecommunications Issues in Public Policy*. Englewood Cliffs, N.J.: Prentice-Hall, 1970.

Technical and Office Protocols Specification Version 1.0. Society of Manufacturing Engineering, November 1985.

Ward, Paul T. and Mellor, Stephen J. *Structured Development for Real Time Systems: Vol. 1: Introduction and Tools*. Englewood Cliffs, N.J.: Prentice-Hall, 1985.

Yourdon, E. *Managing the Structured Techniques,* 3rd ed. Englewood Cliffs, N.J.: Yourdon Press, 1987.

Yourdon, E., and Constantine, L. L. *Structured Design: Fundamentals of a Discipline of Computer Program and Systems Design*. Englewood Cliffs, N.J.: Prentice-Hall, 1979.

CHAPTER 2

MATHEMATICAL DESCRIPTION OF COMMUNICATION PROCESSES

I tend to avoid equations as much as possible. I simply can't manage very complicated equations, so I have developed geometrical ways of thinking instead, and choose to concentrate on problems that can be given geometric, diagrammatic interpretations. This does have the unfortunate aspect that for those of us who don't understand all the details may find some connecting arguments missing.

STEVEN HAWKING
NEW YORK TIMES INTERVIEW

2.1 SYSTEM DESCRIPTION

LINEAR SYSTEMS

The key ideas of data communications processes can be formulated in a few engineering theorems that deal with the shape and form of signals representing information. Although not as intuitive as the familiar way of representing signals as a function of time, signals can be equivalently described with frequency as the independent variable. The principles used for this treatment of signals are lodged in a mathematical framework that may appear to introduce new complexities. However, the mathematics offers a vocabulary shared with other engineers and scientists, whereby the concepts and abstract terms of processes can be given a more quantitative meaning, and there is the added advantage of studying the system's behavior graphically.

Figure 2.1 represents an assembly of interconnected physical components (an engineering system), which, when excited by an input, produces an output response. Regardless of the physical composition of the functional block, the functional relationship between the input and the output describes the system. Stated differently, the physical model of the system can be replaced by a mathematical rule that assigns an output function to each input function. By this approach, attention can be diverted from the details of the hardware and focused on the behavior of the system. Although such a diagram may be used to study processes in all engineering disciplines, the intent here is to use this functional approach to describe communication systems.

Different but logically equivalent mathematical descriptions may be used to model a process. One popular model employed in engineering formulates the process as a **linear system** described by equations whose coefficients do not change with time. In a sense, this model is unrealistic, since it implies that the process cannot contain elements that change the interconnections of the components, elements whose characteristics change over their operating range, or elements that generate energy spontaneously. However, for practical systems designed to operate over a limited range, the model serves and has an analogous form in all engineering disciplines. While the variables and parameters have specialized meaning in each discipline, the structure of the equations remains the same.

In a linear system, if system inputs I_1 and I_2 independently produce output responses θ_1 and θ_2 respectively, then a linear combination of the inputs, $a_1I_1 + a_2I_2$, where a_1 and a_2 represent arbitrary constants, will produce a corresponding linear

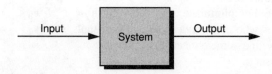

FIGURE 2.1 Functional diagram of a system.

combination of the output responses, $a_1\theta_1 + a_2\theta_2$. The additive property postulated for linear systems can be conveniently used to study the response of a system to an arbitrary, complex input. Equally important to the formulation of processes in this way is that the behavior of the systems can be interpreted graphically. The following steps and an example may make the procedure clearer:

1. Decompose the input into an equivalent linear combination of elementary functional components.

2. Calculate or experimentally measure the system output response to each component of the input.

3. Add together the individual output responses resulting from each of the input components to form the composite output.

Example 2.1

From the two inputs, $I_1(t)$ and $I_2(t)$, and the response of these inputs in a linear system, $\theta_1(t)$ and $\theta_2(t)$, shown below by solid and broken lines, respectively, calculate the output response of the system to the composite sum of these inputs, $I_1(t) + I_2(t)$.

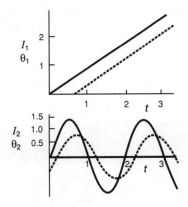

The graphs give the values of $I_1(t)$, $I_2(t)$, $\theta_1(t)$, and $\theta_2(t)$ for each value of t. The composite input, $I_1(t) + I_2(t)$, which is shown by the solid line, is constructed by adding the individual inputs, $I_1(t)$ and $I_2(t)$, point by point. That is, for each value of t—say, t_o—find the values of $I_1(t_o)$ and $I_2(t_o)$ and add these two values together to produce the value of the composite input for this value of t. In a similar fashion, the total response to this input, $\theta_1(t) + \theta_2(t)$, which is shown by the broken line below, is constructed by adding the individual responses, $\theta_1(t)$ and $\theta_2(t)$, point by point.

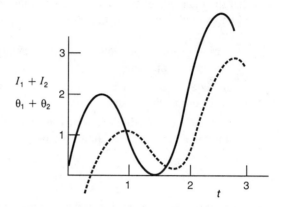

DYNAMIC BEHAVIOR OF A SYSTEM

Figure 2.2 shows some elementary input functions (solid lines) commonly used to study systems, together with a typical output response (broken lines) to each of these inputs. The output response may be viewed as a composite of two components, the transient response and the steady-state response. The transient response is that portion of the total response that reflects the change in the output from its previous stable condition; such as when the input is first applied or when it is removed. The steady-state response is the portion of the total response remaining after the system is given

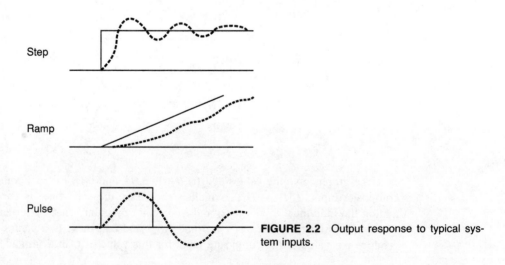

FIGURE 2.2 Output response to typical system inputs.

enough time for the transient to die out, and it often appears as a replica of the input signal in shape and form. Both components are necessary to describe the dynamics of a system; however, the focus here will be only on the steady-state response, and the transient portion will be treated as an aberration of the desired signal.

SINUSOIDAL FUNCTION

A particularly useful and universally adopted elementary function used in conjunction with linear systems is the sinusoidal function given as a function of time. Mathematically, a sinusoidal function can be defined by either the sine or cosine function. Three parameters characterize a sinusoidal function: amplitude, frequency, and phase. For the sine function, these parameters are related by the equation

$$F(t) = A \sin (2\pi f t + \phi) \tag{2.1}$$

Amplitude A gives the maximum variation in magnitude and has the dimension of some measurable physical quantity, such as voltage, current, or displacement from some reference point. Although the value of the amplitude is not essential to the discussion, it can be assumed that when a sinusoidal function is applied to a system, the system's linearity is preserved; that is, the system coefficients remain time-invariant.

The sinusoidal function is periodic, repeating its pattern at fixed periods of time. The time interval between repetitions is called the **period,** denoted by τ. The **frequency** f of the sinusoidal function specifies the number of repetitions per unit of time. The frequency and period form a reciprocal relationship:

$$f = \frac{1}{\tau} \tag{2.2}$$

Frequency is given in units of **hertz** (Hz), replacing the older but more descriptive name of cycles per second. Multiple hertz units may be used as needed for convenience: kHz for kilohertz, representing 10^3 Hz; MHz for megahertz, representing 10^6 Hz; and GHz for gigahertz, representing 10^9 Hz. With no loss of generality, the symbol ω will also be used to denote frequency. The variables ω and f are related by the expression

$$\omega = 2\pi f \tag{2.3}$$

Phase ϕ is the angular delay in the start of the signal and is given in radians, a pure number. The sinusoidal function may be rewritten as $A \sin 2\pi f(t - t_o)$, expressing the delay in units of time. On input, ϕ or t_o will be assumed to be equal to zero, since the phase difference between the input and output, rather than their individual phase values, has importance in the analysis of signals.

The propagation of energy for electrical, radio, light, or sound wave transmission can be assumed to be produced by sinusoidal forces. A parameter needed in these applications is the wave length, defined as the linear distance of one cycle of the sinusoidal wave. If λ is the wave length and c is the transmission velocity of the wave, then

$$\lambda = c\tau = \frac{c}{f} \tag{2.4}$$

For wireless transmission in space, the wave velocity is the velocity of light, which can be approximated by the value 3×10^8 m/s. This value also suffices for many applications under normal atmospheric conditions or wire-coupled transmission, giving the wave length equation

$$\lambda = \frac{3 \times 10^8}{f} \tag{2.5}$$

Exercises

2.1 Plot the sinusoidal function and identify each of the basic parameters of the function.

2.2 Consider the following inputs to a linear system and their individual responses:

INPUT	OUTPUT
$\sin(t)$	$\sin(t - 0.1)$
$\sin(2t)$	$\sin(2t - 0.2)$
$\sin(3t)$	$\sin(3t - 0.3)$

Calculate and draw the composite output response to each of the following composite inputs:
(a) $\sin(t) - \frac{1}{2}\sin(2t)$
(b) $\sin(t) - \frac{1}{2}\sin(2t) + \frac{1}{3}\sin(3t)$

2.3 Given the two inputs and the responses to these inputs shown in Example 2.1, calculate and draw the composite output response to each of the following inputs:
(a) $2I_1 + \frac{1}{2}I_2$
(b) $0.4I_1 + 0.6I_2$

2.4 Given the input I_1 and its response θ_1, and given the composite input $I_1 + I_2$ and its response $\theta_1 + \theta_2$

shown in Example 2.1, calculate and draw the input function I_2 and its response θ_2.

2.5 Find the value of A, f, ω, τ, ϕ, and t_o for each of the following sinusoidal functions:
(a) $5 \sin 6(t - 1)$
(b) $5 \sin(120t + 0.75)$
(c) $6 \sin(2\pi/5)(t - 3)$
(d) $6 \cos(10\pi t - 0.1)$

2.6 Decompose the signal $(1 + 0.1 \cos 5t) \cos 100t$ into a linear combination of sinusoidal functions, and find the amplitude, frequency, and phase of each component. *Hint:* Use the trigonometric identity for $\cos a \cos b$.

2.7 Sound may be modeled as sinusoidal functions. Compare the relative frequency and wave length of the musical notes. Use 330 m/s as the speed of sound and the following frequencies for the musical scale:

Note:	C	D	E	F	G	A	B	C
Frequency:	264	297	330	352	396	440	495	528

2.2   GRAPHICAL DESCRIPTION OF A COMMUNICATION CHANNEL

FREQUENCY RESPONSE CURVES

The central fact for understanding communication signals is that the steady-state response of a linear system to a sinusoidal input is a sinusoidal function of the same frequency. This can be expressed more precisely as follows: An input function of the form $I \sin (\omega t)$ produces an output response of the form $\theta \sin (\omega t + \phi)$, where the amplitude and phase of the input and output have different values but the frequency remains unchanged. Figure 2.3 illustrates on the same coordinate axes the time-versus-magnitude curves for a single sinusoidal signal (bold line) and its output response (light line). The absence of a phase angle in the input signal (i.e., $\phi = 0$) was intentional, since in the analysis of linear systems, the signal delay between the input and output rather than their individual phases is of interest.

Under these mathematical conditions, the steady-state, input-output relationship of multiple sinusoidal signals differing in frequency can be displayed as a three-dimensional plot using time and frequency as the independent variables. Figure 2.4 illustrates the three-dimensional plot for three signals separated by frequency. Normally, both the sinusoidal input signal and the output response would appear as an overlapping curve at the same frequency differing from each other in amplitude and phase.

Rotating Figure 2.4 clockwise about the magnitude axis and looking at the frontal view in the direction of the arrow shown in Figure 2.5, one now sees the multiple signals on the same time-versus-magnitude planar projection. Clearly, when many sinusoidals need to be displayed together, the overlapping curves presented in this view become confusing.

Rotating Figure 2.4 counterclockwise about the magnitude axis and looking at the frontal view in the direction of the arrow shown in Figure 2.6, one now sees the multiple signals on the same frequency-versus-magnitude planar projection. This less confusing view positions the maximum swing in magnitude of each sinusoidal curve

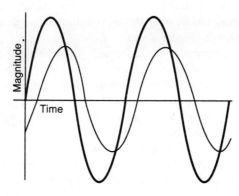

FIGURE 2.3 Steady-state output response to a single sinusoidal input.

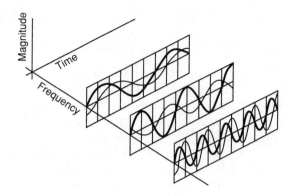

FIGURE 2.4 Multiple sinusoidals displayed as a three-dimensional plot.

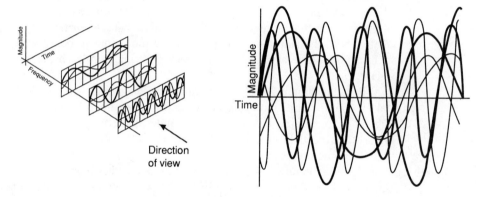

FIGURE 2.5 Time-versus-magnitude view of the three-dimensional plot.

along the frequency axis (Figure 2.6a). However, since the maximum positive and negative swings have equal magnitude, only the maximum positive value, representing the amplitude, need be shown (Figure 2.6b).

The shortcomings of the amplitude-versus-frequency plot are that the input amplitude, output amplitude, and phase change all occupy the same frequency position. A scheme for resolving this problem will be discussed next. But before continuing, another projection that has not been shown should be noted: the time-versus-frequency projection. This view will be dismissed for the time being, but will be reintroduced later, when it serves another purpose in the discussion.

The frequency-preserving property of a linear system with time-invariant coefficients permits a more applicable display of the frequency-versus-amplitude projection for determining system response. Figure 2.7a displays the amplitude response as a

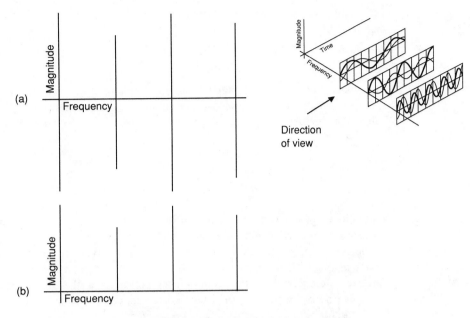

FIGURE 2.6 Frequency-versus-magnitude view of the three-dimensional plot.

ratio of the amplitude of the output (θ) to the amplitude of the input (I). The companion curve, Figure 2.7b, gives the phase change or delay that a sinusoid suffers as it passes through the system. These two curves amply describe the behavior of the system to sinusoidal inputs. Given the frequency and amplitude of an input signal, one can determine the output amplitude by the amplitude response curve and the output phase by the phase response curve. A system described in this way is said to be described in the **frequency domain,** in contrast to the **time domain** of the time-

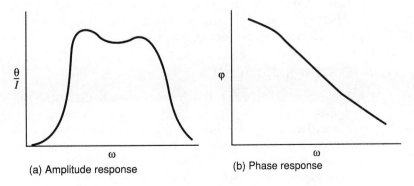

FIGURE 2.7 Frequency response curves.

versus-magnitude projection, where time rather than frequency serves as the independent variable.

DEFINITION OF A DECIBEL

The relative power of two signals, such as the amplitude ratio in the amplitude response curve, is often given on a logarithmic scale. Its basic unit of measurement, called the **decibel** (db), gives the relative power of two signals, P_o and P_i, by the formula

$$R_{db} = 10 \log_{10} \frac{P_o}{P_i} \tag{2.6}$$

The units of power used in this definition, be they watts, milliwatts, microwatts, or horsepower, are irrelevant, since the dimensions cancel out when we take the ratio of the two signals. However, at times it may be convenient to express the absolute power of a signal in decibels. This can be done by comparing the signal to a standard, or reference value. For example, the power level of a signal, P_o, measured in watts can be given in units of decibels by comparing it to a 1 watt reference signal using the formula

$$R_{db} = 10 \log_{10} P_o \tag{2.7}$$

Occasionally, a seemingly contradictory definition appears in the literature, given by the formula

$$R_{db} = 20 \log_{10} \frac{E_o}{E_i} \tag{2.8}$$

where the E values denote the voltage (or current) values of the signals. Since power varies as the square of voltage (or current), equations 2.6 and 2.8 give equivalent definitions. When the factor of 20 rather than 10 appears, it can be assumed that the formula uses voltages (or currents) rather than power.

SYSTEM BANDWIDTH

The response curves display a graphical view of the system behavior to either isolated signals or collections of signals. A system whose amplitude response curve is bounded so that it can only pass signals that lie within a finite range of frequencies is called a **bandpass system.** A bandpass system blocks any sinusoidal signal whose frequency lies outside the bounded range by attenuating its amplitude to an insignificant value.

Figure 2.8 illustrates ideal response curves for a bandpass system. The ideal amplitude response curve (Figure 2.8a) shows a flat response for all frequencies that

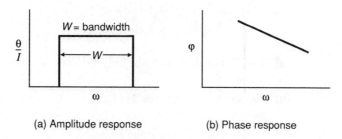

(a) Amplitude response (b) Phase response

FIGURE 2.8 Ideal response curves.

lie between two distinct values and zero response for all frequencies outside this range. The difference between the frequency values where the curve rises and falls is called the system **bandwidth,** designated W. The ideal phase response curve (Figure 2.8b) shows the phase as a linear function of frequency such that all sinusoidals suffer the same time delay when passed through the system. Of course, the delay of any sinusoid outside the bandpass of an ideal system has no significance, since its amplitude has been attenuated to zero.

If all the frequencies in the input signal lie within the bandpass of an ideal system, then the signal will pass undistorted through the system. The output signal, however, will exhibit a change in amplitude and a delay. Although both the amplitude and phase response curves must be used to calculate the output response, only the amplitude response curve will be used so as to expedite the remaining discussion, but keep in mind that a delay accompanies each signal response.

Example 2.2

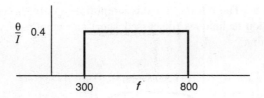

Consider the bandpass response curve shown in the accompanying figure. Find the output response to each of the following input signals:

(a) $5 \sin 2\pi(325t)$

(b) $4.1 \sin 2\pi(723t)$

(c) $52 \sin 2\pi(921t)$

(d) $5 \sin 2\pi(325t) + 4.1 \sin 2\pi(723t)$

(e) $5 \sin 2\pi(325t) + 4.1 \sin 2\pi(723t) + 52 \sin 2\pi(921t)$

(a) The output is $(0.4)(5)\sin 2\pi(325) (t - t_o)$, where t_o gives the delay in the signal.

(b) The output is $1.64 \sin 2\pi(723)(t - t_o)$, where the delay is the same as in part (a).

(c) The output is 0, since the frequency is outside the bandpass of the system.

(d) The output is the sum of the outputs of parts (a) and (b), since the input is the sum of these parts. Graphically, the shape of the input and output will be the same, except that the output signal will be reduced by a factor of 0.4 and delayed in time by t_o.

(e) Since the third term is attenuated to a 0 value, the output will be identical to the output of part (d). ◄

In reality, the shapes of the ideal response curves are unrealistic. Figure 2.9 shows the system response by more realizable curves, although still more desired than achieved. The amplitude response curve would display a more gradual rise and fall, rather than the sharp changes at specific frequencies shown in the ideal response curve, and the response would not be flat within the bandpass nor attenuated to a zero value outside the bandpass. Also, the phase response curve would not give the same time delay for each frequency within the bandpass. These factors cause signals to be distorted as they pass through the system.

For nonideal bandpass systems, engineers define the bandwidth as the difference in frequencies between the points where the power has been attenuated by -3 db, that is, by 50 percent. This one parameter, the bandwidth, characterizes the amplitude response curve of a bandpass system. The other features of the amplitude response curve, the specific value of the frequency spectrum and the value of the amplitude ratio, will be specified only when they are essential to the theoretical treatment. The reasons for this simplification are that signals can be relocated by modulation techniques (discussed later) and amplitude values can be changed by amplification.

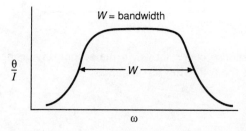

FIGURE 2.9 Realistic bandpass response curve.

VOICE CHANNEL

Although not specifically designed for data communications, the channels used for telephone services can be used for transmitting data. These voice channels are designed to carry a portion of the human audible range. Figure 2.10 shows the frequency power spectrum between 20 and 20,000 Hz as perceived by an average adult; performance, however, varies among persons and deteriorates with age. The bulk of the power associated with this curve lies in the spectral range below 4000 Hz. This lower portion of the audible spectrum serves nicely for the spoken voice, both male and female, and provides the basis for the common telephone channel.

Figure 2.11 shows the frequency response of a telephone channel for voice communications. For calculations, the bandpass will be taken to lie between 300 and 3300 Hz giving a bandwidth of 3000 Hz. Perhaps, more realistically, as everyone has experienced, communication lines obtained for telephone services would not have such desirable characteristics. The response would not have a flat bandpass, and the rise and drop-off would be more gradual.

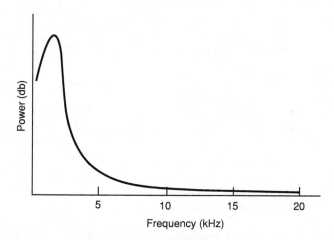

FIGURE 2.10   Human audible spectrum.

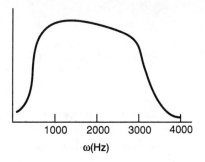

FIGURE 2.11   Voice channel.

Exercises

2.8 Power varies as the square of voltage or current. Show that equations 2.6 and 2.8 give equivalent definitions for the ratio of two signals in units of decibels.

2.9 Consider the following inputs to a linear system and their individual responses:

INPUT	OUTPUT
$5 \sin 2\pi t$	$2 \sin 2\pi(t - 0.1)$
$5 \sin 4\pi t$	$2 \sin 4\pi(t - 0.1)$
$5 \sin 6\pi t$	$2 \sin 6\pi(t - 0.1)$

Plot these curves in the time and frequency domains.

2.10 The input of $A \sin 2\pi ft$ to a linear system produces an output response of $0.2\,A \sin 2\pi f(t - 0.05)$ when $5 < f < 10$ and an output response of zero for all other frequencies. Show the amplitude response and phase response (both as an angle and as a time delay) of this system in the frequency domain.

2.11 Calculate the relative power of two signals in units of decibels when the output power is
(a) twice the input power
(b) half the input power

2.12 Given the relative power in decibels of the individual processes shown in the diagram, calculate the relative power of the sequential combination of these processes in both decibel and absolute units.

2.13 Show that the linear phase response curve of an ideal system results in the same time delay independent of the frequency for any sinusoidal signal that lies within the bandpass of the system.

2.14 Show that an ideal system preserves the shape and form of any linear combination of sinusoids that lie entirely within the bandpass of the system.

2.15 Plot the input $I(t) = \sin 10\pi t + 0.5 \sin 20\pi t$, and compare it to the plot of the output produced from each of the following systems:

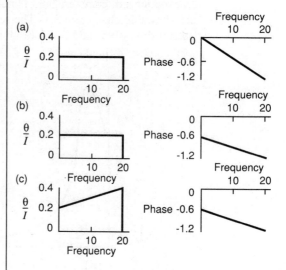

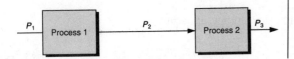

2.3   SPECTRAL REPRESENTATION OF INPUT/OUTPUT SIGNALS

PERIODIC AND APERIODIC SIGNALS

The appeal of using the frequency domain to describe processes is that signals can also be described in this fashion, and together, the two descriptions provide a straightforward graphical interpretation of the system's behavior to both simple and complex inputs. This treatment simply requires a reorientation in looking at signals as collections of sinusoidal components rather than as a variation over time.

Jean Baptiste Fourier, the French mathematician, developed techniques for analyzing two types of signals, called **periodic** and **aperiodic signals,** in the frequency domain. A periodic signal is one whose functional values are repeated at fixed intervals of time. If $F(t)$ represents the signal and (τ) represents the shortest period of time that the functional values recur, then a periodic function may be expressed by

$$F(t) = F(t + \tau) = F(t + 2\tau) = F(t + 3\tau) \ldots$$

The frequency of a periodic signal equals $1/\tau$. A function that is not periodic is called aperiodic.

Figure 2.12a shows examples of periodic functions. Notice how the patterns repeat continuously. The shapes of aperiodic functions, illustrated in Figure 2.12b, differ appreciably from the shapes of periodic functions in that they do not display such repetition. Nevertheless, while the spectral curves and analysis techniques for the two types of signals appear different, the results can be similarly interpreted in the frequency domain.

ANALYSIS OF PERIODIC SIGNALS

A periodic signal can be uniquely decomposed into a linear series, known as a **Fourier series,** consisting of a constant term and a finite or infinite sequence of sine and cosine terms. Algebraically, a periodic signal $F(t)$ whose period is τ can be represented by the series

$$F(t) = a_o + \sum_{k=1}^{\infty} \left(a_k \cos k\frac{2\pi}{\tau}t + b_k \sin k\frac{2\pi}{\tau}t \right) \tag{2.9}$$

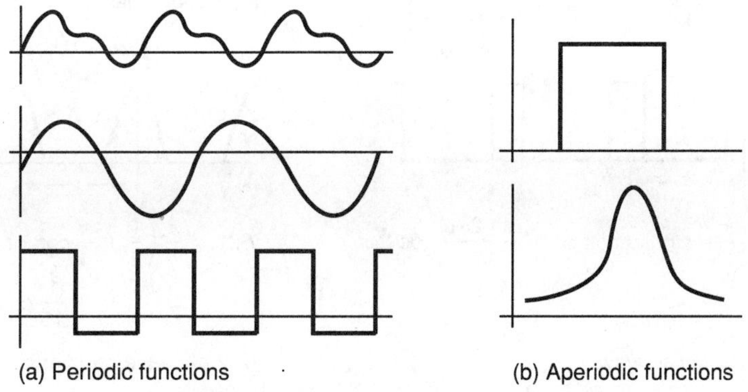

(a) Periodic functions   (b) Aperiodic functions

FIGURE 2.12 Examples of periodic and aperiodic functions.

where the coefficients (*a* and *b* values) are calculated by the Fourier techniques described in Appendix A. The constant term a_o is called the **dc component** from its analog to direct current in electrical systems; the frequency that the pattern of the periodic signal repeats, $1/\tau$, is called the **fundamental frequency;** and the remaining frequencies of the sine and cosine terms are integer multiples of this fundamental frequency, called **harmonics.** While equation 2.9 gives a general formulation of a Fourier series, signals may have missing components (i.e., terms whose coefficients equal 0 do not appear in the series). A few examples of periodic functions will clarify these ideas.

The signals shown in Figure 2.13 all have a period of τ, giving a fundamental frequency of $1/\tau$. While an infinite number of terms are usually needed to represent

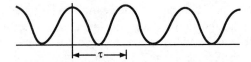

$F(t) = \frac{1}{2} + \frac{1}{2}\cos \omega t$

(a) Finite series

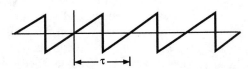

$F(t) = (2/\pi)(\sin \omega t - \frac{1}{2}\sin 2\omega t + \frac{1}{3}\sin 3\omega t - \ldots)$

(b) Sawtooth wave

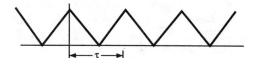

$F(t) = \frac{1}{2} + \frac{4}{\pi^2}(\cos \omega t + \frac{1}{9}\cos 3\omega t +$

$\frac{1}{25}\cos 5\omega t + \ldots)$

(c) Triangular wave

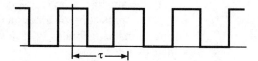

$F(t) = \frac{1}{2} + \frac{2}{\pi}(\cos \omega t - \frac{1}{3}\cos 3\omega t +$

$\frac{1}{5}\cos 5\omega t - \ldots)$

(d) Square wave

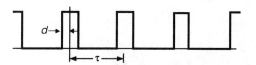

$F(t) = \frac{2}{\pi}\left(\frac{\omega d}{2} + \sin \omega d \cos \omega t + \frac{\sin 2\omega d}{2}\cos 2\omega t + \right.$

$\left. \frac{\sin 3\omega d}{3}\cos 3\omega t + \ldots\right)$

(e) Rectangular pulse wave

$F(t) = \frac{2}{\pi}\left(\frac{1}{2} + \frac{\pi}{4}\cos \omega t + \frac{1}{3}\cos 2\omega t - \right.$

$\left. \frac{1}{15}\cos 4\omega t + \frac{1}{35}\cos 6\omega t - \ldots\right)$

(f) Half-wave rectifier output

FIGURE 2.13 Examples of Fourier series of periodic signals ($\omega = 2\pi/\tau$ and amplitude = 1).

a signal exactly, sometimes, as in Figure 2.13a, all the higher harmonics are missing and a finte series fully describes the signal. For more complex signals, it can be shown that curves that are symmetrical about the magnitude axis [i.e., $F(t) = F(-t)$] can be expressed as an infinite series of cosine terms, while curves that are symmetrical about the origin [i.e., $F(-t) = -F(t)$] can be expressed as an infinite series of sine terms. Figures 2.13b represents a signal whose infinite series consists of only sine terms (the cosine terms are all missing), and the remaining figures represent signals whose infinite series consist of only cosine terms (the sine terms are all missing). The amplitudes of the higher harmonics, however, decrease rapidly, so that each contributes less and less to the shape of the signal. This allows each of these signals to be approximated by truncating the series to a few of the initial terms.

Example 2.3
Draw the approximation to the periodic signal shown in Figure 2.13d using terms up to
(a) the third harmonic
(b) the fifth harmonic

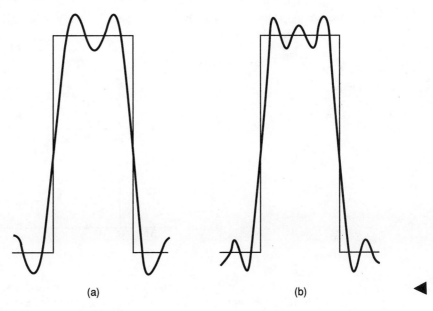

(a)   (b)

The trigonometric identity

$$A \cos \theta + B \sin \theta = \sqrt{A^2 + B^2} \cos (\theta + \phi) \qquad (2.10)$$

where $\phi = \tan^{-1}(-B/A)$, may be used to express equation 2.9 as a series consisting of the dc component and only cosine terms, given by the equation

$$F(t) = a_o + \sum_{k=1}^{\infty} \sqrt{a_k^2 + b_k^2} \cos \left(k\frac{2\pi}{\tau}t + \phi_k \right) \tag{2.11}$$

where $\phi_k = \tan^{-1}(-b_k/a_k)$. Equation 2.11 has the advantage over equation 2.9 in that each frequency component is given by a single term. Together, these components represent a view of the function in the frequency domain that can be shown by two plots. One plot shows the amplitude values, and the other shows the phase values of the signal components at frequencies 0, $1/\tau$, $2/\tau$, and so on, although the phase plot will generally not be shown. Example 2.4 illustrates signals plotted in the frequency domain. The amplitudes are shown as positive values, since a change in the phase angle can convert terms with negative amplitudes, or pure sine terms, into equivalent cosine terms with positive amplitudes.

Example 2.4

Display the sawtooth wave and square wave shown in Figure 2.13 in the frequency domain for a period of 0.1.

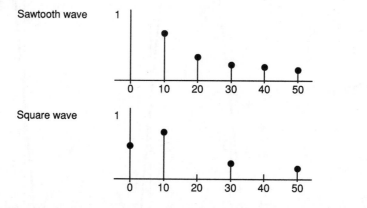

Still another formulation in the frequency domain, and one that will be adopted in much of the presentation, is the expression of the function as an exponential series with imaginary exponents. To show the relationship of this alternative form to the trigonometric Fourier series representation, we will use the following mathematical identities involving the exponential function with a complex exponent and the sine and cosine functions:

$$e^{i\theta} = \cos\theta + i\sin\theta \tag{2.12a}$$

$$\cos\theta = \frac{e^{i\theta} + e^{-i\theta}}{2} \tag{2.12b}$$

$$\sin\theta = \frac{e^{i\theta} - e^{-i\theta}}{2i} \tag{2.12c}$$

Substituting equation 2.12b into equation 2.11 gives the trigonometric Fourier series as an equivalent exponential series:

$$F(t) = a_o + \sum_{k=1}^{\infty} \left[\frac{\sqrt{a_k^2 + b_k^2}}{2} e^{i(k\frac{2\pi}{\tau}t + \phi_k)} + \frac{\sqrt{a_k^2 + b_k^2}}{2} e^{-i(k\frac{2\pi}{\tau}t + \phi_k)} \right] \tag{2.13}$$

Equation 2.13 can be shown in the frequency domain, with the imaginary exponent giving the frequency and phase, and the coefficient giving the amplitude of each component. In the frequency domain, the exponential series resembles the frequency plot of the signal expressed as a trigonometric series, with the following exceptions:

- The phase and amplitude plots have values for both positive and negative frequencies.

- The values in the amplitude plot are one-half the values displayed for the trigonometric series, except for the dc components, where the values are equal.

Example 2.5
Display the sawtooth wave and square wave shown in Figure 2.13 as a two-sided plot in the frequency domain for a period of 0.1.

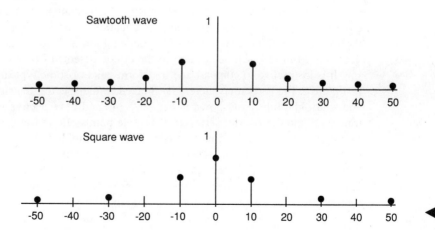

In example 2.5, the plot shown is symmetrical. Indeed, this is always the case for any real signal. Because of this property, the frequency plots will often be shown only in the positive half of the plane, with the understanding that the mirror image of this plot is replicated in the negative half of the plane.

ANALYSIS OF APERIODIC SIGNALS

If the coefficients in equation 2.13 are allowed to be complex values, the phase angles can be removed from exponents. This results in a more concise expression, as shown in equation 2.14:

$$F(t) = \sum_{k=-\infty}^{\infty} c_k e^{ik\omega t} \tag{2.14}$$

The implication is that the phase angles are built into the c_k coefficients rather than being built into the imaginary exponents.

Aperiodic signals do not have the cyclic property of periodic signals, a property that appears essential for modeling a signal by a collection of sinusoidal functions. Yet, by extending the signal's fundamental period to infinity (equivalent to setting the fundamental frequency to zero), an analysis similar to that used for periodic signals can be used for aperiodic signals. The following pair of equations, known as the **Fourier transform pair,** formulate this concept:

$$F(\omega) = \int_{-\infty}^{\infty} f(t)e^{-i\omega t} dt \tag{2.15a}$$

$$f(t) = \frac{1}{2\pi} \int_{-\infty}^{\infty} F(\omega)e^{i\omega t} d\omega \tag{2.15b}$$

Note that $f(t)$ is the given aperiodic function, and $F(\omega)$ is the **Fourier transform** of this function, called the **spectral density.** Mathematically, the summation sign in equation 2.14 and the integration sign in equation 2.15b both form the summation of their respective infinite sequence of exponential terms. This suggests interpreting the values of $F(\omega)$ in a similar fashion to the c_k coefficients of periodic signal.

It is instructive to compare the transform pairs of some typical signals, as shown in Figure 2.14. Particular interest is directed to the spectral density curves of the dc and sinusoidal functions shown in Figure 2.14b and c, respectively. Both the Fourier transform and the Fourier series give discrete points on the frequency plane for these two curves. Technically, this is misleading; the amplitude of any signal component resulting from the Fourier transform is more accurately equated to (the limit of) the incremental areas under the spectral density curve. Although the dimensions of the curves are different, either viewpoint suffices for determining the behavior of the system.

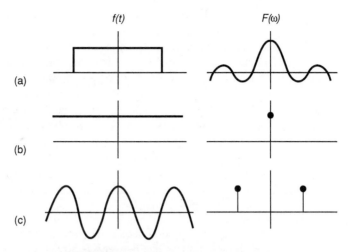

FIGURE 2.14 Fourier transform pairs for some typical signals.

ANALYSIS IN THE FREQUENCY DOMAIN

The essential points for understanding physical systems in engineering terms are as follows:

- The physical characteristics of a system can be described in the frequency domain using two curves representing the changes in amplitude and phase of sinusoidal signals as they pass through the system.

- An arbitrary periodic signal can be decomposed into a linear combination of sinusoidal signals.

- An aperiodic signal, as a variant of periodic signals, can be represented by a continuous spectrum of frequencies.

- The output of each input sinusoidal component can be determined by the system's frequency response curves, using the amplitude response curve to get the amplitude and the phase response curve to get the phase change (although the phase change will be disregarded in this discussion with the understanding that a fixed delay in the signal ensues for an ideal system).

- The outputs can be recombined by summation or integration to put the total response back into the time domain.

A signal whose frequency components lie entirely within a finite frequency spectrum is called a **bandlimited signal.** When convenient, a bandlimited signal whose highest and lowest frequencies are ω_h and ω_l, respectively, can be represented by an equivalent bandlimited signal whose spectral range lies between 0 and $\omega_h - \omega_l$. A system of bandwidth W can be viewed as one whose bandpass lies between 0 and W. In other words, the signal or the system bandpass can be moved in the spectrum without placing any undue restrictions on the theory.

An ideal channel of bandwidth W can be used to transmit and recover a bandlimited signal that lies entirely within its range of frequencies. Normally, however, frequency components out of the range of the bandpass will be present, but the dominant frequencies will be bandlimited within the bandpass and the signal can be transmitted and recovered by the channel with minor distortion.

Example 2.6

Given the following two input signals, one periodic and the other aperiodic, and an ideal channel whose bandpass lies between −500 and 500 Hz, display the output for each input signal.

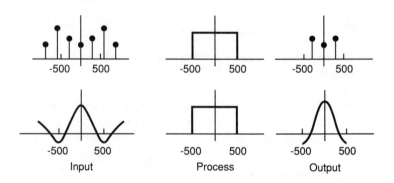

Input   Process   Output

Exercises

2.16 Calculate and plot the shape of a 600 Hz rectangular wave transmitted over an ideal voice line.

2.17 Prove that if $F_1(\omega)$ and $F_2(\omega)$ are the Fourier transforms of $f_1(t)$ and $f_2(t)$, respectively; then $a_1F_1(\omega) + a_2F_2(\omega)$ is the Fourier transform of the linear combination $a_1f_1(t) + a_2f_2(t)$, where a_1 and a_2 are arbitrary constants. Interpret the significance of this theorem.

2.18 Prove that if $F(\omega)$ is the Fourier transform of $f(t)$ and τ is an arbitrary constant, then $e^{-i\omega\tau}F(\omega)$ is the Fourier transform of $f(t - \tau)$.

2.19 Show that $F(\omega - \omega_o)$ is the Fourier transform of the function $f(t)e^{i\omega_o t}$, where $F(\omega)$ is the Fourier transform of $f(t)$. Interpret this result.

2.20 Calculate and draw the approximation to the periodic signal shown in Figure 2.13c, using an increasing number of harmonics to demonstrate that the series represents the given function.

2.21 Displace each of the functions shown in Figure 2.13 by a value of t_o, and find their Fourier series.

2.22 Plot the frequency spectrum of a signal composed of the sum of the output of a half-wave rectifier

Exercises *(continued)*

and the square wave (given in Figure 2.13). Plot the two-sided frequency spectrum for this composite wave.

2.23 Verify that any real function expressed as an exponential series produces a symmetrical function in the frequency domain.

2.24 Plot in both the frequency and time domains the output of an ideal channel for various values of bandwidth for each of the signals given in Figure 2.13 (disregard the signal delay).

2.25 Show the output frequency response through the given channel for each of the following input spectrums:

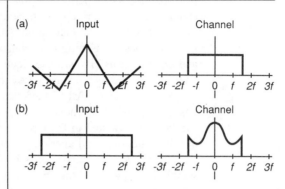

SUMMARY

The operational behavior of communication processes has been lodged in a mathematical framework, which has the advantage of using concepts and abstract terms used in other engineering disciplines, which gives them a quantitative meaning and a graphical interpretation. The relationship between input signals and output signals has been depicted as a black box that acts as a linear system. This external view describes how the system will respond to the individual input signals. To study the system's response to an arbitrary, complex input, the input signal is decomposed into a linear combination of elementary functions whose response is known, and then these individual responses can be reassembled to give the total system response.

The sinusoidal function is particularly useful for the study of linear systems because its response produces an output signal of the same frequency. The response of a system viewed in the frequency domain produces an uncluttered graphical picture. Two curves suffice for describing a system's response in the frequency domain: the ratio of the output and input signals and the time (phase) delay the signal experiences in passing through the system. The amplitude response curve produced by such a display is that of a bandpass system, a system that passes all signals lying within the bandpass, attenuating all other to an insignificant level.

Although the response curves for an ideal channel are unrealistic and could never be duplicated by a physical system, they serve well as a theoretical model of communication processes. The ideal response curves show the system by a flat amplitude response curve and a linear phase response within the bandpass. The well-known commercial telephone channel has been used as an example to put these ideas in perspective.

Signals can also be described in the frequency domain. The frequency analysis of periodic and aperiodic signals has been described (with further details presented in Appendix A). A periodic signal is a signal whose pattern is cyclically repeated. A signal that is not periodic is aperiodic.

A periodic signal can be uniquely decomposed into a linear series, known as a Fourier series, consisting of a constant term and a finite or infinite sequence of sine and cosine terms. By simple algebraical transformation, this series can be equivalently expressed as a cosine series (or sine series) or as a series of exponentials with complex exponents. All of these series can be represented in the frequency domain. Also, by considering the signal's period equal to infinite, an aperiodic signal can be similarly represented in the frequency domain using Fourier transforms. In this manner, both periodic and aperiodic signals can be similarly interpreted.

From response curves of a bandpass system and the composition of the input signal, both given in the frequency domain, the response can be obtained graphically. A bandlimited input signal whose spectrum lies entirely within the bandpass of an ideal channel will appear in the output as an attenuated replica of the input signal with a time delay. An input signal whose spectrum extends outside the bandpass of the channel will appear in the output as a distorted replica of the input signal so long as the dominant frequencies of the input signal lie within the bandpass.

KEY TERMS

Linear system	Periodic signal
Amplitude	Aperiodic signal
Period	Fourier series
Frequency	Dc component
Hertz	Fundamental frequency
Phase	Harmonics
Frequency domain	Fourier transform pair
Time domain	Fourier transform
Decibel	Spectral density
Bandpass system	Bandlimited signal
Bandwidth	

SUGGESTED READINGS

Lucky, R. W., Salz, J., and Weldon, E. J. *Principles of Data Communication*. New York: McGraw-Hill, 1968.

Roden, Martin S. *Analog and Digital Communication Systems*. 2nd ed. Englewood Cliffs, N.J.: Prentice-Hall, 1985.

Martin, James. *Telecommunications and the Computer*. Englewood Cliffs, N.J.: Prentice-Hall, 1969.

Stanley, W. D. *Electronic Communication Systems*. Reston, VA., Reston Publishing Co., 1982.

CHAPTER 3

COMMUNICATION SIGNALS

And if the noise is not caused directly by
these channels, it is indirectly. And even
if it should have no connection with them
whatever, one is not at liberty to make a
priori assumptions, but must wait until
one finds the cause, or it reveals itself.
One could play with hypotheses, of
course, even at this stage . . . .
FRANZ KAFKA
"THE BURROW"

3.1 SIGNAL TRANSMISSION SYSTEMS

TRANSMISSION TECHNIQUES

The structure of communication signals must conform to the bandpass of the communication line used for transmission. Signals whose dominant frequencies lie within the bandpass of the line can be transmitted directly on the line. This form of transmission, called **baseband transmission,** dedicates the entire bandpass of the line to one channel. Another form of transmission, called **broadband transmission,** divides the line's bandwidth into multiple channels so that many independent users may share the line simultaneously. To transmit signals by broadband transmission, the spectrum of each signal must be moved to occupy the transmission spectrum of the channel.

The process of shifting the frequency spectrum of signals to lie within the bandpass used for baseband transmission or to relocate the frequency spectrum of signals to a designated channel for broadband transmission is called **modulation.** Signals that have been modulated may be recovered by a complementary process called **demodulation.** Figure 3.1 shows the placement of the modulator/demodulator in the context of a transmission system. Signals may, however, be modulated and demodulated many times in different ways before they finally arrive at their destination point.

Signals whose spectrum extends outside the bandwidth of the transmission channel become distorted during transmission. Moreover, extraneous noises also enter the communication system. If it weren't for the fact that channel noises and signal distortions can corrupt the signals, the signals could be transmitted and recovered with impunity. To preserve the integrity of the data in the presence of these anomalies, the data values are formatted and transmitted as digital signals.

Ultimately, the question that must be answered is, How fast, in bits per second, can digital information be transmitted in a given channel? To answer this question, the principles of both analog and digital transmission must be understood. A theoretical bound can be placed on the rate of transmission of analog signals in a noiseless, ideal channel. From this vantage point, the rate of transmission of digital information

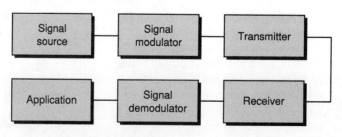

FIGURE 3.1 Schematic view of a signal transmission system.

can also be given for an ideal channel whose noise characteristics have been defined statistically.

TRANSMISSION NOISE AND SIGNAL DISTORTION

Noise is the unpredictable, extraneous fluctuations that are ever present in all communication systems, corrupting the expected signals and causing transmission errors. Under normal usage, voice lines assume intelligence at both ends of the communication channel, permitting either end to interpret the communication signals and correct faulty transmissions by requesting the transmitter to repeat or speak slower, louder, or more clearly, a capability not inherent in a data communication system. Although voice lines are a common source of communication lines for data, their use is limited by the transmission speed possible or by the error rate that can be tolerated. Moreover, line characteristics acceptable for voice communications cause unwanted distortions in digital signals, which from a user's perspective are indistinguishable from noise and further exaggerate the number of transmission errors. We will now take a look at several types of noise (in particular, random noise, interference, echoes, and impulse noise) and sources of signal distortions and, when appropriate, identify special problems introduced when using voice lines.

Random noise is often called **Gaussian noise** because of the mathematically convenient properties of the normal statistical distribution curve studied by Gauss. Random noise whose sources are not correlated to each other is also referred to as white noise because its composition is analogous to white light consisting of a uniform frequency spectrum or as **thermal noise** because of the random variations inherent in the thermal properties of materials. Physically, it is the background noise present in all electronic gear, which can be described statistically by the normal distribution curve over the frequency spectrum.

The physics of thermal noise, in particular, has been studied in detail. The amount of thermal noise is a function of the temperature and bandwidth of the system, although the temperature factor is often removed from design calculations by standardizing the operating conditions at 17°C. When this is done, the amount of thermal noise, N, can then be given by the equation

$$N = kW \tag{3.1}$$

where k is a physical constant and W is the bandwidth of the channel.

Random noise, in general, is given as a ratio of the average power of the transmitted signal over the average power of the noise in the bandpass of the system, called the **signal-to-noise ratio.** This ratio, normally given in decibels using factors of 3 (the reason for this will be given later), characterizes the quality of the transmission channel. The statistical nature of Gaussian noise is such that its standard deviation, σ, is equal to the square root of its average power, P; that is,

$$\sigma = \sqrt{P} \tag{3.2}$$

This equation will be used later in the formulation of a theoretical limit in the speed of noisy channels.

Crosstalk, radio noise, or **static** is caused by interference from radio waves, from signals in adjacent wires, or from natural electronic disturbances in the atmosphere. Although this type of noise has many of the same characteristics as white noise, it usually is more troublesome because its level and duration may change unpredictably over time. An attempt can be made to reduce the amount of noise by shielding the wires or by regenerating and strengthening the signal by repeaters stationed every few miles, techniques that require extraordinary measures.

Echoes are particular disturbances that can be traced back to the actual signals being transmitted. They occur when the electrical characteristics of the lines connecting the terminal points are not properly matched electrically. For example, the telephone line connection to a local exchange consists of a two-wire circuit, while long-distance lines connecting exchanges consist of four-wire circuits, and when these dissimilar facilities are joined together at junction points, line irregularities may occur, resulting in echoes. Echoes even in voice communications can be disturbing and often require stopping the call and redialing to seek a better connection; but in data transmission, the unwanted, delayed echo interferes with the signals transmitted later in the sequence and deteriorates communications.

The effect of echoes may be counteracted by transmitting at reduced power or by installing echo suppressors. Reduced power can be effective when used between intermediate points in the telephone networks. This reduces the loudness of the echoes but does not eliminate them. Echo suppressors installed in the four-wire line (Figure 3.2) act to prevent simultaneous bidirectional transmission by attenuating the softer signal on the line (i.e., the echo) to an undisturbing level. When desired, the echo suppression circuit can be temporarily disabled by maintaining a strong prescribed tone for a period of time that disables the suppressor circuits and keeps them disabled so long as the channel actively uses bidirectional transmission.

Impulse noise is a sudden burst of noise introduced into the system from some external physical activity. Usually, impulse noise is not bothersome in voice communications unless it is of long duration or repetitive. In digital communication, it

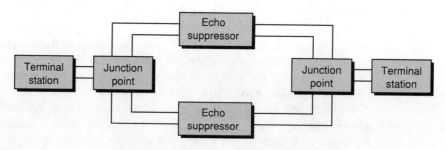

FIGURE 3.2 Echo suppressors in telephone circuits.

can be disastrous. Suppose a noise spike of 0.01-second duration occurs while data are being transmitted at a rate of 1000 bits per second. The result is a 10-bit error, an error that cannot be detected simply. Complicating this further, spikes occur randomly. There are many sources of such noise, including:

- Dirty switch contacts, when older relay circuits are used
- Defective electronic filters in the power supply
- Crosstalk resulting from switching circuits
- Improper shielding and grounding
- Loose connectors
- External noises picked up by inductive or capacitive coupling

If a channel is particularly troublesome with impulse noise, the only solution may be to monitor the circuits with electronic equipment and try to locate its source. Other than correcting the conditions causing the noise, some actions that may be used are to retransmit on a regular basis or use special error detecting–error correcting codes, to be discussed later.

Distortion differs from noise but has similar effects in signal uncertainty and higher error rates. The desired objective of a communication channel is to recover the signals as transmitted. Signal aberrations due to distortion cannot easily be distinguished from noise. Even in the absence of extraneous noise, a transmitted signal may be spoiled by the characteristics of the physical components of the channel. However, once the source of the problem is located, the channel can be improved by physical design unique for each channel, a costly process.

A prevalent form of distortion is due to the nonideal frequency response characteristics of the available channels. In practice, the frequency components of an input signal transmitted over a channel will be attenuated disproportionately and their phase will be shifted in a nonlinear manner. The amplitude response of a communication line varies as a function of distance. To correct for these variations, special circuits are inserted into the lines at regular intervals. These circuits improve the line for voice communication but add further phase delays into the frequency components of the transmitted signals. This solution, while appropriate for voice communication, is troublesome when the line is used for digital transmission because it causes interference between signals that have been sequentially transmitted. When a line is used for digital transmission, a circuit can be inserted to compensate for both amplitude and phase. However, this correction must be specialized for each line, at an added cost and only for lines leased for private use.

The physical components of a transmission channel may introduce other forms of distortion. Two forms are worth mentioning. The power supply acts to convert ac to dc power through suitable circuits. If the conversion is imperfect and not properly isolated from the communication lines, then ripples may appear as an added signal in the output. Another form of signal distortion results when the carrier frequency used to transmit the signal and the frequency used to recover the signal are not matched; in such cases, the frequencies of the expected signal will be shifted and will produce a distorted signal (such distortion can be observed in radio transmission). Both of these problems require an engineering solution.

Exercises

3.1 Show that if the noise in a channel is thermal noise, then the signal-to-noise ratios (given in decibels) of two channels of bandwidths W_1 and W_2 are related by the equation

$$(S/N)_{W_1} - (S/N)_{W_2} = (W_2/W_1)_{db}$$

3.2   BROADBAND TRANSMISSION

SINUSOIDAL MODULATION

A bandlimited signal can be relocated for transmission over a portion of the bandpass spectrum of the transmission channel by continuous-wave modulation. While such modulation techniques are used to share the bandpass among many independent data sources, they also may be necessary to improve the performance of the transmission system. For example, the efficiency of radio transmission depends on the size of the antenna, which in turn depends on the wavelength of the transmitted signals. Antenna sizes of 25 to 50 percent of the wavelength, the nominal sizes recommended for efficient transmission, would be impractical for low frequencies such as those in the audible range. These signals can be moved, transmitted, and recovered by modulating them onto a sinusoidal carrier in the radio frequency range.

A sinusoidal carrier, given by equation 3.3, has three parameters onto which the signals can be superimposed for transmission: amplitude, frequency, and phase.

$$\text{Sinusoidal carrier} = A \sin(2\pi f_c t + \phi_c) \tag{3.3}$$

Amplitude ———⌐

Frequency ————————

Phase ————————————

Sinusoidal modulation techniques are known by the carrier parameter that the signals modulate: **amplitude modulation, frequency modulation,** and **phase modulation,** which perhaps are better known by their acronyms AM, FM, and PM, respectively. The value of the carrier frequency sets the frequency location of the signal in the bandpass of the transmission channel. Demodulation reverses the modulation process and recovers the original signal for use at the receiving station.

AMPLITUDE MODULATION

For amplitude modulation, the source signal, $S(t)$, acts to modulate the amplitude of the carrier to produce the modulated signal T:

$$T = [A + S(t)]\sin(2\pi f_c t) \tag{3.4}$$

Assume, for the sake of discussion, that the signal consists of a pure tone, which may be expressed mathematically by a sinusoid of a single frequency:

$$S(t) = a \sin(2\pi f_s t)$$

Substituting this into equation 3.4 gives

$$T = [A + a \sin(2\pi f_s t)]\sin(2\pi f_c t) \tag{3.5}$$

Using the trigonometric identity

$$\sin x \sin y = \tfrac{1}{2} \cos(x - y) - \tfrac{1}{2} \cos(x + y) \tag{3.6}$$

the spectral composition of the transmitted signal can be shown to consist of three components, the carrier and two replicas of the source signal located above and below the carrier frequency and called the upper sideband and lower sideband, respectively.

$$T = \underset{\text{carrier}}{A \sin(2\pi f_c t)} + \underset{\text{lower sideband}}{(a/2) \sin[2\pi(f_c - f_s)t + \pi/2]} + \underset{\text{upper sideband}}{(a/2)\sin[2\pi(f_c + f_s)t - \pi/2]} \tag{3.7}$$

Figure 3.3a shows the modulated signal given by equation 3.7 plotted in the frequency domain. In a comparable way, a bandlimited signal can be analyzed and displayed as shown in Figure 3.3b. The two replicas of the source signal form mirror images of each other about the carrier frequency. The sidebands of the modulated signal are 90° out of phase with the unmodulated signal, a fact given by the equation but not shown in the figure.

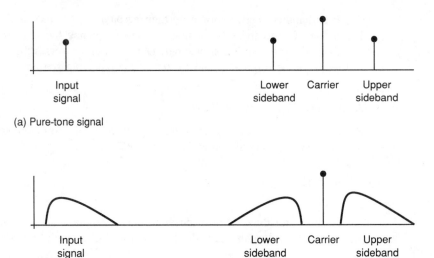

(a) Pure-tone signal

(b) Bandlimited signal

FIGURE 3.3   AM signals in the frequency domain.

Example 3.1

Given a bandlimited signal between 300 and 3300 Hz, transmitted by AM using a 60 kHz carrier, calculate the range of frequencies in the transmitted signal.

60,000 Hz	Carrier
56,700–59,700 Hz	Lower sideband
60,300–63,300 Hz	Upper sideband

In practical AM transmission systems, three variations of amplitude modulation are used to transmit the signals; known as **double-sideband modulation, single-sideband modulation** and **vestigial-sideband modulation.** Double-sideband modulation transmits and recovers the source signals from the two sidebands. Clearly, a double-sideband modulation system requires a bandwidth of twice the source signals' spectrum. The single-sideband modulation method acts to reject one of the sidebands before transmission by filtering and then by recovering the source signals entirely from the other sideband. While this method makes a more economical use of the available bandwidth it introduces phase discrepancies among the transmitted sinu-

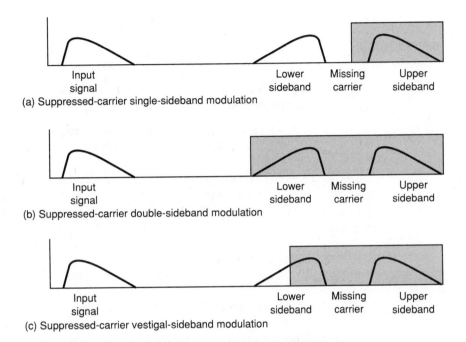

FIGURE 3.4 AM transmission strategies.

soids that distort the signals during recovery. Vestigial-sideband modulation method is a compromise design that transmits one complete sideband and a part of the other sideband.

Vestigial-sideband modulation is an alternative to double-sideband modulation when some distortion in the recovered signals is tolerable or when the signals can be adequately described by some dominant frequencies in their spectrum. This form of AM transmission realizes most of the advantages of double-sideband transmission without doubling the bandwidth needed to transmit the signals. In addition, the carrier in all of these methods is an extraneous signal and is suppressed by filtering. Figure 3.4 graphically compares the three strategies by showing an ideal channel superimposed over the recovered signal.

ANGLE MODULATION

FM and PM are related forms of modulation. They differ from AM in that they both use a constant amplitude carrier and modulate the angular value of the carrier proportional to the source signal. Equation 3.8a shows the formula for modulating the carrier frequency to produce the FM signal. The notation follows that used in equation 3.6 for AM transmission, except that Δf_c represents the maximum variation

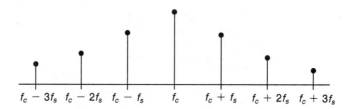

$f_c - 3f_s \quad f_c - 2f_s \quad f_c - f_s \qquad f_c \qquad f_c + f_s \quad f_c + 2f_s \quad f_c + 3f_s$

FIGURE 3.5 Frequency domain description of a signal modulated by FM or PM.

allowed in the carrier frequency. Equation 3.8b shows the formula for PM, which differs from FM in that the phase of the carrier is modulated directly. The term $\Delta\phi_c$ represents the maximum phase change that the source signal can impose on the carrier phase.

$$T = A \sin[2\pi[f_c + \Delta f_c S(t)]t] \tag{3.8a}$$

$$T = A \sin[2\pi f_c t + \Delta\phi_c S(t)] \tag{3.8b}$$

Without further mathematical analysis of FM and PM techniques, an understanding of these techniques is gained from a description of the modulated signals in the frequency domain. Figure 3.5 shows the frequency spectrum resulting from modulating a single sinusoidal signal whose frequency is f_s by FM or PM techniques. The output signal continuously replicates the source signal. With proper design, practical systems rapidly attenuate the sidebands located farther away from the carrier so that the signal can be recovered from a few sidebands. Still, FM and PM systems require a wider bandwidth to recover the transmitted signals than that required for AM systems. The signal fidelity and the superior discrimination against noise that can be achieved by these techniques more than compensate for the complexities they introduce over AM.

Exercises

3.2 The amount of modulation of an AM signal is given by the ratio m of the signal amplitude to the amplitude of the carrier. Plot the waveform of a 1 Hz tone modulated by a 10 Hz carrier for various values of m, where $0 < m \le 1$, and describe envelope of the curves.

3.3 For $\Delta f_c = 1$ Hz, plot the waveform of a 1 Hz tone modulated by FM techniques using a 10 Hz carrier.

3.4 For $\Delta\phi_c = \pi/2$, plot the wave form of a 1 Hz tone modulated by PM techniques using a 10 Hz carrier.

3.5 To transmit radio signals efficiently, an antenna must be at least 25 to 50 percent the size of the wavelength of the transmitted signal. Compare the antenna size needed to recover a 100 Hz signal with that needed to recover a 100 kHz signal.

3.3 PULSE TRANSMISSION

SAMPLER

Up to now, the discussion on signals in the frequency domain has focused on signals that can be represented as a continuous function of time. Signals whose form consists of a time sequence of discrete values can be treated in a like manner. Figure 3.6 depicts a scheme for generating a sequence of discrete values from a continuous function and gives a basis for comparing functions given as a sequence of discrete values with their continuous-function counterparts.

The **sampler** consists of a switch that periodically makes and breaks contact with the input line, producing an output of short pulses. The contact of an ideal sampler can be assumed to be instantaneous and of zero duration, yielding a sequence of discrete pulses whose values equal the values of the continuous function at the time of contact. Although the output appears as a skeletal reproduction of the input, both the input and output represent different versions of the same function.

Mathematically, the output of the sampler, $\theta(t)$, can be formulated as the product of the continuous input, $I(t)$, and a periodic impulse sequence, $p(t)$. The impulse sequence represents the action of the switch, giving a sequence of equally spaced short pulses of equal amplitude. The period and frequency of the impulse sequence, called the **sampling period** and **sampling frequency,** are denoted by τ_s and f_s (where $f_s = 1/\tau_s$), respectively. Equation 3.9 expresses the relationship between these terms algebraically, and Figure 3.7 illustrates their form and shape.

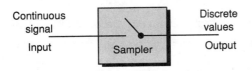

Continuous signal
Input   Sampler   Output

Discrete values

FIGURE 3.6 Scheme for generating discrete values of a continuous signal.

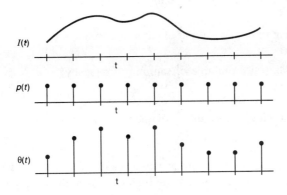

FIGURE 3.7 Sampler input and output.

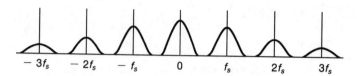

FIGURE 3.8 Frequency spectrum of a sampled signal.

$$\theta(t) = I(t)p(t) \tag{3.9}$$

SAMPLING THEOREM

An interesting result occurs when the output of the sampler (given by equation 3.9 and illustrated in Figure 3.7) is analyzed using Fourier techniques. The output spectrum repeatedly reproduces the input spectrum by replicating a copy of the input spectrum about all multiples of the sampling frequency. Figure 3.8 illustrates this result for a bandlimited signal.

Example 3.2

Find the spectrum of a 5 Hz sinusoidal input signal sampled at a sampling rate of 7 Hz.

A copy of the 5 Hz signal will reappear together with replicas of this signal about multiples copies about multiples of the sampling frequency:

$$5 \text{ Hz (original signal)}$$
$$7 - 5 = 2 \text{ Hz (first multiple of sampling frequency)}$$
$$7 + 5 = 12 \text{ Hz}$$
$$14 - 5 = 9 \text{ Hz (second multiple of sampling frequency)}$$
$$14 + 5 = 19 \text{ Hz}$$
$$21 - 5 = 16 \text{ Hz (third multiple of sampling frequency)}$$
$$21 + 5 = 26 \text{ Hz}$$

etc., continuing at multiples of sampling frequency ◄

An important implication of the frequency analysis of a sampled-data function is the sampling theorem, a theorem by Claude Shannon. This theorem states:

FIGURE 3.9 Frequency spectrum of sampler output.

A bandlimited input signal can be recovered from a periodic sampled sequence of the signal if the sampling frequency is at least twice the highest frequency in the signal's spectrum.

To validate the sampling theorem, refer to Figure 3.9, which gives the output spectrum of a bandlimited signal of bandwidth W sampled at a sampling frequency of f_s. The replicas in the output spectrum can be kept separate from each other when the sampling frequency is at least twice the bandwidth of the input signal; that is,

$$f_s \geq 2W \tag{3.10}$$

The minimum theoretical sampling frequency, $f_s = 2W$, given by equation 3.10, is called the **Nyquist frequency.** When the sampling frequency is at least the Nyquist frequency, then an ideal bandpass process whose bandwidth equals W can recover the input signal from any replica. However, for a sampling frequency less than the Nyquist frequency, frequencies from one replica overlap the frequencies of a neighboring replica's spectrum, called an **alias.** Since a bandpass process cannot discriminate to which replica an alias belongs, the original signal cannot be reconstructed without distorting the reconstruction with an extraneous signal.

PULSE MODULATION AND DEMODULATION

The sampler functions to generate discrete values of a continuous signal for transmission and from which the continuous signal can be later reconstructed. While it was theoretically convenient to assume pulses of zero duration, the assumption was unreasonable in practice. Besides containing the value of the sample to be transmitted, the pulse shape should also have a spectrum suitable for transmission over the bandpass of the communication channel. Figure 3.10 shows the sampler augmented

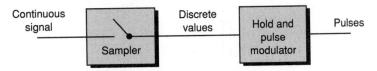

FIGURE 3.10 Pulse modulation.

by a **hold,** which functions to hold the value of the sample while a **pulse modulator** embeds the value of the sample into a pulse for transmission.

But how should the value of the samples be embedded into the pulses? Figure 3.11 compares three techniques used for pulse modulation: pulse-amplitude modulation (PAM); pulse-duration modulation (PDM); and pulse-position modulation (PPM). Flat-topped rectangular pulses will serve to illustrate the pulse shapes.

PAM represents the instantaneous value of a discrete sample by the amplitude of a finite-width rectangular pulse. The height of each pulse is made proportional, between a maximum and minimum value, to the value of the sampled data it represents. The leading edges of the pulses are set at the start of each sampling period so that the signals can be transmitted and later retrieved without having to synchronize the clock at the receiver to detect the arrival of the pulse.

PDM and PPM differ from PAM in that the timing of the pulse conveys its value. PDM uses pulses of constant amplitude but whose duration (i.e., width) convey the values of the samples. The pulse width is made proportional to the maximum time slot allocated for each pulse. As with PAM, the leading edge of each pulse used with PDM clocks the start of the pulse. The disadvantage of PAM and PDM is that the energy of each signal is given by the area under each pulse, which depends on its value. PPM, on the other hand, provides uniformly shaped pulses. With PPM, the position of the pulse from its nominal start represents the value of the sample; in other words, the pulse gives the position of the trailing edge of a corresponding pulse generated by PDM. However, since the leading edge of the pulse is not fixed, PPM requires regeneration of the clock timing at the receiver.

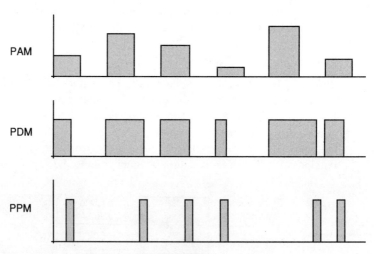

FIGURE 3.11 Pulse modulation techniques.

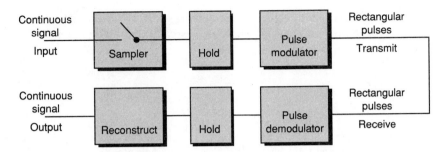

FIGURE 3.12 Pulse modulation and demodulation.

After transmission, the value of the pulses can be fixed by demodulation, and the continuous signal can be reconstructed using more sophisticated holding techniques. The schematic in Figure 3.12 shows the steps for generating and reconstructing a signal using pulse modulation and demodulation techniques.

The degree of polynomials used to approximate a continuous function from discrete values can be used to systematically order the hold circuits used during regeneration. In this way, regeneration can be viewed as piecewise polynomial interpolation. Figure 3.13 illustrates the output of typical hold circuits.

The zero-order hold, shown in Figure 3.13a, generates a flat-topped rectangular pulse whose amplitude equals the discrete value. In contrast with this simple hold a first-order hold, shown in Figure 3.13b, uses two successive samples and approximates the values between successive samples by straight lines. This scheme can be carried out to higher-order approximations, for example; three values for constructing a quadratic approximation (Figure 3.13c), four values for a cubic approximation (not shown), and so on. It might appear that higher-order holds produce better approxi-

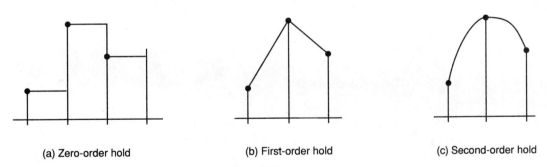

(a) Zero-order hold   (b) First-order hold   (c) Second-order hold

FIGURE 3.13 Signal reconstruction from sampled data.

mations. This is true, but the higher-order holds also introduce added delays in the reconstructed signals. These delays can be partially compensated for by increasing the sampling frequency.

Exercises

3.6 Find all the frequencies of a signal composed of two components at 2 Hz and 5 Hz when it is sampled at a sampling rate of 7 Hz.

3.7 Calculate and plot the samples of a 5 Hz signal using a sampling rate of 7 Hz, and overlay the plot with
(a) a 5 Hz sinusoid signal
(b) a 2 Hz sinusoid signal
(c) a 12 Hz sinusoid signal

Explain the optical illusions that are possible when one looks at every third point of a 5 Hz signal sampled at a sampling rate of 21 Hz.

3.8 Viewed another way, the sampling theorem states that a sampling rate of f_s can theoretically recover any bandlimited signal whose highest frequency is less than $f_s/2$, called the folding frequency. Discuss the relationship of the folding frequency to
(a) the frequency spectrum of the sampler output
(b) aliases

3.9 The highlight of Shannon's theorem is that a band-limited signal can be completely recovered by samples taken at a finite sampling rate. Obviously, given the sampled points, many functions can be con-structed that pass through these same points. Explain the fallacy in this apparent paradox.

3.10 Consider a large amount of noise whose frequency spectrum lies outside the frequency spectrum of a bandlimited input signal to the sampler. Discuss the effect of this noise on the reconstruction of the signal.†

3.11 Sample a 1 Hz signal using a sampling rate of 12 Hz, and represent the data by PAM, PDM, and PPM.

3.12 Repeat exercise 3.11 using a signal that is delayed by 45°. Compare these two results.

3.13 Write a program to piecewise interpolate between successive samples of a 1 Hz signal sampled at a rate of 6 Hz using a zero-order hold, a first order hold, and a second-order hold. Plot the difference (error) between the reconstructed signal and the actual signal.

3.14 Discuss how the signal strength and timing affect the reconstruction of signals generated by PAM, PDM, and PPM.†

†Class discussion exercise.

3.4   DIGITAL TRANSMISSION

PULSE–CODE MODULATION

Sinusoidal and pulse modulation are different forms of analog transmission; one embeds the value of the signal into a sinusoidal carrier and the other into a rectangular pulse. In both cases, transmission noise and distortion degrade the signals from their prescribed values, causing errors and uncertainty in the recovered signals. As an alternative to analog transmission, the signal values can be encoded and transmitted in a digital format to preserve their integrity.

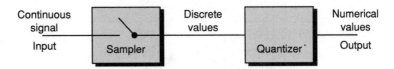

FIGURE 3.14   A/D conversion.

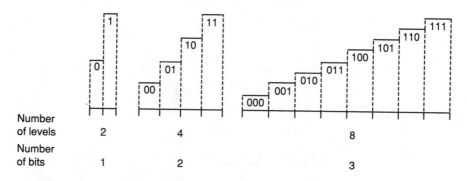

FIGURE 3.15   Number of bits versus number of quantized levels.

Figure 3.14 shows a sampled-data arrangement augmented with a process to quantize the sample values, sometimes known as **analog-to-digital conversion (A/D).** The quantizer assigns a numerical value to each sample by dividing the permissible range of the samples into a finite number of incremental levels.

The number of incremental steps determines the numerical precision of the quantizer. As shown in Figure 3.15, two possible levels can be assigned the value 0 or 1 and can be encoded by 1 bit, four possible levels can be assigned a value from 0 through 3 and can be encoded by 2 bits, eight possible levels can be assigned a value from 0 through 7 and can be encoded by 3 bits, and so on (seven bits is normally sufficient for transmitting voice by digital means). Using this argument inductively, M possible levels can be assigned digital values from 0 to M $-$ 1 and can be encoded by $\log_2 M$ bits. This relation can be easily verified by observing that n bits can represent 2^n numbers.

Example 3.3
Divide an input signal in the range of 0–5 volts (V) into increments for quantizing the samples by a precision of 3 bits. (See art on page 68.)

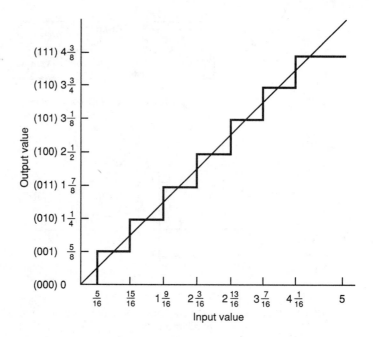

The figure divides the input range into eight levels to give a precision of 3 bits. An output value of 0 V will be produced for any input value between 0 and $\frac{1}{16}$ V. After an input value of $\frac{1}{16}$ V, the quantized output value jumps by $\frac{5}{8}$ V for each $\frac{5}{8}$ V in the input value until $4\frac{1}{16}$ V. Any input value over $4\frac{1}{16}$ V will be quantized to the maximum output value of $4\frac{3}{8}$ V. The numbers in parentheses to the left of the output values represent the equivalent binary values of the quantized values.

The difference between the step function and the linear line is the error in quantization, which in this case never exceeds $\frac{1}{16}$ V up to the upper realistic input value of $4\frac{15}{16}$ V. Commercial A/D converters use a variety of other methods for dividing the range, such as using nonlinear steps to provide greater precision for analog signals that have less than the maximum swing. ◀

By quantifying the samples into a finite number of levels, little has been gained in safeguarding the pulse values against noise or distortion during transmission. However, the incremental levels represent the sample's numerical value, and by encoding this value into a digital format, we can transmit the value by digital transmission. **Pulse-code modulation (PCM)** is the name given to the process for encoding values of the samples for digital transmission. Figure 3.16 shows the sampled-data arrangement for digital transmission.

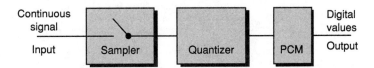

FIGURE 3.16 Sampled-data system for digital transmission.

Pulse-code modulation encodes each value as a sequence of pulses, where each pulse represents one or more binary digits of the value. Digitally encoding the samples for transmission has the advantage that small fluctuations in the signal caused by noise or distortion will not corrupt the value. However, the technique is not achieved without penalty. Depending on the precision used in encoding, each value requires multiple pulses rather than a single pulse. To reduce the number of pulses needed, multilevel pulses can again be used such that each pulse encodes more than one bit of the numerical value. Using 1 and 2 bits per pulse is common (using 2 bits per pulse is referred to as **dibit transmission**). Figure 3.17 illustrates the pulse sequence for the single-bit and dibit transmission of samples using PCM.

SHIFT KEYING

Unlike sinusodial and rectangular pulse modulation techniques for modulating analog signals, pulse-code modulation addresses the issues of digital transmission. PCM conveyed the value of the signal in a digital format by encoding it into a sequence of pulses. The sinusoid can also serve in a similar fashion to encode digital information for transmission, known as **shift keying.**

Figure 3.18 illustrates three possible forms of shift keying—amplitude, frequency, or phase—depending on the sinusoidal parameter used to represent the digital information. **Amplitude-shift keying (ASK)** uses a single frequency and represents the binary value, 0 and 1, by switching a particular frequency on or off. **Frequency-shift keying (FSK)** uses two frequencies to represent a binary value. **Phase-shift keying (PSK)** uses a single frequency and shifts the phase to represent the binary value.

As a practical matter, to make economical use of the bandwidth available, sev-

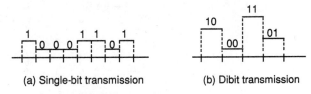

(a) Single-bit transmission   (b) Dibit transmission

FIGURE 3.17 PCM of bit value 10001101.

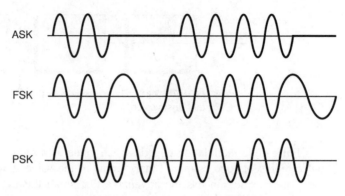

FIGURE 3.18 Shift keying modulation.

eral bits can be encoded together for multiple-bit transmission. The following illustrates some of the many possible variations of this theme.

A common scheme encodes 2 bits into four phase values of a sine for dibit transmission. Table 3.1 shows the assignment of four dibit values using four equally spaced sine phases. Consider, for the sake of discussion, that each dibit is represented by a sinusoidal pulse of one full period of the carrier. The phase value given may be used in two different ways. One way represents the phase at the start of each sinusoidal pulse. Alternatively, the phase assignment may represent the phase change from one pulse to the next. In this later case, the phase change can be measured by storing and comparing successive pulses and detecting the phase difference.

Touch-tone dialing, which was developed to facilitate data communications using the frequency spectrum available in voice lines, can serve to illustrate multivalued FSK. Each button transmits two frequencies simultaneously to encode each bit (Figure 3.19). A touch-tone board can produce combinations of eight different frequencies, using two frequencies for each symbol for a total of 16 possible symbols. Ten of these combinations are used to represent the ten digits, and the remaining six combinations are used for other purposes. The frequencies have been selected to

TABLE 3.1
PHASE ASSIGNMENTS FOR DIBIT
TRANSMISSION

BINARY VALUE	PHASE VALUE
00	135°
01	−135°
10	45°
11	−45°

Frequency	697	941	852	770
1477	1	4	7	
1336	2	5	8	
1209	3	6	9	0
1633				

Frequency	
2050	Zone 0
2150˙	Zone 11
2250	Zone 12

FIGURE 3.19　Multitone transmission.

avoid the in-band control frequencies used by the telecommunications system. This code has also been expanded with a third frequency to transmit the extended code used on punch cards.

Obviously, the preceding schemes lend themselves to other multibit arrangements such as eight equally spaced phase values for tribit transmission. However, for higher transmission speeds over quality voice-grade lines, a combination of modulation methods is often used. For example, one technique uses a combination of PSK and ASK to encode and detect the pulse values. Table 3.2 illustrates a couple of possible phase and amplitude assignments that can be used for quadbit transmission.

TABLE 3.2
COMBINATION OF PSK AND ASK FOR QUADBIT TRANSMISSION

BINARY VALUE	12-PHASE/3-LEVEL		8-PHASE/2-LEVEL	
	AMPLITUDE LEVEL	PHASE VALUE	AMPLITUDE LEVEL	PHASE VALUE
0000	2	22.5	1	22.5
0001	3	45.0	1	67.5
0010	2	67.5	1	157.5
0011	1	45.0	1	112.5
0100	2	157.5	1	− 22.5
0101	1	135.0	1	− 67.5
0110	2	112.5	1	−157.5
0111	3	135.0	1	−112.5
1000	2	− 22.5	2	22.5
1001	1	− 45.0	2	67.5
1010	2	− 67.5	2	157.5
1011	3	− 45.0	2	112.5
1100	2	−157.5	2	− 22.5
1101	3	−135.0	2	− 67.5
1110	2	−112.5	2	−157.5
1111	1	−135.0	2	−112.5

Exercises

3.15 Compare the bandwidth requirements for transmitting a bandlimited signal of bandwidth W using PAM with those of a system using PCM.

3.16 If the pulses used in PCM have three possible levels, how many pulses are required to transmit signals quantized to M levels? Repeat the problem for PCM pulses that have p levels.

3.17 The bandpass of a telephone line allows normal conversational voice to be transmitted, but its bandwidth is too small for transmitting the full acoustic range. Discuss how one might use a telephone line to transmit a symphony.

3.18 Plot the signal for transmitting the following bit patterns by PSK using the phase values given in Table 3.1 to encode each dibit into a sinusoidal pulse of one full period of the carrier. Assume that the phase values represent the phase at the start of each sinusoidal pulse.

(a) 00 01 10 11
(b) 00 00 01 01

3.19 Repeat exercise 3.18 assuming that the phase values represent the phase change at the termination of the previously transmitted dibit.

3.20 Put ASK, FSK, and PSK in the context of AM, FM, and PM using equations 3.4, 3.8a, and 3.8b.

3.5 RATE OF TRANSMISSION

CHANNEL CAPACITY

Now, at last, we will state the central theory for understanding digital transmission. Unfortunately, providing theoretical justification would require mathematical tools beyond the scope of this discussion, and an attempt to introduce the needed material would divert attention from the issues. For this reason, the mathematical rigors of the theory will be bypassed and an intuitive explanation will be attempted based on an understanding of analog signals and processes.

Assume for discussion an ideal, noiseless channel. If the bandwidth of a bandlimited signal and the bandwidth of the channel both equal W, then a sampling rate of $2W$ (the Nyquist sampling rate) suffices for transmitting and recovering the signal. This statement implies that the pulses transmitted at the rate of $2W$ contain all the information to be transferred and that a higher rate would add no further information. It follows from this circuitous argument that an ideal channel of bandwidth W can transmit information by undistorted pulses at a maximum rate of $2W$.

The maximum rate for transmitting information through a channel is called the **channel capacity.** The value of C, the channel capacity for an ideal channel of bandwidth W in pulses per second, is given by the equation

$$C = 2W \tag{3.11}$$

Under these idealized conditions, each pulse can be transmitted and recovered uncorrupted. Without noise or distortion, pulses can be quantized into an arbitrary number of levels, with each level representing a value. Assume M possible levels representing M discrete values. These values can be encoded by $\log_2 M$ bits. Expressed in bits per second, the capacity of an ideal channel can be rewritten as

$$C = 2W \log_2 M \tag{3.12}$$

Equation 3.12 is known as the channel capacity of a discrete noiseless channel, since it assumes that no extraneous frequencies are present in the recovered pulses due to noise or distortion. If noise is present in the channel, then fluctuations about the quantized levels may introduce uncertainty into the shape of the transmitted pulses, limiting the maximum number of possible levels that can be assigned. If the noise is statistically defined and the spacing between the levels is uniform, then the standard deviation of the signal and noise can be used to fix the maximum number of levels. Accordingly, if $S + N$ and σ_{S+N} are the mean and standard deviation, respectively; of the composite signal and noise power transmitted, and if N and σ_N are the mean and standard deviation, respectively; of the noise power in the channel, then the maximum number of statistically defined levels that are separated by one standard deviation of the noise is

$$M = \frac{\sigma_{S+N}}{\sigma_N} \tag{3.13}$$

The **Hartley-Shannon theorem** gives the capacity of a channel in the presence of Gaussian noise. For Gaussian distribution, the standard deviation equals the square root of the signal, and therefore from $\sigma_{S+N} = \sqrt{S + N}$, $\sigma_N = \sqrt{N}$, and equation 3.13; the maximum number of levels are:

$$M = \sqrt{1 + S/N} \tag{3.14}$$

Substituting equation 3.14 into the channel capacity equation (equation 3.12) gives

$$C = W \log_2 \left(1 + \frac{S}{N} \right) \tag{3.15}$$

The signal-to-noise ratio is universally given in units of decibels, often in values divisible by 3 (e.g., 12, 15, or 18 db). Assuming S/N is a reasonably large number compared to 1, then the term $\log_2(1 + S/N)$ can be approximated by $\log_2(S/N)$. Substituting this approximation into equation 3.15 and approximating $\log_{10}2$ to be 0.3, the Hartley-Shannon equation for computing the capacity of a noisy channel can be simplified to

$$C = \frac{W(S/N)_{db}}{3} \tag{3.16}$$

where $(S/N)_{db}$ is the signal-to-noise ratio of the channel in decibels.

LINE SPEED

Line speed and channel capacity are related terms. Line speed refers to the actual data rate of the channel, and channel capacity defines the maximum rate that data can be transferred. According to Shannon's theorem for a noiseless channel, the channel capacity is a linear function of its bandwidth. An increase in bandwidth increases the capacity proportionally, notwithstanding other factors that act to decrease the channel capacity. In the case of Gaussian noise, the Hartley-Shannon theorem for a noisy channel maintains an apparent linear relationship between bandwidth and capacity. But is this so? The amount of thermal noise, a tenacious form of Gaussian noise, has been given by equation 3.1 to be proportional to the bandwidth (i.e., $N = kW$, where k is a known physical constant dependent on the units used). It follows that at least for thermal noise, the capacity is not related linearly to the bandwidth.

The preceding considerations in determining the capacity of a channel are complicated by other practical considerations. The transient signal response, signal and channel distortions, signal modulation, and other types of noise decrease the number of detectable levels that can be assigned to the transmitted signals and so effectively decrease the channel's capacity.

Nevertheless, the capacity given by Hartley-Shannon theorem can be used as a theoretical upper limit for the speed of a channel given in bits per second. Figure 3.20 plots this upper bound on capacity showing C/W as a linear function of the signal-to-noise ratio given in decibels. The slope of the line is $\frac{1}{3}$. All factors considered, a more practical working range for capacity is one-half to one-quarter of the theoretical limit giving a working range of

$$\frac{(S/N)_{db}}{12} \leq \frac{C}{W} \leq \frac{(S/N)_{db}}{6} \tag{3.17}$$

For a comparison with the bound defined by the theoretical limit, this working range is also plotted in Figure 3.20.

The line speed given by the Hartley-Shannon theorem is in bits per second (bps). Line speed is also often quoted in **baud rate,** or in words per minute (wpm).

The term *baud* is often used interchangeably with line speed given in bits per second. This usage is misleading and confusing. The word *baud,* whose origin comes from the telegraph industry, represents the rate the line signal changes electrically. If a change occurs for each bit transmitted, then the two terms have identical meaning; but for multibit transmission, each change results in the transmission of several bits, causing the confusion.

The unit words per minute also come from the telegraph industry. To convert a line speed given in words per minute to bits per second, the number of characters per word and the number of bits per character need to be known. By dimensional analysis,

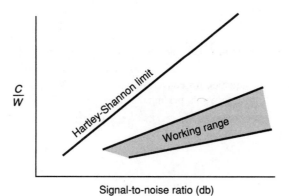

FIGURE 3.20 Bounds on the capacity of a channel.

$$\frac{\text{Bits}}{\text{Second}} = \frac{\text{words}}{\text{minutes}} \times \frac{\text{characters}}{\text{word}} \times \frac{\text{bits}}{\text{character}} \times \frac{1 \text{ minute}}{60 \text{ seconds}} \qquad (3.18)$$

The average word size is uniformly fixed by standard at 6 characters per word. The number of bits per character, however, depends on the character set used (see Appendix B). If n denotes the number of bits per character, then the line speed in bits per second, S_{bps}, can be computed from the line speed given in words per minute, S_{wpm}, by the following equation:

$$S_{bps} = nS_{wpm}/10 \qquad (3.19)$$

Interestingly, when the number of bits per character equals 10 bits, the line speeds given in bits per second and in words per minute are numerically equal.

Exercises

3.21 Plot the percentage error versus the signal-to-noise ratio given in decibels that results from using equation 3.16 instead of equation 3.15 for computing the theoretical capacity of a channel.

3.22 Prove that if the random noise in the Hartley-Shannon theorem is due to thermal noise, then the capacities of two channels of bandwidths W and rW are related by the equation

$$C_{rW} = rC_W - W(r \log_2 r)$$

3.23 Show that the capacity of a channel with thermal noise whose bandwidth is very large can be approximated by the equation

$$C = (S/k)\log_2 e$$

Exercises *(continued)*

where S is the signal strength, k is a physical constant, and $e = 2.71825$.

3.24 Find the conversion equation for converting line speeds from bits per second to words per minute for transmitting

(a)   ASCII characters with parity, represented by 11 bits per character

(b)   baud characters, represented by 7.42 or 7.5 bits per character

SUMMARY

The bandpass of a communication line can be dedicated to a single channel for baseband transmission or divided into multiple channels for broadband transmission. The signal's spectrum must be structured to conform to the bandpass of the channel to which it has been assigned for transmission. The modulation process functions to shift the signal's spectrum to conform to the channel's transmission requirements. Modulated signals may be recovered by demodulation.

When the spectrum of the transmitted signals is bandlimited to pass through the bandpass of an ideal channel, the signals can be theoretically recovered undistorted. However, even undistorted signals can be corrupted by line noises. To safeguard against noises, their source must be located and corrected accordingly or the errors generated from these noises detected and/or corrected by techniques to be discussed later.

Of the three general modulation/demodulation methods covered (i.e., continuous-wave, pulse, and digital), continuous-wave methods deal with techniques used to relocate the spectrum of the signals by a sinusoidal carrier for broadband transmission. The carrier serves to locate the channel used for transmission.

Amplitude modulation is more bandwidth conservative than frequency or phase modulation. Frequency modulation and phase modulation are different forms of modulating the angle of the carrier and lead mathematically to the same spectral representation. Their advantage over AM is that the signal can be reproduced with greater fidelity. Nevertheless, all forms of sinusoidal modulation require a larger bandwidth in the transmission channel than the bandwidth of the bandlimited signal to be transmitted so that the transmitted signal can be recovered without major distortion problems.

Pulse modulation techniques are formulated for shaping sampled-data pulses. For illustrative purposes, the pulses are shaped as flat-topped rectangular pulses, although the concepts apply equally well to pulses shaped to coincide better with the bandpass of the transmission channel. Of the pulse modulation techniques described, PPM seemed best, but unlike PAM and PDM, recovery presents a timing problem.

Digital transmission preserves the value of the data during transmission. PCM explains how data can be transmitted by pulse transmission. The more practical techniques frame the spectrum of the pulses to the bandwidth available for transmission, using three options of shift key encoding: amplitude, frequency, or phase. The higher-speed devices transmit multibits, such as dibits or quadbits, by a combination of these encoding methods.

Finally, the fundamental question of communication signaling and transmission was formulated and answered theoretically. The sampled-data theorem states that a bandlimited signal can be recovered when sampled at least by its Nyquist frequency. From this vantage point, it can be argued that an ideal, noiseless channel can transfer pulses uncorrupted at a rate $2W$, where W is the bandwidth of the channel. This formula translates into a channel capacity of $2W\log_2 M$ bps, where M equals the number of levels used to represent the value of each pulse. For a channel whose source of noise is Gaussian noise, the Shannon-Hartley theorem gives $W(S/N)_{db}/3$ bps as the theoretical bound on capacity, where $(S/N)_{db}$ is the signal-to-noise ratio in decibels. To compensate for modulation techniques, signal distortion, and other line noises, the line speed used in practical transmission systems must be reduced from this theoretical limit.

KEY TERMS

Baseband transmission
Broadband transmission
Modulation
Demodulation
Random noise
Gaussian noise
Thermal noise
Signal-to-noise ratio
Crosstalk
Radio noise
Static
Echoes
Impulse noise
Distortion
Amplitude modulation
Frequency modulation
Phase modulation
Double-sideband modulation
Single-sideband modulation
Vestigial-sideband modulation

Sampler
Sampling period
Sampling frequency
Nyquist frequency
Alias
Hold
Pulse modulator
Analog-to-digital conversion (A/D)
Pulse-code modulation (PCM)
Dibit
Shift keying
Amplitude-shift keying (ASK)
Frequency-shift keying (FSK)
Phase-shift keying (PSK)
Channel capacity
Hartley-Shannon theorem
Baud rate

SUGGESTED READINGS

Davis, D. W., and Barber, D. L. A. *Communication Networks for Computers*. New York: Wiley, 1973.

Lathi, B. P. *An Introduction to Random Signals and Communication Theory*. Scranton, Pa.: International Textbook Co., 1968.

Peebles, P. Z., Jr. *Digital Communications Systems*. Englewood Cliffs, N.J.: Prentice-Hall, 1987.

Shannon, C. E. ''Communications in the Presence of Noise.'' *Proceedings I.R.E.,* vol. 37, no. 1 (1949), pp. 10–21.

Stanley, W. D. *Electronic Communications Systems*. Reston, Va: Reston, 1982.

Stremler, F. G. *Introduction to Communication Systems*. Reading, Mass.: Addison-Wesley, 1977.

CHAPTER 4

COMMUNICATION LINES

And still the Queen kept crying
"Faster, Faster" . . . .
LEWIS CARROLL
THROUGH THE LOOKING-GLASS

4.1   LINE SOURCES

LINE NEEDS

What collection of facts would give a reasonable picture of line technology? Obviously, line speed is an important technical consideration, but there are many other related technical factors concerned with reliability, availability, and maintainability that enter into the choice of lines. Moreover, important design questions cannot always be answered on pure technical grounds, since economy also involves the legal and commercial makeup of the carriers and the enterprise's organizational structure for internal and external communications.

No single taxonomy will suffice for discussing line options. The medium technology used for line construction can serve as one classification, since an enterprise must provide the lines for its own internal communications as well as the interfaces to lines that it procures from common carriers. The important considerations for internal communications would be the type and number of nodes, the distances between nodes, and the transmission speeds required. On the other hand, the choices for external communication depend on the tariffs offered by the commercial carriers. The discussion follows the choice of lines from both of these perspectives.

MEDIUM TECHNOLOGIES

To start with, line choices depend on the physical characteristics of the medium, which in turn depend on whether the medium forms a **wire-line** or **wireless** path. The spider diagram in Figure 4.1 shows the medium technologies that will be covered in this discussion. Two candidates for creating a communication path by wire lines are prominent in today's market: **metallic conductors,** using electrical transmission, and optical fibers, using light transmission. Metallic conductors have been widely accepted in the communications industry, so gradations in the use of this technology exist in practice. The characteristics of **open-wire, twisted-pair,** and **coaxial-cable** construction will be considered separately. Optical-fiber technology, on the other hand, has only recently moved out of the laboratory and into the field. Because this technology is just emerging as a viable means of forming communica-

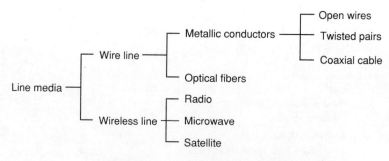

FIGURE 4.1   Line medium technologies.

tion lines, the discussion will include how **optical fibers** are used for transmitting digital signals and their potential in the communication industry.

Wireless transmission requires a clear, line-of-sight path between the communicating nodes. This critical requirement restricts its use in many environments, such as in congested urban areas. Nevertheless, the high transmission speeds that can be achieved, together with the advances that have been made in the technology, make wireless transmission an attractive alternative for long-haul applications. Three variations of wireless technology will be considered: **radio, microwave,** and **satellite.**

COMMERCIAL LINE TARIFFS

To communicate outside its own premises, an enterprise may select line services from those offered by common carriers for commercial use. Vendors package the services that they plan to offer into tariffs, submit the tariffs to the appropriate regulatory agency, and after approval offer the services for public use. The structure of the line charges for these services depend on the vendor, the regulatory agency, and the type and quality of the service. While the tariffs may differ, the general categories of services available and the formats used to package these services give the basis for comparisons.

Common carriers support a wide variety of analog and digital networks from which they package their services. **Digital lines** adopt a particular form of digital signaling that must be used. **Analog lines** can also be used for digital communications, but differ from digital lines in that they leave the form of signaling open and specify the line by its quality and bandwidth. By further enhancing these existing line facilities, value-added networks may provide other services, such as packet network services.

Commercial lines offered by the common carriers may be **leased,** called **private lines,** or **dialed** through the well-known, demand-switching capabilities of the networks, called **public lines.** Contrasted with public lines, which form a temporary connection of short duration between any of the network's subscribers, private lines give dedicated, full-time services between designated stations over a permanent connection. While both classes of lines often coexist on the same switched network, they differ appreciably from each other in services offered, cost, and performance.

The expected usage of public lines is to place short-duration calls intermittently between stations. Any network subscriber may initiate services by sending an "off-hook" signal to the network, such as that generated when a phone handset has been removed from its cradle. After dialing, the network routes the call to the destination point through a series of line connections, alerts the called station by ringing, and completes the end-to-end connection when the ring has been answered. The stations may then use the assigned lines to communicate until disconnected. Following the termination of the call, the network returns the lines to its inventory of available resources for further assignment.

To make and break the frequent line connections needed by dial-up lines, special control signals must be transmitted through the network. Other than for routing, these signals lie within the bandpass of the assigned channel (in-band signals), which must be given special consideration when dial-up facilities are used for data communications. Moreover, since lines are arbitrarily assigned from the vendor's inventory on a demand basis, the frequency response characteristics varies from call to call and may be of marginal use for data communications.

The term *private line* does not mean a privately constructed line that an enterprise may construct on its own premises for its own use, but refers to a line leased from a common carrier for dedicated use. Private lines must still conform to the general network requirements, but unlike public lines, they can be conditioned to improve the quality of transmission and/or be shared by multiple end stations. Higher-speed commercial lines fall into this category.

Exercises

4.1 Make a list of the factors that should be considered in selecting a communication line. Discuss these factors in the context of private construction, lease lines, and dial-up lines.†

---

†Class discussion exercise.

4.2 METALLIC MEDIA

OPEN-WIRE LINES

Open-wire construction is now obsolete, dating well over 100 years, but it is still useful for short runs and even more useful in illustrating the capabilities and problems of other wire-line technologies. Here are some of the characteristics of open-wire construction:

- Open wires are strung on poles in pairs, a forward path and a return path for completing the electrical circuit. As the need for greater communication capacity increases, the number of wires multiply, causing signal interference from other pairs of wires as well as an unsightly mess.

- Construction is costly and maintenance high.

- The resistance of the wire depends, among other factors, on the wire diameter and the distance between nodes. The larger the wire diameter, the greater the amount of copper, the heavier the wire, and the harder it is to work with. But the electrical resistance decreases with the larger wire size, which permits a greater span of wire between nodes. Wire diameter is formed in standard gauges, expressed in American Wire Gauge (AWG), so that for comparable lengths, the resistance of the wire increases and its weight decreases by approximately a

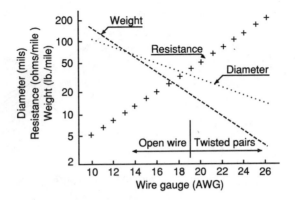

FIGURE 4.2 Physical and electrical characteristics of copper wire.

factor of 10 for each ten gauges. Figure 4.2 compares, on a logarithmic scale, the physical and electrical characteristics of copper wire as a function of the common AWG sizes used for metallic conductor construction.

- At low frequencies, the line losses are primarily a function of distance, limiting the span that can be covered before regeneration and retransmission.

- At high transmission frequencies, the current flow concentrates on the ''skin'' (the outer layer of the conductor), leaving the inner copper core unused and creating a high electrical interference in the immediate environment.

- The power transmitted is equal to the current and voltage in phase with each other. As the signal bandwidth increases, the phase difference of the signal components also increases, necessitating a correction of phase.

- Exposure to natural and human elements, such as rain, storms, heat, birds, corrosion, and BB guns, contribute to a continuous maintenance problem.

- The circuits are especially vulnerable to various kinds of noise and interference from other circuits.

TWISTED PAIRS

To correct the shortcomings of open-wire construction individual strands of wires may be sheathed by color-coded insulation material, twisted into pairs, and the pairs tightly bundled into a common cable (Figure 4.3). Twisting the pairs of wires reduces the amount of electrical interference between the individual strands of the pair. Using a different twist length with each pair housed in the common cable reduces the amount of electrical interference between adjacent pairs. Cables of multiple twisted pairs have the advantage that they can be buried rather than strung to provide better protection against the elements, at the same time reducing construction costs and maintenance and giving better aesthetics.

FIGURE 4.3 Twisted pair wire cable.

Twisted-pair wiring forms the backbone of the voice communication networks. A typical application of twisted pairs is their use in the local-loop circuit connecting the home instrument to the nearest telephone exchange and in interconnecting the exchanges over long distances through intermediate stations. Although designed for voice communications, these analog lines serve admirably for low-speed data communications.

Higher data rates can be achieved when twisted pairs are shielded and used in private construction. Figure 4.4 illustrates typical bit rates that can be expected from commercially available cables using AWG 22 and AWG 24 wires. Through proper balancing of the electrical characteristics of the lines and through the use of amplifiers to regenerate the signals or repeaters to reshape and retime the signals, twisted wires can be used for high-speed digital transmission. For example, a commercial digital network (T1 carrier system) operates at 1.544 Mbps over twisted-pair cables using 22-gauge wires. Still, the problem of transmitting very high frequencies and data rates persists because signal shielding and line balancing have only been partially addressed by twisted-pair technology.

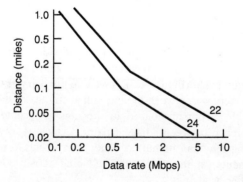

FIGURE 4.4 Typical bit rates for twisted-pair lines.

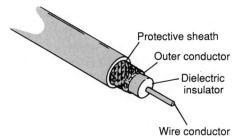

Protective sheath

Outer conductor

Dielectric insulator

Wire conductor   **FIGURE 4.5**   Coaxial cable.

COAXIAL CABLES

Coaxial cables have been heralded as the wherewithal of high-bandwidth, high-data-rate, low-error-rate wire transmission, but they carry higher engineering costs. Physically, coaxial cables consist of a wire braid or a thin, hollow, tubular outer conductor surrounding a copper wire core. These two conductors are separated and spaced by dielectric insulation to form the communication line. For protection from outside elements, an outer sheath covers the cable. Figure 4.5 shows a cross section of the cable construction. Theoretically, this construction can produce a marked improvement in transmitting high frequencies compared to twisted-pair conductors while at the same time shielding the wires from outside electrical disturbances.

The bandwidth and data rate of a coaxial line depend primarily on the wire size of the core, on the diameter, material, and construction (braid or tube) of the outer conductor, and on the type of insulation. Bandwidths up to 500 MHz and bit rates of 50 Mbps can be achieved with special construction, but data rates of 1–10 Mbps would be more common, depending on the span between nodes, which in turn depends on the allowable attenuation of the signals. Another important design parame-

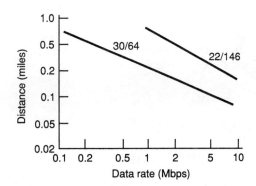

FIGURE 4.6   Typical bit rates for coaxial cable.

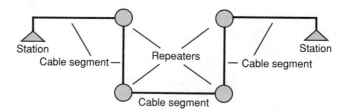

FIGURE 4.7 Extension of link path using repeaters.

ter associated with the data rate is the propagation velocity of the signals in the cable, which for common cables is approximately 78 percent the speed of light.

Figure 4.6 illustrates the typical bit rates for a couple of commercially available coaxial cables. Each cable is partially identified by two of its parameters: The first number gives the AWG wire size of the core, and the second number gives the diameter of the outer conductor in mils.

To achieve greater distance between nodes at high data rates, a cable system can be implemented in segments with electronic repeaters between the segments to reform the signals. For example, Figure 4.7 shows a popular configuration using **CATV (Community Antenna Television)** coaxial cable to transmit 10 Mbps over a modest distance in segments of 500 m for a maximum of five segments with four repeater sets. CATV coaxial cable is the mainstay of cable TV and has the advantage that the peripheral hardware associated with its installation, such as connectors, couplers, amplifiers, and repeaters, are readily available.

Exercises

4.2 Sometimes, multiple circuits use a common wire for the return path to construct each communication circuit. Any electrical circuit needs a forward path and a return path to complete the circuit. Explain the disadvantages of this arrangement.

4.3   OPTICAL-FIBER MEDIA

OPTICAL-FIBER CONSTRUCTION

Like electrical cables, optical-fiber cables can be strung or buried, and they offer many benefits over other communication technologies. Compared to copper cables, optical cables can be easily handled because of their lighter weight, smaller physical size, and greater flexibility. The major engineering obstacles have already been re-

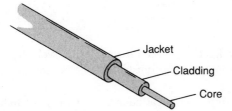

FIGURE 4.8 Optical-fiber cable.

moved, and systems have been constructed whose performance has been impressive. Coupling potentially very high bandwidths with the absence of interference from outside sources and neighboring channels, this media technology promises extremely high data rates for the future of data communications. These many advantages of optical fibers have encouraged industry and government to continue to overcome the remaining problems associated with this technology.

The physical composition of a fiber-optic cable consists of two light-transmitting materials; an inner core for transmitting light signals and an outer cladding for guiding the signal through the core (Figure 4.8). A protective jacket sheaths the core and cadding. This outer coating prevents extraneous light from entering the cladding and core through the skin, absorbs the internal light that has escaped into the cladding from the core so that it does not reenter the core, protects the fiber material from being scratched, since glass and glasslike substances easily break along scratched surfaces, and otherwise gives the cable extra strength for field handling.

The idea of directing light through optical fibers finds its base in the phenomena of light reflection and refraction that occur when two different substances form an optical boundary (Figure 4.9). Reflection and refraction depend on the relative velocities of light through the substances forming the boundary. The velocity of light in any particular substance is often given as a ratio called the **index of refraction,** n defined by

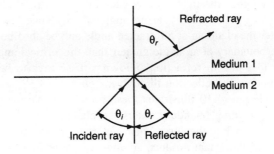

FIGURE 4.9 Reflection and refraction of light.

$$n = \frac{c}{v} \tag{4.1}$$

where c equals the velocity of light in a vacuum and v is the velocity of light in the substance. The value of n for any physical substance must be greater than 1, since v can never exceed c.

When different materials form an optical boundary, the rays of light striking the boundary must be reflected at an angle equal to the angle of incidence, given by

$$\theta_i = \theta_r \tag{4.2}$$

where θ_i equals the angle of incidence and θ_r equals the angle of reflection, or the rays may be refracted according to the well-known law of Snell,

$$\frac{\sin \theta_r}{\sin \theta_i} = \frac{n_2}{n_1} \tag{4.3}$$

where θ_r equals the angle of refraction rather than the angle of reflection and n_1 and n_2 are indices of refraction of medium 1 and medium 2, respectively. The refracted light rays deviate toward the boundary or away from the boundary, depending on whether $n_2 > n_1$ or $n_2 < n_1$, respectively.

For optical fibers, the core and cladding and materials are chosen such that the velocity of light in the core is less than the velocity of light in the cladding and the two velocities are approximately equal, say within 2 percent. Since the ratio of the index of refraction of the cladding to the index of refraction of the core is less than one, Snell's law fixes the maximum angle of incidence for refracted rays (i.e., θ_i when $\theta_r = 90°$) at

$$\theta_{i_{\max}} = \sin^{-1}\left(\frac{n_{\text{cladding}}}{n_{\text{core}}}\right) \tag{4.4}$$

Although some light reflects back into the core at all angles of incidence, most light striking the boundary at an angle of incidence less than this maximum angle will enter the cladding at a refracted angle and be absorbed by the jacket. All rays striking the boundary at an angle greater than this critical angle will be totally reflected, with no loss due to refraction, allowing these rays to be guided back and forth off the boundary by reflection through the core.

Figure 4.10 illustrates these principles. Normally, a ray of light directed to the core-cladding boundary enters the cladding at a refracted angle with some light reflected back to the core. Most important, however, all rays whose angles of incidence exceed those that produce an angle of refraction of 90° will be transmitted by reflection with no loss of light due to refraction.

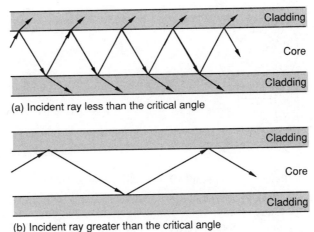

(a) Incident ray less than the critical angle

(b) Incident ray greater than the critical angle

FIGURE 4.10 Light transmission through optical fibers.

SIGNAL COMMUNICATIONS WITH OPTICAL FIBERS

Three variations of fiber technology have found a degree of acceptance in practice: **multimode step-index fibers, multimode graded-index fibers,** and **single-mode (step-index) fibers.** The transmission speed of multimode fibers depends on the amount of spreading a light pulse suffers during transmission. The amount of **pulse spreading** depends on the path the light takes in traversing the fiber and the velocity of light in the fiber, which changes with its wavelength. Single-mode fibers have only one possible path and one wavelength of light, so theoretically the light pulses suffer no spreading during transmission that would limit the rate of transmission. The term *index* in the names of these fibers simply refers to how the index of refraction varies in the cladding and core. These concepts will be explained in the context of multimode step-index fibers, and from this understanding, the performance of the other fiber technologies can be compared.

Multimode step-index fibers use a core with a relatively large diameter composed of material having a uniform index of refraction. Figure 4.11 illustrates the index of refraction profile of step-index fibers, showing the index of refraction n as a function of the radius r. The index of refraction has an abrupt change in value at the **core-cladding boundary.** Much of the light, of course, will be refracted, enter the cladding, and be absorbed by the jacket. The remaining light will strike the boundary at shallow angles relative to the axis of the fiber cable and be guided by reflection through the core.

The rays of a pulse emanating from a light source representing the encoded information will be delayed nonuniformly in arriving at the terminal point, depending on the path each ray takes through the core, which in turn depends on the angle of

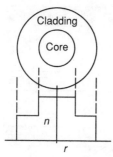

FIGURE 4.11 Index of refraction profile for multimode step-index fibers.

incidence. The amount of spreading that a pulse suffers during transmission can be calculated by the techniques of geometric optics.

While all rays entering the fiber strike the boundary at various angles, only those rays that are totally reflected and propagate through the cable are of interest. Two specific rays bound the totally reflected rays, shown as ray 1 and ray 2 in Figure 4.12. Ray 1 takes the shortest distance through the cable and consequently reaches its destination point in the shortest time, given by the expression L/v_{core}, where L equals the length of the cable and v_{core} equals the velocity of light in the core. Ray 2 represents the ray that strikes the boundary at the critical angle and takes the longest time to reach its destination point, given by the expression $L/(v_{core} \sin \theta_{i_{max}})$. All other reflected rays reaching the terminal point will be delayed proportionally between these two values. Most of the remaining light will be refracted into the cladding and be absorbed by the jacket. Since $\sin \theta_{i_{max}} = n_{cladding}/n_{core}$, the transmitted pulses will be spread in time, Δt, by an amount given by the following expression:

$$\Delta t = \frac{L}{v_{core}} \left(\frac{n_{core}}{n_{cladding}} - 1 \right) \tag{4.5}$$

The amount of light energy that can be focused on the fiber coupled to the loss of light and pulse spreading sets a limit on the operational data rates (see Example 4.1). As a rule, multimode step-index fibers serve reasonably well for short hauls at modest data rates, say, under 1 km at 1–10 Mbps; but for better performance, other fiber technologies must be found that reduce the amount of spreading.

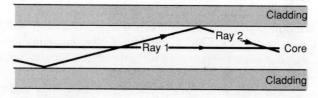

FIGURE 4.12 Light spreading of transmitted light pulses.

Example 4.1

If $v_{core} = 2 \times 10^5$ km/s and $n_{core}/n_{cladding} = 1.02$, calculate the amount of spreading in the transmitted light pulses. How does this affect the maximum rate of transmission?

By equation 4.5, the amount of spreading that a pulse suffers in transmission is

$$\frac{\Delta t}{L} = \frac{1.02 - 1}{2 \times 10^5} = 100 \text{ ns/km}$$

For optical fibers of 1 km length, the pulses must be separated by at least 100 ns if successive pulses traverse the fiber cable without overlapping. This gives a theoretical bound of $1/(100 \times 10^{-9}) = 10$ Mbps for the maximum transmission rate. Pulses transmitted at a data rate greater than this maximum value would overlap, making detection impossible. Other factors considered, practical data rates would be reduced from this optimal value in any operational system.   ◄

Contrasted to multimode step-index fibers, the index of refraction of the core used with multimode graded-index fibers decreases as a function of radial distance from the core center (Figure 4.13). Such a core acts as a lens to compensate for ray spreading due to the different paths the various rays take to the terminal point. This type of fiber offers appreciably higher transmission rates and serves nicely for longer cable runs requiring fewer repeater stations, which partially compensates for its more expensive fabrication.

As the rays pass through the core of a graded-index fiber, they follow a curved, helical path instead of the abruptly changing path caused by reflections that characterizes the step-index fibers. Such a path, illustrated in Figure 4.14 as a two-dimensional, sinusoidal curve, produces a longer path than that followed through a step-index fiber, which gives the impression that nothing could be gained by this config-

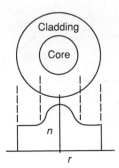

FIGURE 4.13 Index of refraction profile for multimode graded-index fibers.

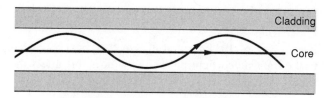

FIGURE 4.14 Paths traversed by rays in multimode graded-index fibers.

uration. However, because the index of refraction decreases along the radial distance, two effects come into play to reduce spreading. First, the worst-case rays form a more shallow angle than those present in step-index fibers. And further compensating for the path length, the speed of transmission increases as the rays traverse the region near the boundary, so that the delay suffered by the rays that follow the helical path approximately equals the delay suffered by the rays that follow a direct path through the center of the fiber.

The difference between single-mode and multimode fibers is not in their index of refraction profiles, but in the relative size of their respective cores. The previous reasoning on pulse spreading was misleading. Not all rays will reflect off the boundary, but only discrete rays, depending on the wavelength of the light. For large core sizes, this argument is academic, since many rays conform to the wavelength requirement and will be transmitted through the fiber. But for very small core diameters relative to the wavelength of light, the rays propagated can be restricted to those that take a direct path through the media (Figure 4.15). Although some pulse spreading may occur in single-mode fibers owing to the relative speeds of light at different wavelengths, the amount of spreading can be controlled by using a monochromatic source. The theoretical bandwidth of single-mode fibers is astronomical, greater than 100 GHz, but aberrations and losses coupled with low, monochromatic light sources result in their use for shorter-length cables, where their performance compares similarly to that of other types of fibers. However, since single-mode fibers have a great deal of potential that has not yet been realized, it is perhaps best to think of this fiber technology as still being developed.

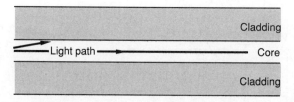

FIGURE 4.15 Path for single-mode optical fibers.

The advantages of fiber optics construction are at least partially offset by the introduction of new complications, including the following:

- Transducers are required to convert electrical signals to light signals, and from light signals to electrical signals.

- As line speed increases, the light source must be more stable and monochromatic, requiring light sources of high spectral quality.

- To fabricate long runs or to repair a line requires complex splicing techniques to maintain line continuity.

- Pin connections are difficult and costly.

- Bends in the line are very prohibited, since they will alter the angle of incident that the rays hit the boundary and change the transmission path.

- The line interface devices cannot be designed or selected independent of the remaining configuration, so each fiber cable has its own interface components and connectors.

- Tapping into a line changes the performance of the system, but in a sense this is an advantage, since security is improved by preventing unauthorized, clandestine taps.

Exercises

4.3 Derive the theoretical limit for the transmission rate per kilometer through a multimode step-index fiber in terms of n_{core} and $n_{cladding}$.

4.4 Calculate the critical angle of refraction that a ray suffers as it passes from air through (a) glass and (b) a diamond, given that $n_{air} = 1.00029$, $n_{glass} = 1.65$ (typically), and $n_{diamond} = 2.417$.

4.5 An important parameter of optical fibers is the numerical aperture, which represents the amount of light admitted into the fiber. For multimode step-index fibers, the numerical aperture is defined by

$$NA = \sqrt{n_{core}^2 - n_{cladding}^2}$$

Show that alternative expressions for the numerical aperture are

$$NA = \sqrt{2n\delta}$$
$$NA = \sqrt{2nc\Delta t/L}$$

where n represents the average index of refraction of the core and cladding, c the velocity of light in free space, $\Delta t/L$ the delay of a pulse per kilometer as given by equation 4.5, and δ the difference in the index of refraction between the core and cladding material. Discuss the implications of these alternative forms for NA in the design of optical fibers.

4.6 Calculate and compare the amount of ray spreading for the fibers whose index of refraction profiles are shown below.

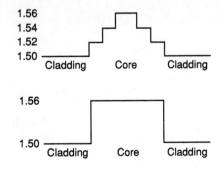

Exercises *(continued)*

4.7 Not all rays that lie between the straight path and the critical angle of refraction will be propagated through the fiber. The term mode is used to indicate the ways a light wave can travel in a given direction. The distinct modes a light wave can propagate through the fiber are separated by a discrete angle give by λ/D, where λ is the wavelength of the source light and D is the diameter of the core. Plot the number of modes of transmission for a light source whose wavelength is $0.75\mu m$. Derive a formula for computing the diameter of the core in terms of the wavelength of light and $n_{\text{cladding}}/n_{\text{core}}$.

4.8 It is known that the speed of light traveling through a transparent medium depends on its color. Given a light source composed of two colors whose indices of refraction in a single-mode fiber are n_1 and n_2, formulate the theoretical limit for the transmission rate for a fiber whose length is 1000 m.

4.4 WIRELESS MEDIA

RADIO

One must be impressed by the progress made in the 100 years since Nobel laureate Marconi demonstrated his thesis that free space, like other substances, was a suitable conductor of electromagnetic waves and invented the apparatus for wireless transmission. The frequency spectrum for radio transmission theoretically extends from the sub-hertz range upward, but in practice it is a different story. The transmission and reception of frequencies at the very high and very low ends of the spectrum cannot be engineered outside the laboratory, which limits the practical spectrum to a more modest size. The challenge is to make the best use of the spectrum that is available.

Responsibility for control of the total spectrum falls on the FCC, which has the authority to assign bands of frequencies (channels) for specific uses and can license users according to the needs of the application. Contending for space is the entertainment industry, other commercial enterprises, government, and private citizens. Figure 4.16 shows the assignments made for commercial broadcasting. For AM broadcasting, stations are assigned a 10 kHz bandwidth between 540 kHz and 1600 kHz.

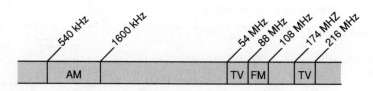

FIGURE 4.16 Frequency assignments for broadcasting stations.

A larger bandwidth is allocated to each station for FM transmission in order to achieve better fidelity during reception. FM stations use a bandwidth of 200 kHz in the frequency range between 88 MHz and 108 MHz. TV broadcasting requires an even larger bandwidth. Each TV station is assigned 6 MHz within two different frequency ranges, from 54 MHz to 88 MHz and from 174 MHz to 216 MHz (note that the frequency assignments made for FM transmission fall between these bands). The remaining spectrum is used to fulfill the needs of other applications.

Radio transmission used for **broadcasting** is omnidirectional using analog techniques. After modulating the signals by an assigned carrier, any receiver within transmission range can receive the broadcast and can reconstruct the signals by demodulation. However, even for an ideal system, the range is limited by the distance between stations and the transmission frequency. Consider the power loss of an antenna system under free-space conditions (Figure 4.17). The power transmitted, P_t, concentrates about the surface of a sphere whose radius equals the distance d between the receiving and transmitting antennas. The power received, P_r, depends on the effective area of the receiving antenna, which for radio waves equals $\lambda^2/4\pi$ (alternatively, $c^2/4\pi f^2$) for radio waves of wavelength λ. Without considering other losses, the attenuation of power can be expressed by the equation

$$\frac{P_r}{P_t} = \left(\frac{4\pi d f}{c}\right)^2 \tag{4.6}$$

Radio transmission operates best along the line of sight between the transmitter and the receiver. However, atmospheric conditions (such as temperature, absorption by air, and rainfall), physical obstructions (such as buildings), and the earth's curvature weakens the signal. For transmission beyond line-of-sight distances, the radio signals can be transmitted by wire lines and rebroadcast.

With a fixed spectrum and a growing number of applications, better sharing of the spectrum becomes essential. For many applications, reception can be restricted

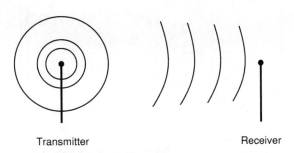

Transmitter   Receiver

FIGURE 4.17 Radio antenna system.

to the immediate area of the transmitter by reducing the transmission power. Another technique that has been proposed would allow commercial broadcast stations to perform double duty by multiplexing data in the unused slices of time during a broadcast, called piggybacking. Finally, transmission can be confined to a narrow angle by use of **beam radio** directed at a specific receiver. This is contrasted with broadcasting that is a one-to-many transmission. Beam radio brings us to the next topic: microwave media.

MICROWAVES

When necessity becomes the mother of invention, the offspring are better disciplined. To make room in the electromagnetic spectrum for more applications, the usable spectrum was extended into the gigahertz range; but use of this spectrum is tightly controlled. Microwaves, so called because of their relatively short wavelengths, occupy this portion of the spectrum. As the wavelength of microwaves approaches the wavelength of light, their behavior exhibit similar properties (i.e., they can be focused, refracted, reflected, etc). Early uses of these shortwaves was to reflect them off the earth's troposphere for transmission to distant points. Modern microwave

FIGURE 4.18 Point-to-point microwave transmission.

construction uses a directed line-of-sight transmission for point-to-point communications, say, from 5 to 50 miles. For longer transmission, the signals are relayed by repeater stations placed along the route of the path.

Figure 4.18 shows two stations creating a microwave path. The shape of the transmitter and receiver is designed as a paraboloidal reflector, called a **dish.** The reflector focuses the microwave beam onto the receiving antenna as it similarly does by the concave mirror of a flashlight. The beam is confined to a narrow angle, typically 1°–2°, giving line-of-sight, point-to-point communications. To increase the distance of transmission, an unobstructed airspace between antennas can be provided by placing the antennas on towers or on top of buildings (in congested urban areas).

The use of microwave transmission also mandates that frequency, bandwidth, and efficiency all be tightly controlled. The frequency spectrum lies between 1 and 300 GHz, although the most useful range at this time is from 1 to 40 GHz, which leaves the upper range for experimentation. Bandwidths are assigned in the range of 0.5–50 MHz. Because of the tight control on efficiency, digital speeds of 0.5–100 Mbps have been reported in using these bandwidths. Although most transmission is by analog technology, more and more services are designed to transmit digital signals directly.

SATELLITES

Microwave technology, like the other technologies, require either a direct connection or a line of sight between stations. When long terrestrial distances must be covered, communications must be structured through many intervening repeater stations. Satellite communications can be looked on as an extension of microwave technology that circumvents the limitations imposed by the curvature of the earth on the line of sight. The satellite appears as a repeater station with an extraordinarily high antenna that can be reached from distant points (Figure 4.19). Unfortunately, however, the

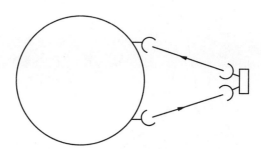

FIGURE 4.19 Microwave communications using satellite repeaters.

satellite's movement relative to the fixed earth positions of the transmitter and receiver presents another kind of problem.

A satellite rotates around the earth in an orbit that (according to Kepler's third law) has a period whose square is proportional to the cube of the mean distance from the earth's center of mass. For a period P expressed in hours and a distance d expressed in miles, Kepler's third law can be written as

$$P^2 = 31.854 \times 10^{-12}d^3 \tag{4.7}$$

where the constant of proportionality depends on the earth's gravitational pull.

The original, experimental satellite was a large, reflective balloon, called ECHO, that was put in a near-earth orbit. Microwaves were transmitted to the balloon, reflected, and received back on earth at another ground station. Later satellites were more sophisticated, with active electronics for reconstructing and retransmitting signals. These space stations were still in near-earth orbit with a period of a few hours. The ground stations had to carefully track these satellites, which could be used for only a short period of time before they would go out of sight and later return.

A satellite placed at a distance of 22,300 miles orbits the earth once every 24 hours. Such a satellite, called a synchronous satellite, appears fixed in space from earth and can be used by ground stations as a repeater. By an arrangement of three such satellites put in circular orbits about the equatorial plane (Figure 4.20), communications can span all the inhabited part of the earth. This technology is not without new problems. For example, the signal suffers noticeable delays, and the space station orbit must be finely controlled to correct for drifts in orbit. Nevertheless, performance has been impressive. Current bandwidths of 0.5–2 GHz will no doubt be expanded many orders of magnitude in the future.

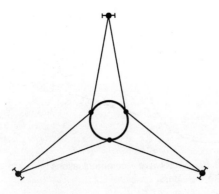

FIGURE 4.20 Placement of synchronous satellites for worldwide communications.

Exercises

4.9 Calculate the range of microwave wavelengths. How do these wavelengths compare with the colors of the light spectrum (7900 Å for red, 5900 Å for yellow, and 4900 Å for blue, where $Å = 10^{-8}$cm)?

4.10 The distance between the transmitter and receiver for terrestrial radio communications depends on the line of sight between the two stations. Assuming the transmitter at ground level, plot the line-of-sight distance of a receiver station as a function of tower height at the receiving station (mean radius of the earth is 3959 miles).

4.11 Show that doubling the transmission frequency or doubling the distance between the transmitting antenna and the receiving antenna will attenuate the power received by 6 db.

4.12 Verify the height of the synchronous satellite.

4.13 Calculate the minimum delay that a signal suffers in being relayed by a synchronous satellite.

4.14 Calculate the maximum distance between ground stations as a function of the height of a satellite.

4.5   COMMERCIAL LINES TARIFFS

END-TO-END TARIFF STRUCTURES

Three tariff schedules make up the end-to-end connection, depicted in Figure 4.21. Common carriers locate major switching stations to service selected metropolitan areas. Of course, not all common carriers service each and every metropolitan area; they choose areas for which they will provide services. From each designated metropolitan area, two local line segments complete the path, one to the central office servicing the customer and the other from the central office to the customer's service area.

A separate tariff applies for each of the line segments, consisting of a one-time installation charge for making the connections, a monthly service charge for maintenance and service options, and a usage schedule. The usage schedule combines a number of factors that include the quality of the line, the distance between the terminal points, and the duration of use. The distance for the long line between the metropolitan switching stations is measured in a variety of ways, depending on the number of stations serviced by the tariff: one to one, many to one, or one to many. For public lines, these rates are discounted for the time of day and the day of the

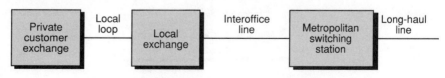

FIGURE 4.21   Major line interconnections.

week, and surcharges are added for special services like operator assistance and credit card use.

For point-to-point traffic, the long-haul distance is determined by assigning co-ordinates H and V to the switching points servicing the terminal area and computing the mileage by the algorithm shown in Figure 4.22, where the subscripts denote designated rate centers. The distance computed by this algorithm can be estimated by using the air mileage between stations obtained from a road map. The tariff de-fines the charges for the connection by giving the cost per mile, with a reduced rate for longer distances.

MULTIPOINT TARIFF STRUCTURES

For connecting many points to a common point, be it many to one or one to many, tariffs use a couple of basic schemes for scheduling charges. One scheme arranges the continental United States into areas (Figure 4.23a) and quotes the rates in the form of a table, depending on the areas servicing the two farthest connecting points. Selected stations located in between the two farthest points may be added at a nom-inal charge per drop. The other and perhaps more familiar scheme divides the geo-graphical points of the United States into six zones from the central point that serves

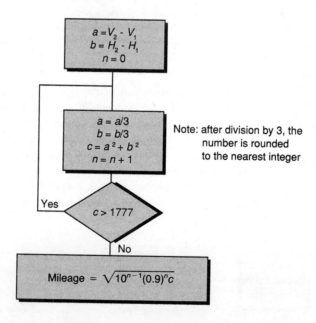

FIGURE 4.22 Point-to-point mileage algo-rithm.

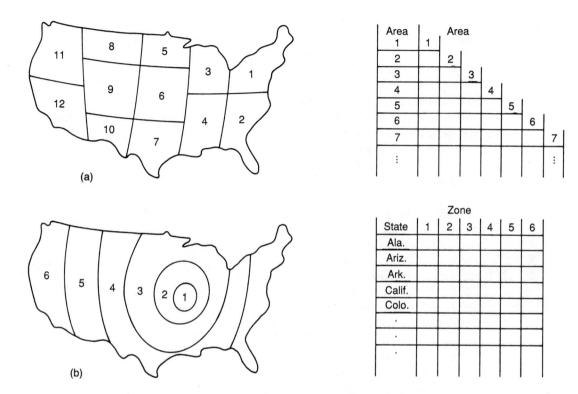

FIGURE 4.23 Multipoint tariff schedules.

the customer. The customer may select a tariff to any zone, which permits the customer to be connected to any point within that zone and all points in the zones less than the designated zone. For example, if zone 3 is selected, then all service points in zones 1, 2, and 3 are included. This arrangement is shown in Figure 4.23b.

ANALOG LINES

When digital information is transmitted over analog lines, equipment at the customer's premises converts the digital signals to analog signals that conform to the frequency spectrum of the channel, and the equipment at the receiving station reconverts the analog signals back into their digital form. Along the network, the transmission facilities reconstitute the signals by amplifying them before they degrade and become unrecognizable. Unfortunately, however, when the transmission facilities amplify the signals, they also amplify the noise in the line and the distortions in the signals.

Digital lines differ from analog lines in that a transmission facilities for digital lines expect the signals to be in a particular electrical form representing digital information. For long-haul transmission, the intermediate line facilities regenerate the signals by reshaping and retiming them rather than simply amplifying them. Digital transmission reduces the expected error rate, typically giving error rates of 10^{-7} compared with rates of 10^{-5} for good-quality analog lines.

Since the major source of analog lines and their associated tariffs have evolved from the lines constructed for telecommunication services, the lines are grouped into three bandwidth grades, using the voice bandwidth as the norm: **narrow-band** for lines whose bandwidth is smaller than voice lines; voice lines; and **wide-band** for lines whose bandwidth is greater than **voice-grade lines.** Narrow-band channels can be realized by subdividing a voice channel into subchannels for low-speed data communications. Unlike narrow-band channels wide-band channels use a consecutive group of voice-grade channels to form a larger bandwidth to support high-speed data communications or can be subdivided in a variety of ways for voice or data. Line quality, on the other hand, depends on the shape of the line's frequency response curves, the amount and types of allowable noise, and the options available for improving these line conditions for data transmission. These factors form the major considerations for packaging the line services.

The familiar DDD **(Direct Distance Dialing)** best characterizes the services for public, voice-grade lines. The DDD tariff serves for occasional calls between arbitrary subscribers; but for sustained traffic to a distant point or points, the common carriers offer tariffs giving bulk rates. **Wide Area Telephone Services (WATS)** and **Foreign Exchange (FX)** typify such tariffs.

WATS lines give subscribers a bulk rate schedule for DDD services. Categorically, the tariffs offer a variety of options whose rates are sensitive to

- The zone or area covered
- Whether the facilities are directly supplied by the vendor or resold by the vendor
- The amount of time usage that can be by measured time or full-time
- Whether the calls originate or terminate on the customer's premises, called OutWATS or InWATS (800 numbers), respectively or both

FX tariffs permit a subscriber to obtain a line connection to a specific distant (foreign) exchange. For a fixed monthly charge based on mileage, the FX line may be connected to the private line-switching station servicing an enterprise's communication equipment so as to treat all calls to the remote exchange as local calls (Figure 4.24).

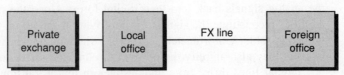

FIGURE 4.24 FX line connection.

Perhaps the options offered with private analog lines better characterize their advantage over public lines for data communications. By choice or design, private lines give better line characteristics and routing. To achieve the higher bit rates, the common carrier will install circuits for echo suppression or will condition the line against noise or distortions due to signal delays. Tariffs define a number of line conditioning levels, called C1, C2, C3, C4, C5, D1, and D2, depending on the type of improvement needed and the number of stations to be connected to the line. While the details of the various levels of conditioning need not be discussed here, it is important to emphasize that conditioning of any type is available only on private lines.

DIGITAL LINES

For digital services, the tariffs quote line rates in bits per second rather than bandwidth. As with other leased lines, three connections must be made (Figure 4.25), but they differ from analog lines in that a line interface unit transforms the input signals into a digital format and the network facilities continue to handle the signals in pure digital form until they arrive at their destination point. This arrangement has the advantage that the network reconstitutes the signals by regeneration rather than amplification so that reduced error rates can be expected. The tariff charges for the long-haul line connections between rate centers consist of a fixed monthly charge and a per-mile charge that depends on the distance and speed of the channel. The networks can accommodate operating speeds of 2.4, 4.8, 9.6, and 56 kbps and 1.544 Mbps and higher.

Alternatively, digital information can be packaged and transmitted as packets of bits using pure digital switching techniques for routing the information to the destination points. Value-added network vendors provide these services with facilities to accept, disassemble, transmit, and reassemble messages of arbitrary lengths. The heart of this service is a special interface device known as a **packet assembler/ disassembler (PAD),** which may be located on the user's premises or integrated into the network. Figure 4.26 illustrates some possible interconnections using commercial lines.

On receiving information for transmission, the PAD disassembles each message into fixed-size units, 128 octets being most common, and directs the units through the network by header information used to identify the source and destination points.

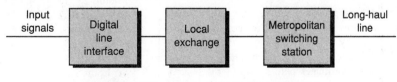

FIGURE 4.25 Digital network line connections.

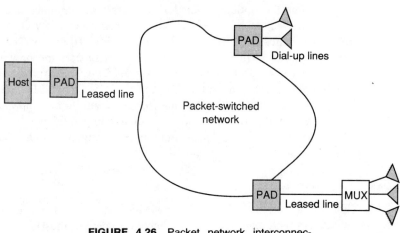

FIGURE 4.26 Packet network interconnections.

These packets may take different paths through the network, depending on the traffic at the intermediate nodes. Since the packets may arrive in a different order than sent, each packet receives a sequential number that can be used by the PAD at the destination point to reassemble the information in the order the packets were sent. The tariff charges for this service depends on the type of interconnection to the network and on the volume of traffic measured in kilopackets.

Exercises

4.15 The mileage between rate centers may be computed by the formula

$$d = \sqrt{[(V_2 - V_1)^2 + (H_2 - H_1)^2]/10}$$

Write a computer program to compute the mileage by this formula and that given by the algorithm in Figure 4.22. How do the values compare?

4.16 Compute the mileage between the rate centers given below. How do these distances compare to the distances found by using a road map to determine the air miles between cities? Using these sample rate centers, plot their coordinates onto a map of the United States and determine the approximate coordinates of other rate centers.

RATE CENTER COORDINATE TABLE

	V	H
Atlanta	7260	2083
Boston	4422	1249
Chicago	5981	3437
Cleveland	5574	2543
Detroit	5536	2828
Miami	8351	0527
New Orleans	8483	2638
New York	5000	1358
Philadelphia	5251	1458
Pittsburgh	5621	2185
St. Louis	6807	3482
Washington	5622	1583

Exercises *(continued)*

4.17 Interconnect the cities shown in exercise 4.16 with a 2400–9600 bps line so that there is a path from any city to any other city. Compute the cost for this interconnection using vendor A's tariff, shown below. Repeat using vendor B's tariff.

MILEAGE BAND	VENDOR A		VENDOR B	
	FIXED RATE	PER-MILE RATE	FIXED RATE	PER-MILE RATE
1–50	80.00	2.27	64.00	1.90
51–100	142.00	1.03	122.00	0.75
101–500	183.00	0.62	145.00	0.52
501–	333.00	0.31	265.00	0.28

4.18 Interconnect New York, Chicago, and Atlanta by 56 kbps lines and the remaining cities given in exercise 4.16 to one of these stations with a 2400–9600 bps line. Compute the cost for this interconnection using vendor A's tariff (the rates are shown below for the 56 kbps line and in the previous exercise for the 2400 bps line). Repeat using vendor B's tariff. Compile a list of reasons for selecting a particular vendor.

MILEAGE BAND	VENDOR A		VENDOR B	
	FIXED RATE	PER-MILE RATE	FIXED RATE	PER-MILE RATE
1–50	297.00	9.81	255.00	8.00
51–100	555.00	4.65	485.00	3.40
101–500	725.00	2.94	580.00	2.45
501–	1370.00	1.65	1100.00	1.50

SUMMARY

To communicate outside its own premises, an enterprise subscribes to the line services offered by commercial vendors who have constructed an inventory of lines through analog and digital networks for public use. For internal communications, an enterprise must construct its own lines. Line technologies have been categorized according to whether they form a wire-line path or a wireless path. Wire-line construction forms a physical connection between communicating stations from metallic conductors or optical fiber. Wireless communication requires a clear, line-of-sight path between the transmitter and receivers. The discussion presented three variations of each of these technologies.

Twisted pairs and coaxial cables provide high rates of transmission by metallic conductors. Twisted pairs help guard against interference from adjacent lines by twisting each pair of wires by a different amount. Coaxial cables are configured to offer large line bandwidths that operate at very high frequencies. Both of these technologies have the advantage that the ancillary hardware components that support installation have been field-proved by the telephone and television industries and are generally available as shelved items.

Optical-fiber technologies were compared based on their mode of propagation (multimode or single mode) and their index of refraction profile (graded index or step index). The amount of spreading that occurs when rays follow different paths through the medium limits the potential rate that light pulses can be transmitted through multimode fibers. Multimode graded-index fibers have a gradual change in the core's index of refraction, so that the worst-case path follows a more shallow angle with the axis of the cable than step-index fibers, resulting in a decrease in the amount of spreading. A very fine core typifies single-mode fibers such that only one wavelength of light taking a straight path through the medium can be transmitted. Potentially, these fibers can achieve astronomical speeds if other problems with their construction can be overcome.

Wireless transmission tries to make the best use of the spectrum that is available among the many contenders for frequency assignments. Broadcast radio is omnidirectional. To better share the spectrum, beam radio using microwaves in the very high spectrum range confines the transmission to a narrow angle directed toward the receiver. In addition, satellites stationed in space act as intermediate nodes to achieve an unobstructed path between communicating nodes. Three satellites located so that they appear stationary relative to earth positions can span all the inhabited parts of the earth.

Common carriers package their services into tariffs that they offer to the public after approval from a regulatory body. The major sources of analog lines are available from those lines constructed for telephone services. Line services are offered according to bandwidth—narrow band, voice channel, or wide band—on a dial-up (public lines) or lease-line (private lines) basis. The line usage charges for long-haul, point-to-point communication depend on the quality of the line and the air mile distance between metropolitan switching stations. For communications between multipoint stations, the tariffs are structured by dividing the continental United States into areas, or zones, from the focal point of the traffic. Public lines are made available on a demand basis and after use are returned to the line inventory. Private lines, on the other hand, are assigned to provide dedicated, full-time services. Private lines may be conditioned to give better performance.

While analog lines leave the form of signaling open and specify the line by its bandwidth and quality, digital lines adopt a particular form of signaling to which the signals must conform. Tariffs for digital lines are quoted in bits per second and are structured similarly to analog line tariffs. However, another type of carrier enters this arena, the value-added network vendors, who package their digital services into packets. To avail oneself of these services, a special line interface device is needed that assembles and disassembles the packet.

KEY TERMS

Wire-line	Optical fibers
Wireless	Radio
Metallic conductors	Microwave
Open wires	Satellite
Twisted pairs	Digital lines
Coaxial cables	Analog lines

Leased lines
Private lines
Dialed lines
Public lines
Community Antenna Television (CATV)
Index of refraction
Multimode step-index fibers
Multimode graded-index fibers
Single-mode (step-index) fibers
Pulse spreading
Core-cladding boundary

Broadcasting
Beam radio
Dish antenna
Narrow-band line
Wide-band line
Voice-grade line
Direct Distance Dialing
Wide Area Telephone Services (WATS)
Foreign Exchange (FX)
Packet assembler/disassembler (PAD)

SUGGESTED READINGS

Chou, W., et al. (eds.). *Computer Communications,* vol. 1, *Principles.* Englewood Clifffs, N.J.: Prentice-Hall, 1983.

Datapro Reports on Data Communications, vols. 1–3. Delran, N.J.: Datapro Research Corp., 1986.

Palais, Joseph C. *Fiber Optic Communications.* 2nd. ed. Englewood Cliffs, N.J.: Prentice-Hall, 1988.

Personick, S. D. *Fiber Optics—Technology and Applications.* New York: Plenum, 1985.

Rosner, Roy D. *Packet Switching.* Belmont, Calif.: Wadsworth, 1982.

Smith, David R. *Digital Transmission Systems.* New York: Van Nostrand Reinhold, 1985.

Spilker, James J. *Digital Communications by Satellite.* Englewood Cliffs, N.J.: Prentice-Hall, 1977.

Technical Staff of CSELT. *Optical Fiber Communication.* New York: McGraw-Hill, 1980.

Techo, Robert. *Data Communications.* New York: Plenum, 1980.

CHAPTER 5

CODING THEORY

O hateful error, melancholy's child, why
dost thou show to the apt thoughts of
men the things that are not? O error, soon
conceived, thou never comest unto a
happy birth but kill'st the mother that
engender'd thee!
WILLIAM SHAKESPEARE
JULIUS CAESAR

109

5.1   CODE REDUNDANCY

CODING STRATEGIES FOR
IMPROVING THE RELIABILITY OF TRANSMISSION

The physical composition of a channel determines its quality, which for digital channels is given as a statistical value representing the average error rate of the channel. For example, an error rate of 10^{-5} indicates the probability of one error, on average, for every 100,000 bits transmitted. One can now ask, Can the reliability of transmission be improved without changing the physical characteristics of a channel by encoding the information, and if so, how? The first part of this question is answered positively by theory; the second part is the subject of this chapter.

Two approaches can be tried to encode the information in order to improve the reliability of transmission. One decreases and the other increases the length of the bit sequence transmitting a fixed amount of information. Although they appear to contradict each other, both approaches work.

Decreasing the number of bits to be transmitted by encoding the information into a minimum-bit sequence decreases the likelihood of an error. To reduce the size of the average bit sequence and still transmit the same amount of information, the more frequent messages are assigned fewer numbers of bits than those transmitted less frequently. But the less expected messages have the greater information content.* Since the less expected messages also have a greater number of bits, and all bits in an average sequence of messages have the same probability of an error, then a random error would most likely destroy a greater amount of information.

It is not clear that increasing the number of bits to be transmitted by repeating or adding redundant information can improve the reliability of transmission. The added **redundancy** will decrease the possibility of an undetected error, but the added number of bits will increase the likelihood of an error. The strategy of adding redundancy is saved from this dilemma by **Shannon's second theorem,** which states that if the rate of transmission is less than the theoretical capacity of a noisy channel, then the reliability of transmission can be arbitrarily improved by coding.

This chapter presents some selected coding techniques found in practice to improve the reliability of transmission by adding redundancy. An algorithm for improving transmission by compressing information into minimum-bit sequences is given elsewhere (Appendix C). Another way to improve the reliability of transmission is for cooperating partners to employ code standards to control the exchange of information. This use of coding will be covered later in the text in context with other

---

*The study of information in a mathematical context is the subject of information theory. The amount of information a message conveys, as R. W. Hamming aptly describes (see Hamming in Suggested Readings), is the amount of "surprise" expressed in the message. From this viewpoint, for example, the notice of a child's birth has less surprise and therefore contains less information than the birth notice of quintuplets.

standards. Nevertheless, all these techniques have the same goal, to preserve the integrity of the data during transmission, which is the essence of data communications.

BASIC CONCEPTS

First, some basic terms and attributes of codes need to be formally fixed by definitions. A **code word** is a finite sequence of symbols from an alphabet used to represent a fragment of information. The alphabet might consist of English letters, the dots and dashes of the Morse code, the binary digits 0 and 1, and so on. The total number of symbols in a code word, called its **length,** must be at least 1. A **code set,** or **code,** is a collection of code words chosen from all possible sequences of the alphabet. Each code word of a code set must be distinct from all other code words of the code set. To be distinct, code words must differ from each other by at least one symbol. **Binary codes** are specialized code sets whose alphabet consists of two symbols, 0 and 1. The discussion throughout this chapter deals exclusively with binary codes of the same length.

The possibilities for codes, even under the constraint that all code words have the same length, are numerous, too numerous to rely on a casual selection of code words. For example, for 2-bit codes, there are $2^2 = 4$ possible code words: 00, 01, 10, and 11. From these possible code words, 11 possible code sets consisting of two, three, or four code words each can be selected. Table 5.1 shows these code sets explicitly. In general, the following equations give the possible code words N and the possible code sets S that can be selected from binary code words of length n:

$$N = 2^n \tag{5.1a}$$
$$S = 2^{2^n} - 2^n - 1 \tag{5.1b}$$

Once a code set is chosen, numerous possibilities exist for assigning the code words to represent the information. For example, ten code words can be assigned 3,628,800 (10!) different ways to represent ten fragments of information; and more generally, k code words can be assigned $k!$ different ways to represent k fragments

TABLE 5.1
POSSIBLE 2-BIT CODE SETS

TWO-WORD CODE SETS	THREE-WORD CODE SETS	FOUR-WORD CODE SETS
00, 01	00, 01, 10	00, 01, 10, 11
00, 10	00, 01, 11	
00, 11	00, 10, 11	
01, 10	01, 10, 11	
01, 11		
10, 11		

of information. With so many possibilities, it behooves one to select and assign code words in a way that will facilitate the use of the code. The exercises will provide some examples of specialized codes.

HAMMING DISTANCE

The premise that the integrity of data transmitted over a channel can be protected by adding redundancy makes this approach viable, but how should the redundancy be added? One way is to transmit multiple copies of each bit sequence and compare the received copies, bit by bit. When two received copies match in all bit positions, then there is some assurance, although not complete certainty, that the received bit sequence has been transmitted correctly. If the two copies do not match, then the receiver has detected an error in either one or both copies, which may be corrected by retransmission. To detect and possibly correct an error without retransmission, at least three copies must be transmitted. This strategy is effective but inefficient. Other means must be sought to achieve redundancy.

Consider the collection of all possible bit patterns of length n, called **n-tuples.** From these n-tuples, the code words of the code set can be chosen. An error in any code word could change the code word into another code word of the set, making the error undetectable, or it could change the code word into one of the unassigned n-tuples, making the error detectable. The latter case not only permits error detection, but also make possible the opportunity for correcting the error. By judiciously associating each unassigned n-tuple with one of the code words, any n-tuple received that had not been assigned can be replaced by its associated code word.

A code designed to detect selected errors when they occur, called an **error-detecting code,** requires retransmission to correct the errors. A code that includes enough redundancy to detect and also correct selected errors without retransmission is known as an **error-correcting code.** Both types of codes require that the difference between any two bit patterns be measured. The number of bit positions in which two n-tuples disagree, known as the **hamming distance,** serves this purpose.

If u and v are two n-tuples, and u_i and v_i represent the value of the ith bit of u and v, respectively, then the hamming distance, $d(u, v)$, can be calculated by the equation

$$d(u, v) = \sum_{i=1}^{n} u_i \oplus v_i \tag{5.2}$$

where $\oplus$ denotes the exclusive-or operator ($0 \oplus 0 = 0$, $0 \oplus 1 = 1$, $1 \oplus 0 = 1$, and $1 \oplus 1 = 0$) and Σ denotes summation with ordinary addition. Defined in this way, the hamming distance satisfies three axioms normally used in mathematics to define a distance. For any n-tuples, say u, v, and w, these axioms are:

$$d(u, v) = 0 \quad \text{if} \quad u = v \tag{5.3a}$$

$$d(u, v) = d(v, u) > 0 \quad \text{if} \quad u \neq v \qquad (5.3b)$$
$$d(u, w) + d(v, w) \geq d(u, v) \qquad (5.3c)$$

This formulation of the hamming distance offers the advantage of manipulating codes algebraically. Moreover, these axioms conform to the common understanding of distance and can be interpreted like other ways of measuring distance, as follows:

- Axiom 5.3a states that the distance of a point from itself is zero.

- Axiom 5.3b states that the distance is a positive number and that it does not matter if it is measured from u to v or from v to u.

- Axiom 5.3c states that any side of a triangle is less than the sum of the other two sides or equal in the degenerative case when the three points are colinear (triangle rule).

Example 5.1
Given the code words 000 and 111, what is the hamming distance from these points to each of the possible 3-tuples?

	000	001	010	011	100	101	110	111
000	0	1	1	2	1	2	2	3
111	3	2	2	1	2	1	1	0

◀

MINIMUM DISTANCE FOR ERROR-DETECTING AND ERROR-CORRECTING CODES

For a code word to be distinct, all the code words of a code must differ from each other by a hamming distance of at least 1. Clearly, when the minimum distance between all pairs of code words equals exactly 1, then a single error could produce an n-tuple that has been assigned to another code word, making the error undetectable. What must be the minimum hamming distance between any pair of code words to detect errors or to detect and correct errors in any arbitrary sequence of code words?

A code used to detect up to q errors is called a q-error detection code. An error of 1 to q bits in any code word, say, c_i, will produce an n-tuple t_i whose distance from the code word is $1 \leq d(c_i, t_i) \leq q$. Figure 5.1 pictures the c_i code word and all versions (i.e., the t_i's) of this code word that have been corrupted by up to q errors as lying inside the circle. In the worst case, the distance between the code word and the damaged code word equals q. To detect the error, any of the n-tuples produced by the damaged code word must also be at least a distance of 1 from any other code

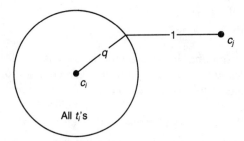

FIGURE 5.1 Minimum hamming distance for q-error detection code.

word in the code, say c_j. The minimum hamming distance needed to detect q errors must therefore be

$$d(c_i, c_j)_{\min} \geq d(c_i, t_i) + d(t_i, c_j) \geq q + 1 \qquad (5.4)$$

A code used to correct up to r errors, called an r-error correction code, must also be able to detect the r errors. But how much more redundancy must an error-correcting code have than an error-detecting code? Following Figure 5.2, an error of $1-r$ bits in any code word, say, c_i, will produce an n-tuple t_i whose distance from the code word is $d(c_i, t_i) \leq r$. In the worse case, the distance between the code word and the damaged code word equals r. Similarly, an error of $1-r$ bits in any other code word, say, c_j, will produce an n-tuple t_j whose distance from the code word is $d(c_j, t_j) \leq r$. Again, for the worst case, the distance between the code word and the damaged code word equals r. To correct for any error, the n-tuples produced by errors in either code word must be distinct and must therefore be a distance of at least 1 from each other, that is, $d(t_i, t_j) \geq 1$. This argument shows that the minimum hamming distance needed for an r-error correction code must be

$$d(c_i, c_j)_{\min} \geq d(c_i, t_i) + d(c_j, t_j) + d(t_i, t_j) \geq r + r + 1 = 2r + 1 \qquad (5.5)$$

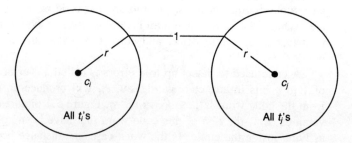

FIGURE 5.2 Minimum hamming distance for r-error correction code.

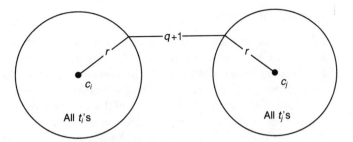

FIGURE 5.3 Minimum hamming distance for an r-error correcton code with an additional q-error detection code.

These results can be expressed concisely by one equation, as follows. Referring to Figure 5.3, consider the minimum distance required between any two code words of a code used to detect and correct r errors and to detect an additional q errors. As before, an error of up to r errors in any of the code words, say, in the code words c_i and c_j, will produce n-tuples, t_i and t_j, respectively, whose distances from the code words are $d(c_i, t_i) \leq r$ and $d(c_j, t_j) \leq r$, respectively, with the worst-case distance equal to r. To correct any of these errors, the n-tuples must be distinct. To detect the additional q errors, all the n-tuples produced by the correctable errors must be at least a distance of $q + 1$ from each other, that is, $d(t_i, t_j) \geq q + 1$. This argument shows that a code for correcting r errors that can also detect an additional q errors must have a minimum hamming distance of

$$d(c_i, c_j)_{\min} \geq d(c_i, t_i) + d(c_j, t_j) + d(t_i, t_j)$$
$$\geq r + r + q + 1 = 2r + q + 1 \quad (5.6)$$

Equation 5.6 states the minimum distance required between all pairs of code words in a code set to detect $r + q$ errors and correct for r of these errors. Table 5.2 summarizes this result together with the previous results.

TABLE 5.2

MINIMUM DISTANCE REQUIRED FOR ERROR CORRECTION AND ERROR DETECTION

CODE	MINIMUM DISTANCE
Distinct	1
q-error detection	$q + 1$
r-error correction	$2r + 1$
r-error correction plus q-error detection	$2r + q + 1$

BOUND ON CODE SIZE

From a code efficiency point of view, the code length should not be increased unnecessarily to achieve redundancy. As a guideline to code design, this concern can be stated as follows: What is the maximum number of code words that can be selected from the 2^n possible n-tuples for correcting r errors?

Each code word of a code set of length n is assigned one of the possible n-tuples. For an r-error correction code, each code word and all n-tuples caused by damaging the word in $1-r$ bits must be associated with the code word. The number of ways an n-bit code word can be damaged by exactly i errors is the number of ways of selecting i bits at a time from n bits, $\binom{n}{i}$. The code word appears undamaged in exactly 1 way, which can also be expressed as $\binom{n}{0}$. Mathematically, the sum of $\binom{n}{i}$ from 0 to r gives the number of n-tuples that must be associated with each code word. For an n-bit code, there are, in fact, 2^n n-tuples available, giving an upper bound for m of

$$m \le \frac{2^n}{\displaystyle\sum_{i=0}^{r} \binom{n}{i}} \tag{5.7}$$

Equation 5.7 gives a necessary condition on the number of code words that can be selected to develop an r-error correction code. However, the code words selected must still be at a hamming distance of $2r + 1$ from each other, and it may not be possible to find m words that have this property.

Example 5.2

Find the maximum number of code words in a 5-bit code that can be used to correct for 1 error.

$$m \le \frac{2^5}{1 + 5} = 5$$

To correct for 1 error, the code words must have a distance of at least 3 from each other. Five code words cannot be found. Four code words that can serve this purpose are

00000, 01011, 10101, 11110   ◀

Exercises

5.1 A code of n bits has 2^n possible code words (see equation 5.1a and 5.1b). Verify the formula giving the possible number of code sets that can be formed from these code words. (*Hint:* How many ways can i items be selected from a collection of N items? How many possible code words of length n can be formed from an alphabet of k symbols, and how many code sets of two words or more can be selected from these code words?)

5.2 A weighted code is a code that assigns a numerical value to each symbol, depending on its position in the code word, and then sums the values to get the code word's numerical value. An example is the code for the binary number system, which assigns 1, 2, 4, 8, and so on, to each of the bit positions.

One way of forming negative numbers is by replacing each digit in the number by it 9's complement. (A digit and its 9's complement equal 9; e.g., 4 and 5 are the 9's complements of each other.) Subtraction using 9's complement arithmetic can be performed by expressing the negative number by its 9's complement and adding it to form the result. A carry outside the range of the added numbers is carried to the rightmost position. Using $85 - 37$, demonstrate 9's complement arithmetic.

There is an obvious advantage in finding a weighted binary code that permits the 9's complement to be formed by changing each 0 to 1 and each 1 to 0. Two such weights for forming 9's complements in binary codes are 5, 1, 1, 1, 1 (the weights in a five-button abacus) and 4, 2, 2, 1. Display 9's complement code using these sample weights.

5.3 A k-out-of-n code represents the decimal digits by exactly k 1's in an n-bit code. It is an example of a code developed to detect an error if a bit position is "picked," that is, changed accidentally from 0 to 1 or from 1 to 0. Find a weighted binary code that selects k-bits out of n that can encode the decimal numbers in 9's complement. (*Hint:* Try the weights 7, 4, 2, 1, 0 and the weights 6, 3, 2, 1, 0 and see which values cannot be represented. Also, try using a code with a negative weight, e.g., 5, 4, 3, 2, -2.)

5.4 A unit distance code changes in one and only one bit position in the normal counting sequence; that is, only one bit position is changed in the transition from 0 to 1, from 1 to 2, from 2 to 3, and so on. The Gray code is such a code. The numerical value of a code word in the Gray code can be computed by assigning the weights 1, 3, 7, . . . , $2^n - 1$ to the bit positions and then alternating between adding and subtracting the weighted value each time a 1 is encountered in a bit position, starting at the high-weight bit position. For example, 11011 has the value $31 - 15 + 3 - 1 = 18$.

(a) Enumerate the values 0–15 in the Gray code.

(b) Calculate the decimal value of the Gray code word 10110101.

(c) Write a computer algorithm to calculate the value of a Gray code word if the bits are scanned sequentially by low order first. By high order first.

(d) Illustrate by example the formula $g_i = b_i \oplus b_{i+i}$ for converting a binary number to its Gray code equivalent, where g_i and b_i denote the ith bit position in the Gray code and binary code, respectively, and where $\oplus$ denotes the exclusive-or operator.

(e) Illustrate by example the equation $b_i = b_{i+1} \oplus g_i$ for converting a Gray code of length n to its binary value, where $b_{n+1} = 0$.

5.5 Calculate the hamming distance between the following code words:

(a) 00000, 10101, 01010

(b) 000000, 010101, 101010, 110110

5.6 Verify the third hamming distance axiom for any 3-tuple from the code words 010 and 101.

5.7 Find the hamming distance between any two code words in a 2-out-of-5 code (see exercise 5.3).

5.8 Verify graphically the hamming distance axioms by plotting the 3-tuples as corner points on a three-dimensional cube.

5.9 Develop a 5-bit code that can correct for 2 errors, a 4-bit code that can detect 3 errors, and an 8-bit code

Exercises *(continued)*

that can correct for 2 errors and detect 3 additional errors.

5.10 Find the maximum number of code words in a 7-bit code that can be used to correct for 1 error. Try to find an instance of such a code.

5.2 HAMMING SINGLE-ERROR CORRECTION CODES

PARITY CHECK CODES

The systematic development of codes containing redundancy to enhance the integrity of the transmitted data can be most effectively described mathematically. Central to this treatment is the concept of parity. A **parity bit** is a bit used to record whether a group of selected bits in the code word contains an even or odd number of 1's. This permits the receiving station to check the transferred data.

For discussion, the practice will be adopted of recording a 1 for the parity bit whenever the group of selected bits has an odd number of 1's, and 0 for an even number of 1's. Since this parity scheme always makes the total number of 1's in the selected bits and the parity bit an even number, it is called **even parity.** Even parity has the advantage of admitting the all zero word in the code set. Although **odd parity** will not be used, its definition should be obvious; with only minor theoretical revision, odd parity serves equally well in applications.

If n is the number of bits used to encode k information bits, denoted by (n, k), then the remaining $n - k$ bits are used to form the parity sums for checking the information bits. One can deduce from these parameters that 2^k code words can be constructed out of the possible 2^n n-tuples. The value k/n gives the code efficiency for an **(n, k) code.**

But where in the sequence of bits should the parity bits be located? Consider two choices. A **block code** disburses the parity bits among the checked information bits. The illustrations used throughout this discussion will follow this format. Alternatively, the parity bits of one block may be included with the information bits transmitted in later blocks; this is known as a **convolution code.** Since noise most likely will cause multiple errors to occur within the same block, such codes have the advantage of avoiding many undetected errors.

ENCODING HAMMING CODES

The inherent elegance possible with parity check coding can now be illustrated by presenting the Hamming coding/decoding algorithm for structuring code redundancy. The **Hamming coding** algorithm constructs specific code sets that can detect and

	i_7	i_6	i_5	p_4	i_3	p_2	p_1
Row 1	1	0	1	0	1	0	1
Row 2	1	1	0	0	1	1	0
Row 3	1	1	1	1	0	0	0

FIGURE 5.4 Bit designations for a (7, 4) Hamming code.

correct for 1 error. Before delving into the reasons why it works, let us first describe the mechanics of the technique.

Refer to Figure 5.4. The bit positions are numbered consecutively, starting at the right end. The letters p and i designate the parity check bits and information bits, respectively. The parity bits are placed at the 2^j bit positions (i.e., at bit positions 1, 2, 4, 8, 16, etc.). The number in the column below each bit position simply restates the bit position number in binary notation. The binary bit number, however, is not of interest itself; rather, the interest is on the pattern of 0's and 1's in each row. This pattern will serve as a templet for selecting which information bits to use in calculating each parity bit.

The 1's in each row of the binary numbers below the bit positions identify the bit positions selected to compute the parity bit associated with that row. Each row includes one and only one parity bit, a fact that can be confirmed by the (7, 4) code shown in the figure. Row 1 selects bit positions i_7, i_5, and i_3 to calculate the value of parity bit p_1. Similarly, row 2 selects i_7, i_6, and i_3 to calculate p_2. Row 3 selects i_7, i_6, and i_5 to calculate p_4. This scheme allows the parity bits to be set independently of each other. For even parity, the parity bit settings can be expressed concisely by the following equations:

$$p_1 = i_7 \oplus i_5 \oplus i_3$$
$$p_2 = i_7 \oplus i_6 \oplus i_3 \qquad\qquad (5.8)$$
$$p_4 = i_7 \oplus i_6 \oplus i_5$$

Example 5.3 may help clarify the procedure.

Example 5.3

Encode the information bits 1010 using a 7-bit Hamming code. Placing the information bits in their respective bit positions gives:

$1\ 0\ 1\ p_4\ 0\ p_2\ p_1$
$1\ 0\ 1\ 0\quad 1\ 0\quad 1$ sets $p_1 = 1 \oplus 1 \oplus 0 = 0$
$1\ 1\ 0\ 0\quad 1\ 1\quad 0$ sets $p_2 = 1 \oplus 0 \oplus 0 = 1$
$1\ 1\ 1\ 1\quad 0\ 0\quad 0$ sets $p_4 = 1 \oplus 0 \oplus 1 = 0$

The encoded Hamming code is 101$\underline{00}$1$\underline{0}$. The underlined values serve only to highlight the parity bits in this example.   ◀

DECODING HAMMING CODES

For decoding, the same group of information bits used to set each parity bit are checked together with their respective parity bit, recording a 0 into a check bit when the sum is even, and a 1 otherwise. Referring again to Figure 5.4, the following equations can be easily verified for forming the check sum bits for an even parity (7, 4) code:

$$c_1 = i_7 \oplus i_5 \oplus i_3 \oplus p_1$$
$$c_2 = i_7 \oplus i_6 \oplus i_3 \oplus p_2 \tag{5.9}$$
$$c_4 = i_7 \oplus i_6 \oplus i_5 \oplus p_4$$

If all check bits equal 0, then the received n-tuple can be assumed correct (i.e., a single error has not damaged the received code word). When any of the check bits do not equal 0, then an error has occurred and the bit pattern $c_4 c_2 c_1$ gives the binary value of the bit position of the damaged bit. It should be reemphasized that the Hamming code can detect and correct for 1 and only 1 error; if more than 1 error occurs, then the check sum would result in a misleading value.

Example 5.4
Suppose the bit in the fifth bit position in the Hamming code word shown in Example 5.3 has been damaged during transmission (i.e., the code word has been received as 1000010). Use the Hamming decoding scheme to find the damaged bit.

$$c_4 = 1 \oplus 0 \oplus 0 \oplus 0 = 1$$
$$c_2 = 1 \oplus 0 \oplus 0 \oplus 1 = 0$$
$$c_1 = 1 \oplus 0 \oplus 0 \oplus 0 = 1$$

The check sum, $c_4 c_2 c_1$, equals 101 (the binary value for 5), pointing to an error in the fifth bit position. Magic!

It should be noted that in this example, multiple errors could also give a check sum of 101. For example, if bit positions 1 and 4 were both damaged, then the check sum would misleadingly point to an error in the fifth position.   ◀

MATRIX CODING AND DECODING

The coding and decoding operations can be recast into a more concise form by using matrix operations, substituting the and-operator for multiplication and the exclusive-or operator for addition. The logic operators and the arithmetic operators yield the same results if modulo 2 arithmetic is used for addition. Using the (7, 4) Hamming code as an example, the coding algorithm can be described as follows:

- The individual information bits can be selected by multiplying the row of information bits into a column vector with a single 1 located in an appropriate position. For the (7, 4) Hamming code, the following matrix composed of three unit column vectors will select bits i_7, i_6, and i_5 as the first three bits:

$$(i_7 \ i_6 \ i_5 \ i_3) \begin{pmatrix} 1 & 0 & 0 \\ 0 & 1 & 0 \\ 0 & 0 & 1 \\ 0 & 0 & 0 \end{pmatrix} = (i_7 \ i_6 \ i_5)$$

- The fourth bit in the Hamming code is a parity bit calculated by the exclusive-or addition of bits i_7, i_6, and i_5. A column vector with a 1 in each row corresponding to the selected information bits, and 0 otherwise, will form the parity bit, as illustrated by the fourth column of the following matrix:

$$(i_7 \ i_6 \ i_5 \ i_3) \begin{pmatrix} 1 & 0 & 0 & 1 \\ 0 & 1 & 0 & 1 \\ 0 & 0 & 1 & 1 \\ 0 & 0 & 0 & 0 \end{pmatrix} = (i_7 \ i_6 \ i_5 \ p_4)$$

- The next bit is the i_3 information bit, again selected by the appropriate unit vector:

$$(i_7 \ i_6 \ i_5 \ i_3) \begin{pmatrix} 1 & 0 & 0 & 1 & 0 \\ 0 & 1 & 0 & 1 & 0 \\ 0 & 0 & 1 & 1 & 0 \\ 0 & 0 & 0 & 0 & 1 \end{pmatrix} = (i_7 \ i_6 \ i_5 \ p_4 \ i_3)$$

- The last two bits are parity bits, calculated by the exclusive-or addition of bits i_7, i_6, and i_3, and bits i_7, i_5, and i_3:

$$(i_7 \ i_6 \ i_5 \ i_3) \begin{pmatrix} 1 & 0 & 0 & 1 & 0 & 1 & 1 \\ 0 & 1 & 0 & 1 & 0 & 1 & 0 \\ 0 & 0 & 1 & 1 & 0 & 0 & 1 \\ 0 & 0 & 0 & 0 & 1 & 1 & 1 \end{pmatrix} = (i_7 \ i_6 \ i_5 \ p_4 \ i_3 \ p_2 \ p_1)$$

Example 5.5

Encode information bits 1101 using the encoding matrix for the Hamming code.

$$(1 \ 1 \ 0 \ 1) \begin{pmatrix} 1 & 0 & 0 & 1 & 0 & 1 & 1 \\ 0 & 1 & 0 & 1 & 0 & 1 & 0 \\ 0 & 0 & 1 & 1 & 0 & 0 & 1 \\ 0 & 0 & 0 & 0 & 1 & 1 & 1 \end{pmatrix} = (1 \ 1 \ 0 \ 0 \ 1 \ 1 \ 0)$$

◀

The encoding matrix, called the **generator matrix,** describes in a convenient notation the mechanics of constructing the code word for transmission. In general, an $(n, \ k)$ code can be described by a generator matrix with n columns and k rows. For the Hamming code, the position of the information and parity bits were located such that any single error could be identified by the numerical value of the check bits. While this result was interesting, one need not strictly adhere to this convention.

After the parity bits have been generated, they need not be treated any differently than the information bits. The standard format for parity-checking codes displays the parity bits following the information bits. Since each column of the generator matrix corresponds to a bit position, the encoded bits can be positioned arbitrarily by switching the matrix columns. The matrix for generating the bits in the standard format consists of an identity matrix, a matrix composed of 1's on the diagonal and 0's elsewhere, followed by the matrix for encoding the parity bits. Using this structure, a standard generator for the (7, 4) Hamming code can be constructed by switching columns 3 and 4 as follows (note that the bit-numbering scheme that had been used has now lost its original significance):

$$(i_7 \ i_6 \ i_5 \ i_3) \begin{pmatrix} 1 & 0 & 0 & 0 & 1 & 1 & 1 \\ 0 & 1 & 0 & 0 & 1 & 1 & 0 \\ 0 & 0 & 1 & 0 & 1 & 0 & 1 \\ 0 & 0 & 0 & 1 & 0 & 1 & 1 \end{pmatrix} = (i_7 \ i_6 \ i_5 \ i_3 \ p_4 \ p_2 \ p_1)$$

Example 5.6

Encode the information bits 1101 using the Hamming generator matrix in standard format.

$$(1 \ 1 \ 0 \ 1) \begin{pmatrix} 1 & 0 & 0 & 0 & 1 & 1 & 1 \\ 0 & 1 & 0 & 0 & 1 & 1 & 0 \\ 0 & 0 & 1 & 0 & 1 & 0 & 1 \\ 0 & 0 & 0 & 1 & 0 & 1 & 1 \end{pmatrix} = (1 \ 1 \ 0 \ 1 \ 0 \ 1 \ 0)$$

◀

The standard generator matrix for an (n, k) code can be written as (IP), where I denotes the identity matrix of order k, and P denotes a parity bit submatrix with k rows and $n - k$ columns. The decoding matrix associated with this generator matrix can be written as $\binom{P}{I}$, where P is the same parity bit submatrix given in the generator matrix, and I is another identity matrix of order $n - k$. The generator matrix for the (n, k) code consists of n columns and k rows. The associated decoding matrix consists of $n - k$ columns and n rows. For example, the decoding matrix D associated with the encoding matrix used in Example 5.6 is

$$D = \begin{pmatrix} 1 & 1 & 1 \\ 1 & 1 & 0 \\ 1 & 0 & 1 \\ 0 & 1 & 1 \\ 1 & 0 & 0 \\ 0 & 1 & 0 \\ 0 & 0 & 1 \end{pmatrix}$$

Figure 5.5 shows the organization for the encoder used to generate the code from the information bits available at the data source and the decoder used to extract the information bits from the received n-tuple. The encoder and decoder can be represented as matrices that have been designed for error detection or error correction or a combination of both. For error detection, any detected error of the type embedded in the design causes a signal to be sent back to the transmitter asking for a retransmission of the bit sequence. For an error-correcting code, any error of the type embedded in the design can be corrected by the receiver, making it unnecessary to retransmit. Errors that cannot be detected will persist throughout the application.

The form of the decoding matrix can now be justified. When given in a matrix format, the encoder multiplies the row of information bits into the generator matrix, creating a code word for transmission. Formally, if d denotes the vector of information bits, and (IP) denotes the generator matrix in standard format, then $d(IP)$ gives the generated code word. The decoder receives an n-tuple representing the code word or a bit pattern that has been damaged in a manner anticipated by the design. The received n-tuple is multiplied into the decoding matrix, giving a bit sequence equal in length to the number of parity bits. In the event of no error, the output of the

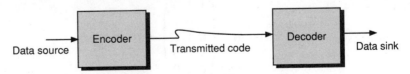

FIGURE 5.5 Schematic diagram for the encoding and decoding process.

decoder is $d(IP) \binom{P}{I} = d(P \oplus P)$. $P \oplus P$ consists of a matrix of k rows and $n - k$ columns whose elements all equal 0, giving

$$d(IP)\binom{P}{I} = 0 \tag{5.10}$$

This can be illustrated by multiplying the (7, 4) Hamming generator and its associated decoding matrix in standard format to get the following null 4×3 matrix:

$$\begin{pmatrix} 1 & 0 & 0 & 0 & 1 & 1 & 1 \\ 0 & 1 & 0 & 0 & 1 & 1 & 0 \\ 0 & 0 & 1 & 0 & 1 & 0 & 1 \\ 0 & 0 & 0 & 1 & 0 & 1 & 1 \end{pmatrix} \begin{pmatrix} 1 & 1 & 1 \\ 1 & 1 & 0 \\ 1 & 0 & 1 \\ 0 & 1 & 1 \\ 1 & 0 & 0 \\ 0 & 1 & 0 \\ 0 & 0 & 1 \end{pmatrix} = \begin{pmatrix} 0 & 0 & 0 \\ 0 & 0 & 0 \\ 0 & 0 & 0 \\ 0 & 0 & 0 \end{pmatrix}$$

The product of the received n-tuple and the decoding matrix is called the **syndrome.** It has just been demonstrated that an all-zero syndrome indicates that no error of the type embedded in the design has occurred. A syndrome other than the all-zero syndrome characterizes the error.

Example 5.7

Find the syndrome for the following received n-tuples, which have been encoded by the (7, 4) Hamming generator in standard format.

(a) 1110101

(b) 1101010

(a)

$$(1 \; 1 \; 1 \; 0 \; 1 \; 0 \; 1) \begin{pmatrix} 1 & 1 & 1 \\ 1 & 1 & 0 \\ 1 & 0 & 1 \\ 0 & 1 & 1 \\ 1 & 0 & 0 \\ 0 & 1 & 0 \\ 0 & 0 & 1 \end{pmatrix} = (0 \; 0 \; 1)$$

(b)

$$(1\ 1\ 0\ 1\ 0\ 1\ 0) \begin{pmatrix} 1 & 1 & 1 \\ 1 & 1 & 0 \\ 1 & 0 & 1 \\ 0 & 1 & 1 \\ 1 & 0 & 0 \\ 0 & 1 & 0 \\ 0 & 0 & 1 \end{pmatrix} = (0\ 0\ 0)$$

◀

For the Hamming code, a nonzero syndrome equals the bit pattern of the decoding matrix row corresponding to the bit position that has been damaged. This conclusion can be demonstrated by noting the effect of any single error on an otherwise correct code word. When a row bit in the decoding matrix equals 0, then any single error changing the corresponding received bit from either a 0 to a 1 or from a 1 to a 0 would have no effect on the syndrome and would leave the syndrome bit equal to 0. On the other hand, if the corresponding row bit is a 1, then a change in the received bit will change the syndrome bit to a 1. The effect can be summarized by saying that any single error will duplicate the row of the decoding matrix corresponding to the bit position of the error.

Example 5.8

Correct the code word 0000110, which has been encoded using the Hamming coding matrix in standard format.

$$(0\ 0\ 0\ 0\ 1\ 1\ 0) \begin{pmatrix} 1 & 1 & 1 \\ 1 & 1 & 0 \\ 1 & 0 & 1 \\ 0 & 1 & 1 \\ 1 & 0 & 0 \\ 0 & 1 & 0 \\ 0 & 0 & 1 \end{pmatrix} = (1\ 1\ 0)$$

The detected error was in the second bit, since the syndrome equals the second row of the decoding matrix. Changing the second bit of the received n-tuple gives 0100110 as the correct code word. ◀

Exercises

5.11 Calculate and append one parity bit for each of the following patterns of information bits, using all the bits to calculate the parity bit:
(a)   100 011
(b)   1100 1001
(c)   1001 0001 1000

5.12 List all the possible ways the code words can be damaged and the error detected for the (5, 4) code set.

5.13 A rectangular code is one that appends a separate parity check to each row and each column of a collection of bits arranged in a rectangular manner, e.g., as in a block of data on magnetic tape. Add the parity bits to the following array and discuss the possible errors that this code can detect and correct;

        1000 1001
        0011 1011
        1010 0110
        1101 1000
        0101 0010

5.14 Discuss the advantage of a convolution code when spike noise is expected on the line.†

5.15 Encode the following information bits using the Hamming code:
(a)   0 001
(b)   10 001
(c)   10 001 100 011
Repeat using the Hamming generator matrix.

5.16 Locate the error in each of the following Hamming codes:
(a)   1 011 010
(b)   11 101 011 010

(c)   110 001
Repeat using the Hamming decoding matrix.

5.17 Express equations 5.8 and 5.9 when using odd parity.

5.18 Plot the efficiency versus the number of information bits for the Hamming code.

5.19 Encode the information bits 1010 using the Hamming coding procedure. Assuming that the bits in the resultant code word are information bits, encode these bits again using the Hamming coding procedure. Discuss the error-correcting capabilities of this arrangement. Compare the number of possible code words with the upper limit derived for codes of length n.

5.20 List all combinations of errors in the (7, 4) Hamming code that result in a 000 value of the check bits $c_4 c_2 c_1$. Explain why the value of the check bits gives the bit position damaged when a single error occurs. What happens to the value of the check bits when more than one error occurs?

5.21 Find the coding and decoding matrices in standard format for each of the following Hamming codes:
(a)   (3, 1)
(b)   (6, 3)
(c)   (9, 5)
(d)   (15, 11)

Show that the product of the coding matrix and associated decoding matrix for each of these code sets is the null matrix.

---

† Class discussion exercise.

5.3   CYCLIC REDUNDANCY CODES

CYCLIC CODE THEOREM

It seems natural to interpret a code word, say, the code word $c_{n-1} c_{n-2} \cdot \cdot \cdot c_2 c_1 c_0$, as a binary number representing the value

$$c_{n-1}2^{n-1} + c_{n-2}2^{n-2} + \ldots + c_2 2^2 + c_1 2^1 + c_0 2^0$$

With added generality, a code word can be represented as a polynomial with the same coefficients by simply replacing the radix 2 with the variable x, giving

$$c_{n-1}x^{n-1} + c_{n-2}x^{n-2} + \ldots + c_2 x^2 + c_1 x + c_0$$

For example, the code polynomial for the code word 10010001 is $x^7 + x^4 + 1$. This formulation of code words as code polynomials makes possible the use of the extensive theoretical foundation of algebra for the study of coding.

A **cyclic code** is a code in which every rotation of a code word is also a code word of the code. Rotation is performed by shifting each bit 1 bit position to the left, except for the leftmost bit, which is shifted around to the rightmost position. Algebraically, for a code polynomial $c(x)$, of length n, a rotation of i positions can be expressed by the equation

$$c(x) = x^i c(x) \bmod (x^n + 1) \tag{5.11}$$

The modulo operator (mod) computes the remainder of division. Consistent with coding as it has been presented up to this point and with the algebraic theory, the *exclusive-or* and *and* operators replace the numerical operators of addition and multiplication, respectively.

Example 5.9
Find the code words of the cyclic code for which 1011 is a code word.

The code word 1011 is represented by the code polynomial $x^3 + x + 1$. Every rotation of the code word 1011 is also a code word of the code. Algebraically, this can be computed by using the exclusive-or operator and the and operator to compute the remainder of each of the following expressions. The remainder is a code word of the cyclic code.

$$\frac{x^0(x^3 + x + 1)}{x^4 + 1} \quad \text{represents 1011}$$

$$\frac{x^1(x^3 + x + 1)}{x^4 + 1} \quad \text{represents 0111}$$

$$\frac{x^2(x^3 + x + 1)}{x^4 + 1} \quad \text{represents 1110}$$

$$\frac{x^3(x^3 + x + 1)}{x^4 + 1} \qquad \text{represents } 1101$$

Each expression is formed by multiplying the code polynomial by a power of x and dividing by $x^4 + 1$. The exponent 4 in $x^4 + 1$ represents the length of the code word. Further powers of x simply repeat the cycle. To illustrate the operations, consider the following:

$$\frac{x^2(x^3 + x + 1)}{x^4 + 1}$$

$$\begin{array}{r} x \\ x^4 + 1 \overline{)\; x^5 + x^3 + x^2} \\ \underline{x^5 + x} \\ x^3 + x^2 + x \end{array}$$

The remainder $x^3 + x^2 + x$ represents the code word 1110. Note that the higher powers of the remainder (up to x^3 in this example) may be missing from the remainder. When this occurs, leading zeros may have to be inserted in the leftmost positions to maintain the code length, as in the code word 0111.   ◀

Cyclic codes are a special form of block codes, offering the advantage that they can be readily implemented in practice and analyzed mathematically. The central theorem for generating cyclic codes, **cyclic code theorem,** can be stated, without proof, as follows:

Every cyclic (n,k) code (called a **cyclic redundancy code, CRC**) is generated by a factor of $x^n + 1$ of degree $n - k$, and conversely, every factor of $x^n + 1$ of degree $n - k$ generates a cyclic (n,k) code.

Table 5.3 lists the **primitive factors** of $x^n + 1$ for various values of n. Primitive factors are factors that are not composites of other factors. Other factors may be derived by forming products of these primitive factors to satisfy the condition of the cyclic code theorem.

Example 5.10
Prove that $x^7 + 1$ can be factored by the primitive code polynomials given in Table 5.3.

$$x^7 + 1 = (x + 1)(x^3 + x + 1)(x^3 + x^2 + 1)$$

By modulo 2 arithmetic:

$$
\begin{array}{l}
x^3 + x + 1 \\
\underline{x\ \ + 1} \\
x^4\qquad + x^2 + x \\
\underline{\qquad x^3 \qquad\quad + x + 1} \\
x^4 + x^3 + x^2 \qquad\quad + 1
\end{array}
\qquad\qquad
\begin{array}{l}
x^4 + x^3 + x^2 + 1 \\
\underline{x^3 + x^2 + 1} \\
x^7 + x^6 + x^5 \qquad\quad + x^3 \\
\quad\ x^6 + x^5 + x^4 \qquad\qquad + x^2 \\
\underline{\qquad\qquad x^4 + x^3 + x^2 + 1} \\
x^7 \qquad\qquad\qquad\qquad\quad + 1
\end{array}
$$

◀

TABLE 5.3
PRIMITIVE FACTORS OF $x^n + 1$

$x^n + 1$	PRIMITIVE FACTORS
$x^3 + 1$	$x + 1$
	$x^2 + x + 1$
$x^7 + 1$	$x + 1$
	$x^3 + x + 1$
	$x^3 + x^2 + 1$
$x^{15} + 1$	$x + 1$
	$x^2 + x + 1$
	$x^4 + x + 1$
	$x^4 + x^3 + 1$
	$x^4 + x^3 + x^2 + x + 1$
$x^{31} + 1$	$x + 1$
	$x^5 + x^2 + 1$
	$x^5 + x^3 + 1$
	$x^5 + x^3 + x^2 + x + 1$
	$x^5 + x^4 + x^2 + x + 1$
	$x^5 + x^4 + x^3 + x + 1$
	$x^5 + x^4 + x^3 + x^2 + 1$
$x^{63} + 1$	$x + 1$
	$x^2 + x + 1$
	$x^3 + x + 1$
	$x^3 + x^2 + 1$
	$x^6 + x + 1$
	$x^6 + x^3 + 1$
	$x^6 + x^4 + x^2 + x + 1$
	$x^6 + x^4 + x^3 + x + 1$
	$x^6 + x^5 + 1$
	$x^6 + x^5 + x^2 + x + 1$
	$x^6 + x^5 + x^3 + x^2 + 1$
	$x^6 + x^5 + x^4 + x + 1$
	$x^6 + x^5 + x^4 + x^2 + 1$

Example 5.11

Find a generator polynomial for encoding the following (n, k) cyclic codes:

    (a) $(7, 4)$

    (b) $(15, 7)$

    (a) A factor of degree $7 - 4 = 3$ is needed from the polynomial $x^7 + 1$. Either primitive factor $x^3 + x + 1$ or $x^3 + x^2 + 1$ will serve the purpose.

    (b) A factor of degree $15 - 7 = 8$ is needed from the polynomial $x^{15} + 1$. The factor $x^8 + x^7 + x^5 + x^4 + x^3 + x + 1$ constructed from the product of the primitive factors $x^4 + x + 1$ and $x^4 + x^3 + 1$ will serve the purpose. Note that either of these primitive factors could have been replaced by the primitive factor $x^4 + x^3 + x^2 + x + 1$ to construct other factors that would have been equally applicable. ◀

POLYNOMIAL ENCODING AND DECODING

The algorithm for the polynomial encoding of a message is given explicitly in Figure 5.6. For an (n, k) code, a factor of $x^n + 1$ of degree $n - k$, represented by $G(x)$, is selected as the **generator polynomial.** Multiplying the message polynomial $M(x)$ by x^{n-k} shifts the message left by $n - k$ bit positions. After dividing the shifted message by the generator polynomial using modulo 2 arithmetic, the remainder represents the $n - k$ parity bits. The code word is formed in standard code format by shifting the information bits left by $n - k$ positions and appending the parity bits to the right of the message bits.

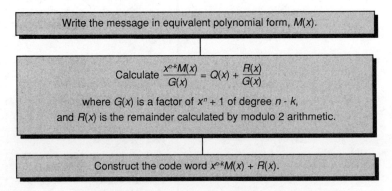

FIGURE 5.6 (n, k) polynomial encoding.

Example 5.12

Encode the information bits 1001 with 3 parity bits.

The number of information bits, k, equals 4, and the number of parity bits, $n - k$, equals 3, giving a value of $n = 7$. The expression $x^3 + x + 1$, a factor of $x^7 + 1$, is selected as the generator polynomial (alternatively, the factor $x^3 + x^2 + 1$ could have been selected).

Step 1 $M(x) = x^3 + 1$

Step 2   Calculate $x^3(x^3 + 1)\bmod(x^3 + x + 1)$.

$$
\begin{array}{r}
x^3 + x \\
x^3 + x + 1\overline{)\,x^6 \qquad\;\; + x^3} \\
x^6 + x^4 + x^3 \\
\overline{\hphantom{x^6 + x^4 + }x^4} \\
x^4 + x^2 + x \\
\overline{\hphantom{x^4 + }x^2 + x} = 110
\end{array}
$$

Step 3   Shift the information bits 3 places and append the parity bits.
$$
\begin{aligned}
x^{n-k}M(x) + R(x) &= x^3(x^3 + 1) + x^2 + x \\
&= x^6 + x^3 + x^2 + x \\
&= 1001\ 110
\end{aligned}
$$
◀

The algorithm outlined in Figure 5.7 checks the received n-tuple and produces the syndrome of the transmitted n-tuple. The n-tuple, in equivalent polynomial for-

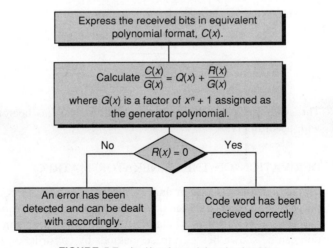

FIGURE 5.7 (n, k) polynomial code checking.

mat, is divided by the same generator polynomial used to encode the transmitted message using modulo 2 arithmetic. The remainder of this operation gives the syndrome. A nonzero remainder indicates a detected error that can be dealt with accordingly. If a zero syndrome is calculated, it can be assumed that the bits have been transmitted correctly. No errors other than those embedded in the design can be handled.

Example 5.13

Check the following received n-tuples generated by the generator polynomial $x^3 + x + 1$.

(a) 1001 110

(b) 1001 010

(a)
$$
\require{enclose}
\begin{array}{r}
x^3 + x \\
x^3 + x + 1 \enclose{longdiv}{x^6 + x^3 + x^2 + x} \\
\underline{x^6 + x^4 + x^3} \\
x^4 + x^2 + x \\
\underline{x^4 + x^2 + x} \\
0
\end{array}
$$

The zero syndrome indicates that the code word has been transmitted correctly (see Example 5.12).

(b)
$$
\begin{array}{r}
x^3 + x \\
x^3 + x + 1 \enclose{longdiv}{x^6 + x^3 + x} \\
\underline{x^6 + x^4 + x^3} \\
x^4 + x \\
\underline{x^4 + x^2 + x} \\
x^2
\end{array}
$$

The syndrome $x^2 = 100$ indicates that an error has been detected and can be dealt with accordingly. ◀

DERIVATION OF THE GENERATOR MATRIX

Throughout the discussion and exercises on Hamming codes, coding matrices, and polynomial coding, an attempt has been made to show some connection between the various coding methods so that they would not appear unrelated. A stronger connection can be shown between these methods by constructing the (n, k) generator matrix that will produce the equivalent code generated from an (n, k) generator polynomial.

Figure 5.8 give an algorithm for constructing a set of $n - k$ polynomials from

$p_k(x) = G(x)$
$i = k-1$

Repeat
    $S(x) = xp_{i+1}(x)$
    If coefficient of x^{n-k} term in $S(x)$ equals 0,
        Then $p_i(x) = S(x)$
        Else $p_i(x) = S(x) \oplus G(x)$
    $i = i-1$
Until $i = 0$

FIGURE 5.8 Algorithm for forming an equivalent generator matrix from a generator polynomial.

a generator polynomial $G(x)$ of degree $n - k$ selected from the factors of $x^n + 1$. These polynomials represent the rows of a standard generator matrix for generating a code equivalent to that generated by the (n, k) generator polynomial.

Following the algorithm, the first polynomial of the set, which is numbered by the subscript k, is the generator polynomial itself. Subsequent polynomials, $p_i(x)$, are formed by multiplying the polynomial that has just been formed by x. Recall that multiplying a code polynomial by x amounts to shifting its associated binary representation one place to the left and appending a 0 on the right side. The new, shifted polynomial may or may not contain the x^{n-k} term. When this term is missing, the shifted polynomial is retained in the set. However, when the shifted polynomial contains the x^{n-k} term, it is replaced by another polynomial constructed by adding the shifted polynomial to the generator polynomial using the exclusive-or operator. Since the generator polynomial also contains the x^{n-k} term, this process guarantees that the x^{n-k} term has been eliminated in the replaced polynomial. The algorithm continues until k polynomials have been formed. The reason for numbering the polynomials as shown in the algorithm will become clear shortly.

Example 5.14
Derive the polynomials representing the rows of a standard generator matrix for the $(7,4)$ generator polynomial $x^3 + x + 1$ using the algorithm given in Figure 5.8.

From this generator polynomial, $k = 4$ polynomials can be constructed as follows:

    Set $p_4(x) = G(x)$
        $p_4(x) = x^3 + x + 1$

Calculate $S(x) = x(x^3 + x + 1) = x^4 + x^2 + x$. Since the coefficient of x^3 in $S(x)$ equals 0, then $p_3 = S(x)$.

$$p_3(x) = x^4 + x^2 + x$$

Calculate $S(x) = x(x^4 + x^2 + x) = x^5 + x^3 + x^2$. Since the coefficient of x^3 in $S(x)$ equals 1, then $p_2(x) = S(x) \oplus G(x)$.

$$\begin{aligned} p_2(x) &= (x^5 + x^3 + x^2) \oplus (x^3 + x + 1) \\ &= x^5 + x^2 + x + 1 \end{aligned}$$

Calculate $S(x) = x(x^5 + x^2 + x + 1) = x^6 + x^3 + x^2 + x$. Since the coefficient of x^3 in $S(x)$ equals 1, then $p_1(x) = S(x) \oplus G(x)$.

$$\begin{aligned} p_1(x) &= (x^6 + x^3 + x^2 + x) \oplus (x^3 + x + 1) \\ &= x^6 + x^2 + 1 \end{aligned} \qquad \blacktriangleleft$$

The generator matrix can be constructed from the k polynomials created by the algorithm in Figure 5.8 by simply expressing the coefficients of each polynomial by their associated bit patterns and collecting these bit patterns to form the matrix generator. The polynomial number corresponds to the row number of the generator matrix. Note that each of the k polynomials has one and only one term with an exponent greater than or equal to $n - k$; therefore, the resulting generator matrix will be in standard format. This can be clarified with an example.

Example 5.15
Given the k polynomials created in Example 5.14, construct the generator matrix.

$p_4(x) = x^3 + x + 1$	which translates into row 4: 0001 011
$p_3(x) = x^4 + x^2 + x$	which translates into row 3: 0010 110
$p_2(x) = x^5 + x^2 + x + 1$	which translates into row 2: 0100 111
$p_1(x) = x^6 + x^2 + 1$	which translates into row 1: 1000 101

Collecting these rows together will produce the following equivalent generator matrix:

$$\begin{pmatrix} 1000 & 101 \\ 0100 & 111 \\ 0010 & 110 \\ 0001 & 011 \end{pmatrix} \qquad \blacktriangleleft$$

The generator matrix can be constructed more directly by bypassing the explicit formulation of the polynomials representing the rows. Starting with the bottom row representing the given polynomial generator, the leftmost bit corresponds to the x^{n-k} term that forms part of the identity matrix. Each new row can be formed by shifting the previous row one position to the left and appending a 0 in the rightmost position. If after shifting, a 1 appears in the bit position corresponding to the x^{n-k} term, then the shifted row is replaced by adding it (using the exclusive-or) to the bottom row. This process continues until all k rows have been formed. A little time can be saved in the exercises by not writing the bits representing the identity matrix until after the portion representing the parity bits has been completed, as illustrated in the following example.

Example 5.16

Form the (7, 4) generator matrix from the generator polynomial $x^3 + x + 1$.

Row 4: Convert the generator polynomial to its equivalent bit pattern and place it at the bottom row of the matrix.

1 0 1 1

Row 3: Shift row 4 by one position to the left. Since the bit corresponding to the x^3 term equals 0, no further manipulation is required.

0 1 1 0
1 0 1 1

Row 2: Shift row 3 by one position. A 1 has now been shifted into the bit position corresponding to the x^3 term. Row 2 is formed by adding the shifted row (1 1 0 0) to the bottom row (1 0 1 1) bit by bit.

0 1 1 1
0 1 1 0
1 0 1 1

Row 1: Shift row 2 by one position. Since a 1 appears in the bit position corresponding to the x^3 term, row 1 is formed by adding the shifted row (1 1 1 0) to the bottom row (1 0 1 1).

0 1 0 1
0 1 1 1
0 1 1 0
1 0 1 1

The generator matrix can be formed by inserting the identity matrix in front of the parity matrix.

$$\begin{pmatrix} 1 & 0 & 0 & 0 & 1 & 0 & 1 \\ 0 & 1 & 0 & 0 & 1 & 1 & 1 \\ 0 & 0 & 1 & 0 & 1 & 1 & 0 \\ 0 & 0 & 0 & 1 & 0 & 1 & 1 \end{pmatrix}$$ ◀

Exercises

5.22 Express the following code words as code polynomials:
(a) 101
(b) 1011
(c) 1011 1011

5.23 Assume that the following code words are code words of a cyclic code. By algebraic manipulation, find the other code words of the code.
(a) 101
(b) 1011
(c) 1011 1011

5.24 Prove that the primitive factors given for $x^{15} + 1$ are correct.

5.25 Prove that the factors given for $x^7 + 1$ are primitive factors.

5.26 Show that $x^n + 1 = (x^{n/2} + 1)^2$ if n is even. Find the primitive factors for $x^{30} + 1$.

5.27 Encode the following information bits:
(a) 1000, using a (7, 4) generator polynomial
(b) 10 110 100 101, using a (15, 11) generator polynomial
(c) 1 001 101, using a (15, 7) generator polynomial

5.28 Write a computer program to find all the primitive factors of $x^n + 1$ for any given n.

5.29 Check the following received n-tuples:
(a) 1 011 101 generated by $x^3 + x^2 + 1$
(b) 110 111 100 000 101 generated by $x^4 + x^3 + 1$

5.30 Find all polynomials that can generate 15-bit cyclic codes.

5.31 Polynomial encoders can be implemented by an attractively simple hardware circuit consisting of a shift register equal in size to the number of parity bits (i.e., degree of the generator polynomial). The following diagram shows the bits of the shift register as rectangular blocks. The value shifted into each bit depends on whether the feedback switch connected to the exclusive-or gate has been closed or has been kept open. Shown here are the connections for an mth-degree generator polynomial, $x^m + a_{m-1}x^{m-1} + \ldots + a_1 x + 1$. The feedback switches are closed for $a_i = 1$ and open otherwise.

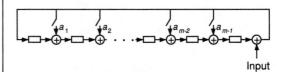

Input

The shift register starts with all zeros. As the input signals arrive, the line is set according to the value in the shift register bit position and the feedback signal and then shifted into the next position in sequence. After all the information bits have been entered, the shift register contains the parity bits for completing the code word.

Set up encoder for the generator polynomial $x^3 + x + 1$, and verify that the operation of the circuit will give the correct parity for the information bits 1001.

5.32 A polynomial decoder has a simplicity equal to that of a hardware encoder as given in exercise 5.31. The circuit for an mth-degree generator polynomial

Exercises *(continued)*

decoder is shown below. As for the encoder, the feedback switches are closed when $a_i = 1$ and open otherwise.

Input

Set up the decoder circuit for the generator polynomial $x^3 + x + 1$, and verify the syndrome for the input n-tuples 1001011 and 1000110.

5.33 Three important cyclic redundancy codes (CRC) used to discriminate multiple errors are

(a) CRC-12: $\quad x^{12} + x^{11} + x^3 + x^2 + x + 1$
(b) CRC-CCITT: $x^{16} + x^{12} + x^5 + 1$
(c) CRC-16: $\quad x^{16} + x^{15} + x^2 + 1$

Show the encoding and decoding circuits for these polynomials by extending the circuits shown in exercises 5.31 and 5.32.

5.34 Use an appropriate generator polynomial to generate the following generator matrices:

(a) (7, 4)
(b) (15, 11)
(c) (7, 3)
(d) (31, 26)
(e) (31, 21)

SUMMARY

Even though the error rate of a digital channel is fixed by its physical construction, the reliability of transmission can be improved by encoding the information with redundant data. For binary codes, this can be done by appending parity bits to the information. A parity bit simply records whether a selected group of bits has an odd or even number of 1's. The correctness of a code word can be checked when it is received if all the code words in a code set differ from each other by a minimum hamming distance. The hamming distance measures the number of bit positions in which two n-tuples differ. A code set whose code words differ from each other by a hamming distance of $q + 1$ can detect up to q errors. A code set whose code words differ from each other by a hamming distance of $2r + 1$ can detect for r errors but can also correct these errors without retransmission.

These concepts have been illustrated with a classic code developed by R. Hamming that can detect and correct for 1 error. The Hamming code places the parity bits at specific positions in the code word, and each parity bit is used to record the parity of a specific group of information bits to be transmitted. For decoding, each parity bit is checked together with the same information bits that had been used to set it. A check sum records the result of each of these checks. If a single error has occurred, then the check sum gives the bit number of the bit that has been damaged.

The formulation of the Hamming encoding procedure can be concisely given in a matrix format. By simply exchanging the columns of the matrix, the code word groups the information bits in front of the parity bits. The matrix in this format can be identified by an identity matrix followed by the parity bit check matrix, *IP*. The decoding matrix can be formed from the encoding matrix by placing the parity bit check matrix on top of an identity matrix, $\binom{P}{I}$. The decoding matrix gives the syndrome of the transmitted n-tuple, which for this code can also be used to correct for a single error.

The more general class of codes used in practice for detecting errors or for detecting and correcting errors is called a cyclic redundancy code. A cyclic code is a code in which every rotation of a code word (whereby each bit is shifted one place to the left except the leftmost bit, which is shifted to the rightmost position) is also a code word in the code set. Cyclic codes have been formulated into code polynomials, and from this formulation the following theorem was stated for generating cyclic codes:

> Every cyclic (n, k) code is generated by a factor of $x^n + 1$ of degree $n - k$, and conversely, every factor of $x^n + 1$ of degree $n - k$ generates a cyclic (n, k) code.

A table of primitive factors for various size codes was given, from which factors could be developed for illustrating this theorem. The generator polynomial used to encode the code words was also used for decoding, giving the syndrome as a result. Although the technique was not discussed, the syndrome could be used to correct errors expected by the specific code. An algorithm was given for the construction of the generator matrix from the generator polynomial. The treatment of these techniques was left for the exercises, where a more practical implementation by coding and decoding circuits could be formed directly from the generator polynomials.

KEY TERMS

Code redundancy	(n, k) code
Shannon's second theorem	Block code
Code word	Convolution code
Code length	Hamming code
Code set	Matrix coding/decoding
Binary code	Generator matrix
n-tuples	Syndrome
Error-detecting code	Cyclic code
Error-correcting code	Cyclic code theorem
Hamming distance	Cyclic Redundancy Code (CRC)
Parity bit	Primitive factors
Even parity	Generator polynomial
Odd parity	

SUGGESTED READINGS

Hamming, R. W. *Coding and Information Theory*. Englewood Cliffs, N.J.: Prentice-Hall, 1980.

Lucky, R. W., Salz, J., and Weldon, E. J., Jr. *Principles of Data Communication*. New York: McGraw-Hill, 1968.

Peterson, W. W., and Weldon, E. J., Jr. *Error Correcting Codes*. 2nd ed. Cambridge, Mass.: MIT Press, 1972.

Rabiner, L. R., and Schafer, R. W. *Digital Processing of Speech Signals*. Englewood Cliffs, N.J.: Prentice-Hall, 1978.

CHAPTER 6

NODAL INTERFACING TECHNOLOGY

Interface . . . the means by which
interaction or communication is effected
at an interface.
WEBSTER'S NINTH NEW COLLEGIATE
DICTIONARY

141

6.1 SIGNAL COORDINATION BETWEEN NODES

TRANSMISSION MODES

Data devices normally transfer information in bit groups whose composition represents a character, a block of characters, or an arbitrary collection of bit patterns. The bits of a group may be transmitted simultaneously in a **parallel mode** or sequentially in a **serial mode.** Parallel transmission is indigenous to the internal operations of a computing system where short lines can be assigned for transferring the bits individually. On the other hand, it would be impractical to connect remotely located stations with multiple lines. A single line transmitting serially provides a more reasonable alternative. Ultimately, the equipment at a station must be able to convert between these two modes of communications.

To coordinate the transfer of the data between communicating stations, the transmitter needs to alert the receiver when it has data ready to send. In parallel transmission, a separate control wire in addition to the data wires couples the transmitter and receiver. Whenever data bits become available for transfer, the transmitter alerts the receiver through a signal in the control line to probe the data wires and record the transmitted bit pattern into a register. In serial transmission, no separate wire controls the recovery of the signals. The transmitter sends the bits one after the other at carefully timed intervals, and the receiver recovers the transmitted signals by sampling the signals on the line at time intervals synchronized with the timing used by the transmitter.

In serial transmission, carefully timed signals flow through the line in both directions either simultaneously or one direction at a time, or exclusively in only one direction when the exchange of information does not require two-way communications. The communicating nodes may use two alternative schemes for timing the signals. One scheme, called **asynchronous** or **start-stop transmission,** uses independent but identically timed clocks at the transmitter and receiver and a separate start signal and stop signal to frame the bits representing a character during transmission. For transmitting larger blocks, the stations use **synchronous transmission,** whereby a common clock is established between the communicating stations.

Lines, whether procured through commercial vendors or strung by private construction, are costly, and it is unlikely that a single pair of nodes can justify the cost. Justification lies in sharing the lines among many independent users. A line can be shared in two ways, by **switching** or by **multiplexing.** Switching pools the lines into an available bank of resources and assigns them as needed on a demand basis. Multiplexing, on the other hand, partitions the channel's bandwidth into subbands or time slices and allocates resources to the individual users according to their needs.

Besides these considerations on which the communication nodes must agree, the interface is fraught with other problems dealing with the quality of the line, the speed of transmission, and the shape and form of the transmission signals. These problems have been delegated to a special line-interfacing device called the modem. Over a period of time, many salient features have been embodied into this device to provide greater interfacing flexibility.

PARALLEL AND SERIAL TRANSMISSION INTERFACES

A station in the network uses parallel transmission internally when communicating among its components and serial transmission when communicating with devices at other remote stations. In fact, the speed of a machine depends on the number of parallel lines it uses for internal communications and the size of the shift register it uses for external communications. For example, a machine might use 32-bit circuits for internal operations and a 16-bit I/O bus. Common shift register sizes are 8, 16, or 32 bits, which are commensurate with the data sizes of byte-structured machines.

Figure 6.1 shows the logical circuit for conversion of one mode to the other. When a group of bits becomes available for transfer, a signal on the control wire probes the bit wires, which causes the bits to be transferred simultaneously into the shift register. Bits flow serially out of the output end of the shift register at the transmitting station, through the communication line, and into the input end of the shift register at the receiving station. As each bit is transmitted, the remaining bits are shifted one place in the shift register to position the next bit for transmission. In a like manner, the receiving station shifts the bits in its shift register as each bit is received. After all the bits have been received, the receiver transfers the content of its shift register in parallel into the communication bus of the computer and prepares to receive the next group of bits.

DIRECTION OF TRANSMISSION

Serial information may be transferred between points over a network

- In one direction only, called a **simplex line**
- In both directions, but only one direction at a time, called a **half-duplex line**
- In both directions simultaneously, called a **duplex** or **full-duplex line**

Data communications networks seldom employ simplex lines, simply because

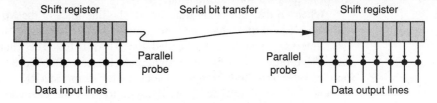

FIGURE 6.1 Conversion between parallel and serial transmission.

they do not provide a return path for acknowleding receipt of the information or for requesting a retranmission in the event that an error has been detected. However, there are applications where a simplex line sufffices, as in printing data from a computer or automatically reading instruments located at a remote site. Moreover, the validity of the data even in simplex lines can be checked. Faulty transmission can be detected by periodically transmitting a standard message such as time of day or by transmitting the data with error detection codes, and errors can be corrected by transmitting multiple copies of the messages or by transmitting the data with error correction codes.

The choice between a half-duplex line and a full-duplex line is a more complex issue. Often, the receiving station echoes back to the transmitter error control information after all the data have been received and checked. A half-duplex line suffices for this operation. However, in switching from a receiving mode to a transmitting mode, a time delay ensues, called the **line turn around time.** To eliminate the need to turn the line around for acknowledging the received data, a full-duplex line can be installed, even though there is no other need to transmit and receive simultaneously.

To fully utilize the simultaneous feature of a full-duplex line requires more complex interfacing equipment, which further adds to the cost. Various compromise solutions are possible for applications requiring full-duplex operations. For example, the bandwidth of a line may be divided into two separate subchannels, one for transmitting and the other for receiving. When a line transmits a large amount of information in one direction and a small amount of control information in the other direction, then the bandwidths of the subchannels need not be equal, and there is no great reduction in line capacity. Another scheme designates a single supervisory channel for returning control information from a group of lines.

ASYNCHRONOUS TRANSMISSION

Figure 6.2 illustrates the format of a typical character transmitted in the asynchronous mode together with the nomenclature used to describe the signals. The line may be in one of two states: the MARK state, equivalent to a 1, or the SPACE state, equivalent to a 0. Although the figure illustrates the MARK and SPACE states by levels, the actual physical conditions representing these states depend on the electrical conventions adopted for transmission.

When no data are being transferred, the line idles in the MARK state. To signal the transmission of a character, the line condition changes to the SPACE state for a time interval equal to 1 bit, called the START bit. The character bits follow in successive order, with the least significant bit first after the START bit. Depending on the code, 5 to 8 bits compose the character, using MARK to send a 1 and SPACE to send a 0. A parity check bit, if used, follows the character bits. By agreement between the transmitter and receiver, either odd or even parity is adopted, or the parity bit may not be used but may be uniformly set to 1. Transmission terminates by returning the line to the MARK state, called the STOP bit. The minimum length of the STOP bit varies depending on the standard from 1 to 2 bit intervals which gives the transmitter and receiver the opportunity to act on the data and stabilize the circuits. After the STOP bit, another character may follow immediately. If another character is not ready for transmission after the STOP bit, then the line is kept in the MARK state (ready condition) until a character becomes ready for transmission.

Asynchronous transmission finds its roots in the standards and conventions of the early teletypewriter industry. The bits representing a character are formatted together and transferred one character at a time at a rate that is commensurate with slow-speed devices such as keyboards and printers. While the two stations do not share a common clock, their timing must nevertheless be coordinated. The receiving station continuously samples the signals on the input line many times the effective bit rate, say 8 or 16 times the bit rate, seeking to find a transition in the line's current or voltage that identifies the START pulse from its normal idle condition. After finding the START pulse, the receiver counts off enough samples to locate the center of the pulses representing the character's bits and uses these central samples to record the bit values.

The simplicity of start-stop transmission pays a high overhead penalty for synchronizing the receiver and transmitter during transmission. For example, each 7-bit ASCII character requires a parity bit for checking and at least two extra bit times for the START and STOP pulses. Also, the use of separate clocks at the two stations dictates that only a few bits can be transmitted before the stations must be resynchronized. For slow-speed, intermittent communications, this is tolerable; but for communications at computer rates, efficiency requires larger blocks of bits. This is achieved by synchronous transmission.

SYNCHRONOUS TRANSMISSION

For synchronous transmission, the transmitter formats bits into larger groups than a character and transmits the bits as a block. It would be prohibitive to try to precisely time the transmissiion and receipt of such blocks by separate clocks, as with asynchronous transmission, even if the clocks were almost identical. For example, to correctly identify the bits in a 1000-bit block would require that the clocks at the two stations not drift from each other even momentarily by more than 0.1 percent. Therefore, a common clock must be established between the transmitter and the receiver

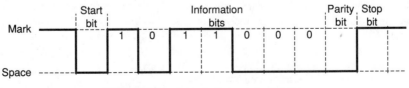

FIGURE 6.2 Asynchronous transmission.

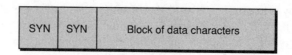

FIGURE 6.3   Character synchronization.

to achieve synchronization, which justifies the term *synchronous transmission*. In practice, the timing of the bits may be superimposed by the transmitter directly on the waveform of the data signals or on the carrier used to transmit the signals, or it may be transmitted as an independent signal on a subband of the channel.

The exact signaling techniques used for synchronous transmission will be discussed later; for now, assume that a block of characters has been prepared for transmission. Figure 6.3 depicts the block of characters prefixed by SYN characters. The specific combination of bits defining the SYN character depends on the code set used (see Appendix B). By agreement between the transmitter and receiver, the receiver can determine the beginning of the block once it has detected the SYN characters. The end of the block is determined by other control characters embedded in the format. The bit pattern for the SYN character is especially chosen to minimize the possibility of a line error putting the receiver into false synchronization. For example, the 8-bit ASCII-1968 code defines the SYN character by the bit pattern 01010110, which has multiple symmetries.

During operations, the receiver is put in the sync-search mode, looking for the SYN character. To avoid false synchronization, at least 2 SYN characters mark the beginning of the block so that the receiver does not inadvertently mistake line noise for the SYN character. As each bit is received, it is concatenated with the bits already received, and an attempt is made to match these bits with the SYN character's unique bit pattern. Upon recognizing 1 SYN character, the receiver collects the next group of bits representing a character to confirm that it is another SYN character. If successful, the receiver acts to recover the block of data that follows; otherwise, the receiver assumes that the first SYN character was due to erroneous transmission and returns to the sync-search mode.

Exercises

6.1 During asynchronous transmission, the receiver samples the line many times the effective transmission rate. When it detects the transition of the START pulse, it attempts to sample the middle of each of the successive pulses to determine the value of each bit. Calculate the percentage discrepancy between the receiver's clock and the transmission rate that would be tolerable to correctly receive the bits for various size codes. How is this related to the rate at which the receiver samples the line?

6.2 START-STOP bits are not required when characters are transmitted in the synchronous mode, if present, they are removed by the line-interfacing equipment. Moreover, a separate parity bit is not ap-

Exercises *(continued)*

pended to each character transmitted in the synchronous mode, but either two or a four character CRC field for the entire block is appended at the end of the block. Compare the overhead penalty associated with synchronous and asynchronous modes of transmission.

6.3 Given two end stations interconnected with a full-duplex line, discuss the problem of line turn around for this communication channel when an echo

suppression circuit is installed in the line.

6.4 Suppose that 2 SYN characters are transmitted in a row. What possible combination of 1 to 8 bits immediately preceding these SYN characters could signal false synchronization?

6.5 Given multiple stations that can exchange data simultaneously using two channels, A and B, how can a station decide which channel to use for transmission and which to use for reception?

6.2 SWITCHING

SWITCHING STRATEGIES

The expected usage of the line facilities in a network is to place calls of short duration intermittently between stations. Switching allows the lines to be shared among users by assigning the lines to users on a demand basis for the duration of time needed, then returning the lines back to the bank of available resources after communications have been completed. By a combination of manual and mechanized operations, switching has been a part of the telephone and telegraph industries since their inception. Without switching, stations would have had to be permanently wired to each other, making line costs prohibitive. Paralleling other advances in electronics, more and more switching functions are being delegated to computer or computer-like devices, not only to eliminate inefficiencies in the circuits of past technology, but also to provide a more flexible and robust network environment.

Networks can be categorized by the switching strategy that they use as **circuit-switching, message-switching,** or **packet-switching** networks. The ideas of circuit switching find their roots in the telephone industry, where the network establishes a path when a subscriber places a call and dedicates that path to the calling parties for the duration of the call. When high data rates can be sustained during the entire session, circuit switching can also be efficiently used for data communications. Unlike the telephone industry, the telegraph industry used message switching. Messages, prefixed by their destination address, were transmitted in their entirety from station to station through the network until they finally arrived at their destination. In the process of automating message switching, it proved more manageable to segment the messages into small, fixed-size blocks called packets. Packet switching works in a pure digital form of transmission, which when embellished with suitable features can replace circuit and message switching in many applications, including telephone services.

CIRCUIT SWITCHING

Circuit switching, exemplified by the telephone network, shares transmission facilities among users by establishing a dedicated path from source to destination when any network subscriber places a call. Each node of the network interconnects a link to a successive node in the direction of the destination node to form the end-to-end path by a sequence of point-to-point links. Once established, the physical path becomes transparent to the end nodes, so that both parties can communicate without interruptions. At the completion of the call, the path is disconnected and the links are returned to the bank for further assignment.

Figure 6.4 illustrates the well-known manual procedures for establishing and terminating a call placed on the public telephone network. When the node at point A wishes to place a call to the node at point B, point A initiates the call setup procedure by picking up the handset from its cradle, an action that indicates the off-hook condition of the phone to an operator at a private exchange by ringing or an indicator light. After receiving instructions, the switchboard operator selects a line to the central exchange, known as a trunk line, by inserting a jack into the switchboard which adds the first link to the final path. The operator at the central exchange adds a link to the called station or to other relay points as needed to complete the path to the destination node. At each node of the path, the operator is alerted to an incoming

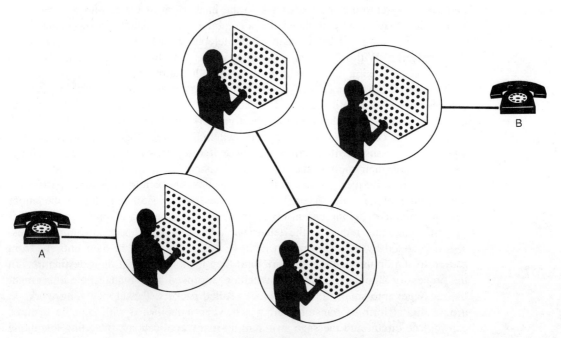

FIGURE 6.4   Circuit switching.

call by a light or a ring. After completing the communication, the end stations hang up the phones, causing an on-hook condition of the phones, which alerts all intervening stations to disconnect the links and return them to the inventory of available resources for reassignment. The essential point in this arrangement is that a physical, contiguous path between the calling and called stations is established and maintained only for the duration of the call.

The preceding manual steps may be automated by using preassigned frequencies as control signals to create the communication path. Most control signals lie outside the bandpass of the voice channel, but some lie within the bandpass; they are called out-band and in-band signals, respectively. Out-band signals cause no interference with the communictions taking place within the line. However, the frequencies assigned for in-band signals, such as dial tone, touch tones, ringing, off-hook signals, call waiting signal, and recording alert signal, must be given special consideration especially when using the line for data communications. For example, a prominent in-band frequency used in the U.S. telephone system has a frequency of 2600 Hz. Normally, this signal, like the other in-band signals, has a tight design tolerance on duration and signal strength so as not to cause any undue problems when used with voice communications, but adds complications for digital communications.

The calling party initiates automatic line switching by picking up the handset, causing a connection to be established with the local switchboard. An off-hook dial tone confirms that the connection has been made. The address of the called party can now be electrically identified by touch tones, and the switchboard creates the necessary path. If the called station lies outside the switchboard's own address structure, the address dialed is prefixed by extra digits to locate the switchboard where the address can be serviced.

The switching offices, as well as the other intervening stations forming the telephone network seek an optimal path between the calling and called stations by maintaining and referencing a routing table. Based on the routing table, links are selected by out-band signaling, and intermediate links are connected to create the physical path. A ringing tone confirms the establishment of a dedicated physical path through the network. When the called party picks up the phone, end-to-end communication can proceed without further switching delays. However, if the called station is already in use or if there is no available line out of the switching station, a busy tone is sent rather than a ringing tone. (Although they are hard to distinguish, different tones are used to indicate whether the station or all the trunk lines are busy.) After the call is terminated, each link in the path is returned to the bank of available resources for further assignments.

Until the advent of local area networks, the support of communications within an enterprise had been delegated to circuit-switching equipment that acted as the central node in a star network, called **private branch exchange (PBX).** In addition, the PBX was vested with limited communications outside the enterprise through trunk lines connected to a switchboard office serviced by the national telephone network (governmental or commercially owned). Gradually, the functions of the PBX

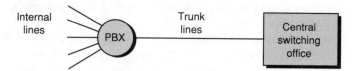

FIGURE 6.5 PBX line interface.

were improved upon by computer-controlled programmable switches, and the system was renamed **private automatic branch exchange (PABX).** Figure 6.5 shows the private branch exchange as the interface among the internal stations and between the internal stations and the external switching stations.

MESSAGE SWITCHING

To contrast message switching with circuit switching, especially as it affects line usage and routing, the following outline gives the manual steps used in early systems for sending telegrams between points. Assume that A originates a message destined for point B (see Figure 6.6). The message, prefixed by the address of the destination point, is transmitted to an intermediate station, where it is punched onto a paper tape. An operator at the intermediate station edits the incoming message, tears the segment of paper tape containing the message from the receiving terminal, and directs the message toward its destination by retransmitting it through another terminal (paper tape reader). This process may be repeated at several intermediate nodes until the message arrives at its destination.

To automate message switching, a header giving the source and destination addresses is inserted into the message. Each receiving station stores the message, examines the header by a computer or a computer-like device, and transmits the message to the next station toward its destination point based on a routing table. This process continues until the message arrives at its destination address.

Messages must be received in their entirety at each node before they can be retransmitted to the next station, using a computer to **store and forward** the mes-

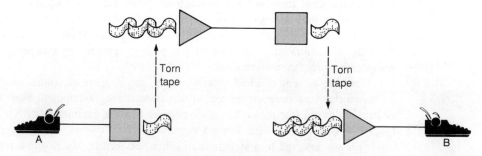

FIGURE 6.6 Message switching.

sages. Messages normally differ in length, so managing the storage at a node becomes complex. Since messages arrive at a node randomly and wait in a queue before being retransmitted, a delay ensues, depending on the congestion. For long messages, the delays may be intolerable. Moreover, traffic may be too high for the amount of storage available, making it necessary to either postpone transmission or retransmit any lost messages, both requiring two-way communications before the message can be validated.

PACKET SWITCHING

To make storage at intervening nodes of a store-and-forward system manageable, messages can be segmented into small, fixed-size blocks called **packets.** The packet size determines the number of bits that can be transmitted as a unit. While messages up to the maximum size of the packet may be transmitted as a unit, larger messages must be segmented into several packets, which must be numbered and individually transmitted. In addition to containing data and error-checking information, some packets contain control information for establishing and terminating end-to-end connections.

Two schemes that have been devised to route packets through the nodes of a network are **virtual circuits** and **datagrams.** In both cases, the header contains the source and destination addresses. For virtual circuits, special control packets establish the physical path. Once established, the path is transparent to the end nodes, and the packets can be directed toward their destination without any further routing decision. However, the virtual circuit may be temporarily assigned between nodes, in which case it is called a **switched virtual circuit,** or, analogous to circuit switching, it may be assigned without requiring further call connect or call termination, in which case it is called a **permanent virtual circuit.** Datagrams, on the other hand, need not take the same path through the network. At each intermediate station, a routing table decides which forward station has the least congestion and can best direct the packet toward its destination.

Since packet technology transmits messages in fix-size pieces, it greatly simplifies the management of intermediate storage and queuing. Each receiving node checks the packets and confirms their arrival before erasing the packets from the transmission node buffer. However, packets may arrive at their destination in a different order than sent and must be reassembled in their correct order before the information can be used. Packets may be lost, and in the event of congestion, packets thought to be lost may have been merely delayed. The end stations must deal with problems of lost or duplicate packets.

With the addition of more computer components, the private branch exchange servicing the communications of an enterprise has again been renamed **computer branch exchange (CBX).** The functions have evolved into packet switching rather than circuit switching, which allows not only data but also voice to be transferred in a digital format and permits both voice and data to share the same network.

Exercises

6.6 Assuming that long messages are stored with short messages in a message-switching system, explain how the memory can become fragmented and unusable. Give possible solutions for alleviating this potential problem.

6.7 The number of bits on a line that are in the process of actively being transmitted between two nodes (i.e., the number of bits that have been transmitted but have not yet been received) is called the line storage. Plot the line distance versus the transmission speed for a line storage of 1000 bits.

6.8 Track how lines are switched to create a communication path using extra digits (0, 1, 01, 9, area code, etc.) appended to the address of a called station.*

6.9 Using the area code map given in the telephone directory, connect the 200 sequence of numbers; the 300 sequence of numbers; and so on. Determine the various rules for assigning numbers.

6.10 The following figure shows a schematic of a crossbar switch, whereby a contact engages at the cross-points to enable an input line to be uniquely connected to an output line. If there are n input lines and m output lines, then the crossbar switch requires $n \times m$ semiconductors or metallic contacts to be available at the contact points. Such a switch makes a distinction between input and output lines. How many contact points would be required if there were no distinction between the input and output lines (i.e., if any line could be interconnected to any other line serviced by the crossbar)? Show the minimum configuration.

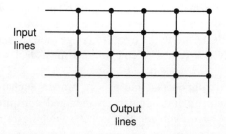

Input lines

Output lines

6.11 A switching array (see exercise 6.10) is said to be nonblocking if a path from the input to the output

is always available. Obviously, in the rectangular array shown in exercise 6.10, this is always true when $n \leq m$. For very large values of n and m, the number of cross-points becomes extraordinarily large.

The following figure shows a three-stage switch, whereby each crossbar connector at stage 1 is connected by a line to a stage 2 crossbar, and each stage 2 output line is connected to a stage 3 crossbar. Such a configuration may be blocking or nonblocking. To be nonblocking, it can be shown that the number of stage 2 crossbars must equal $2n - 1$, where n is the number of input lines to the stage 1 crossbar. Following this argument, the number of cross-points among all the crossbar switches is $(2n - 1)[2N + (N/n)^2]$, where N is the total number of input lines.

(a) Illustrate a three-stage configuration that will block an input from being connected to an output, even though the output line has not been already allocated.

(b) Show that the optimal number of cross-points for a nonblocking configuration is $4N\sqrt{2N}$ for large values of N.

(c) Plot the number of input lines for 10^2 to 10^6 versus the number of cross-points for both a single-stage switch and a three-stage switch.

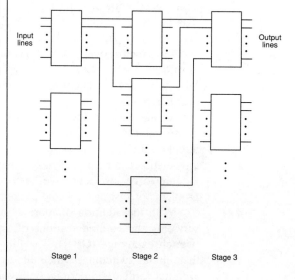

Input lines

Output lines

Stage 1   Stage 2   Stage 3

---

*See footnote, page 7.

6.3 MULTIPLEXING

REPRESENTATION IN THE FREQUENCY-TIME PLANE

Notwithstanding that a channel's bandwidth, quality, and time in use determines its cost, several low-speed channels cost more than a single high-speed channel of equivalent bandwidth. Since most applications need only sporadic access to the channel, it makes sense, when possible, to use a single channel and spread the cost by sharing its capacity among several independent applications. Multiplexing is the name given to the process by which signals from several, independent applications can be combined and transmitted together over a shared common channel.

Multiplexing devices, called **multiplexers (MUXs),** organize the spectrum of the shared line according to two different strategies. The difference in strategies can be visualized using the frequency-time plane shown in Figure 6.7 (the top view of the three-dimensional frequency response curve given in Figure 2.3). One strategy, called **frequency-division multiplexing (FDM),** divides the channel's bandwidth into several frequency slots and gives each user the exclusive use of one of the subchannels. The other, called **time-division multiplexing (TDM),** divides the channel's available time into time slots and gives each user the exclusive use of the channel's entire bandwidth during allocated time slots. As one might surmise, FDM lends itself better than TDM for combining analog signals, while TDM lends itself better for digital signals.

FDM and TDM differ also in how each employs the channel's spectrum for transmitting signals. FDM uses broadband transmission, the transmission of several bandlimited signals modulated by separate carriers. TDM, on the other hand, uses baseband transmission, the transmission of bandlimited signals unmodulated by a carrier (although they may be modulated by other means to fit within the bandpass of the channel).

FREQUENCY-DIVISION MULTIPLEXING

Figure 6.8 illustrates the arrangement for sharing the bandwidth of a communication line among three independent users by dividing the bandwidth into frequency slots and using FDM. In this case, each user receives an equal portion of the available bandwidth. Before combining the input signals for transmission, the individual sig-

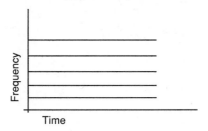

FIGURE 6.7 Frequency-time domain (top view of Figure 2.3).

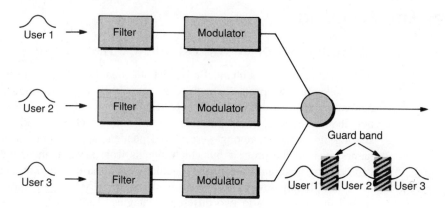

FIGURE 6.8 Frequency-division multiplexing.

nals are filtered to fit within their assigned bandwidth and modulated by carriers that are judiciously chosen to properly locate the signals within the spectrum so that they do not infringe upon adjacent subchannels. The receiving multiplexer recovers the individual signals by demodulation. Radio broadcasting is a good example of how FDM works in practice.

Figure 6.9 shows the channel assignments using FDM in the frequency-time plane, again showing three users sharing the channel equally. The arrangement of the channel allows the users the exclusive use of their respective subchannnels, and yet all may transmit concurrently. To protect the integrity of the input signals, an unassigned gap called the **guard band** is left between the bandpass of adjacent subchannels. For commercial lines, the guard bands at the ends of the bandpass have already been allocated, and so a guard band need be assigned only between subchan-

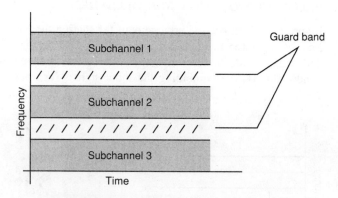

FIGURE 6.9 FDM shown in the frequency-time plane.

nels that further divide the channel. The guard bands act together with the filters to shield the applications from crosstalk by preventing signal components that lie outside their assigned frequency slot from infringing upon neighboring subchannels. However, noise caused by other sources, such as impulse noise due to spikes, may still spill over from a neighboring subchannel to cause errors and degrade performance. Filtering before modulation removes much of this type of noise.

The bandwidths and carrier frequencies assigned to the subchannels are normally fixed at the time of installation. The bandwidth sizes, of course, need not be equal, but assigned according to the transmission speed needed by each user. It might appear advantageous to change the size of a subchannel's bandwidth after communications have been initiated, but this would be difficult, if not impractical, since the carrier frequencies depend on the bandwidth, and all the subchannel frequencies would have to be changed accordingly.

One advantage of FDM is that no local intelligence (i.e., internal logic in each user's device) is needed in the nodes to provide for addressing. In effect, the filter and carrier assigned to each subchannel suffice to separate the signals and direct them to their destination nodes. Figure 6.10 shows several nodes configured onto a shared line whereby the demodulator and filter assigned to each node reject all signals other than those destined to the node it serves. After demodulation, the signals appear as they were before transmission, making the multiplexing process transparent to the end users.

TIME-DIVISION MULTIPLEXING

The channel arrangement for the alternative scheme, TDM, assigns each user a buffer area for inserting input data as available and provides a mechanism for scanning the buffers sequentially (Figure 6.11). In the figure, the commutator represents the scanner, and the input points to the commutator represent the buffered sources. The commutator services the buffers in a fixed order, converts the data into electrical signals, and transmits the signals using the full bandwidth of the channel. Conceptually, TDM interleaves data from several low-speed input sources onto a high-speed line, allowing multiple users to share the channel's bandwidth without interfering with each other.

TDM can be viewed as a digital communication scheme, interleaving data from several independent devices into a common frame for transmission. In its simplest

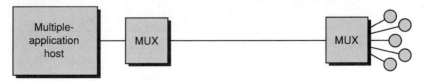

FIGURE 6.10 FDM MUX front end serving a
cluster of terminals.

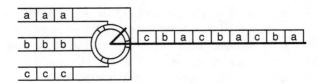

FIGURE 6.11   Time-division multiplexing.

form, the size of the time slots are fixed to contain a predetermined number of bits, say, a single bit, single character, or multiple characters. The combined sizes of the input buffers correspond to the size of the frame, so that by cyclically polling the buffers, the multiplexer interleaves the data into the frame's time slots and moves the data sequentially over the transmission line. After the data have been moved out of the buffers, the buffers are initialized by holding marks such as null characters when TDM uses character interleaving. Until new data arrive, the multiplexer fills the unused time slots of successive frames with the holding marks. Another multiplexer at the receiving end of the link redistributes the interleaved bit patterns into buffers accessible by the designated destination nodes.

Figure 6.12 depicts the blocking and deblocking of several input channels communicating by character interleaving. The objective, of course, is to make the most efficient use of the high-speed line connecting the MUXs. The multiplexer frames the characters and transmits the frames to the demultiplexer at the remote site by synchronous transmission. Communications between the terminal devices and the multiplexer may proceed either in the synchronous or asynchronous mode. However, when using asynchronous transmission, the start-stop bits need not be retained. In this situation, the transmitting multiplexer strips off these bits before interleaving the characters, and the receiving multiplexer reinserts them to reform the asynchronous frames. Effectively, the internal operations of the multiplexers and the synchronous transmission between the MUXs are transparent to the user, so the end devices can transmit synchronously, asynchronously, or by a mixture of the two modes to the MUX interface.

The delays in TDM resulting from the timing and control data are shown in the frequency-plane in Figure 6.13 as a gap between cycles, called the **guard time,** albeit short. It may appear that TDM offers facilities with a negligible overhead;

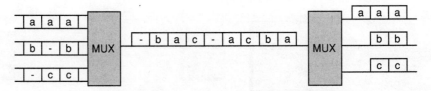

FIGURE 6.12   TDM blocking and deblocking.

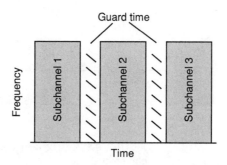

FIGURE 6.13 TDM in the frequency-time plane.

however, this is not the case. In addition to the guard time, some input channels will probably be idle while others are actively transmitting, so many of the time slots would be filled with holding marks. This can be partially compensated by allocating a higher proportion of the time slots to the higher-speed input devices and using a variable scan multiplexer to give each input channel the amount of line access it can use efficiently. Nevertheless, the intermittent nature of data flow makes it improbable that the input devices can continuously replace the holding marks with data.

A more sophisticated TDM device, known as a **statistical multiplexer,** assigns time slots to the active users on a demand basis rather than designating the time slots permanently to particular users (Figure 6.14). A similar device sometimes called a **concentrator** also serves this purpose. Although the terms *statistical multiplexer* and *concentrator* are often used interchangeably, the term *concentrator* normally connotes a device that has enhanced intelligence embedded into the logical circuits to select and control the transmission lines. In either case, the aggregate capacities of the input lines to these devices can exceed the capacity of the high-speed service line, since these devices service only those nodes that have data ready for transmission, and most nodes would be active a small percentage of time. By storing incoming data in the buffer area, framing the data with the identification of the destination node, and programming line controls using the local logic embedded in the multiplexer, the multiplexer transmits whatever data the input devices have ready for transmission. However, the data suffer an added overhead and delay in passing

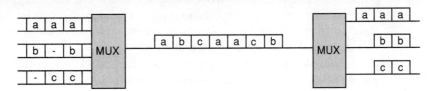

FIGURE 6.14 Statistical multiplexer.

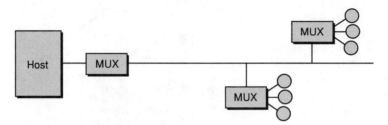

FIGURE 6.15 MUX configuration as a front-
end processor.

through the multiplexer for assembling, disassembling, and interpreting the control
characters needed to handle the channels.

In a network configuration, multiplexers serve as intermediate nodes rather than
as source or sink nodes. By their location in the network, they can enhance the
connected terminals with features that might not be obvious. Figure 6.15 illustrates
a possible configuration. The front-end unit to the host interconnects the individual
stations onto a multidrop line and pools the combined communications over the common long-haul line. The maxim of end-to-end communications dictates that the
source and sink agree in mode and speed. The remote interface unit allows the terminal devices to conform to this dictate, while at the same time they can share the
capacity of the long-haul line. For example, it might be convenient to transmit to a
high-speed device (say, a computer) synchronously and at the same time pace an
output device (say, a printer) operating at a lower speed in the asynchronous mode.
In addition, the interface unit can provide dumb terminals (terminals that do not have
embedded logic) with local intelligence. Vendors refer to such MUX interface units
as bus interface units, controllers, or front-end processors.

Not surprisingly, since TDM requires data processing, vendors combine other
related and useful functions with the multiplexing functions within the same operational unit. For example, commercial models might by programming or hard logic
include the facilities to interface the line (thereby eliminating the need for a separate
unit), combine voice and data signals, provide self-testing and report diagnostics in
case of failure, pool share the buffers and signal the inputs when the buffers are all
full, compress data before transmitting to increase line efficiency, or encrypt the data
for security. In fact, with enhancements, it is often difficult to distinguish a multiplexer from a front-end processor (a separate communications processor that interfaces multiple-end devices to the line).

Multiplexers do not need to be pure FDM or TDM, but may through programming achieve a hybrid of the two forms. Figure 6.16 shows the frequency-time plane
of a multiplexer dividing a channel into several subchannels by FDM and then subdividing one of the subchannels into more subchannels by TDM.

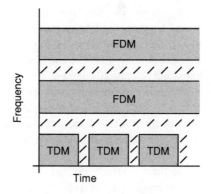

FIGURE 6.16 Hybrid combination of FDM and TDM.

Exercises

6.12 Divide a voice grade line into 2 and 3 subchannels using 20 percent of the channels bandwidth for guard bands. Discuss problems that would result if the size of a subchannel is changed after communications have been initiated.

6.13 Explain when FDM filtering can and cannot prevent spike noise from infringing on a neighboring subchannel.

6.14 Show a configuration whereby several multidrop lines can share a common long-distance line.

6.15 Show the configurations whereby analog signals to a phone and the digital signals to a line printer input can be combined on the same line, first by FDM and then by TDM.

6.16 For TDM, a delay ensues at each relay station until a complete frame has arrived. Assuming 100 in-puts with an average message length of L, a line transmission speed of S, and no queuing, compare the delay resulting by framing the messages using bit interleaving, character interleaving, and statistical multiplexing.

6.17 Contrast TDM and statistical TDM by comparing the overhead associated with each.

6.18 The following figure depicts a statistical multiplexer with several slow-speed lines on one side and a high-speed, long-haul line on the other. Explain why the combined capacities of the slow-speed lines can exceed the capacity of the long-haul line.

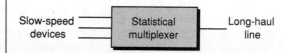

6.4   LINE-INTERFACING DEVICES

MODEMS

The equipment used to transmit or receive digital information over a communication line, either on a switched commercial line or on a privately owned line, must form and maintain the physical signals so they conform to the other facilities in the network. Digital networks define the equipment needed to cast the signals into the proper physical form, but analog networks dictate only the frequency content of the signals and not their exact form. A variety of devices have been adopted over the years to interface analog lines, some acting to provide digital-to-analog conversion from the transmitting station's logical circuits to the line and vice versa at the receiving station. The role that these devices have assumed to interface commercial, voice-grade lines will be illustrated in this section.

One class of interfacing device, known generically as **modems**, convert the digital signals representing the 0's and 1's into electrical signals conforming to a network's transmission facilities, a process called modulation, and then restore these signals back to their original form at the receiving end, a process called demodulation. The word *modem* is derived from the prefix of the words *modulation* and *demodulation*. In addition to the data signals, these devices provide the control and timing signals needed to coordinate the exchange of data and have other capabilities for creating a more flexible network environment. When a modem is not required, a simpler device that does not alter the signals by any form of modulation or demodulation, but simply provides the interface between the node and the line, can replace the modem. These modem-like devices, although not modems, ensure that the line connection and the signals on the line conform to the nodal requirements.

Modems operate in pairs, with each unit functioning as the front end of a node and providing the mechanical connection between the nodes's digital equipment and the communication line. Figure 6.17 shows the placement of the modem functions relative to a computer or terminal device. The actual physical arrangement can be implemented in a variety of ways:

- Integrating the modems with the equipment electronics so that no external wiring is needed between the two units
- Placing the modems on a circuit board that can be inserted into one of the expansion slots available in many models of computers
- Implementing the modems on a chip (i.e., microcomputer) that can be connected to the handset of a conventional telephone
- Enclosing the modems into a free-standing unit and directly coupling the unit to the computer or terminal by cable

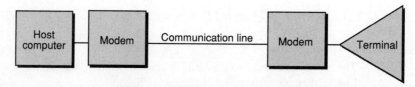

FIGURE 6.17   Node interfacing by modems.

The mechanical connection of the communicating equipment to the line depends on the line technology used. For voice lines, the line connection may be made by inserting a connector wired to the modem into a wall jack that has been connected to a dial-up line or a leased line. Another form of line connection to dial-up services uses a modem that can be acoustically coupled to a telephone headset by rubber cups attached to the modem. Acoustically coupled modems operate at lower speeds than electrically coupled modems, but offer the advantage of making every phone a potential node in the network.

In addition to providing for the exchange of data, timing, and control signals, other options are often embedded into modems that in cooperation with the remaining equipment extend the node's capabilities. To exchange information, stations must agree on communication parameters, including parameters needed by any of the added options. It is not unusual, however, that one node dictates the general requirements used by the remaining nodes serviced by the network. For example, a host computer might be required to process information emigrating from many different terminals, so that the configuration of the host predetermines the parameter settings at terminal stations.

MODEM OPTIONS

Although on some models the needed features are selected by manual switches, the trend is to select features by software-driven electronics. As with more complex equipment, hardware and software must be chosen as a package. Without reference to specific products, the more popular options can be organized into the following categories:

- Selectable baud rate
- Mode of transmission
- Error checking
- Auto call
- Auto answer
- Self-test

Other features notwithstanding, nodes cannot communicate unless they agree on their transmissiion speeds. When a node must communicate with many partners whose transmission speeds differ from each other, the modem's transmission speed may be set by the user. The transmission speed might be given in either baud rate or bit rate. Normally, when a modem transmits multibits (e.g., dibits), its line speed is quoted in bauds, resulting in a bit rate that is a multiple of its baud rate.

Transmission speed is so critical in the selection of a modem that modem products, more often than not, are classified by their speed range:

- Low speed for bit rates up to 600 bps
- Medium speed for bit rates from 600 to 4800 bps
- High speed for bit rates from 4800 bps to 19.2 kbps
- Wide band for bit rates over 19.2 kbps

As might be expected, most models operate with commercial lines at low or medium speeds. While not as plentiful, other models operate at high or wideband speeds or with less conventional media, such as fiber optics, microwave links, or coaxial cables, or with special tariffs such as T1 lines. T1 carrier services exemplify transmission by a digital line. Modems for T1 tariffs accept bit streams of 64 kbps PCM signals over 24 channels and after adding the information for proper interpretation can achieve the T1 line speed of 1.544 Mbps by time-division multiplexing.

Modems can operate either synchronously or asynchronously and as simplex, half duplex, or duplex. Normally, synchronous transmission uses the higher bit rates, and asynchronous transmission uses the lower rates. For communication in only one direction, say, from an on-line instrument to a computer or from the computer to a printer, simplex transmission suffices. However, most nodes require two-way communications, which may be implemented by either full- or half-duplex lines. Often, the terms *four-wire circuit* and *full duplex* are used interchangeably, as are the terms *two-wire circuit* and *half duplex*. This practice can be misleading. Modems may transmit over a two-wire circuit in the duplex mode by dividing the available bandwidth of the transmission line into two separate bands; or, as has been previously described, a four-wire circuit with echo suppression can restrict communications to the half-duplex mode.

For asynchronous transmission, three communication parameters must be agreed on between the communicating stations: the format of the data characters (e.g., AS-CII, EBCDIC, or Baudot), the length of the stop signal (e.g., 1, 1.5, or 2 bit times), and the parity setting (odd, even, or none). On the other hand, for synchronous transmission error-checking techniques and the separation of the individual characters take advantage of the added capabilities offered by the block format. This topic will be discussed later when specific formats used with synchronous transmission are presented.

Increasingly included as options within the capabilities of modems are features that allow the communicating nodes to operate without human intervention, called auto call and auto answer. These features work in conjunction with the software at the end stations. Using a directory of numbers, auto call allows a station to automatically dial a remote node, and auto answer allows a host station to automatically respond to the ring. After the connection has been completed, the handshaking operations normally performed by a human operator can be automatically executed by software driven procedures. For example, the procedures for log on, password entry, entry of program parameters, execution of an application task, and sign-off can be

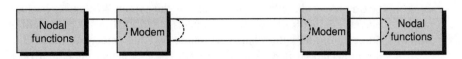

FIGURE 6.18 Self-testing loops.

performed by an unattended node. These features are a valuable asset for delivering computing services at off hours when the network would not normally be busy.

Embedded electronics allow a modem to self-test possible points of trouble within the communication devices or within the communication paths connecting the nodes. Such electronics work in conjunction with software for performing and reporting the automatic tests. Figure 6.18 shows the interconnections between two communicating nodes and isolates the paths that can be separately tested. These tests may be initiated automatically or under operator control and may operate concurrently with normal communications functions.

ECHOPLEXING

The terms *half duplex* and *full duplex* take on another meaning when applied to terminal devices that differs from their use with modems and communication lines. A half-duplex terminal implies that the character source, typically the terminal's key-

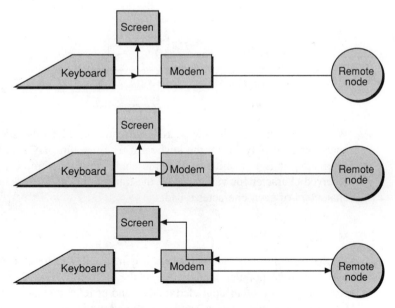

FIGURE 6.19 Possible paths used to display each character generated.

board, has a directly coupled path to the screen so that each character can be displayed automatically when generated (called local echo on). Contrasted with a half-duplex terminal, the character source and the screen of a full-duplex terminal are disconnected (called local echo off). The characters generated on a full-duplex terminal can be optionally displayed after they have been transmitted by looping them back to the display screen from the modem or the remote node, a process called **echoplexing.** Figure 6.19 shows three possible paths whereby the generated characters can be displayed on the screen: one by directly coupling the keyboard to the screen, and the other two by echoplexing the transmitted characters from the modem or from the remote node.

Echoplexing offers a positive check on the validity of the transmission path. However, its use (or perhaps its misuse) can produce multiple copies of each character generated. The following example gives a configuration by which the text appears on the screen as a garbled composition of three characters for each character typed.

Example 6.1

Draw the schematic and explain the configuration whereby three copies of each character typed on the terminal's keyboard will be displayed on the terminal's screen.

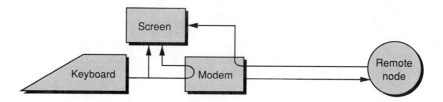

With local echo on, the keyboard is directly wired to the screen, displaying each character as it is typed on the keyboard. The modem may also loop back each character after it is transmitted. If at the same time the remote node retransmits each received character for validation by the transmitter, then the screen will display three characters of each character typed.   ◄

MODEM TYPES

To make modem operations clearer, it is instructive to look at modulation techniques used by some popular modem types: the Bell 103, Bell 202, and Bell 212 units. Notwithstanding other upgraded models and/or related standards and models supplied by different vendors, these models serve as the industrial prototypes for modem operations through the public telephone network.

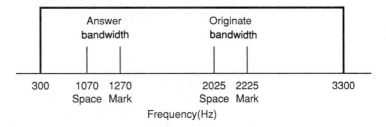

FIGURE 6.20 Bell 103 FSK tone assignments.

The Bell 103–type unit is designated for low-speed, duplex communications over a conventional, switched, voice-grade line operating in an asynchronous mode. Two-way communications are arranged by dividing the available spectrum into two subchannels. Figure 6.20 shows the assignment of frequencies using FSK for representing the information. At the lower subchannel, the 1070 Hz tone represents a 0 (space), and the 1270 Hz tone represents a 1 (mark). At the upper subchannel, the frequency of 2025 Hz represents a 0 (space), and the frequency of 2225 Hz represents a 1 (mark). It will be noted that the frequencies assigned avoid the 2600 Hz signal used by the public telephone for in-band signaling.

Consider the issues involved for orderly, two-way, duplex communications. There must be agreement between the two stations as to which station will use the lower subchannel to transmit and the upper subchannel to receive. As shown in Table 6.1 for the Bell 103–type modems, the channel assignments are prearranged, assigning the station initiating communications, known as the **originate node,** the lower subchannel for transmitting and assigning the called station, known as the **answer node,** the upper subchannel for transmitting. Clearly, the assignments are reversed for the call station. This arrangement serves when each node has an independent role in the network; but often, one station serves as a central node for processing information from many tributary nodes, and in this case, the subchannels may be permanently preassigned to the nodes according to their use. The advantage of fixing the transmitting and receiving frequencies at a modem is that the modem frequencies

TABLE 6.1
BELL 103 SUBCHANNEL ASSIGNMENTS FOR
DUPLEX COMMUNICATIONS

	ORIGINATE NODE	ANSWER NODE
Transmit	1070 (space) 1270 (mark)	2025 (space) 2225 (mark)
Receive	2025 (space) 2225 (mark)	1070 (space) 1270 (mark)

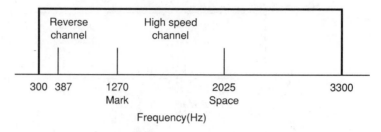

FIGURE 6.21 Bell 202 frequency assignments.

need not be switchable between the originate mode and the answer mode, resulting in a considerable simplification in modem design.

In contrast with the Bell 103–type modem, the Bell 202–type modem operates at medium speed over a public or leased switched line that can support half- or full-duplex communications in either synchronous or asynchronous modes. Figure 6.21 shows the frequency assignments using a single pair of frequencies for representing the binary digits by FSK. The modem defines one other frequency at the low end of the spectrum (387 Hz) that can be used for returning error information to the transmitter by simply on-off signaling. This frequency is normally turned on during normal operations to confirm that the communicating modems are still connected, however, it can also be used to ask for a retransmission of the data in the event of an error.

The Bell 212–type unit combines many of the ideas of the other two modems to provide medium-speed, full-duplex operations over a public telephone line. Like the Bell 103–type modem, it achieves full-duplex capabilities over a single-channel arrangement by dividing the channel into two subchannels, as shown in Figure 6.22 and Table 6.2. It differs from the other modem types discussed, however, in that it encodes the data by PSK using dibits. Table 6.3 shows the four phase differential shifts assigned to the dibit values. While supporting both synchronous and asynchronous modes, depending on the type of terminal used, the Bell 212–type modem is primarily used for asynchronous transmission. Also, it is interesting to note that

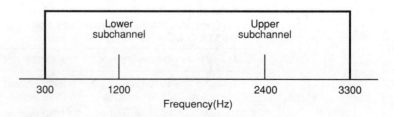

FIGURE 6.22 Bell 212 tone assignments.

TABLE 6.2

BELL 212 SUBCHANNEL FREQUENCY ASSIGNMENTS

	NODE	
	ORIGINATE	ANSWER
Transmit	1200	2400
Receive	2400	1200

TABLE 6.3

BELL 212 PSK ASSIGNMENTS

DIBITS	PHASE DIFFERENTIAL
00	$-135°$
01	$-45°$
10	$+45°$
11	$+135°$

high-speed modems for synchronous transmission almost always include multibit, PSK technology.

Because modem costs can become significant, a device is available that allows several terminals to share a common modem by either a multidrop or star configuration (Figure 6.23). Although several terminals are connected simultaneously to the device, only one terminal may be active at any particular time. **Modem sharing** is merely a scheme to save on the cost of interfacing devices.

It may appear that if signals did not degenerate and become unrecognizable during transmission, there would be no need for special line-interfacing considerations. However, even for short cable runs between devices, a problem remains. The input/output points on devices such as data terminals and computers are normally configured to be connected by a multiline male connector. Minimally, when terminal devices need to be directly connected to each other using a standard connector such as the RS 232-C Standard (described later in the text), the connecting cable must connect two male connectors to each other. The wires which the two devices normally use to transmit and receive data must be interchanged so that each device looks

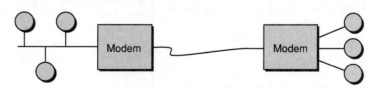

FIGURE 6.23 Modem sharing.

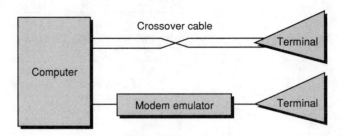

FIGURE 6.24 Direct-line interfaces.

like it is connected to a modem. This can be accomplished by crossing the wires within the cable connecting the two devices, called a **crossover cable.** Alternatively, the crossover function can be achieved by the use of a line-interfacing unit sometimes referred to by the lofty name **modem emulator.** The objective, of course, is to reduce cost when the end devices are relatively near each other and do not need the full capabilities of modems. Figure 6.24 shows these possible interconnections.

When private lines are used to make the interconnections between host nodes located in close proximity to each other yet over a longer distance than would normally be allowed, **line drivers** may be used instead of the modems (Figure 6.25). Line drivers augment and strengthen the signals for transmission; and although strictly speaking they are not modems, some models perform other functions typically assigned to modems, such as allowing for both synchronous and asynchronous transmission. Whether classified as modem-like devices or not, line drivers allow the distance between nodes to be extended.

Exercises

6.19 Show in tabular form the number of characters displayed for each character generated as a function of local echo (on, off), loopback from modem (yes, no), and loopback from remote node (yes, no), and give the schematic for each of these configurations. Explain each configuration and justify the number of characters displayed for each typed character.

6.20 Several related standards describe the cable interface used to connect the nodal equipment to the modem; e.g., Mil-188C, EIA RS 232-C, and CCITT V.24. Refer to the RS 232-C standards and flowchart the procedures for automatically establishing and terminating communications between two nodes.*

6.21 *Datapro Reports on Data Communications* (see Suggested Readings) lists approximately 125 vendors that produce line-interfacing equipment. Based on these reports and/or vendor-supplied literature, compare products that are compatible to the Bell 103, 201, and 212 modems and describe any added features.*

---

*See footnote, page 7.

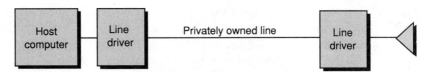

FIGURE 6.25 Line drivers.

SUMMARY

As a practical matter, remotely separated nodes exchange information by transmitting groups of bits in the serial mode over a single line. Serial transmission may be in one direction only (simplex line), bidirectional transmission but only one direction at a time (half duplex), or simultaneous bidirectional transmission (duplex). In addition to the direction of transmission, the communicating stations must agree on how bits are timed. Asynchronous transmission uses independent but identically timed clocks at the transmitter and receiver and serves admirably for transmitting short blocks of bits. For transmitting larger blocks of bits, synchronous transmission must be used that establishes a common clock between the communicating stations by embedding timing information within the bit signals being transmitted.

To efficiently use costly line resources, it makes sense to share them among independent users who can collectively supply a suitable work load. Lines can be shared by switching or by multiplexing. The spider diagram in Figure 6.26 summarizes the different ways line resources can be shared.

Multiplexing has been described in the frequency-time domain. Frequency-division multiplexing divides the available bandwidth into subchannels. A suitable carrier places the signals in the assigned subchannel for broadband transmission over the channel. Time-division multiplexing divides the total bandpass into time slots. Each user's data are placed into individual time slots that are transmitted as a block using baseband transmission.

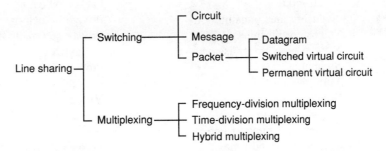

FIGURE 6.26 Line-sharing techniques.

Switching pools the lines into an available bank of resources and assigns them to the users for making short, sporadic calls between stations. Circuit switching interconnects point-to-point links from the collection of available lines to form a dedicated physical path between the communicating partners. Message switching transmits messages in their entirety from station to station through the network. Each station stores the message as it is received and examines the destination address in the header to direct the stored message toward its destination point. To make storage at intervening nodes manageable, messages can be segmented into small, fixed-size packets that must be numbered and individually transmitted.

Packets may be routed by virtual circuits or by datagrams. For virtual circuits, special control packets establish the physical path, and once established, the path either is transparent to the end nodes or can direct the packets toward their destination with an abbreviated address (permanent or switched virtual circuits, respectively). The packets for datagram transmission need not take the same path through the network, but each intermediate station decides which forward station has the least congestion and directs each packet toward its destination.

The remaining discussion deals with modem operations. Modems operate in pairs, with each unit functioning as the front end of a node and providing the connection between the nodes's digital equipment and the communication line. In addition to the data signals, these devices provide the control and timing signals needed to coordinate the exchange of data, and they may have other capabilities for creating a more flexible network environment. To make modem operations clearer, three basic modem types that serve as the industrial prototypes for modem operations have been singled out for discussion: the Bell 103, Bell 202, and Bell 212 units. The interface between the nodal equipment and the line is so intimately associated with modem operations that manufacturers provide devices that solve special interfacing problems; these include shared modems, modem emulators, and repeaters.

KEY TERMS

Parallel mode	Message switching
Serial mode	Packet switching
Asynchronous transmission	Private branch exchange (PBX)
Start-stop transmission	Private automatic branch exchange
Synchronous transmission	(PABX)
Switching	Store-and-forward
Multiplexing	Packets
Simplex line	Virtual circuits
Half-duplex line	Datagrams
Duplex (full-duplex) line	Switched virtual circuits
Line turn around time	Permanent virtual circuits
Circuit switching	Computer branch exchange (CBX)

Multiplexer (MUX)
Frequency-division multiplexing (FDM)
Time-division multiplexing (TDM)
Guard band
Guard time
Statistical multiplexer
Concentrator
Modems

Echoplexing
Originate node
Answer node
Modem sharing
Crossover cable
Modem emulator
Line driver

SUGGESTED READINGS

Chou, W., et al. (eds.) *Computer Communications, vol. 1, Principles.* Englewood Cliffs, N.J.: Prentice-Hall, 1983.

Datapro Reports on Data Communications, vols. 1–3. Delran, N.J.: Datapro Research Corp., 1986.

Ellis, Robert L. *Designing Data Networks.* Englewood Cliffs, N.J.: Prentice-Hall, 1986.

McNamara, J. E. *Technical Aspects of Data Communication.* 2nd ed. Bedford, MA: Digital Equipment Corp., 1982.

Smith, David R. *Digital Transmission Systems.* New York: Van Nostrand Reinhold, 1985.

Spilker, James J. *Digital Communications by Satellite.* Englewood Cliffs, N.J.: Prentice-Hall, 1977.

Stallings, William. *Data and Computer Communications.* New York: Macmillan, 1985.

Techo, Robert. *Data Communications.* New York: Plenum, 1980.

CHAPTER 7

DATA COMMUNICATION NETWORK ARCHITECTURE

Whenever perfect works of art
   are planned,
The craftsman always makes a
   model to be
The first simple part from which
   shall grow
The finished object underneath his hand.
MICHELANGELO
SONNET XIV

7.1 NETWORK LAYER ARCHITECTURE

LAYER MODEL

Architecture defines the harmonious relationships of the elements of a structure. In a real sense, there is no such thing as architecture, since the relationships are embedded into parts of the system's structure that perform other useful services. There are, however, architects. Architects look at the parts of a system and, by abstraction, identify and reorganize the interconnections and interactions that form a substructure of the system. In a similar way, data communications network architecture deals with the relationships within a distributed system that make up the substructure that provides for the exchange of data between the parts of a system.

Figure 7.1 depicts two applications (processes) that need to cooperate to accomplish their respective tasks. When the equipment and information of the applications reside at the same node, the applications cooperate by sharing a common bank of data or by directly exchanging the data each needs from the other. However when the applications are located at geographically distributed nodes, then the equipment at each node must be augmented to allow the exchange of data. This portion of the equipment (hardware and software) forms the communication substructure.

The modeling of the communication substructure starts by packaging the entities representing the communication facilities at a node into a **modular layer architecture.** The functions defined at each layer are abstractions of the operations performed by real facilities, but need not be identified with any specific hardware or software product. In fact, the implementation of a layer may not only be different at different nodes, but may also be replaced by a new implementation as the technology advances.

Figure 7.2 illustrates a node structured into three hierarchical layers, where the entities assigned to each layer perform some well-defined functions. The entities residing at a layer provide communication services to the layer above or may request the services available from the layer below. For example, the entities at layer 2

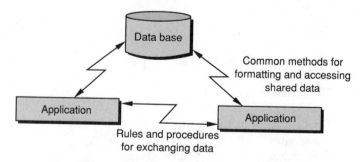

FIGURE 7.1 Nodes cooperate by sharing data or exchanging data.

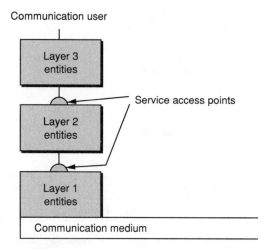

FIGURE 7.2 Communication layer structure at a node.

provide services to layer 3 or may request the services available from layer 1. The services requested and services provided are accessible only at specific points, called **service access points,** identified by addresses at the boundaries that interface the adjacent layers.

Under this arrangement, the topmost layer provides no communication services to the other layers but may request and use the services offered by the layer below through the designated service access points. This topmost layer serves to interface the other, noncommunicating functions performed by the node; and in this sense, the functions it performs depend on the needs of the specific application. The facilities above the top layer, be they people, programs, or devices, call on the communication functions needed by the actual application (labeled the communication user), but themselves are not part of the communication substructure.

The bottom layer is also unique, since it does not have a lower layer through which services are available. Entities at the bottom layer must create and recognize the physical signals used to exchange communications with the entities at the bottom layer of a partner. The communication medium simply creates the path between adjacent nodes for the transfer of signals to the service access points serviced by their respective bottom layers. The communication medium, however, is outside the scope of the layer model, although at times it may be convenient to think of it as layer 0.

PROTOCOLS

Using the layer model, Figure 7.3 illustrates the communication modes between nodes. The collection of entities at each layer level, called **peer entities,** furnish the services needed by the layer above. When entities residing at a node cannot by them-

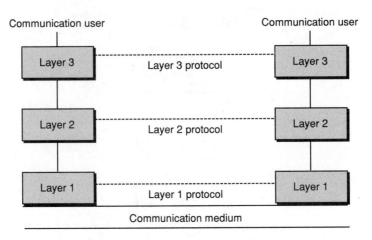

FIGURE 7.3 Network architecture layer structure.

selves provide the services needed, they call on peer entities at another node to cooperate in providing the services by exchanging information. The exchange of information between peers must conform to a common, acceptable set of rules and conventions called the **layer protocol.** Entities at each layer assume that they are exchanging information with their peers. This peer-to-peer communication is virtual communication except at the bottom layer, where the physical signals are formed and transported over the medium. Physical communications proceed from the top layer of the sending node, down the lower layers, through the communication medium connecting the nodes, and then up from the bottom layer to the upper layers of the receiving node.

DATA UNITS

As information passes through the layer structure, each layer appends control and error-checking data to the information received from the layer above. The added information, shown schematically in Figure 7.4, is formatted into a header (annotated by H) and possibly a trailer (annotated by T). The bottom layer does not add control and error-checking data to the data it receives from the layer above, but strictly converts the data, bit by bit, into physical signals and transports them over the physical connection. Conceptually, the header and possible trailer form an envelope enclosing the information received from the adjacent layer above. Each layer treats all the information received from the layer above, including the appended envelopes, as the message to be transmitted.

As the data units pass through a node, they must be buffered at each level of the layer structure. To accommodate the data units into the buffer sizes which have been provided, several data units may be combined into a single data unit or a single data

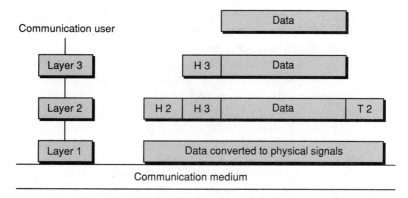

FIGURE 7.4 Nesting of data envelopes for transmission between layers.

unit may be split into several data units, each with its own header and possible trailer. At the receiving node, each layer uses the header and trailer information put on by its peer, and separates combined data units or recombines split data units before passing the communications to the adjacent higher layer.

Example 7.1

The French prime minister and the Chinese prime minister need to come to an agreement. The ministers, however, speak only their respective languages, so they arrange to use English translators. Describe their hypothetical phone conversation using the layer model, and identify the interfaces and protocols between the various layers.

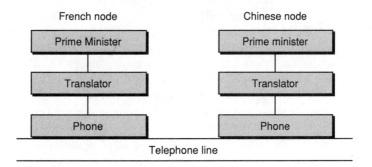

Although the PMs do not speak each other's language, they assume that they are speaking directly to each other. For example, when the French PM speaks, he addresses his remarks directly to the Chinese PM. However, since the Chinese PM does not speak French, the message is actually passed to the translator. The translator translates the message into English and communicates it to the Chinese PM's translator, who in turn renders the message into Chinese for the benefit of the Chinese PM. Both translators assume that they are talking fact to face. Since the translators are remotely located from each other, the phone system and the protocol established for using the phone system must be followed. The phone system converts the audio conversation into electrical signals, uses the medium to transmit the signals to their destination point, and then reproduces the audio conversation from the electrical signals.

Each layer assumes that it is communicating with its peer using the appropriate protocol for exchanging information. Actual communication proceeds from a PM to the translator, through the phone system, which uses the communication medium to transmit the physical signals, and then from the second translator to the other PM.

◀

HOST-TO-HOST COMMUNICATIONS

Why form a communication network except to provide the functions and facilities for accessing application nodes that are remotely located from each other? **Application nodes,** otherwise known as **end nodes, host nodes,** or **workstations,** house the facilities supporting the end uses of the network, such as information-processing programs, file servers, messaging, input/output monitors, and control processes. These nodes serve as the source and sink nodes.

Besides the end nodes, the network may include **intermediate nodes,** whose activities are less concerned with the actual application but which act to relay information through the interconnecting paths in the network. These nodes transfer data from one node to the next, monitor the traffic, and validate the correctness of the transferred data. The collection of end nodes and intermediate nodes together with their interconnections constitute the data communications network.

These nodal considerations suggest that a two-layer model suffices for partitioning the functions and facilities at a node. Later, each of these layers will be subdivided into several layers for convenience in implementing a more workable arrangement. The upper layer of the two-layer model provides the communication facilities that service the end users whose applications are cooperating. The lower layer provides the facilities for creating suitable physical signals and the path for transporting these physical signals through the communication links. When the end nodes are connected to a subnetwork (Figure 7.5), the bottom layer must conform to the dictates of the subnetwork while the top layer is concerned with the needs of the applications.

Generally, both layers are needed at host nodes; however, only the bottom layer is normally needed at the intermediate nodes, since these nodes are concerned with

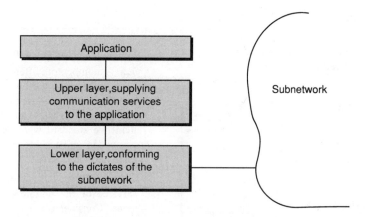

FIGURE 7.5 Communication interface between end nodes and subnetwork.

transporting the communications and not with the operations of the applications. Figure 7.6 shows communication between two host nodes directed through an intermediate node. An **end-to-end protocol** disciplines the internodal communications between the upper layers of the host nodes, while a **point-to-point protocol** disciplines the communications between the lower layers of hosts and the intermediate relay nodes (or any two adjacent intermediate nodes). The protocols, shown by broken lines, define the virtual communications between peer entities that reside at a particular layer level. Actual communications, however, shown by the solid line, follow the path through the layers of the hosts and intermediate nodes and through the communication medium. To reverse communications, the source and sink nodes exchange roles.

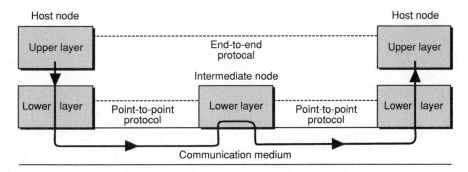

FIGURE 7.6 Communication path between two hosts nodes through an intermediate node.

Exercises

7.1 Using the following layer model, describe the ordering and delivering of a pizza.

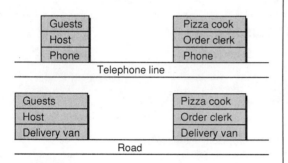

7.2 Model a data entry system, list in detail the communication functions and facilities that must be located at each of the host nodes, and assign these functions and facilities to the layers of the two-layer model.†

7.3 Give reasons why you might or might not consider the communication medium to be layer 0.†

7.4 Using a layer model, describe how letters are sorted and packaged as they pass through the postal services. Carefully identify the virtual and physical communications between layers.

7.5 A number of different standards have been defined for each of the layers. However, a single standard is usually adopted for use in a particular network architecture. What would be the difficulties if more than one standard were used at any layer, and how can nodes supported by different communication protocols be interfaced?

7.6 In the two-layer model, the top layer uses the services of the bottom layer in performing its services. Consider two data base management systems, each housed at a different node. Discuss the functions assigned to the application, the upper layer, and the lower layer for transferring a file from one data base to the other.

7.7 Suppose the Chinese PM translator in Example 7.1 can render a translation between Chinese and Japanese, and the French PM translator can render a translation between French and German. Augment the translation services that must be made available to the PMs, and describe the hypothetical phone conversation.

_____

†Class discussion exercise.

7.2 ISO REFERENCE MODEL FOR OPEN SYSTEMS INTERCONNECTION

PURPOSE OF THE MODEL

The set of protocols and communication services provided by the layers at a node specifies the network architecture. Each of these is a proper subject for standardization. To coordinate and expedite the development of standards by independent teams of experts, the International Organization for Standardization (ISO) has described a layer model for network architecture, called the **Reference Model for Open Systems Interconnection (OSI).** The term _open systems_ refers to systems that can be interconnected to communicate with each other by conforming to common implementation standards.

Although itself a standard, ISO OSI is not an implementation standard. Instead, it partitions the communication functions into layers so that each layer's functions can be independently standardized. Without such a model, vendors could and would package the communication functions in different ways, which would prohibit the interconnection of devices from different vendors. The objective of this model is to guarantee the interoperability of products selected from different suppliers by virtue of the fact that they conform to a common suite of standards.

GUIDELINES FOR CREATING LAYERS

It may appear that the number of layers and the grouping of functions assigned to each layer is arbitrary, and indeed this is the case. To guide the development of standards, ISO used a number of principles for partitioning the functions into layers. In addition to the principles that ISO used to partition the reference model, it also gave principles for creating sublayers within each layer, as needed. Later some standards will be presented that have been developed by partitioning a layer into sublayers.

The driving principle used by ISO was to keep the number of layers to a number that would make the task of describing and integrating the layers manageable. To achieve this, layers and boundaries were created that conformed to the following guidelines:

- Locate boundaries where
  past experience has proved successful
  the number of interactions between layers can be kept to a minimum
  an interface standard may prove useful
  a different layer of abstraction is needed to handle data (e.g., morphology, syntax, or semantics)
  an upper or lower layer exists and only at these points
- Locate layers where
  similar functions should be collected
  the functions or technology is manifested differently
  functions can be localized so that the layer can be redesigned without changing the services expected from or provided to other layers
  functions can be changed without affecting other layers

SEVEN-LAYER MODEL

Figure 7.7 shows the structure developed under the auspices of ISO together with the name given to designate the collection of entities and functions located at each layer. It should be reemphasized that the partitioning itself is not intended to be an implementation standard, nor does it provide a basis for appraising existing implementations or match the partitioning of existing networks. However, the model gives an orderly view of the communication functions and facilities at each node, as well

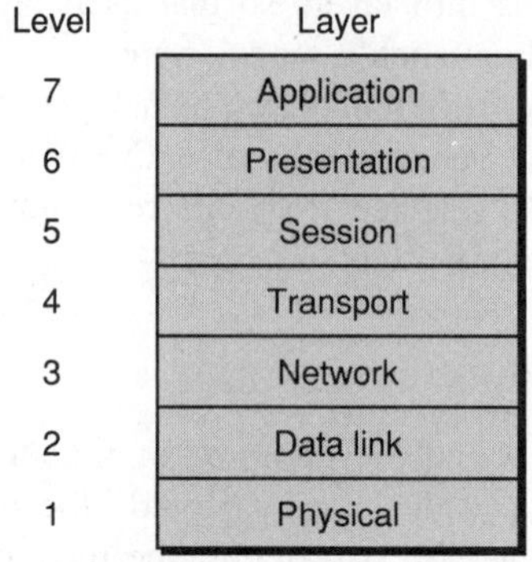

Level	Layer
7	Application
6	Presentation
5	Session
4	Transport
3	Network
2	Data link
1	Physical

FIGURE 7.7 ISO OSI layer model.

as the opportunity for developing implementation standards for integrating open systems products.

The ISO OSI is a seven-layer model. The four top layers (layers 4 to 7) offer the end-to-end services needed by nodes supporting applications. The three bottom layers (layers 1, 2, and 3) provide the functions for creating the physical signals and transporting them over the network lines. Not all the layers, however, need to be implemented at every node. For example, the upper layers need not be implemented at intermediate nodes, which have no direct interactions with the applications. Nevertheless, since each layer provides services only to the adjacent layer above, any layer implemented must include the implementation of the layers below.

LAYER SERVICES AND FUNCTIONS

Starting with the bottom layer, we will briefly describe the services and functions assigned to each layer, but the specific details will be delayed until they can be put in context with specific standards. Since the entities at each layer both transmit and receive data, the protocol between peer layers must supply both the input and output data, depending on the direction of transmission.

The **physical layer** generates and detects the physical signals needed to communicate between nodes and safeguards the integrity of the signals against faulty transmission or lack of synchronization. The major concern of this layer is to provide for the electrical recognition of the signals and mechanical connection of the node to the network, including the identification of the connection points used by the upper layers to control the data circuits during transmission. In addition, the physical layer monitors the quality of service, such as the transmission rate, error rate, and transmission delays, and notifies the upper layers of faulty conditions when detected.

Data may be transferred either in serial or parallel modes, but the emphasis of this and the following discussion will deal exclusively with serial transmission. In serial transmission, the data unit is the bit, while in parallel transmission, the number of bits is exactly equal to the number of transmission lines. In either case, however, the lines transmit the physical signals representing the bits independent of their interpretation. This philosophy follows for all layers whereby each layer provides its services independent of the protocol used by the layer above.

While the physical layer is concerned with the transfer of bits, the **data link layer** is concerned with the transfer of information that has been organized into larger blocks (e.g., characters, packets, frames) by creating and recognizing the block boundaries. It ensures accurate data transmission between adjacent nodes by providing error detection and possibly error correction techniques, controlling the rate that data flow between nodes, and sequencing the information to the upper layers in the same order as transmitted. To support these activities, the data link layer must recognize bit patterns controlling and delimiting the transfer of information and deal with errors resulting from the loss, duplication, disordering, or transit delays of the blocks.

The **network layer** provides for the establishment, maintenance, and release of the route whereby the nodes direct the information toward its destination. It is the highest layer involved in point-to-point communications between adjacent nodes. Perhaps it is misleading to talk of point-to-point communications, since the routing may include intermediate nodes used to establish connections between subnets that have different characteristics (e.g., between a private local area network and the public wide area network). Within a subnetwork, the network layer supports this service by uniquely identifying each end point of the network so that it can create the necessary interconnections through an appropriate routing table using the node addresses. In addition, it provides ancillary services, such as detecting unrecoverable errors, sequencing information that might not be in the order needed by the higher layers, controlling flow so as to avoid congestion between a fast transmitter and a slow receiver, and maintaining quality-of-service parameters (error rate, service availability, throughput, transit delay, etc.).

The **transport layer** establishes (and releases) the connections between itself and transport layers at other nodes to provide end-to-end data transfer services. The transport end points, identified by unique addresses, are mapped by the transport layer onto end addresses used by the network layer, where the required grade of service may be selected. The selected services include throughput, transit delays, connection setup delays, error rate control, and availability of resources. To optimize the required services, several transport addresses may be mapped onto the same network layer end address, or alternatively, a transport address may be mapped onto different network layer end addresses.

The **session layer** coordinates the dialogue between nodes. It acts without concern for any of the other communication interactions that must be performed as a result of nodes being remotely located from each other (these interactions are delegated to the lower layers). There may be a many-to-one mapping of the session layer's addresses and the transport layer's addresses; however, at any given time, there is a one-to-one connection. This arrangement allows several sessions to use the same transport connection, but only one at a time. Moreover, in the event of a transport connection failure, the transport connection may be replaced by another.

The data exchange services supported by the session layer may be in both directions, whereby the nodes can transmit and receive simultaneously or take turns, or they may be unidirectional, whereby only one node transmits and the other receives. In addition, two related services are cited, called quaranting and session connection synchronization. Quaranting refers to the facilities embedded in the session layer that allow it to withhold data elements from the presentation layer until explicitly released by its communication partner. Session connection synchronization allows the presentation layer to identify points in the dialogue where the session can be reinitialized in the event of an abnormal condition. These services circumvent actions and partial actions (e.g., when transmitting data files) that can lead to unrecoverable errors.

The **presentation layer** relieves the **application layer** of the need to conform to particular syntactical representations of the data. Not only may the syntax used by the application layer in the transmitter and receiver differ, but a different syntax may also be used for exchanging data. The presentation layer provides for the conversion of character sets and the modification of the data layout to conform to the formats needed by the application layer for processing and interpreting the exchanged information. While not concerned with the semantics of the data, a concern only to the application layer, it makes the transfer of information efficient. For example, it may perform code compression for file transfers, as well as providing code compatibility between different devices.

As the highest defined layer in the ISO model, the application layer provides no services to other layers, but serves as the interface where the processes of the actual application may request services of the communication substructure. Application processes may be one or more intelligent users, computer processes (programs), or integrated control processes. Typical services performed by the application layer for these processes include file transfer services, message handling services, virtual terminal services or job transfer, and control services.

Since the number and variety of specific applications with which the network must deal are almost unlimited, the functions performed by the application layer must be tailored to specific applications. The responsibility for the semantics (i.e., intended meaning) of the information resides with this layer. For processes to exchange information, they must agree on the semantics they will share, called the **universe of discourse.** Figure 7.8 gives an example of the universe of discourse between an

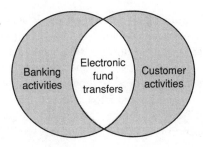

FIGURE 7.8 Universe of discourse for an electronic fund transfer system.

application and the communication substructure. If the left and right circles represent the relevant semantics of a bank and banking customer, respectively, then the common area in the middle represents the universe of discourse for an electronic fund transfer system.

NETWORK MANAGEMENT FUNCTIONS

One other aspect of the ISO architecture needs to be addressed, specifically, the functions dealing with the management of the network. Of these activities, however, only those implying the exchange of information between cooperating entities need to be considered within the framework of the communication substructure. Under the purview of this general guideline, three categories of management functions have been identified: **application management, system management,** and **layer management.**

The layer management functions relate to those functions performed by the individual layers, such as those dealing with the activation of the layer entities for error control. The application and system management functions, on the other hand, reside within the application layer and relate to the management of the application processes and control of the system's resources, respectively. Table 7.1 lists some typical activities associated with these categories of network management.

TABLE 7.1
TYPICAL NETWORK MANAGEMENT ACTIVITIES

APPLICATION MANAGEMENT ACTIVITIES	SYSTEM MANAGEMENT ACTIVITIES
Setting application process parameters	Initialization and modification of system parameters
Initiation, maintenance, and termination of application processes	Establishment, maintenance, and release of management entity connections
Allocation and deallocation of resources assigned to application processes	Activation, deactivation, and termination of the distributed resources
Detection and prevention of resource interference and deadlocks	Monitoring system status and status changes
Integrity and commitment control	Reporting system statistics
Security control	Program loading
Checkpointing control	System error detection and diagnostic reporting
Recovery control	System reconfiguration and restarts

Exercises

7.8 Refer to the literature and compare the proprietary network architecture offered by various suppliers [e.g., SNA by IBM, DECNET by Digital Equipment Corp., BNA by Burroughs (UNISYS), etc.] to the ISO OSI model.*

7.9 Describe the protocols in terms of the ISO OSI model for establishing, transmitting, and terminating the transactions for common stock with a broker.†

7.10 Each layer of the reference model builds on the services of the layer below. Starting with the top layer, explain the complications that would result if particular layers were bypassed.

7.11 Discuss the universe of discourse of each of the following applications:
(a)   airline reservation systems
(b)   student registration system
(c)   robotic painting system
(d)   bill of material system

7.12 The physical layer does not have a lower layer from which it can request services. Discuss peer-to-peer communications that occur at this level.

*See footnote, page 7.
†Class discussion exercise.

7.3   LAYER SERVICE STRUCTURE

SERVICE PROVIDER

Figure 7.9 depicts the essential communication paths between two layers at the same level. Although the entities lodged in the layers are remotely located from each other, they can cooperate in providing the services needed by their respective users by exchanging information under control of the layer protocol. The term user in this diagram simply identifies the layer immediately above the service layer as the service user. However, since the layer protocol exchanges information by virtual communications, each layer uses the service access points of the adjacent lower layer to form the necessary physical path. The medium creates the physical connection between the service access points for the entities at the bottom layer.

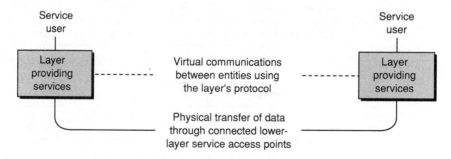

FIGURE 7.9 Communication between peer entities.

FIGURE 7.10 Peer entities combined to form the service provider.

Entities supplying services at a particular layer level, regardless of the node in which they reside, can be represented as a single functional unit, called the **service provider.** Figure 7.10 shows the service provider placed in the center of the figure as a logical reorientation of the diagram shown in Figure 7.9. The service provider embeds the rules and conventions that make up the layer's protocol for exchanging information between entities. Although not shown explicitly, the service provider builds its services from the hierarchy of lower-layer services and together with the medium forms the intrinsic path through which peer entities exchange information.

TIME SEQUENCE DIAGRAM

Figure 7.11 replicates the previous figure as a working diagram, called the **time sequence diagram.** When a user needs to communicate with its peer, it uses the services of the service provider by issuing commands that may include optional parameters and/or data through the service access points at the interface boundaries. In the diagram, the command arrows indicate the direction of the command into and out of the service provider. The sequence of the commands from top to bottom gives their temporal order.

When a user issues a request for service, the time sequence diagram can be used to track the intervening operations of the service provider. Following Figure 7.12, assume that the user at the left node issues a command requesting services from the service provider. The direction of the arrow identifies the sender and receiver, and the label on the arrow identifies the command. The command may be modified by parameters and/or data. The local entities of the service provider cooperate with the

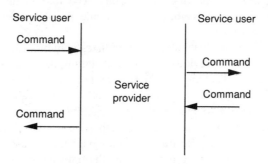

FIGURE 7.11 Time sequence diagram.

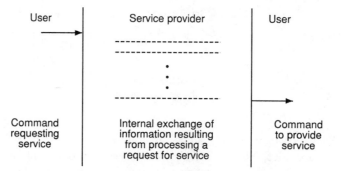

FIGURE 7.12 Communications between peer
entities of the service provider.

entities at the remote site to interpret and process the command according to the
service provider's protocol. This is shown as a series of operations performed by the
service provider to execute its protocol. Ultimately, the service provider responds by
issuing a command directed either back to the user that issued the request for service
or to its correspondent user at the remote node.

COMMUNICATION PHASES

The dialogue between users can be structured into phases, with a specific collection
of commands supporting each phase. Figure 7.13 gives the interrelationships of the
phases. In the event of transmission loss due to a malfunction or error during any
phase, procedures are invoked to gracefully recover and reset the communication
mechanisms for continuing the operations.

The dialogue begins with the **connect phase,** which acquires the links connecting the stations. After the connection has been confirmed, the connected stations may
exchange information until the **clear phase** terminates the dialogue and deallocates
the links connecting the stations. The middle three phases—**establishment, data
transfer,** and **termination**—provide for the orderly exchange of information between stations.

The establishment phase initiates communications with a request to transmit to a
partner in a previously connected station, and if granted, sets the control mechanisms
for error checking and the maintenance of the link even under faulty operations. The
data transfer phase immediately follows the establishment and continues by allowing
the stations to repeatedly exchange information, acknowledging the receipt of the
data, and, when needed, requesting the retransmission of the data. After all the data
that were ready for transmission have been transferred, the termination phase notifies
the communicating partners that the transmission has ended and allows either partner
to establish communications with any other partner at the connected station. So long
as the facilities are not disconnected by the final clear phase, the establishment, data

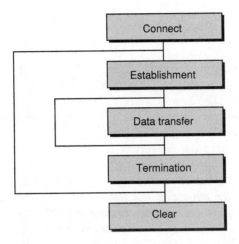

FIGURE 7.13 Communication phases.

transfer, and termination phases may be cycled repeatedly without the need to reconnect the facilities after each cycle.

Exercises

7.13 Describe telephone communications in terms of the five phases given in Figure 7.13.

7.14 Describe the transactions exchanged during a computer session in terms of the five phases given in Figure 7.13. Be especially careful to talk only about the communications that are independent of the applications.

7.15 Host-to-host communications can proceed without explicit commands for connecting and clearing the lines. How can this be organized? Explain why this arrangement might be advantageous.

7.16 The following diagram depicts a three-layer model as an embedded set of service providers. Use this diagram to describe in narrative form how physical communications proceed between users.

7.4 LAYER SERVICE SPECIFICATIONS

PRIMITIVE COMMANDS

Functionally, layer entities can be specified by:

- The commands issued by the service provider to the layer above or the request for services of the service provider from the layer below

- The data structures transmitted between peer entities
- The set of internal mechanisms implemented in the service provider

The commands characterize the available layer services. A set of four service primitives describe the possible actions for each service, although not all four need to be included for all services. The four primitives associated with each service are generically named **request, indication, response,** and **confirm.** An illustration using the time sequence diagram may help in understanding their individual roles.

The request primitive passed from the service user to the service provider initiates a particular service. For example, in the connect service illustrated in Figure 7.14, the request primitive asks that a logical connection be established between the local service access point and the remote service access point at the same layer level.

The indication primitive passes from the service provider to the user and indicates that a significant event has occurred requiring the user's attention. In the illustration, the request primitive that had asked for a connection has caused the indication primitive to be passed to the correspondent user, indicating whether the connection attempt was successful or not, and in case it was not, giving the reason for the failure.

Having received and processed the indication primitive, the correspondent user may reply to the service provider with a response primitive. The reply gives the status of the connection and may include parameters to control the information flow back to the user.

The confirm primitive gives the user that requested the connection the status of the connection attempt. The service provider internally generates this command as a result of one of the previous commands. When it comes from the request, it confirms that a request for service has been sent; when it comes from the indication, it confirms that the request has arrived; and when it comes from an explicit response, it confirms that the request has been received.

A service primitive may be issued by the service provider as a result of some activity in the lower layer or as a result of a previous service primitive issued by a user. When it is important to show the cause-and-effect relationship between service primitives, it can be done by connecting them with a dotted line. Figure 7.15 shows some possibilities.

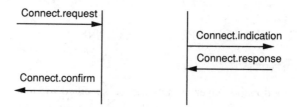

FIGURE 7.14 Command service primitives.

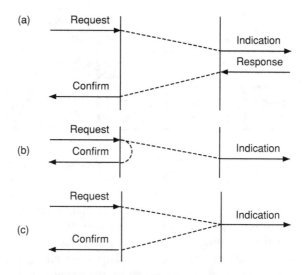

FIGURE 7.15 Some possible relationships between service primitives.

Figure 7.15a shows a user making a request, which results in the service provider indicating the outcome to the correspondent user. The correspondent user may in turn formulate a response, which is passed to the user who had made the request to confirm the results of the request.

Figure 7.15b shows that the confirmation may be issued by the lower layer of the node requesting the service, but gives no confirmation from the correspondent user on whether it has arrived. The correspondent node, however, still receives an indication that a request has been made.

Figure 7.15c shows a logical variation of the events illustrated in Figure 7.15a. This time, the lower layer of the correspondent node internally issues the confirmation that the request has arrived rather than as an explicit response from the correspondent user.

PROTOCOL DATA UNITS

The data format used by the protocol to transfer information between peer entities is an integral part of the protocol specifications. Structurally, these data units, called **protocol data units (PDU),** consist of two components: the **protocol control information (PCI)** and the **service data unit (SDU).** The service data unit represents the data transferred between peer entities of the service provider on behalf of the user (i.e., the layer above the service provider). The protocol control information, on the other hand, represents the information transferred between peer entities to coordinate their joint activities. While both components may be included as needed within a

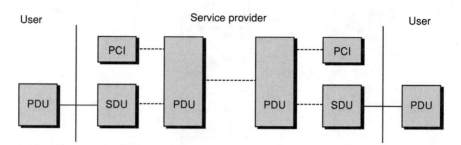

FIGURE 7.16 Mapping protocol data units between layers.

protocol data unit, some protocol data units serve only to coordinate the joint operations of peer entities and contain no user data.

Communication proceeds between layers by mapping the protocol data unit into a service data unit that acts as a buffer for the service provider. Although not germane at this point in the discussion, the actual transfer of information between layers may occur in pieces or as multiple data units. Figure 7.16 shows the construction of protocol data units from one layer to the next and the transfer of data between peer entities. The service data unit is packaged with the protocol control information to form the protocol data unit of the service provider. When the protocol data unit arrives at the receiving end of the service provider, the service provider separates the two components and uses the protocol control information to coordinate the activities of the peer entities. A mapping then re-forms the service data unit into one or more protocol data units for the layer above.

Since the structure of the protocol data units is specified separately for each layer, its size need not be preserved at the various layers. Using the service data unit as a buffer, Figure 7.17 illustrates the possibilities for reformatting the data units into other sizes. The end effect, however, is always the same: The mapping and transfer of the data through the lower layers are transparent to the user.

Figure 7.17a shows the concatenation of several protocol data units into a single service data unit. The service data unit acts to buffer several protocol data units mapped into the lower layer. The service data unit is then combined with the protocol control information to format the layer's protocol data unit. At the receiving end, the process is reversed, using the protocol control information to separate and map the user data into the protocol data units meaningful to the user.

Figure 7.17b illustrates the data normally associated with several protocol data units being blocked within the service provider and transported to a peer as a single unit. The peer entities deblock the data.

Figure 7.17c illustrates the opposite of blocking, whereby the data in the service data unit are segmented into several protocol data units. At the receiving end, the user data from the protocol data units are reassembled into the service data unit.

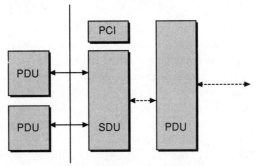

a. Concatenation/Separation

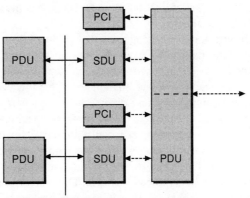

b. Blocking/Deblocking

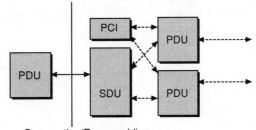

c. Segmenting/Reassembling

FIGURE 7.17 Techniques for reformatting protocol.

SPECIFICATION OF SERVICE PROVIDER INTERNAL MECHANISMS

It may appear that the time sequence of commands and the structure of their associated data units should suffice to complete the layer's protocol specifications. However, one aspect of the specifications remains, namely, the set of internal mechanisms implemented in the service provider. These mechanisms perform the actions, track the sequence of events, and manipulate the data units that transfer the information between entities. Effectively, the internal mechanisms specify how the service provider interprets the commands issued at the interfaces or how it generates the commands issued back to the users.

Ultimately, the layer entities must be implemented by programming or equivalently by hardware logic, so some formal method is needed to organize their complexity and describe the layer functions in a precise manner. Moreover, the specifications for standardization must be presented in a form that allows vendors to adopt any viable technology.

It has long been recognized that protocols can be treated as finite-state machines. Finite-state machines are a family of abstract machines that can be used to organize the interconnections needed between simple components to produce a deterministic behavior. They have the advantage of having been extensively studied mathematically and applied in many diverse fields of science and engineering. The focus here, however, will be on their use in protocol specifications.

Two forms that are especially attractive for describing finite-state machines are **state transition diagrams** and **state transition tables.** Either of these forms may be used in practice. State transition diagrams depict the finite state machine by circles interconnected by directed arrows. The circles, called states, represent stable conditions of the machine during its operation. The number of states is finite. The interconnecting arrows are labelled in two ways; by the events causing the transition of the components from one stable state to the next, and by the sequence of actions

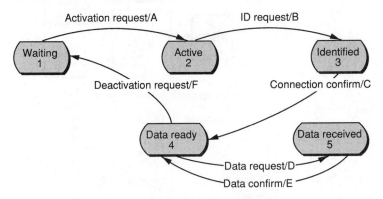

FIGURE 7.18 Example of finite-state diagram.

taken as a result of the event. The state transition table gives this same information, but in tabular form.

The state transition diagram in Figure 7.18 illustrates by a simple, intuitive example the ideas used to describe the internal mechanism of a layer. Assume that the layer activities start in stage 1 (waiting), depicting the entities as inactive and currently unconnected to the entities at another node. This is a stable state, as are the remaining states in the diagram.

An activation request puts the machine into a new stable state given as state 2 (active) and executes a sequence of actions labeled A. The actions usually are quite extensive, so the label simply identifies them and they are listed elsewhere. A number of schemes can be used to specify the actions including flowcharts, structured English, and programming languages such as PASCAL. It is immaterial in the representation on whether the actions are implemented by hardware, software, or a combination of both. The actions taken in making the transition from state 1 to state 2 results in activating the correspondent node.

From state 2, the sending user initiates a request for connection with a specific service access point identified by its address. This request causes a transition from state 2 to the next stable state, state 3 (identified). In a like manner, the transition from state 3 to state 4 (data ready) confirms the connection between users. The series of transitions from state 1 to state 2 to state 3 to state 4 and their associated actions result in making the communication connections and verifying that the machine is ready for the transfer of data.

From state 4, two possible events may occur: Data may be transferred when ready, or the machine may be returned to the waiting state. Data ready for transfer

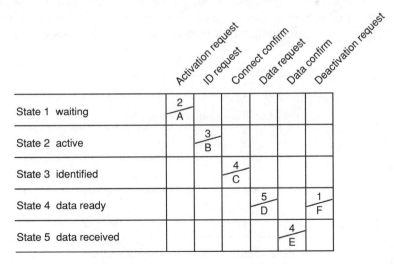

FIGURE 7.19 Example of a state transition table.

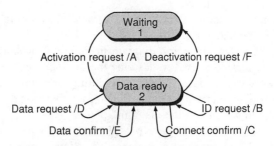

FIGURE 7.20   Reducing the number of states by using flags.

cause the actions transferring the data that accompany the transition to state 5 (data received). The transition from state 5 back to state 4 confirms the data transfer. This data cycle continues until all the data have been transferred. The final transition from state 4 back to state 1 returns the machine to the waiting state and terminates the connection between users.

Figure 7.19 shows the same information given in Figure 7.18, but as a state transition table. This format allows more details to be included without crowding the diagram. Each entry contains two labels. The top label gives the next state, and the bottom label identifies the detailed sequence of actions that accompany the transition. Empty entries in the table indicate that an error condition has occurred.

The number of states can become very large, complicating the machine. To reduce the number of states, the transition actions can set flags in addition to performing the other operations and these flags can then be examined during subsequent transitions. Figure 7.20 illustrates Figure 7.18 as a two-state machine. Implicit in this arrangement is that programming flags are set and checked whenever a transition occurs, permitting only legitimate transitions with each event.

Example 7.2

Organize the state transition information given in Figure 7.20 into a state transition table.

	Activation request	ID request	Connect confirm	Data request	Data confirm	Deactivation request
State 1 waiting	2 / A					
State 2 data ready		2 / B	2 / C	2 / D	2 / E	1 / F

◀

Exercises

7.17 Expand each of the diagrams in Figure 7.17 to show separation, deblocking, and reassembling.

7.18 Show the relationship between service primitives that confirms the message

(a)   has been sent
(b)   has arrived
(c)   has been received

SUMMARY

ISO has instituted a reference model to guide independent teams of experts in coordinating and expediting the development of implementation standards for communications. The model is structured into seven layers, whereby each layer provides the services needed by the adjacent layer above or can request the services provided by the adjacent layer below. The services are available at the service access points located at the boundary of adjacent layers. When the layer entities at a node cannot by themselves provide the services that have been requested, they may call on peer entities at another node to cooperate in providing the services.

Peer entities exchange information by virtual communications using the rules and conventions of the layer protocol. Physical communications proceed from the top layer of the sending node through the adjacent lower layers through the communication medium, and then up the layers of the receiving node.

Entities at the bottom layer of a node do not have a layer below from which they can request services, but they can exchange information with peer entities through the physical medium connecting their respective service access points. The physical medium itself is not part of the layer structure. The top layer is also unique in that it services the actual application, which is not part of the layer model.

The OSI architecture distributes the communication functions into four upper layers that have end-to-end significance and three lower layers that have point-to-point significance. Accordingly, the layers have been assigned the following roles:

Layer 7, the application layer, provides the services that are directly comprehensible to the actual application.

Layer 6, the presentation layer, transforms the data to the format needed by the application layer.

Layer 5, the session layer, synchronizes and manages the dialogue between cooperating end nodes.

Layer 4, the transport layer, ensures reliable data transfers between end points.

Layer 3, the network layer, routes the data between adjacent nodes.

Layer 2, the data link layer, blocks or frames the bits for reliable data transfer between adjacent nodes.

Layer 1, the physical layer, physically encodes the bits and provides the mechanical connections to the medium for transferring the bits between nodes.

The time sequence diagram depicts each layer as a service provider and the interface with its users (the layer above). Through this model, the functionality of the entities can be better pictured. The layer specifications are given by the service commands issued to or from the users, the data structures transmitted between peer entities, and the internal mechanisms implemented in the service provider.

The specific commands depend on the layer and the communication phase where they are issued. There are four possible generic commands: request, indication, response, and confirm, which may or may not be included with each service. The commands may pass data and/or control parameters from the users. As they pass through the service provider, the data units may be reformatted into other sizes by concatenation, blocking, and segmenting. After passing the data units, the service provider reconstitutes them by separating, deblocking, and reassembling them, respectively, so as to make these services transparent to the user (i.e., the layer above).

Ultimately, the layer entities must be implemented by programming or equivalently by hardware logic. Although there are many methodologies that can specify the control flow independent of the technology used, a combination of structured programming and state transition diagrams serves particularly well.

KEY TERMS

Layer architecture
Service access points
Peer entities
Layer protocol
Application node
End node
Host node
Workstation
Intermediate node
End-to-end protocol
Point-to-point protocol
Reference Model for Open Systems
    Interconnection (OSI)
Physical layer
Data link layer
Network layer
Transport layer
Session layer
Presentation layer
Application layer

Universe of discourse
Application management
System management
Layer management
Service provider
Time sequence diagram
Connection phase
Establishment phase
Data transfer phase
Termination phase
Clear phase
Request
Indication
Response
Confirm
Protocol data unit (PDU)
Protocol control information (PCI)
Service data unit (SDU)
State transition diagram
State transition table

SUGGESTED READINGS

Green, Paul E. (ed.). *Computer Network Architectures and Protocols*. New York: Plenum, 1982.

Halsall, Fred. *Introduction to Data Communications and Computer Networks*. Reading, Mass.: Addison-Wesley, 1985.

Information Processing Systems-Open Systems Interconnection-Basic Reference Model, ref. no. ISO 7498-1984 (E).

Kuo, Franklin F. (ed.). *Protocols and Techniques for Data Communication Networks*. Englewood Cliffs, N.J.: Prentice-Hall, 1981.

Peeters, Anton Meijerand Paul. *Computer Network Architectures*. Computer Science Press, 1982.

Schwartz, Mischa. *Telecommunication Networks: Protocols, Modeling and Analysis*. Reading, Mass.: Addison-Wesley, 1987.

Stallings, William. *Data and Computer Communications*. New York: Macmillan, 1985.

Tanenbaum, Andrew S. *Computer Networks*. Englewood Cliffs, N.J.: Prentice-Hall, 1981.

LOCAL AREA NETWORK STANDARDS

The ability to integrate and effectively
transfer information in a timely manner,
within a factory, within an office, and
between the two has become a key factor
in improved quality and productivity and
a key to the future of American industry.
ROBERT DRYDEN
FORWARD TO TOP SPECIFICATIONS

8.1 THE IEEE 802 PROJECT

RELATIONSHIP OF ISO OSI MODEL TO THE IEEE 802 PROJECT

The goal here is to illustrate the data communication principles that are an inherent part of LAN architecture. LANs provide an enterprise the opportunity to interconnect remotely separated facilities that need to cooperate in accomplishing their assigned tasks. It would be a mistake to think that one type of LAN suffices for all applications. The facilities servicing the office applications have critical deadlines, but differ from those on the shop floor that have a real-time constraint and require a deterministic response time. Yet, the devices servicing the applications need to cooperate with each other regardless of the LAN to which they are connected.

Standards provide the basis for integrating the communication substructure. The development of voluntary standards and, equally important, the adoption of such standards into products allow an enterprise to select products from different vendors without the cost of tailoring them to conform to each other's specifications. The principles drawn into standards usually come from operational systems after they have been field-tested and have been proved effective. A standard reaches national prominence when it becomes widely accepted or sometimes when it refines the thinking on the subject matter with which it deals. When the theory and experience embodied in the recommendations reach this status, there is some assurance that they have more than just a passing academic interest.

The ISO OSI model gives the framework for developing standards, but itself is not an implementation standard. Using the ISO model, the IEEE 802 project has recommended a family of related implementation standards for different LAN configurations. In particular, these standards partition the physical and data link layers into sublayers that conform to the functionality specified for these layers by the ISO OSI model. Each sublayer is subsequently defined in terms of the data frame it uses, the services it provides at the interfaces, its electrical and mechanical connections as appropriate, and the actions its entities perform. Although the standards do not mention the upper layers, it is implied that they, too, will conform to the ISO model.

IEEE 802 PROJECT SUBLAYERS

Figure 8.1 shows the lower portion of the ISO model as it has been substructured by the 802 project. In particular, the functions normally performed by the data link layer have been distributed over two sublayers; a **logical link control (LLC)** upper sublayer and a **medium access control (MAC)** lower sublayer. The upper sublayer generates and interprets the link control commands, while the complementary, lower sublayer frames the data units and acquires the right to access the medium. Above the bottom two layers, the layers specified by the ISO should operate without requiring any additional features. The purpose of this substructuring is to provide the partitioning for describing a family of modular standards normalizing the functions, features, and protocols for use with a variety of LANs.

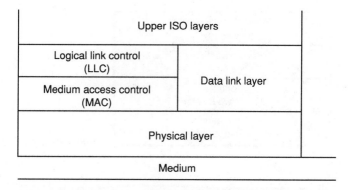

FIGURE 8.1 802 project sublayer model.

Within this structure, four standards have been defined: a logical link control standard and three standards that have been named according to the method each uses to control the access of the medium:

- **Carrier sense multiple access with collision detection**
- **Token-passing bus access**
- **Token ring access**

Even though these accessing methods differ from each other, they all control the right to transmit on the LAN by distributing the control to all the nodes attached to the communication medium, in contrast to other methods that delegate the control to a central, master station.

Effectively, this substructuring partitions the services provided by the data link layer into a common interface between the upper ISO layers and the lower substructure that can be implemented by different medium-accessing technologies. In addition to substructuring the data link layer, each of the MAC sublayer standards also gives guidance for implementing the mechanical, electrical, functional, and procedural characteristics of an associated physical layer, and the physical properties of the medium layer, sometimes referred to as layer 0.

8.2   LOGICAL LINK CONTROL

LLC PROTOCOL DATA UNIT

At the outset, Figure 8.2 gives the format of the protocol data unit used by the LLC sublayer. The protocol data unit is organized into fields, with each field containing an integral number of octets (i.e., 8-bit units). Independent of the services rendered,

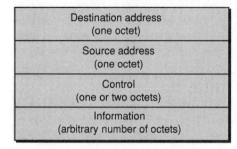

FIGURE 8.2　LLC protocol data unit format.

all data units require two addresses—the address of a local service access point and the address of a remote service access point—and a control field.

- The destination address identifies the LLC access service point to which the data unit is directed. One bit designates the address as either an individual or a group address, and the remaining 7 bits allow the address to uniquely identify 128 individual or group access service points.

- The source address identifies the entity that initiated the data unit. For consistency, the source and destination addresses must use the same addressing scheme.

- The control field specifies the action or the response to be performed. The field length may be either one or two octets, depending on whether or not the data units are numbered.

- The information field consists of the data to be passed between entities and may contain an arbitrary number of octets, including zero.

TYPES OF LINK CONTROL SERVICES

Two types of link control services have been identified for exchanging information between nodes: unacknowledged connectionless and connection-oriented. **Unacknowledged connectionless services** provide the means by which nodes can exchange information without first establishing a data link connection. It is the simpler of the two services and applicable when a guarantee for the delivery of every data units is not essential for the proper functioning of the nodes. **Connection-oriented services,** on the other hand, not only require that the path between the sending and receiving nodes be preestablished before exchanging information, but also specify the mechanisms for establishing the connections, the sequence of communication frames exchanged, and the error checks needed.

　　The LLC standard defines two classes of LLCs, simply called class I and class II, depending on the type of link control services allowed. Both classes of LLCs support unacknowledged connectionless services, while class II LLCs also support connection-oriented services. The procedures for each type of service operate unilat-

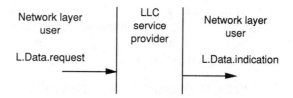

FIGURE 8.3 Unacknowledged connection-less primitives.

erally, allowing a class II LLC to switch freely from one type of service to the other. The description that follows of the command primitives passed between the network layer and the LLC sublayer will make these operations clearer.

LLC UNACKNOWLEDGED CONNECTIONLESS PRIMITIVES

Figure 8.3 illustrates the primitives defined for an unacknowledged connectionless type of operation, and Table 8.1 lists the parameters associated with these primitives. Since the addresses in the data units imply the connection between nodes for this type of service, and no flow control is required, only two primitives are defined for the transfer of information: request and indication. The L.Data.request primitive initiates the transfer of a service data unit to a remote service access point (actually,

TABLE 8.1

PARAMETERS ASSOCIATED WITH LLC
UNACKNOWLEDGED CONNECTIONLESS
SERVICES

	local.address	remote.address	l.sdu	service.class
L.Data.request	X	X	X	X
L.Data.indication	X	X	X	X

Parameters:
local.address—service access point used to transfer
          service data units
remote.address—service access point used to receive
          service data units
l.sdu—service data unit to be transferred
service.class—priority

the transfer may be to a group of service access points). No acknowledgment passes back to the sending node to confirm that the service data unit has been successfully transmitted; however, at the receiving station, the LLC entity indicates the arrival of the service data unit by passing the L.Data.indication primitive to the network layer.

LLC CONNECTION-ORIENTED PRIMITIVES

As expected, a much richer set of commands are defined for connection-oriented services. Figure 8.4 illustrates the commands for the three basic phases of operations—connection establishment, data transfer, and connection termination—and Table 8.2 lists the parameters associated with these primitives.

The L.Connect.request primitive specifies a request from the network layer for a local LLC entity to establish a connection with a remote LLC entity. The L.Connect.indication primitive results directly from the request primitive and communicates to the network layer whether or not the connection attempt for a specified service class was successful. The status parameter associated with this primitive specifies a successful connection or otherwise encodes the reasons that the connection attempt has failed, such as an unacceptable connection priority or lack of access permission. L.Connect.confirm conveys the results of the connection request back to the network layer.

The L.Data.Connect set of primitives serves a similar purpose as the corresponding primitives for unacknowledged connectionless operations, except in this case, it can be presumed that a connection has been made beforehand by the connect primitives. The additional primitive, L.Data.Connect.confirm, communicates the success

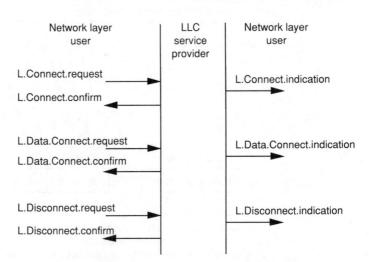

FIGURE 8.4 Connection-oriented primitives for establishment, data transfer, and termination.

TABLE 8.2
PARAMETERS ASSOCIATED WITH LLC CONNECTION-ORIENTED SERVICES

	local.address	remote.address	l.sdu	service.class	status	reason	amount
L.Connect.request	X	X		X			
L.Connect.indication	X	X		X	X		
L.Connect.confirm	X	X		X	X		
L.Data.Connect.request	X	X	X				
L.Data.Connect.indication	X	X	X				
L.Data.Connect.confirm	X	X			X		
L.Disconnect.request	X	X					
L.Disconnect.indication	X	X				X	
L.Disconnect.confirm	X	X			X		
L.Reset.request	X	X					
L.Reset.indication	X	X				X	
L.Reset.confirm	X	X			X		
L.Connect.Flowcontrol.request	X	X					X
L.Connect.Flowcontrol.indication	X	X					X

Parameters:

local.address—service access point used to transfer
service data units
remote.address—service access point used to receive
service data units
l.sdu—service data unit to be transferred
service.class—priority
status—verifies connection completion or the
reason for failure
reason—reason for disconnect
amount—amount of data an LLC entity is permitted
to pass

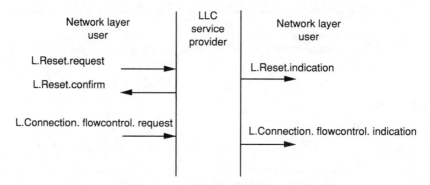

FIGURE 8.5 Reset and Flowcontrol primitives for connection-oriented operations.

or failure the remote LLC has had in receiving the service data unit. After all the data units have been transferred, the set of L.Disconnet primitives terminates the connection between the LLC entities, acting in an analogous fashion to the other sets of primitives.

To supplement the services shown in Figure 8.4, two other sets of primitives are included for connection-oriented services: reset and flowcontrol. Figure 8.5 illustrates these primitives, and the parameters associated with these primitives have been included in Table 8.2. The L.Reset primitives allow the network layer to reset the connection to the initial state. As a consequence of a request for reset, data that have been transferred but not yet acknowledged may be lost. The L.Connection.Flowcontrol primitives serve a distinctly different function. Working with the L.Data.Connect primitives, these commands control the amount of data that may be passed between the LLC entities.

MAC SUBLAYER SERVICES

As data pass through the layer structure, the MAC sublayer provides services to allow the LLC sublayer to exchange information. The three primitives shown in Figure 8.6 initiate these services, and Table 8.3 lists the parameters associated with these primitives. In addition to specifying the service data unit exchanged between addressed entities, the service primitives specify the priority (i.e., service class) and give the success or failure of the transmission or receipt of the data units for error control.

Exercises

8.1 Contrast the sets of primitives for unacknowledged connectionless and connection-oriented services, and explain how they relate to the various switching methods previously described.

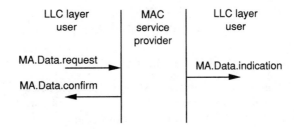

FIGURE 8.6 Service primitives between LLC and MAC sublayers.

TABLE 8.3

PARAMETERS ASSOCIATED WITH SERVICES THAT THE MAC SUBLAYER PROVIDES THE LLC SUBLAYER

	source.address	destination.address	m.sdu	service.class	transmission.status	reception.status
MA.Data.request		X	X	X		
MA.Data.indication	X	X	X			X
MA.Data.confirm					X	

Parameters:

source.address—service access point used to transfer service data units

destination.address—service access point used to receive service data units

m.sdu—service data unit to be transferred

service.class—priority

transmission.status—verifies completion of transmission or reason for failure

reception.status—verifies completion of reception or reason for failure

8.3   CARRIER SENSE MULTIPLE ACCESS WITH COLLISION DETECTION METHOD

CSMA/CD LAYER SUBSTRUCTURE

Carrier sense multiple access with collision detection (CSMA/CD) refers to the access method developed by Xerox Corporation under the trademark Ethernet and standardized by the 802 project. Stations communicate by this accessing method by transmitting any message ready for transmission by broadcasting it to the other stations with which they share a common line after detecting that the line is free of traffic. The term *carrier* in this case may be misleading. It does not imply any form of sinusoidal modulation, but simply signifies the presence of the physical signals during active transmission. In fact, the stations operate by baseband transmission.

Nodes attached to a CSMA/CD bus, shown in Figure 8.7, operate like a telephone party line. When a node needs to transmit, it listens and waits for the line to become free of other traffic before initiating transmission. All stations in the network hear every message transmitted, but accept only those messages addressed to themselves. However, since the transmitted signals take a finite amount of time to propagate along the communication line, the stations hear the signals at different times after transmission. In the interval of time it takes the signals to traverse the line after a station starts to transmit, one or more stations may sense the line free of traffic and initiate transmission. When signals from multiple stations coexist on the line, they ultimately collide and produce a detectable change in the energy level present on the line. In this event, the transmitting stations continue to transmit before abandoning transmission to ensure that all stations can detect a collision, wait a random amount of time to hopefully avoid another collision, and then attempt to retransmit. To ensure that all stations can detect a collision, all data frames must be of sufficient length to be simultaneously present on the line as they pass each station.

Figure 8.8 shows the functional sublayering of the CSMA/CD physical layer and the relationship of these components to the remaining layers and sublayers at a station. This partitioning is partially motivated by the physical separation of components needed at a node. As a practical constraint, most hardware and software at a station are usually placed at a convenient location away from the communication line. The remaining part of the nodal configuration consists of a small amount of circuitry that taps the node to the communication line. This separation of the equipment divides the physical layer into two sublayers, designated in the figure as the **physical signal-**

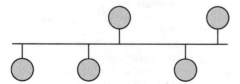

FIGURE 8.7   CSMA/CD bus structure.

ing (PLS) and **medium access unit (MAU)** sublayers. A short drop cable using a 15-pin connector at both ends specifies the interface between these two sublayers. A separate connector on the MAU sublayer attaches the node to the communication line.

Figure 8.9 is a repeat of Figure 8.8 but shows the sublayers as operational units. Using this figure and starting with a service request from the LLC sublayer for transmitting data to a peer entity, the essence of CSMA/CD communications can be tracked. The MAC sublayer first encapsulates the data passed from the LLC sublayer into the format for transmission. The frame structure for the data is organized into fields composed of an integral number of octets. When the MAC sublayer senses the line free of other traffic, it can then initiate passing the encapsulated data to the PLS sublayer. The MAC sublayer sends the octets bit by bit to the PLS sublayer, using an alphabet of 0 and 1 to encode the data and a special parameter value called *data complete* to mark the end of the encapsulated data.

The PLS sublayer generates the physical signals and sends them via the drop cable to the MAU component for transmission over the medium at a data rate of 10 Mbps, although the standard speaks of other possible data rates up to 20 Mbps. Meanwhile, the physical layer at all stations constantly monitors the signal activities on the line and can sense a free line, other traffic, or when a collision has occurred (by sensing the energy level on the line). This line status information passes to the MAC sublayer. The MAC component avoids a signal collision by delaying the encapsulated data when other traffic is present on the line. However, because of the delay in propagating the signals through the network, collisions can still occur.

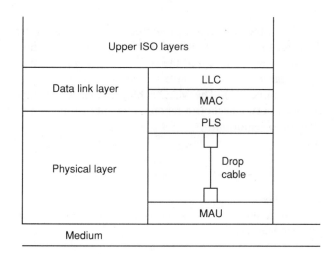

FIGURE 8.8   CSMA/CD layer structure.

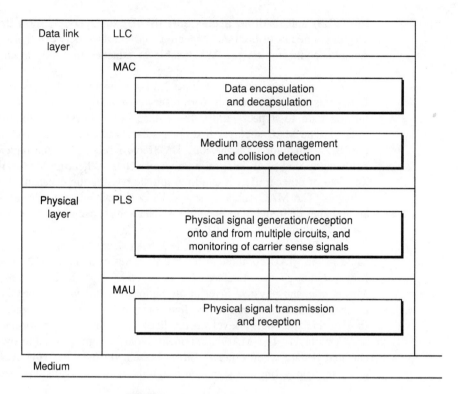

FIGURE 8.9 CSMA/CD transmission.

When the physical layer senses a collision, it informs the MAC sublayer, which then stops transmission after it has transmitted enough of the data frame to guarantee that all nodes have sensed the collision. The minimum frame size is equivalent to the time it takes a signal to make a round-trip between the extreme points in the network (see Example 8.1). The MAC sublayers that are attempting a transmission when the collision occurs backoff a random amount of time to avoid another collision and then attempt to retransmit.

Example 8.1
Plot the minimum frame size needed to transmit data versus the maximum distance between stations.

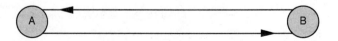

In the above figure, a signal initiated by node A must traverse the line to reach node B before its presence can be detected. In the worst case, node B still senses the line free of traffic the instant before the signal arrives from node A and can start its own transmission. Immediately afterward, node B can detect the collision. For Node A to detect the collision, it must keep transmitting until the signal from Node B arrives. Consequently, all messages must be of sufficient length to span twice the distance between any two stations sharing the line (so that a signal can traverse the line and return before transmitting the end of the message). If d is the length of the line using a coaxial cable transmitting at 0.77 the velocity of light (where the velocity of light is 3×10^5 km/s), n is the number of bits being transmitted at the data rate of 10 Mbps, and t is the round-trip time for transmitting a signal, then

$$(0.77 \times 3 \times 10^5)t = 2d$$
$$10^7 t = n$$
$$n = 86.6d$$

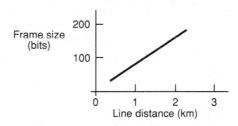

CSMA/CD DATA FRAME FORMAT

Figure 8.10 summarizes the structure of the data frame transmitted over the medium. Specifically, it contains the following information fields:

- The preamble, composed of the bit pattern 10101010 transmitted at least seven times to allow the circuitry to reach a steady state before receiving other data
- The start-of-frame delimiter, which follows immediately after the preamble and has a similar bit pattern except that the last bit is a 1 (i.e., 10101011), indicating the end of the preamble and the start of meaningful data
- The destination address, giving the address of the destination service access point(s) formatted into two or six octets, depending on the choice made in implementing the network
- The source address, giving the address of the source service access point, which has been formatted identically to the destination address
- A length field, consisting of two octets whose value gives the number of data

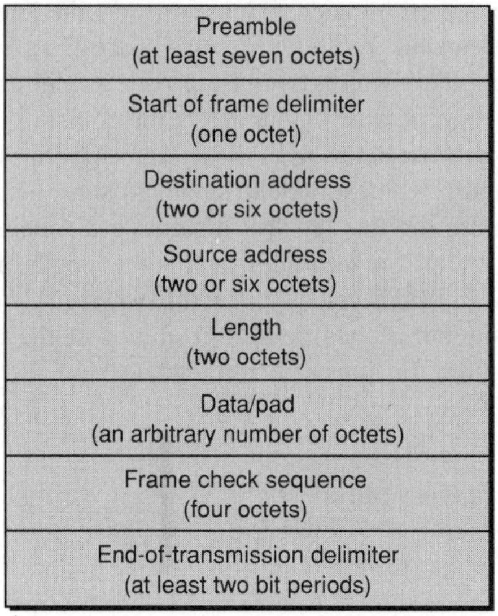

Preamble (at least seven octets)
Start of frame delimiter (one octet)
Destination address (two or six octets)
Source address (two or six octets)
Length (two octets)
Data/pad (an arbitrary number of octets)
Frame check sequence (four octets)
End-of-transmission delimiter (at least two bit periods)

FIGURE 8.10   CSMA/CD data frame format.

octets transmitted on behalf of the LLC and includes the number of pad octets used to extend the frame so as to guarantee that any possible collision with another frame will be detected while the transmitting nodes are still actively transmitting

- The data transmitted on behalf of the LLC sublayer, including any padding that has been reported in the length field

- A frame check sequence of four octets (i.e., CRC), which has been calculated using the address fields, the length field, and the data/pad field by the generator polynomial

$$G(x) = x^{32} + x^{26} + x^{23} + x^{22} + x^{16} + x^{12} + x^{11} +$$
$$x^{10} + x^8 + x^7 + x^5 + x^4 + x^2 + x + 1$$

- The end-of-transmission delimiter to indicate the end of the frame (this delimiter makes use of a nondata signal pattern, called IDL)

SERVICE PRIMITIVES

Before transmitting any of the bits received from the MAC sublayer, the physical layer first transmits the preamble and the start-of-frame delimiter. The encapsulated fields pass from the MAC sublayer serially, bit by bit, and the PLS sublayer generates appropriate physical signals. After all the encapsulated data have been passed from the MAC sublayer, the MAC sublayer signals the PLS sublayer that the data

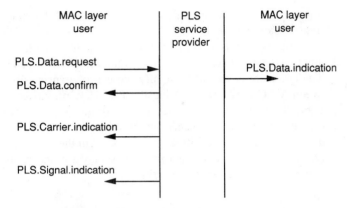

FIGURE 8.11 Service primitives between MAC and PLS sublayers.

TABLE 8.4

PARAMETERS ASSOCIATED WITH SERVICES THAT THE PLS SUBLAYER PROVIDES THE MAC SUBLAYER

	output.unit	output.status	input.unit	carrier.status	signal.status
PLS.Data.request	X				
PLS.Data.indication		X			
PLS.Data.confirm			X		
PLS.Carrier.indication				X	
PLS.Signal.indication					X

Parameters:

output.unit—giving bit value 0, 1, or data complete (signifying end of data)

output.status—indicating whether PLS is ready for another bit value

input.unit—giving a single-bit value of 0 or 1

carrier.status—indicating whether carrier is on or off

signal.status—indicating whether there is an error in the signal transfer has been completed, which causes the PLS sublayer to generate the end-of-transmission delimiter.

The data units passed between the MAC and PLS sublayers are in single-bit units. After the encapsulated data frame has been transferred, the parameter value data.complete is passed to signify the end of transmission. Data are transferred between MAC peer entities using the PLS.Data primitives shown in Figure 8.11 and Table 8.4 shown on page 215. These primitives cause the PLS sublayer to generate the physical signals, indicate the arrival of the data unit, and coordinate the flow of data. Besides these primitives, which perform the activities associated with the transfer of the data, the two other primitives shown in the figure transfer the status of the line signals during active operations.

MANCHESTER SIGNAL ENCODING

Ultimately, the signals generated by the PLS sublayer pass through the 15-pin drop cable connectng the PLS and MAU sublayers and then through the medium. The 15-pin cable supports four circuits, one circuit each for data signal in, data signal out, control signal in, and control signal out. Absent from this multicircuit arrangement is a separate circuit for timing the data. By a special encoding scheme called **Manchester encoding,** which embeds clocking information within the data signals, it becomes unnecessary to supply separate timing signals.

Manchester encoding represents each bit to be transferred by one of three signal forms to denote the numerical values 0 and 1 and the nondata IDL symbol. Figure 8.12 illustrates the waveforms used to encode these data values together with the embedded timing information. Each data period contains two signaling levels. Zero (0) starts with a high during the first half of the signal period and then makes a transition to a low to complete the signal. The inverse of this pattern, starting with a low and ending with a high, represents the value 1. In both of these waveforms, the transition in the middle of each signal provides the bit timing. The IDL, on the other hand, has a high in both halves of the signaling period and thus has no transition in the middle of the bit period. Normally, this does not present a timing problem, since only a couple of IDL bits are required to mark the end of transmission.

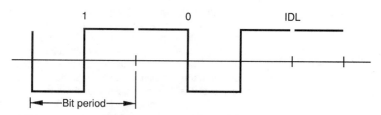

FIGURE 8.12 Manchester encoding.

Exercises

8.2 A CSMA/CD configuration model consists of five segments of coaxial cable of 500 m each and transmits at a data rate of 10 Mbps using minimum frame lengths of 512 bits. Explain the apparent discrepancy between this configuration and the calculations shown in Example 8.1.

8.3 Discuss why the performance of a CSMA/CD LAN seriously degrades (i.e., become unstable) when the amount of traffic exceeds a relatively low percentage of the network's load capacity. (see Appendix E).

8.4 When a station has sensed a collision, it delays its attempt to retransmit in order to avoid another collision. The standard prescribes the amount of delay in units of time intervals called the slot time, which is largely determined by the round-trip propagation time of a signal and an added time used to ensure that the signal has been heard (called the jam size). Each station acts to backoff a random number of slot times after each collision before it attempts to retransmit. To give each station a fair chance to transmit, the standard specifies that each station's backoff be decided by a random number r such that $0 \le r < 2^{\min(n,\ 10)}$, where n is the number of times the retransmission has failed up to maximum value of 10, after which retransmission is abandoned (called truncated binary exponential backoff). Given a slot time of 5000 bit times, what would be the maximum amount of time in the worst-case scenario after the transmitter first tries to transmit and the receiver hears the message?

8.5 In addition to the backoff process given in exercise 8.4, the standard prescribes that the algorithm used to generate the random number r be designed so as to minimize the correlation between the numbers generated by any two stations. What is the purpose of this prescription?

8.6 Explain why CSMA/CD is not recommended for real-time applications.

8.7 Show the Manchester waveforms for the following bit patterns:
(a) 0000 0000
(b) 1111 1111
(c) 1010 10 IDL IDL
(d) 0011 01 IDL IDL

Notice that when a 0 follows a 0, a 1 follows a 1, and the IDL symbol follows a 0; a transition occurs between the two signals. This extraneous transition, however, occurs at the beginning rather than the middle of the bit period so that the integrity of the data and timing information is preserved.

8.4   TOKEN-PASSING BUS ACCESS METHOD

TOKEN-PASSING BUS LAYER SUBSTRUCTURE

Like CSMA/CD, the token-passing bus access method communicates by broadcasting the signals generated at each station to all stations attached to the medium. The medium serves as a common bus through which the attached stations can transmit their respective signals. The **token,** a specific control frame, circulates sequentially from station to station, giving each station the exclusive right to transmit on the bus. When a station receives the token, it may transmit any data frame it has ready for transmission; and after it has completed transmission, or if it had no data frame ready for transmission, it passes the token to the next station in the ring.

Figure 8.13 illustrates the arrangement for circulating the token among the stations attached to the common bus. The broken line connects the stations into a logical

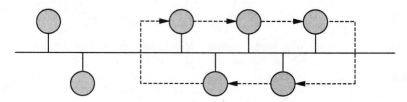

FIGURE 8.13 Token bus logical ring.

ring according to their turn in receiving the token. In a **logical ring,** a station's successor does not have to be its nearest neighbor, and in fact, the configuration of the ring may be changed during the network's operations by patching stations into or out of the ring independent of their location. Moreover, as implied by the figure, stations that have no need to transmit, such as printers, can be part of the network without being part of the logical ring.

    While active in the ring structure, each station must keep track of three addresses: its own, that of the next station to receive the token, and that of the previous station, from which the token was received. To put order into a potentially chaotic situation, the token passes from one station to the next in descending numerical order of their addresses, except that the station with the lowest address passes the token to the station with the highest address. For example, if there are three stations in the ring, with addresses 30, 25, and 20, then station 30 passes the token to station 25, station 25 passes the token to station 20, and station 20 passes the token back to station 30, where the cycle repeats.

    Figure 8.14 gives the layer configuration for the token-passing bus access method as structured by the 802 project. The standard defines the mechanisms embedded into the equipment below the LLC sublayer: the MAC sublayer for controlling the medium access; the physical layer for generating the physical signals; and

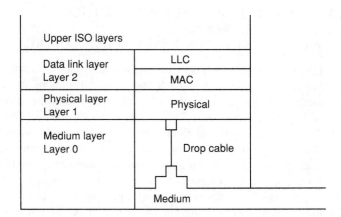

FIGURE 8.14 Token-passing bus layer structure.

the medium layer, designated as layer 0, which describes the characteristics of the communication bus. Layer 0, although not part of the ISO layer model, has been introduced into the standard for ensuring the interoperability of the physical layer entities.

The functions performed by the MAC sublayer are distributed among five machines, namely, the interface machine, the access control machine, the receive machine, the transmit machine, and the regenerative repeater machine. Figure 8.15 shows the interconnections among these five machines. By this modular partitioning of the functions, the operations performed on the data units as they pass through the MAC sublayer can be tracked.

The interface machine, as the name implies, interfaces the LLC sublayer with the MAC sublayer. It provides the mechanisms for interpreting the incoming service primitives from the LLC sublayer and generating the outgoing service primitives back to the LLC sublayer. Besides these services, mechanisms are included to handle the priority of the data frames (i.e., service class) and, when appropriate, to buffer the data units of different priorities into separate queues on a first-in-first-out (FIFO) basis.

The first order of business of the access control machine is to handle the token used to control the right to transmit. In addition, this machine provides the protocol procedures for:

- Recovering the ring structure when a station leaves the ring either intentionally or through a node failure

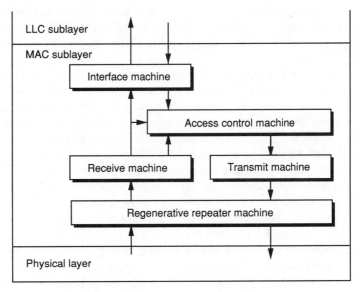

FIGURE 8.15 Internal structure of the MAC sublayer.

- Establishing the membership of a new station into the ring structure
- Initializing the logical ring

Procedures for handling these tasks are complicated by the fact that no station is designated to coordinate the stations participating in the ring structure and each station must contribute equally to accomplishing the ring's maintenance tasks. Without these procedures, the ring would collapse and communications would cease.

Three types of control data units passed between peer entities support the crucial activities of the access control machine, namely, the *token* control frame, the *solicit-successor* control frame, and the *who-follows* control frame. Normally, when a station passes the token, it gives up its right to access the medium until all the other stations have had a chance to transmit their information. However, a station may temporarily delegate its right to transmit to another station and then regain control of the token after the delegated station has finished transmitting. The solicit-successor control frame is used to initialize the logical ring or restructure it when a new station wants to enter the network. The who-follows control frame is used to restructure the logical ring when a station drops out of the network either intentionally or through a malfunction. The solicit-successor and who-follows frames keep the bus free of other traffic while the stations delegate among themselves the order for the right to transmit (i.e., the order in which each station receives the token).

After a station passes the token to its successor, it listens for the station receiving the token to send a valid frame. When the station passing the token hears a valid frame, it can assume that the token has passed correctly. If after sending the token the line remains silent, then the station that has passed the token attempts to pass the token again. If the line still remains silent, then the station assumes that its successor has failed, and it attempts to reestablish the ring by sending a who-follows control frame.

An example will illustrate how the ring can be restructured when a station fails. Assume three stations in a ring with addresses 30, 25, and 20. Normally, station 25 would receive the token from station 30, and would respond by either transmitting any data it has ready for transmission or passing the token to its successor. However, if station 25 does not respond, then station 30, hearing silence on the line, assumes that station 25 might have failed, tries again, then takes it upon itself to reestablish the ring by sending out a who-follows-25 control frame. Station 20 knows that its predecessor station was 25, so it sets its predecessor station to 30 and responds with an instruction to station 30 to set its next station to 20. Having reestablished the ring, station 30 continues by sending the token to station 20.

From the scenario we have just presented, it may appear that when a station wants to patch itself out of the ring, it may do so simply by remaining silent after its predecessor has attempted to send the token. Indeed, this is the case; however, a more orderly procedure is for the station wishing to leave the ring to take it upon itself to restructure the ring by sending a control frame giving the address of the new successor. In the preceding example, station 25 could receive the token, send a control frame to station 30 to reset its successor station to station 20, pass the token to station 20, and then immediately leave the ring.

A station that is not in the ring waits, listening for a solicit-successor control frame from a node that does not know its successor. Suppose, for example, station 25 wants to reenter the ring. It waits until station 30 sends a solicit-successor control frame that contains station 30's own address and that of its previous successor (i.e., station 20). Station 25 sets its successor to station 20 and can now contend for the token by responding to station 30. If successful (i.e., if no other station between 30 and 25 contends for the token), station 30 will respond by setting its successor to 25 and sending station 25 the token.

To initialize or reinitialize the ring, all stations listen for a period of inactivity on the bus. The stations then contend for the token through a complex algorithm. The station that wins the token can then start to reestablish the ring using the procedure for allowing new stations to enter the ring, whereby the nodes put themselves in numerical order.

When a station has the token, giving it the right to transmit, the access control machine forwards any frame ready for transmission to the transmit machine. The transmit machine formats the frame from the data passed from the access control machine, but unlike the CSMA/CD method, the transmit machine of the MAC sublayer, rather than the physical layer, brackets the information with start and end delimiters and adds the proper amount of preamble. The frame is organized into octets and is passed to the physical layer, symbol by symbol, for conversion into physical signals and transmission over the medium.

Although the transmitted data are still organized into octets, several different symbols are used to encode the bits, depending on the octet being transmitted. In particular, the alphabet consists of 0 and 1 for representing binary data, a nondata symbol used in conjunction with 0's and 1's for encoding the start-of-frame and end-of-transmission delimiters, a pad-idle symbol used for generating the preamble, and a silent symbol used for separating frames transmitted by the same station. Ultimately, the physical layer generates different physical signals for each of these symbols.

The receive machine accepts the symbols from the physical layer and reconstructs the frames. The physical layer uses one additional symbol to indicate the reception of a bad signal. After validating the frame, the receive machine passes the information to the access control or interface machine, depending on the control information embedded in the frame.

The regenerative repeater machine is optional and need not be included in all stations. A LAN segment can span only a limited distance before the physical signals must be regenerated. When extended beyond these distances and to avoid implementing the complete MAC sublayer, the regenerative repeater machine in cooperation with the transmit and receiver machines gives an economical solution to this problem.

TOKEN-PASSING BUS DATA FRAME FORMAT

Figure 8.16 gives the arrangement of the frame fields as formatted by the transmit machine and passed to the physical layer for transmission over the communication medium. The preamble allows the receiver machine to lock in on the level and phase of the received signals. However, whether receiving the silence or the preamble signals, a sufficient amount of time must be allowed to elapse between frames to permit the receiver machine to complete processing the previous frame. Here are some salient feature of the fields:

- The preamble is composed of pad-idle symbols whose representation depends on the modulation scheme and the data rate chosen for transmission.

- The start-of-frame delimiter starts the frame with a uniquely recognizable pattern (nondata, nondata, 0, nondata, nondata, 0, 0, 0).

- The frame control gives the code whereby frames can be distinguished according to their use as MAC control frames or LLC data frames.

- The destination address is formatted, as for CSMA/CD, into two or six octets.

- The source address is formatted like the destination address.

- The data field contains the information the MAC sublayer transmits on behalf of the LLC sublayer or it may contain control information generated internally by the MAC sublayer.

- The frame check sequence consists of a cyclic redundancy code using the same generator polynomial as used for CSMA/CD.

- The end-of-transmission delimiter is similar to the start-of-frame delimiter, ex-

Preamble (at least one octet)
Start-of-frame delimiter (one octet)
Frame control (one octet)
Destination address (two or six octets)
Source address (two or six octets)
Data (an arbitrary number of octets)
Frame check sequence (four octets)
End-of-transmission delimiter (one octet)

FIGURE 8.16 Token-passing bus data frame format.

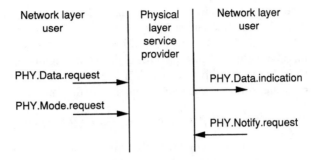

FIGURE 8.17 Service primitives between MAC sublayers and the physical layer.

cept that the first two 0's are replaced by 1's and the last two 0's may be either 0 or 1 (nondata, nondata, 1, nondata, nondata, 1, 0 or 1, 0 or 1).

SERVICE PRIMITIVES

Figure 8.17 and Table 8.5 give the communication primitives for passing information between the MAC sublayer and the physical layer. The data pass in single-symbol units, using any of the legitimate symbols: 0, 1, nondata, pad-idle, or silence. In the

TABLE 8.5

PARAMETERS ASSOCIATED WITH
SERVICES THAT THE PHYSICAL LAYER
PROVIDES THE MAC SUBLAYER

	symbol	mode
PHY.Data.request	X	
PHY.Data.indication	X	
PHY.Mode.request		X
PHY.Notify.request		

Parameters:
symbol—specifying the symbol
        used within an octet
mode—indicating whether MAC entity
        shall act as a regenerative
        repeater or not

case of the indication primitive, the bad-signal symbol may be added to the list that is used to indicate one MAC symbol period during which inappropriate signaling was received. The PHY.Notify primitive notifies the physical layer that the end-of-transmission delimiter has just been detected, signifying the end of the frame. The PHY.Mode primitive serves as a special command to switch the role of a station back and forth between an originating station and a repeater station.

TOKEN-PASSING BUS SIGNALING TECHNIQUES

At the physical layer, three different techniques have been defined for generating the physical signals, and with each technique a corresponding medium layer with suitable characteristics for transmitting the signals using the token-passing bus access method. Table 8.6 summarizes some features associated with the different pairs of layers, which in turn dictate the functional, electrical, and mechanical characteristics of each. The following paragraphs will highlight these differences from an operational viewpoint.

Phase-continuous FSK is a form of FSK whereby the transition smoothly changes between signaling frequencies as opposed to changing frequencies by discrete switching. Two signaling frequencies at 3.75 and 6.25 MHz and the absence of either frequency are used to represent the symbols. Transmission occurs over a single baseband channel operating at a rate of 1 Mbps.

The basic network topology consists of a single coaxial cable routed to all the stations. A very short drop cable connects the equipment at a station to a simple line tap on the transmission cable. To extend the length of the transmission line beyond that normally allowed for unassisted signals, a regenerative repeater can be used. Such a device restores the signal's amplitude, waveform, and timing so as to preserve the integrity of the signals during transmission. In addition to extending the distance between stations, the regenerative repeater can also provide branching to other network segments, allowing the formation of a tree-structured network as illustrated in Figure 8.18.

TABLE 8.6
SIGNALING TECHNIQUES AND MEDIUM ACCESS
USED WITH TOKEN-PASSING BUS ACCESS METHOD

SIGNALING TECHNIQUE	BUS	CHANNEL	DATA RATE
Phase-continuous FSK	Baseband	Single	1 Mbps
Phase-coherent FSK	Baseband	Single	5 or 10 Mbps
Multilevel AM/PSK	Broadband	Dual	1, 5, or 10 Mbps

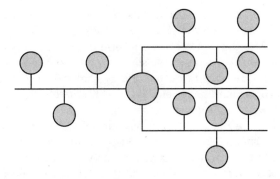

FIGURE 8.18 Tree-structured network using regenerative repeaters.

In **phase-coherent FSK,** the transitions between the two signaling frequencies occur only when the sinusoidal waveform makes a zero crossing so as to prevent any sudden signal jumps. This signaling method operating over a single baseband channel can be supported at two data rates, one at 5 Mbps and the other at 10 Mbps. At the 5 Mbps data rate, the two tones at 5 and 10 MHz or the absence of either tone represents the symbols received from the MAC sublayer. At the 10 Mbps data rate, the tones are at 10 and 20 MHz. To maintain a compatible period with the data rates, signaling periods are integrally related to each other, applying a full period for the lower tone and a half period for the higher tone.

The cable and construction used for the network are similar to those used by the cable TV industry. A smaller-diameter, flexible cable connects the station equipment to the line. Like the topology used with phase-continuous FSK, a regenerative repeater may extend the length of the line to prevent signal degradation due to line losses or to provide for branching. However, even for short lines, a regenerative repeater may be necessary to restore the signals when the number of stations exceeds the number permitted by the electrical characteristics of the line.

A simpler component that may also be used for branching is the line splitter (Figure 8.19). The splitter consists of one input port and two output ports. The signal

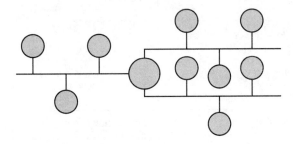

FIGURE 8.19 Line splitter used for branching.

power is not regenerated, but simply divided into equal parts and passed to the separate branches using passive elements.

Multilevel AM/PSK is a form of modulation whereby the carrier is both amplitude modulated and phase-shift keyed to conserve on bandwidth. A set of three pulse shapes are used to encode the symbol, which for convenience can be called high level, medium level, and low level. The physical and medium layers specified for use with this signaling technique operate on dual channels (either on the same or different cables) by broadband transmission and allow a variety of data rates.

Table 8.7 summarizes and compares the encoding of the symbols by the rudimentary physical signals generated by the three signaling techniques. Implicit in each of these techniques is the ability to extract timing information. With the AM/PSK technique, a scrambler randomizes long sequences of identical symbols by dividing the data with a generator polynomial that guarantees a better distribution of spectral components in the signals. A corresponding descrambler is used to recover the data. While the three physical signals encode each symbol in each of these techniques, the two FSK techniques divide the bit period into two parts, a front end and back end, and use a combination of these two physical signal parts for each symbol.

Like the other LAN technologies, the medium layer for the broadband bus utilizes CATV technology to take advantage of proved commercial products such as tap connectors, amplifiers, and power supplies. A single cable or a dual cable may be used, depending on the amount of communications needed to support an enterprise. The channel assignments are themselves subject to other national standards. Figure 8.20 illustrates the allocation nomenclature of one particular channel configuration known as a **single-cable mid-split** configuration.

TABLE 8.7
SYMBOL ENCODING BY PHYSICAL SIGNALS

SYMBOL	PHASE-CONTINUOUS FSK	MULTILEVEL AM/PSK	PHASE-COHERENT FSK
0	High tone, low tone	Low level	High tone, high tone
1	Low tone, high tone	High level	Low tone, low tone
Nondata	Symbols occur in pairs: low tone, low tone; high tone, high tone	Medium level	Symbols occur in pairs: high tone, low tone; low tone, high tone
Pad-idle	Symbols occur in pairs: low tone, high tone; high tone, low tone	Symbols occur in pairs: high level, low level	Low tone, low tone
Silence	No tone, no tone	Four-symbol sequence: medium level, medium level, low level, high level	No tone, no tone

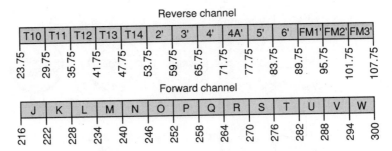

FIGURE 8.20 CATV single-cable mid-split channel assignments into 6 MHz channels.

For phase-continuous FSK and phase-coherent FSK signaling methods, a single channel along an omnidirectional bus propagates the signals in either direction. However, the multilevel AM/PSK signaling method uses two simplex channels (transmitting in opposite directions) that are offset from each other by 192.25 MHz. The lower-frequency channel carries the signals generated by any active stations to a common node, called the **head-end remodulator;** and the head-end remodulator retransmits the signals back to the receiving stations using the higher-frequency channel (Figure 8.21). The particular channels assigned for LAN operations depend on the data rate according to the following scheme (see Figure 8.20 for channel nomenclature):

- For a 10 Mbps data rate, two 12 MHz channels are formed by combining the adjacent channels P and Q, and 3′ and 4′.

- For a 5 Mbps data rate, the P channel is paired with the 3′ channel; or the Q channel is paired with the 4′ channel.

- For a 1 Mbps data rate, the P, Q, 3′, and 4′ channels are subdivided into four subchannels each; and any of these subchannels may be paired with the subchannel separated from it by 192.25 MHz.

- For a dual-cable system, channels of the same frequency are paired; that is, P with P, Q with Q, and so on.

- For multiple LANs on the same cable system, all but the above-named channels are used by assigning channels separated from each other by 192.25 MHz.

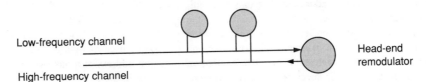

FIGURE 8.21 Directional transmission used by a broadband bus.

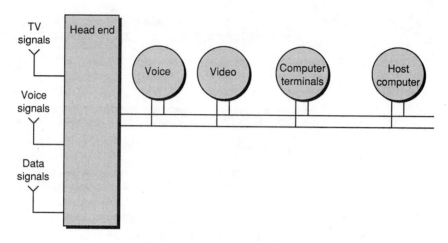

FIGURE 8.22   Diverse applications served by
a coaxial cable.

The available spectrum on the cable system makes possible the assignment of multiple channels, which in turn allows different forms of communications, such as video, voice, data, and multiple LANs, to coexist on different channels on the same cable. Figure 8.22 depicts the role of the head-end remodulator in such a system.

Exercises

8.8 Four stations whose addresses are 20, 30, 40, and 50 are connected to a token-passing bus.
(a) Give the scenario that would normally be followed when station 30 leaves the ring because of a malfunction.
(b) Give the scenario that would normally be followed when station 30 leaves the ring intentionally. What are the advantages of this procedure over that used in part (a)?

8.9 With the solicit-successor frame, the sending station gives the range of addresses that may respond. When several stations respond to this solicitation, the sending station hears "noise" on the line resulting from the garbled frames, assumes that more than one station has responded, and sends a resolve-contention frame to identify a single successor. The resolve-contention frame is followed by four time slots during which a potential successor may respond. Each sta-

tion wishing to respond chooses a 2-bit value (i.e., 0, 1, 2, or 3) based on its address and enters its response in that time slot. However, if it hears a response to an earlier time slot, it eliminates itself from arbitration. Go through a procedure to determine the successor station when contention occurs in response to a solicit-successor frame.

8.10 Two different solicit successor frames are specified in the standard, called solicit successor 1 and solicit successor 2. The solicit successor 1 frame has one time slot that allows any station whose address lies between solicitor's address and the destination address of the token to respond. The solicit successor 2 frame uses its own address as the source and destination address and has two time slots that allow any station in the system to respond. The solicit successor 2 frame is used by the station that has the lowest station address and the solicit 1 successor frame is used

Exercises *(continued)*

by the other station in the logical ring. Go through an algorithm to determine the successor when such frames are sent.

8.11 The recovery of the clocking information depends on the signaling technique used. For phase-continuous FSK, the receiving station recovers the clock from the transitions generated by the Manchester encoding; for the phase-coherent FSK, the receiving station recovers the clock from the zero crossings in the signals; and for multilevel AM/PSK, the receiving station recovers the clock from the level tran-

sitions within the signals. Using various signal patterns, graphically demonstrate how timing is recovered by each of these signaling techniques.

8.12 The token-passing bus method is recommended when stations need a deterministic schedule for transmitting many short messages, and CSMA/CD is recommended when stations need to transmit long messages sporadically. Discuss the basis of these recommendations.†

---

†Class discussion exercise.

8.5   TOKEN RING ACCESS METHOD

TOKEN RING LAYER SUBSTRUCTURE

Unlike the token-passing bus access method, the token ring access method connects the active stations into a **physical ring** rather than a logical ring. Information flows in only one direction from station to station. When a station has the token, it may start to circulate any data it has ready for transmission. Each station repeats the information it receives by regenerating it, bit by bit, and passing it to the next station in sequence, while at the same time copying and processing any information destined for itself. The station that has transmitted the information retains the token until the information has been returned uncorrupted. After removing the transmitted message from circulation, the originating station sends the token to the next station in sequence.

Figure 8.23 illustrates the idea of the ring structure. Physically, each station is linked to two neighbors, one on the downstream side of the direction of communications and the other on the upstream side. A failure in any station makes the entire ring inoperative. Each station, in addition to containing the mechanisms for normal operations, contains a monitoring function that can, by sensing the traffic in the ring, isolate a failure in the medium or in a particular station. In the event of a failure, or when a station needs to enter or leave the ring, service commands are provided to purge the old token and restructure the ring.

Although the token normally passes the right to transmit sequentially from station to station in a round-robin fashion, a station may assign the token a priority level whereby only those stations that have information at that priority level are given the right to transmit. Priority assignments are made by agreement among network users, and perhaps more importantly, by application; for example, digital voice and other real-time applications take precedence over other less demanding applications.

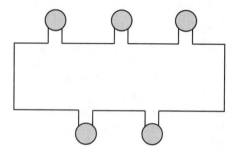

FIGURE 8.23 Token ring access method ring structure.

When a station has priority data to transmit, it can initiate a request for a priority token. Unless some intervening station requests a higher priority, the next token the station receives allows the station to transmit all information it has at that priority level before relinquishing the token to the next station. As the request for a token priority passes each station, the station modifies the request with its own priority whenever it is higher. The mechanisms at a station operate such that when a station changes the token's priority, it also keeps track of the previous requests for lower-level priorities so that each station can restore the token's priority in a fair and orderly manner.

Figure 8.24 shows the layer substructuring as modeled for the token ring access method. Below the physical layer is the mechanical and electrical interconnections between the station equipment and the communication cable. The medium interface connector has four pins for attaching two twisted pairs, one for the receiving circuit and the other for the transmitting circuit. The connector may be attached to the

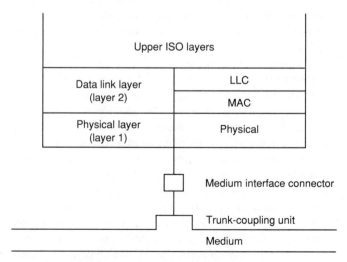

FIGURE 8.24 Token ring layer structure.

station equipment directly or on a pig tail as shown in the figure. At the other end, the connecting cable couples the station equipment to the communication line through the trunk-coupling unit. When a station needs to be removed or bypassed, it may be simply disconnected, which causes the trunk-coupling unit to automatically close the line and reestablish the line's continuity. These connections can support either a 1 Mbps data rate over a 1 MHz bandwidth line or a 4 Mbps data rate over a 4 MHz bandwidth line.

As information passes through the layer structure, the MAC sublayer encapsulates the data it transfers on behalf of the LLC sublayer or the data that is internally generated within the MAC entities and then passes these data units to the physical layer, bit by bit. Upon receiving each bit, the physical layer generates an appropriate physical signal for transmission over the medium.

The alphabet consists of four symbols, two representing data values 0 and 1 and two representing different forms of nondata values distinguished by the letters J and K. The nondata symbols always occur in pairs in the sequence JK. The reason for this will become obvious shortly.

TOKEN RING DATA FRAME FORMAT

Figure 8.25 shows the field structure of the frames transferred between nodes. The transmitter sends the fields in the order depicted in the figure, starting with the most significant bit first. Between frames, a continuous stream of 0's and 1's are transmit-

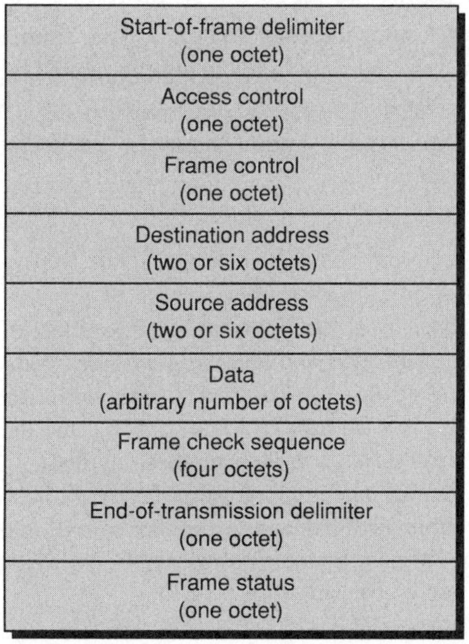

Start-of-frame delimiter (one octet)
Access control (one octet)
Frame control (one octet)
Destination address (two or six octets)
Source address (two or six octets)
Data (arbitrary number of octets)
Frame check sequence (four octets)
End-of-transmission delimiter (one octet)
Frame status (one octet)

FIGURE 8.25 Token ring data frame format.

ted so that the nodes are not misled by noise into diagnosing a false failure. The following describes the frame fields and their functions:

- The start-of-frame delimiter uses a unique bit pattern composed of 0's and non-data symbols, specifically, JK0JK000, to indicate the start of the frame. This field and the end-of-transmission delimiter are the only fields using nondata symbols.

- The access control indicates whether the token or an information frame is being communicated. The token consists of three fields: the start-of-frame delimiter, the access field, and the end-of-transmission field. Within the access field, two subfields of 3 bits each are assigned to the token priority and the request for upgrading the priority to a higher level (up to eight priority levels).

- The frame control gives further details on the substructuring of the frame and, specifically, whether it is directed to the LLC or the MAC sublayer.

- The destination address is formatted into two or six octets.

- The source address, consisting of two or six octets, is formatted like the destination address.

- The data field contains the information the MAC sublayer transmits on behalf of the LLC sublayer or it may contain control information generated by the MAC sublayer.

- The frame check sequence (four octets) consists of a cyclic redundancy code using the same generator polynomial as used for CSMA/CD.

- The end-of-transmission delimiter indicates the end of the frame. This field and the start-of-frame delimiter are the only fields using the nondata symbols. In this particular case, the first 6 bits in the field are the sequence JK1JK1.

- The frame status code indicates the partial status of the frame as its passes through the stations.

SERVICE PRIMITIVES

The MAC sublayer uses the services of the physical layer to transfer its information between peer entities using the primitives shown in Figure 8.26. Table 8.8 gives the parameters associated with these primitives. The MAC sublayer passes the data symbol by symbol using the four-symbol alphabet 0, 1, J, and K, and the physical layer generates an appropriate physical signal for each of these symbols. Upon reception of the physical signal at the remote site, the physical layer notifies and passes the decoded signal to the MAC sublayer by the indication primitive. The confirmation primitive synchronizes the flow of data by alerting the MAC sublayer to pass another symbol or by confirming the end of transmission.

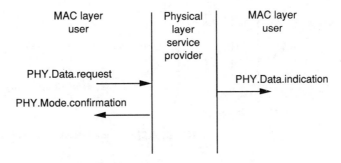

FIGURE 8.26 Service primitives between MAC sublayers and the physical layer.

DIFFERENTIAL MANCHESTER ENCODING

The physical layer employs a scheme called **differential Manchester encoding** for converting the symbols into physical signals. This scheme has the advantage of encoding the four symbols with a two-state circuit and also embedding timing information within the generated signals. Figure 8.27 illustrates the scheme.

TABLE 8.8

PARAMETERS ASSOCIATED WITH SERVICES THAT THE PHYSICAL LAYER PROVIDES THE MAC SUBLAYER

	symbol	transmission.status
PHY.Data.request	X	
PHY.Data.indication	X	
PHY.Data.confirmation		X

Parameters:

symbol—specifying the symbol used within octet

transmission.status—indicating the completion of transmission

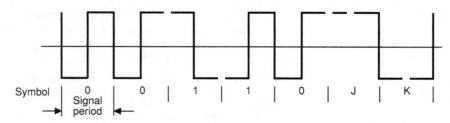

| Symbol | 0 Signal period | 0 | 1 | 1 | 0 | J | K |

FIGURE 8.27 Differential Manchester signaling scheme.

First it is noted that a line transition occurs in the middle of the signal period for each data signal (i.e., 0 and 1). As before, the transition provides the timing information. To represent the data values, a transition also occurs at the beginning of the signal period for the value 0, and no transition occurs at the beginning of the signal period for the value 1. On the other hand, for the nondata symbols, no line transition occurs in the middle of the signal period. A transition occurs at the beginning for the K symbol, and no transition occurs at the beginning for the J symbol; but since the nondata symbols always occur in pairs and in the sequence JK, the encoding scheme always ensures at least one line transition per signal pair. Table 8.9 summarizes the transitions for the various symbols.

Exercises

8.13 Why can't the token-passing bus method use a logically simpler medium interface connector to remove or insert a station into the network?

8.14 Show the differential Manchester waveforms for the following bit patterns:
(a)   0000 0000
(b)   1111 1111
(c)   1010 1010
(d)   0011 0110
(e)   JK0J K000
(f)   JK1J K100

TABLE 8.9

POINTS OF SIGNAL TRANSITION FOR DIFFERENTIAL MANCHESTER SIGNALING

	AT MIDDLE OF SIGNAL PERIOD	AT BEGINNING OF SIGNAL PERIOD
J	No	No
K	No	Yes
0	Yes	No
1	Yes	Yes

Exercises *(continued)*

8.15 Why must the same station that raised the to-ken's priority return the priority to its original level?

8.16 The competitor of the token ring method for the transfer of large, office automation files in CSMA/CD, and for the transfer of real-time data on the shop floor is the token-passing broadband bus. Compare

these three accessing methods for these applications.

8.17 The access field has two 3-bit subfields giving the ring service priority P and a reservation request for a token of appropriate priority R. Develop an algorithm using these subfields for raising and lowering the priority level of the token.

SUMMARY

Data communications principles that are an inherent part of local area networks have been examined through a family of related implementation standards. These standards partition the functions assigned to the data link layer over two sublayers consisting of a logical link control (LLC) upper sublayer and a medium access control (MAC) lower sublayer. Three different accessing methods have been defined for the MAC sublayer, all of which use a common LLC sublayer. Each of these standards also gives guidance for implementing the signaling and mechanical connections of the physical layer and the characteristics of the medium that is applicable.

The LLC protocol data unit has been organized into octet fields that include destination and source address fields. The primitives used to transport these data units depend on whether a guarantee for their delivery is essential for the proper functioning of the nodes. Unacknowledged connectionless services, the simpler of the two services, provide the means by which nodes can exchange information without first establishing a data link connection. For connection-oriented services, the sets of primitives must be expanded to establish and maintain connections, sequence the communication frames, and augment the error control facilities.

CSMA/CD operates by broadcasting the messages to all stations in the network whereby each station hears every message transmitted but accepts only those messages addressed to itself. When a node needs to transmit, it listens for the line to become free of other traffic before initiating transmission. However, because of the delay in transferring the physical signals, two or more stations may sense the line free of other traffic and initiate transmission, which will ultimately cause a collision. When a collision occurs, the transmitting stations wait a random amount of time to hopefully avoid another collision and then attempt to retransmit.

The token-passing bus access method structures the nodes into a logical ring whereby a specific control frame, the token, circulates sequentially from one station to the next. When a station receives the token, it has the exclusive right to transmit any data frame it has ready for transmission. Like the CSMA/CD method, the signals generated are broadcast to all stations attached to the common bus. The procedures for initiating and maintaining the ring structure are complicated by the fact that no station is designated to coordinate the stations participating in the ring structure and each station must contribute equally to accomplishing the ring's maintenance tasks through the use of special control data units.

Unlike the token-passing bus access method, the token ring access method connects the active stations into a physical rather than a logical ring. When a station receives the token, it circulates any data it has ready for transmission to the next connected station. Each station regenerates and passes the data it receives to the next station in sequence, while keeping a copy of the data destined to itself. The station that had first transmitted the information retains the token until the information has been returned uncorrupted. After removing the transmitted message from circulation, the originating station sends the token to the next station in sequence. A station may assign the token a priority level whereby only those stations that have information at that priority level are given the right to transmit. When a station needs to be removed from the ring, it may simply be disconnected, which causes the trunk-coupling unit to which it had been connected to automatically close the line and reestablish the line's continuity.

The partitioning of the physical layer in all of these methods is partially motivated by the physical separation of components needed at a node. The MAC sublayer passes the encapsulated data to the physical layer in single-bit units from an alphabet of 0, 1, and other symbols used to identify the beginning and ending of the frame. Each standard identifies how the physical layer generates signals with embedded timing information.

KEY TERMS

Logical link control (LLC)
Medium access control (MAC)
Carrier sense multiple access with
    collision detection
Token-passing bus access
Token ring access
Unacknowledged connectionless service
Connection-oriented service
Physical signaling (PLS)
Medium access unit (MAU)

Manchester encoding
Token
Logical ring
Phase-continuous FSK
Phase-coherent FSK
Multilevel AM/PSK
Single-cable mid-split
Head-end remodulator
Physical ring
Differential Manchester encoding

SUGGESTED READINGS

Chorafas, Dimitris N. *Designing and Implementing Local Area Networks*. New York: McGraw-Hill, 1984.

Derfler, F. J. *Microcomputer Data Communication Systems*. Englewood Cliffs, N.J.: Prentice-Hall, 1982.

Green, Paul E. Jr. *Computer Network Architectures and Protocols*. New York: Plenum, 1982.

Halsall, F. *Introduction to Data Communications and Computer Networks*. Reading, Mass.: Addison-Wesley, 1985.

Hammond, Joseph L. and O'Reilly, Peter J. P. *Performance Analysis of Local Area Networks*. Reading, Mass.: Addison-Wesley, 1986.

IEEE Std 802.2-1985 (ISO DIS 8802/2), Local Area Network Standard—Logical Link Control.

IEEE Std 802.3-1985 (ISO DIS 8802/3), Local Area Network Standard—Carrier Sense Multiple Access with Collision Detection.

IEEE Std 802.4-1985 (ISO DIS 8802/4, Local Area Network Standard—Token-Passing Bus Access Method.

IEEE Std 802.5-1985 (ISO DIS 8802/5), Local Area Network Standard—Token Ring Access Method.

Kuo, F. F. *Protocols & Techniques for Data Communication Networks*. Englewood Cliffs, N.J.: Prentice-Hall, 1981.

Schwartz, Mischa. *Telecommunication Networks*. Reading, Mass.: Addison-Wesley, 1987.

Stallings, William. *Data and Computer Communications*. New York: Macmillan, 1985.

Tanenbaum, Andrew S. *Computer Networks*. Englewood Cliffs, N.J.: Prentice-Hall, 1981.

CHAPTER 9

INDUSTRIAL DATA COMMUNICATIONS STANDARDS

For this great blessing we are wholly
indebted to systems and abstracts in
which the modern fathers of learning, like
prudent usurers, spent their sweat for the
ease of us their children.

JONATHAN SWIFT

"A TALE OF A TUB"

239

9.1   INTERNETWORKING

PRODUCT COMPATIBILITY

Few vendors, if any, can provide the full range of user products. Moreover, users want to avoid the exclusive use of a single vendor's approach to products so that they can remain free to select the best products they need regardless of the manufacturer. This multisource procurement philosophy fosters a competitive market through which a better, more economical, and wider selection of products can be made available. An open systems environment provides the framework for developing products that can be interconnected through standards.

The ISO OSI model, while not itself an implementation standard, assigns the communication functions to specific layers for which individual voluntary standards for open systems can be developed. However, not all standards that conform to the model are new. Many recommendations that had been proposed prior to the formulation of the model can still be used. This discussion focuses on some practical standards (both old and new) at the lower layers of the architectural hierarchy that have been built into a wide variety of existing products or on which the newer data networks have been planned.

Contrary to popular belief, products based on standards, even on the same standard, may still be incompatible. Voluntary standards are formulated as a grab bag of features that leaves to the vendors' discretion the options they want to implement. The ISO OSI model, however, gives a modular approach for developing compatible products and implicitly gives guidelines for interconnecting incompatible products. These guidelines can be summarized as follows:

- All seven layers must be implemented at an end node.

- Not all seven layers need to be implemented at intermediate nodes.

- The implementation of a layer at a node requires that all layers below that layer be implemented.

- The distribution of communication functions in proprietary systems may differ from how they are assigned to the layers in the ISO model and may differ from each other.

- Nodes whose layers conform to the ISO model may still be incompatible if their protocols are based on different standards or on different options of the same standard.

- When two nodes are incompatible at layer N, an intermediate node between the two nodes is required to convert all the protocols up to and including layer N from one node to the other.

PROTOCOL CONVERTER

Figure 9.1 illustrates two cooperating end nodes whose protocols differ at the third layer. The end nodes, say, a terminal and a host computer, must both house all seven

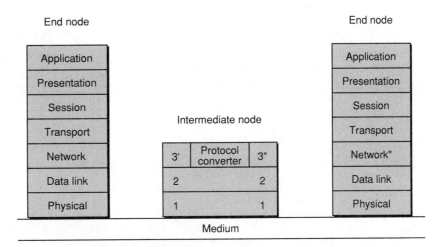

FIGURE 9.1 Protocol converter intermediate node.

communication layers to support the application. The layers below layer 3 may or may not be compatible. However, since the nodes are incompatible at layer 3, a **protocol converter** must include the three bottom layers to convert the protocol of one node to that of the other.

Information flows from the upper layers to the lower layers, through the communication medium, and then up to the three layers of the protocol converter. The data converter repackages the data units at layer 3 into the format needed by the receiving node and then transfers the data down the layer structure, through the medium, and up the layer structure of the cooperating node.

CLASSIFICATION OF INTERNETWORKING DEVICES

Consider the placement of the protocol converter between two homogeneous networks, networks whose nodes conform to a common set of protocols. Any two cooperating end nodes must be compatible at all seven layers. When devices attached

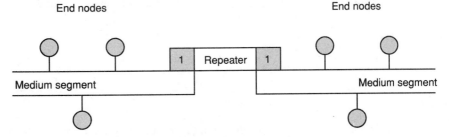

FIGURE 9.2 Repeater connection of multiple communication segments.

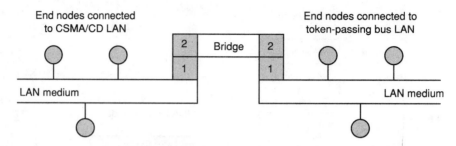

FIGURE 9.3 Bridge connection between two different LANs.

to a network need to communicate outside the network's geographical boundary to reach the devices attached to another network, the two networks can be interconnected with a protocol converter. The protocol converter can be a repeater, bridge, router, or gateway, depending on the amount of incompatibility between the networks.

As the name implies, **repeaters** act as relay points to amplify or regenerate the data signals before they degrade and become unrecognizable. Strictly speaking, however, the repeater is not an internetworking device, but an intranetworking device. It interconnects media with different physical characteristics or extends communications beyond the limitations imposed by a single segment of the same medium. In either case, the repeater provides for the mechanical, electrical, functional, or procedural differences needed to interface multiple line segments (Figure 9.2).

A **bridge** provides the internetworking device for connecting networks that differ at the data link layer, as shown in Figure 9.3. For example, an enterprise may use different LANs for internal communications, say, a CSMA/CD LAN for the office and a token-passing bus access LAN for the shop floor; but to avoid creating isolated islands of automation, these networks need to be interconnected. A bridge can interconnect multiple LANs whose nodes exchange information with a common addressing scheme and frame size. When a device connected to one LAN addresses a device on the other LAN, the bridge captures the communications, reframes it into the required data link format, and passes it to the destination address.

Example 9.1

Given the following bridge connection, describe the action of the bridge when either LAN addresses a node attached to the other LAN.

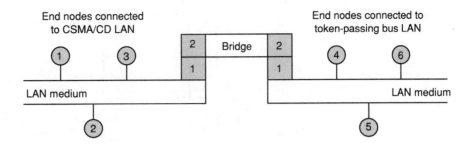

When any of nodes 1 to 3 addresses any node from 4 to 6, the bridge acts as a node in both networks, accepts the communications destined to any node in the token-passing bus network, reformats the data to the form required by the token-passing bus network, and then transmits the data to the appropriate node. In the other direction, the bridge accepts the communications destined for nodes 1 to 3 and converts them to the format required for transfer through the CSMA/CD LAN. ◀

For efficient and effective wide-area communications over public lines, commercial vendors have implemented new packet-switching networks and have adopted the interfaced standards for these networks. Figure 9.4 shows the WAN backbone stripped of the internal interconnections that provide the paths for transporting the traffic. A well-structured backbone dictates the electrical and mechanical interface with the line, the framing of the data, the initialization and operating procedures for the reliable transfer of data between point-to-point or multipoint paths, and the routing of the data through the network from its source to its destination point. These are the functions that the ISO model has assigned to the bottom three layers. When an enterprise needs to communicate outside its internal premises, it can interconnect its internal network to the backbone of the WAN by a **router.** The router splices a virtual circuit through the network using the distinct addresses of each network to direct the communications.

Networks may differ by the protocols required at some or all of the upper four layers. For example, not only might proprietary networks differ at all seven layers,

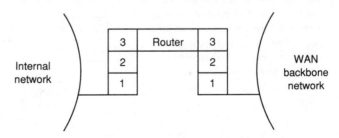

FIGURE 9.4 Internetworking through a router.

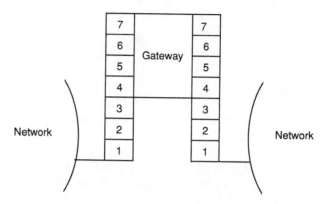

FIGURE 9.5 Internetworking through a gateway.

but the layer structure may not conform to the ISO model. To connect networks, a **gateway** can be used to convert the protocols of one network to that of the other (Figure 9.5). The term *gateway* is the generic name used for a device that interfaces two networks, and in fact, when bridges and routers interface different networks, they are also sometimes called gateways, implying that protocol converters and gateways are synonymous terms.

Exercises

9.1 Using the ISO OSI model, describe the protocol conversion handled by each level of the model.

9.2 Describe the action of a bridge interconnecting two token-passing bus LANs using different signaling techniques.

9.3 The term campus network is often used to denote a network designed to handle the internal communication between devices on the premises of an enterprise. The implementation of such a network often calls for several LANs that are interconnected by protocol converters. Discuss how the devices attached to these LANs differ when a bridge or a router is used as the interfacing device.

9.4 The following diagram depicts a collection of MUXs attached to a CSMA/CD LAN. Each multi-plexer accepts asynchronous inputs from as many as four dumb terminals and transmits the information through the network to one of the two computers. Explain protocol conversion performed by the MUXs.

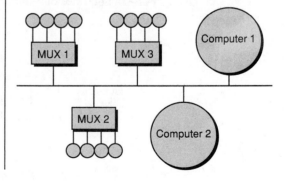

9.2 LINE-INTERFACING STANDARDS

MECHANICAL AND ELECTRICAL CONNECTIONS

The standards at the bottom layer of the ISO model provide the engineering specifications for the mechanical, electrical, functional, and procedural interactions between the nodal equipment and the line. As a practical matter, the circuits generating and receiving the physical signals at a station must be located relatively near the line and connected to the bulk of the equipment by a drop cable. This separation of the nodal equipment was illustrated in the previous discussions on modems and LAN standards. On one side of the configuration, a data terminal was located that ranged in complexity from a dumb terminal to a sophisticated computer; and on the other side, the circuits (modem) were housed that connected the data terminal and the line used to transport the raw signals. The standards address this interface in terms of these two units, which are known generically by their acronyms **DTE** (for **data terminal equipment**) and **DCE** (for **data communication equipment** or **data circuit-terminating equipment,** depending on whether analog or digital technology is used, respectively).

Functionally, four categories of functions—data, control, timing, and ground—specify the interface between the DTE and DCE (Figure 9.6). The standards employ two philosophically different schemes for assigning interface functions. The older, more common scheme assigns a function to each line connecting the two units. Such is the popular **EIA RS-232-C** and its upgraded standard, the **EIA RS-449.** The trend, however, is to make use of fewer circuits and select the functions by passing coded strings of characters between the DTE and DCE. Such an arrangement makes possible a sizable increase in the number of allowable functions and accomplishes this with fewer interconnecting lines. **CCITT's X.21** exemplifies this technology.

So long as the constraints on the interchange circuits are not violated, devices are said to comply with the standard. However, a caveat remains; devices may comply with the standard and still not be interchangeable with each other, since the interchange circuits may be used or unused according to dictates of the product.

To accommodate the interface circuits, a **multipin connector** has been assigned to each of the standards. By agreement, the male connector is fixed to the DTE, and

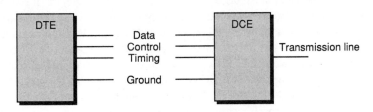

FIGURE 9.6 DTE-DCE interface.

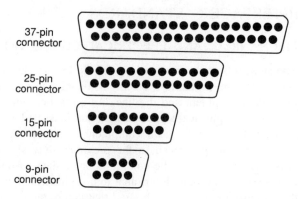

37-pin connector

25-pin connector

15-pin connector

9-pin connector

FIGURE 9.7 DTE-DCE multipin connectors used to make the mechanical and electrical connections.

the female connector is fixed to the DCE. Figure 9.7 shows the connectors that are indigenous to the RS-232-C, RS-449, and X.21 standards.

The RS-232-C is the most widely used standard (in the United States) that addresses the issues of the interconnections between the DCE and the DTE. This standard limits the size of the extension cable tying together the DTE and DCE to no more than 50 feet, although sometimes a greater length may be used when permitted by the amount of local electrical interference. While most often used at lower data rates, the RS-232-C standard applies to data rates up to 20 kbps, supporting both synchronous and asynchronous transmission operating in simplex, half-duplex, or full-duplex modes.

RS-232-C specifies 25 electrical circuits. Of the 25 circuits, 20 are assigned specific functions for data, control, timing, and ground, and the remaining 5 circuits are reserved for device testing (2 circuits) or are left unassigned to allow for extensions by mutual agreement between the DTE and DCE devices.

RS-449 offers a 37-pin connector in place of the RS-232-C 25-pin connector. By redefining the interface circuits, RS-449 removes some of the obstacles that limit the data rates and the permitted separation of devices. In addition to the 37-pin connector, this standard also specifies a 9-pin connector for servicing an optional secondary channel (i.e., the interconnections for the secondary channel and primary channel use a different connector rather than the same connector as specified for RS-232-C). While the mechanical connections, names, functions, and pin assignments differ between these two standards, the RS-449 is intended as an orderly replacement for upgrading the RS-232-C.

With X.21, the DCE and DTE operate in a purely digital mode and use a 15-pin connector for connecting the interface circuits. The functions are implemented within these units by electronic logic and selected by coded character strings transmitted over the interface circuits.

DTE-DCE CIRCUITS STANDARDS

Table 9.1 lists the function designation pin assignments for the RS-232-C circuits. The following briefly describes these circuits in terms of their intended use.

There are two ground circuits, circuits AA and AB. Circuit AA (protective ground) is normally tied to the chassis of the equipment and may be used to maintain

TABLE 9.1
RS-232-C CIRCUITS

25-PIN	CIRCUIT	FUNCTION	SIGNAL SOURCE DTE	SIGNAL SOURCE DCE
		Ground		
1	AA	Protective ground		
7	AB	Signal ground		
		Data		
2	BA	Transmitted data	•	
3	BB	Received data		•
		Data Control		
4	CA	Request to send	•	
5	CB	Clear to send		•
8	CF	Received line signal detector		•
		Other Controls		
6	CC	Data set ready		•
20	CD	Data terminal ready	•	
22	CE	Ring indicator		•
21	CG	Signal quality detector		•
23	CH/CI	Data signal rate selector	•	•
		Timing		
24	DA	Transmitter signal element timing	•	
15	DB	Transmitter signal element timing		•
17	DD	Receiver signal element timing	•	
		Secondary Channel Data		
14	SBA	Secondary transmitted data	•	
16	SBB	Secondary received data		•
		Secondary Channel Data Control		
19	SCA	Secondary request to send	•	
13	SCB	Secondary clear to send		•
12	SCF	Secondary received line signal detector		•
		Others		
9		Reserved for data set testing		
10		Reserved for data set testing		
11		Unassigned		
18		Unassigned		
25		Unassigned		

a common ground potential between all the equipment of a configuration by tying it to the ground wire of the power line connector. Circuit AB (signal ground) establishes the common return for all the other interchange circuits.

The standard provides for two data channels, designated the primary and secondary channels. Both channels need not be used. When different data rates are assigned to the two channels, then the primary channel is assigned the higher data rate. The secondary channel may be used either as an independent channel or in conjunction with the primary channel for returning response signals to the data transmitted over the primary channel. In the latter case, the channels transmit their signals in opposite directions to each other.

Circuits BA (transmitted data), CA (request to send), and CB (clear to send) are used to carry and control the transfer of data through the primary channel from the DTE to the DCE and then through the communication line. Circuit BB (received data) transfers data received on the communication line through the primary channel from the DCE to the DTE. Circuit CF (received line signal detector) is used in conjunction with circuit BB to indicate to the DTE that a data signal has been received. Circuits SBA, SBB, SCA, SCB, and SCF serve similar functions for the secondary channel.

The remaining control signals are used to establish and control communications, especially when the standard is used with a switched line. Circuit CC (data set ready) indicates that the connection to the communication line has been established and that all timing functions have been completed. Circuit CD (data terminal ready) indicates to the DCE that the data terminal is ready to respond to incoming data. Circuit CE (ring indicator) alerts the DTE that a ringing signal is being received on the communication line by the DCE. Circuit CG (signal quality detector) indicates to the DTE that the DCE may have detected an error. Circuit CH/CI (data signal rate selector) is used to select one of two signaling rates when dual rates are available on the DCE. CH or CI indicates if the source signal is the DCE or the DTE, respectively.

Two circuits work in conjunction with circuit BA (transmitted data) to provide timing information. In particular, circuit DA (transmitter signal element timing) indicates the center of the data signal transmitted, and circuit DB indicates the transition of the data signal. Only one of these circuits is used in any particular implementation. The other timing circuit, circuit DD (receiver signal element timing), is used in conjunction with circuit BB (received data), indicating the center of the received data signal. These timing circuits suffice to support both synchronous and asynchronous transmission.

Based on these interchange circuits, 13 configurations simply labeled A through M have been defined by the standard. The primary distinction between these configurations is the mode of transmission on the primary and (when used) secondary channels. For example, the configurations D and L may employ either half- or full-duplex transmission on the primary channel. In the case of simplex transmission, the configuration makes the distinction on whether the channel transmits or receives. Figure 9.8 gives a breakdown on channel employment in each of the configurations.

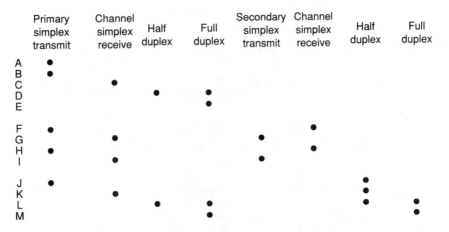

FIGURE 9.8 RS-232-C data transmission configurations.

The interface lines of the EIA Standard RS-232-C share the ground line as a common return line for completing all the circuits. Such circuits, called **unbalanced circuits,** impose undesirable electrical characteristics on the transmitted signals, especially when the ground potential differs at the two units (e.g., for long-distance separation between the DTE and DCE). **Balanced circuits,** on the other hand, use two separate conductors for each interface circuit. RS-232-C does not support balanced circuits.

RS-449 allows for both balanced and unbalanced circuits. Two supplementary standards specify the circuit standards, RS-422-A and RS-423-A for balanced and unbalanced circuits, respectively. For unbalanced circuits, data speeds and allowable separation between the units are comparable to those specified for RS-232-C. However, for balanced circuits, data speeds up to 2 Mbps at 200 feet can be used.

Table 9.2 lists the circuit designations and functions for the 37-pin and 9-pin connectors used with RS-449. The functions are similar to those assigned to RS-232-C, but many of the functions require two pins to establish the circuit.

Like RS-449, X.21 permits balanced or unbalanced interface circuits. Balanced circuits are specified by the X.27 standard, similar to the RS-422A standard, and recommended for DTE-DCE line speeds between 9600 bps and 10 Mbps. For line speeds at or below 9600 bps, unbalanced circuits may be specified by the X.26 standard, similar to the RS-423A standard. The actual speeds depend on the maximum cable length used, which can extend up to 1000 m.

Figure 9.9 shows the line interconnections between the DTE and DCE. While the functional capabilities are grouped similarly to the other two standards, X.21 assigns functions by a sequence of signals on specific lines that is used to activate the logical functions embedded in the two units. Table 9.3 lists the circuit designations for the 15-pin connector used with the X.21 standard, giving the designations for both balanced and unbalanced circuits.

TABLE 9.2
RS-449 CIRCUITS

9-PIN	37-PIN	CIRCUIT	FUNCTION	SIGNAL SOURCE	
				DTE	DCE
			Ground		
1	1		Shield		
5	19	SG	Signal ground		
6	20	RC	Receive common		●
9	37	SC	Send common	●	
			Data		
	4 & 22	SD	Send data	●	
	6 & 24	RD	Receive data		●
			Data Control		
	7 & 25	RS	Request to send	●	
	9 & 27	CS	Clear to send		●
	13 & 31	RR	Receiver ready		●
			Other Controls		
	11 & 29	DM	Data mode		●
	12 & 30	TR	Terminal ready	●	
	15	IC	Incoming call		●
	33	SQ	Signal quality		●
	16	SR	Signal rate selector	●	
	2	SI	Signal rate indicator		●
			Timing		
	17 & 35	TT	Terminal timing	●	
	5 & 23	ST	Send timing		●
	8 & 26	RT	Receive timing		●
			Secondary Channel Data		
3		SSD	Secondary send data	●	
4		SRD	Secondary receive data		●
			Secondary Channel Data Control		
7		SRS	Secondary request to send	●	
8		SCS	Secondary clear to send		●
2		SRR	Secondary receiver ready		●
			Others		
	10	LL	Local loopback	●	
	14	RL	Remote loopback	●	
	16	SF	Select frequency	●	
	18	TM	Test mode		●
	28	IS	Terminal in service	●	
	32	SS	Select standby	●	
	34	NS	New signal	●	
	36	SB	Standby indicator		●
	3		Unassigned		
	21		Unassigned		

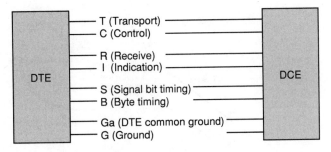

FIGURE 9.9 DTE-DCE lines in X.21.

Signals on the T, C, R, and I circuits put the units into a number of states that are used to step through four operational phases: quiescent, call control, data transfer, and clearing. After the DCE and DTE enter a state, either the DTE or the DCE may provide the permissible source signals to change the state using the T or C circuits or the R or I circuits, respectively. In fact, each state is identified by a particular combination of signals on these circuits. In the event of a problem in the equipment, the state can also indicate the source of the problem. The state transition diagram for the quiescent phase may help clarify the relationship of the state transition diagram to the input signals (Figure 9.10).

TABLE 9.3
X.21 CIRCUITS

X.26		X.27			SIGNAL SOURCE	
15-PIN	CIRCUIT	15-PIN	CIRCUIT	FUNCTION	DTE	DCE
				Ground		
1		1		Shield		
8	G	8	G	Signal ground		
9 & 10	Ga			DTE common ground	•	
				Data		
2	T	2 & 9	T	Transmit	•	
4 & 11	R	4 & 11	R	Receive		•
				Control		
3	C	3 & 10	C	Control	•	
5 & 12	I	5 & 12	I	Indication		•
				Timing		
6 & 13	S	6 & 13	S	Signal element timing		•
7 & 14	B	7 & 14	B	Byte timing		•
				Other		
15		15		Unassigned		

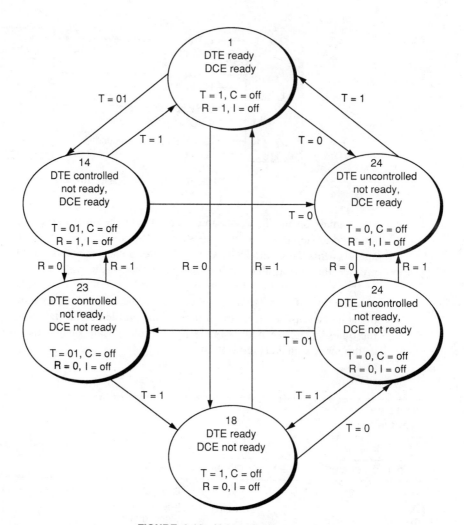

FIGURE 9.10 X.21 quiescent states.

The DTE and DCE wait in the quiescent phase until both are ready to enter either the call control phase or the data transfer phase (the transitions to these phases are not shown in the diagram). The DTE may be in the ready state, uncontrolled not ready state, or controlled not ready state. The DTE uncontrolled not ready state indicates that the DTE is unavailable because of some abnormal condition that must be corrected. The DTE controlled not ready state indicates that the DTE will become available under normal operations but is currently unavailable as a result of some temporary condition. After entering a state, the DTE signals its readiness on the T circuit by a continuous stream of 1's for ready, a continuous stream of 0's for un-controlled not ready, or a continuous stream of alternate 0's and 1's for controlled not ready. On the other hand, the DCE may be ready or not ready, depending on whether it is temporarily in use. The DCE signals its readiness on the R circuit by a continuous stream of 0's for not ready or by a continuous stream of 1's for ready. The state transition diagram gives the changes in the T and R circuits that will put the DTE and DCE into one of the other quiescent states. Other changes in the T, C, R, and I circuits will put the DTE and DCE into one of the permissible states in the other phases.

Table 9.4 (see next 2 pages) gives the X.21 states together with the permissible transitions through which the salient features of the standard can be studied. Note, for instance, that states 6A and 6B and states 10 and 10bis are defined by identical signals on the T, C, R, and I circuits. These states have been included to allow the specification of another standard, called **X.21 bis,** within the framework of X.21. X.21 bis is recommended for use by DTE's that have been designed to interface modems using the RS-232-C standard. Also, note that no transition has been shown to enter the clearing phase. The reason for this is that states 16 and 19 of the clearing phase can be entered from any other state except from state 1, to which the clearing phase exits. Other features of this table will be explored in the exercises.

Communications normally start with the quiescent phase. This phase indicates the readiness of the DCE or DTE to exchange signals. When the equipment is ready, the call control phase establishes communication by an exchange of control signals. Character sequences for call control are selected from CCITT International Alphabet No. 5 (basically the ASCII code) using 7 bits plus odd parity for checking. To synchronize the timing in the devices, sequences of byte-size characters must be preceded by 2 or more SYN characters. After the equipment is put in the data transfer phase, information may be exchanged. The clearing phase returns the devices to the quiescent phase.

Exercises

9.5 When two terminal devices (DTE's) are relatively close to each other they can be directly interconnected to communicate without transmitting through intervening modems (DCE's). How are the RS-232-C lines interconnected to allow these devices to function properly?

9.6 Give the sequence the RS-232-C lines are signaled for transmitting data asynchronously between a terminal and a computer.

9.7 Compare the pin assignments made for the RS-232-C and the RS-449 standards.

9.8 Using Table 9.4, draw the state transition diagram for the clearing phase.

9.9 It is possible that a call request and an incoming call are signaled at the same time at an X.21 interface. Track the state transitions that would result from this situation until the conflict is resolved.

TABLE 9.4
X.21 STATES AND PHASE TRANSITIONS

| PHASE | STATE NUMBER | STATE NAME | SIGNALS ON T, C AND R, I CIRCUITS | | | | PHASE TRANSITION SIGNALED | | | | | | | |
| | | | T, C | | R, I | | BY DTE ON T, C CIRCUITS | | | | BY DCE ON R, I CIRCUITS | | | |
			T	C	R	I	Q	CC	DT	C	Q	CC	DT	C
Q	1	Ready	1	off	1	off	14, 24	2	138	..	18	8	13R	..
Q	14	DTE controlled not ready and DCE ready	01	off	1	off	1, 24	..	..	..	23	..	..	..
Q	18	DTE ready, DCE not ready	1	off	0	off	22	..	..	..	1	..	..	..
Q	22	DTE uncontrolled not ready and DCE not ready	0	off	0	off	18	..	..	..	24	..	..	..
Q	23	DTE controlled not ready and DCE not ready	01	off	0	off	18, 22	..	..	..	14	..	..	..
Q	24	DTE uncontrolled not ready and DCE ready	0	off	1	off	1	..	..	..	22	..	..	..
CC	2	Call request	0	on	1	off	..	4, 5	..	..	..	3, 15	..	..
CC	3	Proceed to select	0	on	+	off	..	5	..	..	..	..	..	..
CC	4	Selection signal	IA5	on	+	off	..	..	..	..	..	..	..	..
CC	5	DTE waiting	1	on	+	off	..	..	..	..	..	6A, 11, 12	..	..
CC	6A	DCE waiting	1	on	SYN	off	..	..	..	..	..	7, 10, 11, 12	..	..
CC	6B	DCE waiting	1	on	SYN	off	..	..	..	..	..	10 bis, 11, 12	..	..
CC	7	Call progress signal	1	on	IA5	off	..	..	..	..	..	6A, 10, 11, 12	..	..
CC	8	Incoming call	1	off	BEL	off	..	9, 15	..	..	..	6B, 11, 12	..	..
CC	9	Call accepted	1	on	BEL	off	..	..	..	..	..	..	..	..

Phase	No.	Name					Next states
CC	10	DCE provided information	1	on	IA5	off	6A, 11,12
CC	10bis	DCE provided information	1	on	IA5	off	6B, 11,12
CC	11	Connection in progress	1	on	1	off	12
CC	12	Ready for data	1	on	1	on	13
CC	15	Call collision	0	on	BEL	off	3
DT	13	Data transfer	D	off	D	on	13R, 13S
DT	13R	Receive data	1	on	D	on	13
DT	13S	Send data	D	on	1	off	7
C	16	DTE clear request	0	off	x	x	17
C	17	DCE clear confirmation	0	off	0	off	21
C	19	DTE clear indication	x	x	0	off	20
C	20	DTE clear confirmation	0	off	0	off	21
C	21	DCE ready	0	off	1	off	

Phases

Q	Quiescent
CC	Call control
DT	Data transfer
C	Clearing Circuits
T	Transmit
C	Control
R	Receive
I	Indicate

Values

0	Steady 0's
1	Steady 1's
01	Steady alternate 0's and 1's
on	Steady signal (0's)
off	Steady signal (1's)
IS5	Any character from CCITT alphabet #5
+	IS5 graphic character
BEL	IS5 control character
SYN	IS5 control character
D	Data
x	Any IS5 character

9.3   DATA LINK CONTROL

PROTOCOL VARIATIONS

The entities of the data link layer act to reliably transfer blocks of data between adjacent nodes that have been connected by a preacquired link. The main issue that must be dealt with by this layer is that of maintaining control of the link for error-free communications while transferring an arbitrary stream of data bits. For example, data composed of instrument readings, graphical outputs, or computer programs must be handled unambiguously as data although some bit patterns appear identical to those assigned to perform control actions. That is, the protocol must allow data to be transmitted transparently in the same block as other code groups that function to control the maintenance of the link. Three methods for achieving transparency will be described: character-oriented, byte count, and bit-oriented protocols.

CHARACTER-ORIENTED PROTOCOL

IBM's **Binary Synchronous Communications protocol,** known as **BISYNC,** exemplifies the **character-oriented protocol.** This popular protocol has been modified to give a number of variations that have been adopted by other networks (e.g., ARPANET).

Figure 9.11 shows the format of a BISYNC data unit as transmitted between nodes. The combination of capital letters indicates a specific control character or in some cases a sequence of 2 characters from a code set. Specifically, BISYNC supports three different code sets (given in Appendix B): EBCDIC, represented by 8-bit

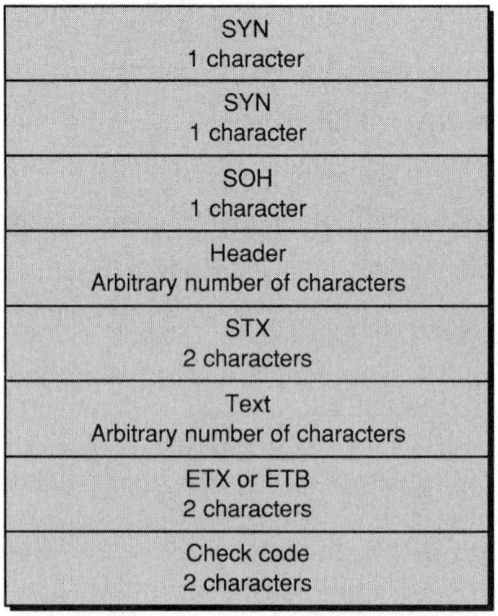

SYN 1 character
SYN 1 character
SOH 1 character
Header Arbitrary number of characters
STX 2 characters
Text Arbitrary number of characters
ETX or ETB 2 characters
Check code 2 characters

FIGURE 9.11 BISYNC Data frame format.

characters; ASCII, represented by 7-bit characters with an odd parity bit; and the 6-bit Transcode. Needless to say, any code set used in a modification of this technique must have the necessary control characters to frame and transmit the data.

Each frame is prefixed by at least two SYN characters. The SYN characters alert the receiver that a legitimate frame follows. Header information preceded by a SOH character may optionally follow the SYN characters. The STX control code (the size of this and the other control codes given in the figure will become obvious shortly) serves two purposes: to terminate the header information, when used, and to indicate the start of the text data. An arbitrary number of text characters follow until terminated by an end-of-text delimiter, which may be either the ETX or ETB characters. The ETB character acts like the ETX character to terminate the text, but in addition indicates that more related data follow in successive frames.

A check code used to detect errors finally ends the frame. The check code is composed of bit patterns commensurate with the character set used, for example, an 8-bit longitudinal check sum, a 16-bit cyclic redundancy code formed from standard polynomials such as $x^{16} + x^{15} + x^2 + 1$ (CRC-16) or $x^{16} + x^{12} + x^5 + 1$ (V.41), or a 12-bit cyclic redundancy code formed from the standard polynomial $x^{12} + x^{11} + x^3 + 1$ (CRC-12).

Figure 9.12 illustrates the phases for exchanging information between two stations. After the stations have been connected, either station can initiate communications by calling the other station with an ENQ character followed by the called station's address. The called station, when ready to receive communications, responds with an acknowledgment (ACK). Once communications have been established, the

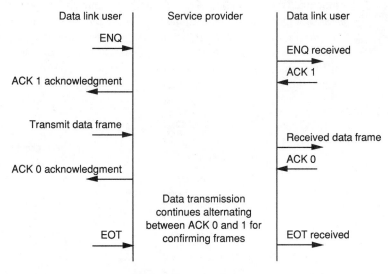

FIGURE 9.12 Protocol phases.

calling station may transmit frames of information to the called station, which in turn acknowledges each received frame. During the course of communication, the receiving station confirms the received frames by alternating between two forms of acknowledgment, ACK 1 for odd-numbered frames and ACK 0 for even-numbered frames, giving the communicating partners a further safeguard against frames that may be lost or damaged in transit. After all the frames have been transmitted, the calling station terminates communications with an EOT signal, which may or may not initiate the clear phase.

There are a number of variations to the preceding theme, some of which use other communication control characters. For example, when a station receives a damaged frame, it may notify the transmitting station with a negative acknowledgment (NAK character) requesting a retransmission. Alternatively, the receiving station may not respond at all to the damaged frame, but may simply wait for the transmitting station to time-out while waiting for an acknowledgment and automatically retransmit or inquire as to the status of the transmitted frame. The following example and the exercises illustrate this and other possibilities.

Example 9.2
Illustrate and explain the communication phases when a station polls another station.

The master station uses the ENQ control code to poll each tributary station by its address. When the polled station has information to transmit, it may start transmitting immediately after it recognizes the polling inquiry. The polling station receives and acknowledges the received frames. After all the information that had been prepared for transmission has been transmitted (the illustration assumes that the polled station had two frames to transmit), the polled station terminates communications by sending an EOT character.

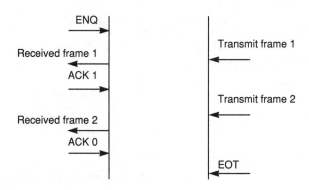

When the polled station has no frames to transmit, it may simply respond with an EOT and allow the polling station to continue to poll other stations. ◀

One remaining problem is how the BISYNC protocol resolves ambiguities in the interpretation of the characters transmitted within the text data. Suppose, for example, that the receiving machine recognizes the bit group corresponding to the character ETX (or ETB) in the data text. In this situation, the receiving machine would be unable to decide whether the bit group represents data within the text or the expected ETX (or ETB) control character used to terminate the text. This problem is further complicated by the fact that a limited number of other control characters are also meaningful within the data text and can be misinterpreted as data.

To circumvent the problem of misinterpreting bit patterns that look alike, BISYNC transmission delimits bit patterns representing control codes by preceding them with a DLE character, so that each control code is represented by a character pair (e.g., DLE STX, DLE ETX, or DLE ETB). This convention leaves the bit patterns that look like the single control characters (e.g., STX and ETX or ETB) free to represent data.

Confusion can still surround the DLE character, since the receiver cannot distinguish if the DLE bit pattern represents data or the DLE control character. To indicate the DLE bit group as data rather than as a control character, the transmitting machine stuffs an extra DLE character in front of any bit group that looks like the DLE character, giving the character pair DLE DLE.

The transparent operations can be best described from the point of view of the receiving machine. A DLE character will always be followed by a control character or another DLE character. When the receiving machine detects a DLE character, it throws it away and looks at the following character. If the following character is another DLE character, then this bit pattern is treated as data; otherwise it is treated as a control character.

BYTE COUNT PROTOCOL

The **byte count** scheme is another character-oriented protocol that allows the text to contain an arbitrary bit pattern of data. The Digital Equipment Corporation's Digital Data Communication protocol (DDCMP) exemplifies this scheme. By using an explicit character count (representing each character in 8-bit byte units), it eliminates the need for the special treatment of any character, such as the DLE character in the BISYNC protocol. DDCMP, in addition to handling the transparency problem by byte count, has other interesting features. Figure 9.13 gives the fields of the frame format, which can be described as follows:

- The SOH character indicates the start of the header, which is mandatory for each frame. Embedded in this character is the code classifying the frame according to its use as a data frame, control frame, or maintenance frame.

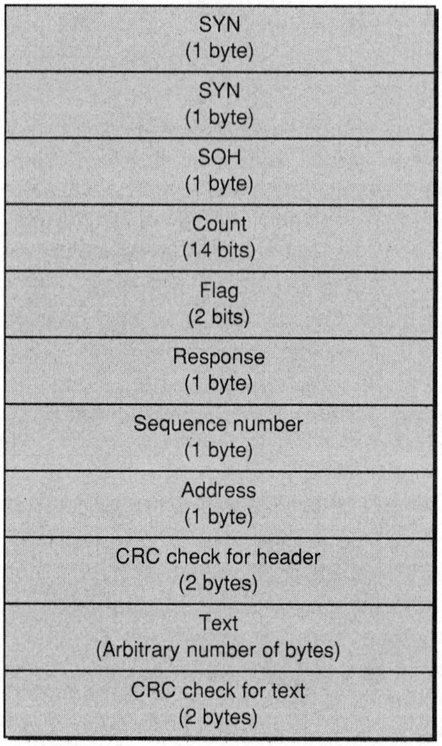

SYN (1 byte)
SYN (1 byte)
SOH (1 byte)
Count (14 bits)
Flag (2 bits)
Response (1 byte)
Sequence number (1 byte)
Address (1 byte)
CRC check for header (2 bytes)
Text (Arbitrary number of bytes)
CRC check for text (2 bytes)

FIGURE 9.13 DDCMP Data frame format.

- The next 2 bytes are divided between the count field and the flag field. The count field gives the number of bytes in the text field, allowing for a length of up to 16,383 characters. The flag field serves two purposes. One purpose is to alert the receiving station when the last message is being transmitted so that the receiving station can begin its own transmission. The other is to inform the receiving station that the transmitted frame will be followed by SYN characters so that the receiving station can avoid filling its buffers with SYN characters.

- The response field gives the sequence number of the last frame within 255 frames that the transmitter has correctly received. The use of this field will be described shortly.

- The sequence field gives the sequence number modulo 256 of the frame transmitted. Separate frame sequence numbers must be tracked for each station to which frames are sent and for each station from which frames are received. For example, if station A sends and receives frames from stations B and C, then it must keep track of four different sequence numbers.

- The address field is used to identify the station whenever a multipoint system is used.

- The code check field forms a cyclic redundancy code to verify the combined previous fields representing the header information. This extra check is used because the header information is critical to the handling of the frames. Later in the frame, another cyclic redundancy code verifies the text.

- The text may be arbitrarily long, up to a maximum length of 16,383 bytes.

- The final cyclic redundancy code verifies the text.

Since it can be expected that most frames will not be damaged during transit, the DDCMP format makes it unnecessary to acknowledge each frame individually, especially during half-duplex operations that require the line to be turned around to change the roles of the transmitting and receiving stations. Instead, each station piggybacks the last frame sequence number that it has received onto the frames it transmits. In the event a machine has not correctly received all the frames that have been transmitted, the missing frames will be retransmitted at the first opportunity.

Although normally the preceding arrangement makes it unnecessary to require separate control frames to acknowledge the frames as received, sometimes, especially when there is little or no reverse traffic by which the correct reception of the frames can be acknowledged, it may be desirable to use explicit control frames to control the data flow. Three such control frames are:

- ACK, to positively confirm the last data frame sequence number that has been correctly received

- NAK, to notify the transmitter of an error, the reason for the error, and to confirm the last sequence number that has been correctly received

- REP, to request the receiving station to acknowledge the reception of data frames which have been sent but have not yet been confirmed.

The following example illustrates the use of these commands.

Example 9.3

Study the exchange of data given in the following diagram, and explain the decisions made at each of the labeled points. The parameters given are the frame sequence number and the sequence number in the response field.

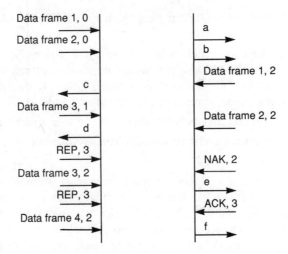

(a) Received frame 1 undamaged.

(b) Received frame 2 undamaged.

(c) Received frame 1 undamaged and confirms that its previously transmitted frames 1 and 2 had been received correctly.

(d) Received frame 2 undamaged and confirms that its transmitted frames 1 and 2 had been received correctly, but that there is the possibility that transmitted frame 3 could have been lost in transit.

(e) Received frame 3 undamaged, but there is an unusually long delay in notifying the transmitter.

(f) Received frame 4 undamaged and confirms that its transmitted frames 1 and 2 were received correctly.   ◀

BIT-ORIENTED PROTOCOL

The character-oriented and byte count schemes achieve transparency by restricting the characters either to a specified length or to specific code sets. **Bit-oriented protocols** not only remove this restriction but offer other advantages, such as an easier hardware implementation of the protocol as well as efficient protocol operations (given by the ratio of the number of data bits to the number of control bits).

As might be expected, there are many variations of bit-oriented protocols offered by commercial products or defined by the various agencies recommending standards. Table 9.5 lists some of these variations by name, although the basic idea among them for handling the transparency problem remains the same.

Figure 9.14 gives the data frame format defined for the ADCCP protocol, which will be used to explain how the bit-oriented protocol handles the transparency prob-

TABLE 9.5
BIT-ORIENTED PROTOCOLS

NAME	ACRONYM	SPONSORING ORGANIZATON
Synchronous Data Link Control	SDLC	IBM
High-Level Data Link Control	HDLC	ISO
Universal Data Link Control	UDLC	Sperry Univac
Advanced Data Communication Control Procedures	ADCCP	ANSI
Borrough Data Link Control	BDLC	Burroughs
Link Access Procedures–Balanced	LAPB	CCITT

lem. With the exception of the text field, which contains an arbitrary number of bits, the remaining fields are organized into octets (8-bit units) that have specific meaning. Briefly, the fields, as shown, represent the following information:

- The flag delimits the start of the frame with the unique bit pattern 01111110. This bit pattern can occur only here and in the field terminating the frame.
- The address field specifies the frame's destination address(es). The encoding scheme allows for simple addresses using a single octet or more complex addresses using multiple octets.
- The control field encodes the functions to be performed and specifies the type of frame. Specifically, each frame is one of three types: information transfer, numbered supervisory commands, and unnumbered commands. Information transfer frames number the frame sent modulo 8 and can piggyback the acknowledgment

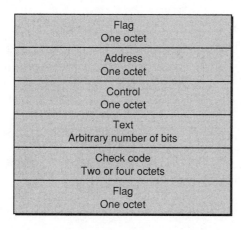

Flag One octet
Address One octet
Control One octet
Text Arbitrary number of bits
Check code Two or four octets
Flag One octet

FIGURE 9.14 ADCCP Data frame format.

of the frame number that has last been correctly received. For command frames, there are two formats for the control field, numbered and unnumbered. The numbered commands allocate 3 bits for explicit acknowledgment of the frames correctly received, while the unnumbered commands use these bits to extend the possible control functions.

- The text field is part of an information frame, but is not present in a command frame. Specifically, it contains the bits that are to be transferred across the data link.

- The check code appears just before the terminating flag. Normally, it uses the CCITT V.41 generator polynomial to generate a two-octet code from all bits except the flag bits and any 0's stuffed elsewhere in the frame (which will be explained shortly). Optionally, when greater protection against errors is required, the following 32-bit generator polynomial is used:

$$x^{32} + x^{26} + x^{23} + x^{22} + x^{16} + x^{12} + x^{11} + x^{10} + x^8 + x^7 + x^5 + x^4 + x^2 + x + 1$$

- The terminating flag, composed of the unique 01111110 bit pattern, marks the end of the frame.

The ability to transmit an arbitrary number of bits in the text hinges on the unique bit pattern that flags the beginning and end of the frame. The transmitter will transmit this pattern only when it is to be interpreted as the flag and alters any other bit pattern that may potentially appear as the flag. Whenever five successive 1's appear elsewhere in the frame, the transmitter automatically stuffs a 0 after them. The receiver removes any 0 after five successive 1's and in this way restores the data to their original form. By this scheme, the bit pattern for the flag cannot reappear anywhere in the frame except in the terminating field.

Exercises

9.10 Compare the bit patterns assigned to the ASCII control characters to the equivalent EBCDIC control characters, and highlight the subset used for communication controls (see Appendix B).

9.11 The following diagram depicts a collection of MUXs attached to a CSMA/CD LAN. Each multiplexer accepts character-oriented synchronous inputs from as many as four computer devices and transmits the information through the network to one of the two computers. Explain in detail the actions of the multiplexer as a protocol converter.

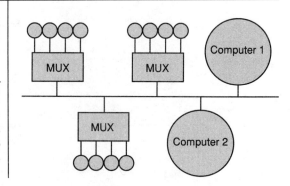

Exercises *(continued)*

9.12 Insert the missing acknowledgment commands in the following diagram and explain how the stations recover communications control.

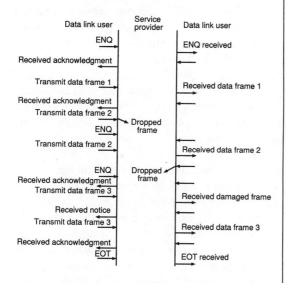

9.13 In BISYNC transmission, the receiving station may respond with a DLE sequence called WACK (Wait Before Transmitting Positive Acknowledge) to temporarily halt further transmission when it is not ready to receive. The transmitting station responds with ENQ, to which it expects either another WACK or notice that it can continue transmission. Modify Figure 9.12 to temporarily halt transmission with the WACK command and then later reinitiate transmission.

9.14 Flowchart the transmission and reception of control characters using a character-oriented protocol.

9.15 Flowchart the transmission and reception of bits using a bit-oriented protocol.

9.16 The receiving machine finds the following characters in a BISYNC data frame text, where DTE represents the bit pattern for the data link escape character, Cco a control character in the code set, and Cda any other character bit pattern. Using the number of the bottom of each character, classify the characters as data, control, throw-away, or an error.

DLE	DLE	DLE	Cco	Cco	DLE	DLE
1	2	3	4	5	6	7
Cda	Cco	DLE	DLE	DLE	Cda	DLE	Cco
8	9	10	11	12	13	14	15

9.17 The transmitting machine finds the following octets in the text to be transmitted by a bit-oriented protocol. How would it alter the bit sequence for transmission?

01110011 11110000 00111100 11111011 11111111 11111100

9.18 Through the literature, obtain the details of two or more of the bit-oriented protocols listed in Table 9.5 and describe how they differ from each other.*

---

*See footnote, page 7.

9.4 NETWORK CONTROL

PUBLIC PACKET-SWITCHING NETWORK STANDARD

The primary function of the network layer in the ISO model is to route the data toward their final destination. An integrated set of standards at the three bottom layers, known as **CCITT X.25** and used to implement the interface to a public packet-switching network, illustrates the role of the network layer. The X.25 nomenclature for the layers differs from that used for the ISO model, but it must be remembered that the X.25 names—the physical level, link access level, and packet level—predate the ISO model. This evolving standard has been put forward as a recommendation for connecting terminals and computers to a public packet-switching network.

The goal of a public packet-switching network is to provide data services analogous to those provided for voice services by the public telephone network, whereby a subscriber presents to the network certain data destined for another subscriber without concern as to how the network handles the transfer of the data. Figure 9.15 shows the relationship of the user's station to a public packet-switching network as defined by the X.25 standard. This suite of standards has only local significance at the end points of the network, which act as data sources or sinks among users. Effectively, X.25 defines the interface between the equipment at a user's station and the network. The network, however, exchanges data internally by other protocol standards, mainly X.75, which serves as the standard for delivering the packets over the network interconnections until they arrive at their final destination.

X.25 defines three peer protocols between two classes of equipment, the equipment at the user's site and the network equipment. The user's equipment may or may not directly support the X.25 interface. However, when the equipment does not support X.25, a packet assembler/disassembler (PAD) must be placed at the interface to act as a protocol converter and properly construct the packets for transmission.

Although the services at the three levels act in unison, they are distinct and are specified by separate protocols. The standards at the two bottom layers can be dealt with briefly, since they have already been considered. Specifically, X.21 is the peer protocol at the physical level. This standard gives the electrical, mechanical, functional, and procedural characteristics of the DTE-DCE interface using coded characters over the circuits connected by a 15-pin connector. However, because of the overwhelming number of computing devices based on the RS-232-C standard oper-

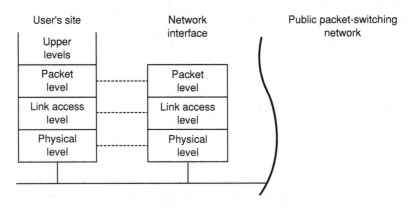

FIGURE 9.15 User's interface to a public packet-switching network.

ating in the field, X.25 permits an interim recommendation at the physical level that allows pin assignments similar to those used on the RS-232-C standard, called X.21bis. The use of X.21bis assumes that the electrical and mechanical connection to the line is made by a baseband modem. At the link access level, the protocol adopted is the ISO high-level data link control (HDLC). Other than to recall that HDLC uses a bit-oriented protocol, there is no need to expand on the features of this protocol.

PACKET-LEVEL STRUCTURE

At the packet level, X.25 defines the data packets and control packets for both switched virtual circuits and permanent virtual circuits. The control packets establish and terminate the virtual circuits, control the data flow, and reset the connections when needed. The data packets are delivered in the same sequence as they had been submitted. X.25 also permits datagram services, which allow the packets to arrive at their destination points in a different order than they were submitted for transmission, but these services need not be implemented and usually are not.

Figure 9.16 repeats the frame structure given in Figure 9.14 as it would be formatted for packet transmission. The text of the frame consists of the packet composed of the packet header and user data, which have been formatted according to the dictates of the upper layers. Three octets portray the basic control information needed for the packet. Specifically, the information content of these octets is as follows:

- The general format identifier indicates by specific bit patterns the format for the remaining part of the header.

- The channel group number, together with the logical channel number given in

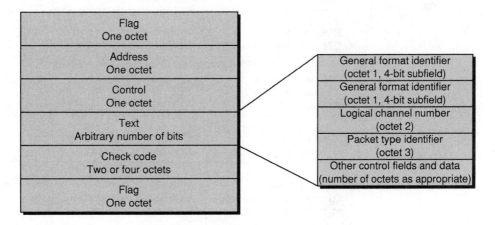

FIGURE 9.16 Format of packet-level header.

the next octet, provides the routing information needed to direct the packet over one of the logical channels in the network.

- The logical channel number is used with the previous subfield.
- The packet type identifier encodes the command associated with the packet.

Depending on the packet type given by the third octet, the packets provide services for call setup, clearing, data transfer, interrupt, flow control, reset, restart, and diagnostics. Table 9.6 lists the packet types as they relate to the services provided. It is understood that the commands may contain parameters given in successive octets, depending on the format used for the particular packet type. The names for

TABLE 9.6
PACKET TYPES RELATED TO SERVICES

DTE→DCE	DCE→DTE	Switched Virtual Circuit	Permanent Virtual Circuit
Call Setup			
Call request	Incoming call	x	
Call accepted	Call connected	x	
Clearing			
Clear request	Clear indication	x	
DTE clear confirmation	DCE clear confirmation	x	
Data			
DTE data	DCE data	x	x
Interrupt			
DTE interrupt	DCE interrupt	x	x
DTE interrupt confirmation	DCE interrupt confirmation	x	x
Flow Control			
DTE receive ready	DCE receive ready	x	x
DTE receive ready	DCE receive ready	x	x
DTE reject		x	x
Reset			
Reset request	Reset indication	x	x
DTE reset confirmation	DCE reset confirmation	x	x
Restart			
Restart request	Restart indication	x	x
DTE restart confirmation	DCE restart confirmation	x	x
Diagnostic			
	Diagnostic	x	x

these services, like those of the layers themselves, may differ from those adopted for the ISO OSI model.

Exercises

9.19 Give the sequence of commands for the call setup, data transfer, and call termination phases using virtual call services, and describe the effect of these commands.

9.20 What are the advantages of a packet-switching network over a circuit-switching network.

9.21 Describe the protocol conversions needed to connect a LAN to an X.25 network.

9.22 CCITT has recommended a number of X series standards for use in making packet-switching connections. Locate one or more of these standards in the literature and report their relationship to the X.25 standard.*

---

*See footnote, page 7.

SUMMARY

The ISO OSI model, in addition to giving the framework for developing open systems products through standards, also provides guidelines on how to interconnect incompatible products. Incompatible communicating partners can be interfaced by a protocol converter that repackages the data units at and below the layer where they differ. An enterprise can interconnect the different homogeneous networks supporting its operations into a larger, integrated network structure by a protocol converter, so that the end nodes can communicate past the geographical boundary of the network to which they are connected.

The remaining discussion dealt with features that have been embodied into various industrial standards, either because they have been built into existing products or because they supply the interface for the new packet-switching networks.

At the bottom layer, the standards address the interface circuits between DTE and DCE units. Two philosophically different methods are used for assigning the interface functions. One assigns the functions to the circuits (RS-232-C and RS-449), and the other assigns the functions by coded strings of characters (X.21). The circuits for these standards have been identified and classified according to their use as data, control, timing, and ground. RS-449 and X.21 permit balanced circuits, which make possible higher transmission rates and a greater physical separation between the two units.

At the data link layer, three schemes—character-oriented, byte count, and bit-oriented protocols—were presented, whereby arbitrary patterns of data can be transmitted without being misinterpreted as control information. These three schemes have been exemplified by BISYNC, DDCMP, and ADCCP, respectively.

BISYNC transmission prefixes the DLE character to any character that is to be interpreted as a control character and to any data character that looks like the DLE character. When the receiving machine detects a DLE character, it removes it from the character stream and treats the following character as a data or control, depending on whether or not it is another DLE character. To provide for reliable transmission between stations, BISYNC transmission expects the communicating partners to acknowledge reception of each frame transmitted.

Byte count protocol uses a rigid format with an explicit character count to remove any ambiguity between control and data characters. By adding special fields to the data unit format, the transmitting stations can piggyback the last frame sequence number that has been correctly received onto any transmitted frame, reducing the number of times the line needs to be turned around for acknowledging the individual frames.

The bit-oriented protocol uses a unique bit pattern (01111110) to flag the beginning and the end of the frame. To prevent the flag from appearing anywhere else in the frame, the transmitter stuffs a 0 after any bit pattern consisting of five consecutive 1's. The receiver restores the data to their original form by removing any 0 after five consecutive 1's. A scheme similar to the byte count protocol is used so that the frames need not be acknowledged individually.

The primary function of the network layer in the ISO model is to route the data toward their final destination. X.25 defines a suite of three peer protocols between the user's equipment and the public network, of which the third layer, named the packet layer, performs the functions of the network layer. At the two bottom layers, X.25 uses standards that have been previously defined. The packet layer defines the format for the control packets and data packets to provide for call setup, clearing, data transfer, interrupt, flow control, reset, restart, and diagnostics. Data packets must be delivered in the same sequence in which they have been submitted. Although X.25 permits the packets to arrive at their destination point in a different order than submitted, implementation of this feature increases the amount of overhead. When the equipment does not support X.25, a protocol converter that assembles and disassembles the packets (PAD) must be inserted at the interface to properly construct the packets for transmission.

KEY TERMS

Protocol converter	Data communication equipment (DCE)
Repeater	Data circuit-terminating equipment
Bridge	(DCE)
Router	EIA RS-232-C
Gateway	EIA RS-449
Data terminal equipment (DTE)	CCITT X.21

Multipin connector
Unbalanced circuit
Balanced circuit
X.21 bis
Binary synchronous communications
  (BISYNC)

Character-oriented protocol
Byte count protocol
Bit-oriented protocol
CCITT X.25

SUGGESTED READINGS

CCITT X-Series Recommendations. CCITT Yellow Book, vols. VIII.2 and VIII.3, Data Communications Networks, 1981.

EIA Std. RS-232-C. "Interface Between Data Terminal Equipment and Data Communication Equipment Employing Serial Binary Data Interchange," August 1969.

EIA Std. RS 449. "General Purpose 37 Position and 9 Position Interface for Data Terminal Equipment and Data Circuit-Terminating Equipment Employing Serial Binary Data Interchange," November 1977.

Green, Paul E. (ed.). *Computer Network Architectures and Protocols*. New York: Plenum, 1982.

McNamara, John E. *Technical Aspects of Data Communication*. 2nd ed. Bedford, Mass.: Digital Press, 1982.

Schwartz, Mischa. *Telecommunication Networks*. Reading, Mass.: Addison-Wesley, 1987.

Tannenbaum, Andrew S. *Computer Networks*. Englewood Cliffs, N.J.: Prentice-Hall, 1981.

SPECTRAL ANALYSIS OF COMMUNICATION SIGNALS

The purpose here is to present the mathematical tools developed by Fourier whereby communication signals can be decomposed into a collection of sinusoidal functions. For periodic signals, two forms of analysis may be used. One form expresses the signal as a sine-cosine series that can be graphically represented as a one-sided frequency spectrum, and the other form expresses the signal as an exponential series that can be graphically represented as a two-sided frequency spectrum. Both forms and the relationship between them will be shown. Also, the analysis that leads to expressing periodic signals as exponential series can be extended to lay the foundation for the analysis of aperiodic signals. By this approach, the discussion will digress briefly from the main theme to show the similarities between periodic and aperiodic signals so as to provide a basis for treating both types of signals in a similar fashion.

FOURIER SERIES OF SINE-COSINE TERMS

Following the discussion in Chapter 2, a periodic signal can be uniquely decomposed into a Fourier series consisting of a linear combination of a constant term and a finite or infinite sequence of sine and cosine terms whose frequencies are multiples of the fundamental frequency. Algebraically, a periodic function, $f(t)$, whose period and fundamental frequency are τ and $1/\tau$, respectively, can be expressed by the series

$$f(t) = a_o + \sum_{k=1}^{\infty} \left(a_k \cos k\frac{2\pi}{\tau}t + b_k \sin k\frac{2\pi}{\tau}t \right) \qquad (A.1)$$

The coefficients for this series can be calculated independently of each other using the following equations:

$$a_o = \frac{1}{\tau} \int_{-\tau/2}^{\tau/2} f(t)dt \qquad (A.2a)$$

$$a_k = \frac{2}{\tau} \int_{-\tau/2}^{\tau/2} f(t)\cos k\left(\frac{2\pi}{\tau}t\right)dt \qquad (A.2b)$$

$$b_k = \frac{2}{\tau} \int_{-\tau/2}^{\tau/2} f(t)\sin k\left(\frac{2\pi}{\tau}t\right)dt \qquad (A.2c)$$

Besides offering the cyclic features needed to reconstruct the periodicity of the function, the constant, sine, and cosine terms have the property of **orthogonality,** which is given by the following collection of identities:

$$\frac{1}{\tau} \int_{-\tau/2}^{\tau/2} dt = 1 \qquad (A.3a)$$

$$\frac{2}{\tau} \int_{-\tau/2}^{\tau/2} \sin\left(k\frac{2\pi}{\tau}t\right) dt = 0 \qquad \text{for all } k \tag{A.3b}$$

$$\frac{2}{\tau} \int_{-\tau/2}^{\tau/2} \cos\left(k\frac{2\pi}{\tau}t\right) dt = 0 \qquad \text{for all } k \tag{A.3c}$$

$$\frac{2}{\tau} \int_{-\tau/2}^{\tau/2} \sin\left(n\frac{2\pi}{\tau}t\right)\cos\left(m\frac{2\pi}{\tau}t\right) dt = 0 \qquad \text{for all } n \text{ and } m \tag{A.3d}$$

$$\frac{2}{\tau} \int_{-\tau/2}^{\tau/2} \sin\left(n\frac{2\pi}{\tau}t\right)\sin\left(m\frac{2\pi}{\tau}t\right) dt = \begin{matrix} 0 & \text{if } n \neq m \\ 1 & \text{if } n = m \end{matrix} \tag{A.3e}$$

$$\frac{2}{\tau} \int_{-\tau/2}^{\tau/2} \cos\left(n\frac{2\pi}{\tau}t\right)\cos\left(m\frac{2\pi}{\tau}t\right) dt = \begin{matrix} 0 & \text{if } n \neq m \\ 1 & \text{if } n = m \end{matrix} \tag{A.3f}$$

These identities may at first appear complex but in fact, they make the computations of Fourier series coefficients manageable. The equations for computing the a and b coefficients (equations A.2a–c) follow directly from equation A.1 and identities A.3. The derivation of these equations not only demonstrates the convenience of orthogonality, but also makes more obvious the ideas embedded in Fourier analysis of signals.

Equation A.2a can be shown by normalizing equation A.1 by $1/\tau$ and integrating both sides of the resulting equation over a period of the signal. The range of the period has been arbitrarily chosen from $-\tau/2$ to $\tau/2$, although any other range would have served equally well. By application of the appropriate identities, all terms except the dc term vanish, giving equation A.2a.

To derive equation A.2b for computing the coefficients of the cosine components, multiply both sides of equation A.1 by the cosine of any harmonic $\left(\text{i.e., } \cos k\frac{2\pi}{\tau}t\right)$, integrate over a period, simplify the resulting equation using identities (equation A.3a–f) to remove terms equal to 0, and finally, normalize the result by the factor $2/\tau$. In a similar way, using the sine of any harmonic $\left(\text{i.e., } \sin k\frac{2\pi}{\tau}t\right)$, equation A.2c for computing the coefficients of the sine components can be derived.

Example A.1
Calculate the Fourier series of the rectangular wave shown in the diagram.

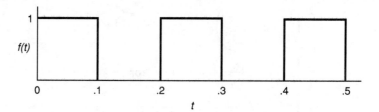

Shown below is the waveform for the period from -0.1 to 0.1, which will be used for this analysis. Any other period of the wave would have served equally well.

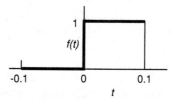

Starting with the formal equation (A.1) for Fourier series,

$$f(t) = a_o + \sum_{k=1}^{\infty} \left(a_k \cos k\frac{2\pi}{\tau} + b_k \sin k\frac{2\pi}{\tau}t \right)$$

it remains to calculate the coefficients (i.e., a's and b's). To calculate the constant term, multiply both sides of the formal equation by $1/\tau$ and integrate over the period:

$$\frac{1}{\tau}\int_{-T/2}^{T/2} f(t)dt = a_o\frac{1}{\tau}\int_{T/2}^{T/2} dt + \sum_{k=1}^{\infty} \left\{ a_k\frac{1}{\tau}\int_{-T/2}^{T/2} \cos\left(k\frac{2\pi}{\tau}t \right)dt + b_k\frac{1}{\tau}\int_{-T/2}^{T/2} \sin\left(k\frac{2\pi}{\tau}t \right)dt \right\}$$

By the orthogonality identities, all terms except the a_o term equal zero, giving the equation for calculating a_o:

$$a_o = \frac{1}{\tau}\int_{-T/2}^{T/2} f(t)dt$$

$$= \frac{1}{0.2}\int_{-0.1}^{0.1} f(t)dt$$

$$= 0.5$$

To expedite the calculations of the cosine term coefficients, multiply both sides of equation A.1 by $(2/\tau)\cos n(2\pi/\tau)$, and integrate over the period:

$$\frac{2}{\tau}\int_{-T/2}^{T/2} f(t)\cos\left(n\frac{2\pi}{\tau}t\right)dt = a_o\frac{2}{\tau}\int_{-T/2}^{T/2}\cos\left(n\frac{2\pi}{\tau}t\right)dt$$

$$+ \sum_{k=1}^{\infty} a_k \frac{2}{\tau}\int_{-T/2}^{T/2}\cos\left(k\frac{2\pi}{\tau}t\right)\cos\left(n\frac{2\pi}{\tau}t\right)dt$$

$$+ \sum_{k=1}^{\infty} b_k \frac{2}{\tau}\int_{-T/2}^{T/2}\sin\left(k\frac{2\pi}{\tau}t\right)\cos\left(n\frac{2\pi}{\tau}t\right)dt$$

giving $a_n = 0$ for all n. After multiplying the formal equation by $(2/\tau)\sin n(2\pi/\tau)$, the coefficients of the sine terms can be calculated in a similar way:

$$\frac{2}{\tau}\int_{-T/2}^{T/2} f(t)\sin\left(n\frac{2\pi}{\tau}t\right)dt = a_o\frac{2}{\tau}\int_{-T/2}^{T/2}\sin\left(n\frac{2\pi}{\tau}t\right)dt$$

$$+ \sum_{k=1}^{\infty} a_k \frac{2}{\tau}\int_{-T/2}^{T/2}\cos\left(k\frac{2\pi}{\tau}t\right)\sin\left(n\frac{2\pi}{\tau}t\right)dt$$

$$+ \sum_{k=1}^{\infty} b_k \frac{2}{\tau}\int_{-T/2}^{T/2}\sin\left(k\frac{2\pi}{\tau}t\right)\sin\left(n\frac{2\pi}{\tau}t\right)dt$$

$$b_k = \frac{2}{\tau}\int_{-T/2}^{T/2} f(t)\sin\left(n\frac{2\pi}{\tau}t\right)dt$$

$$= 10\int_{-0.1}^{0} 0\,\sin(10n\pi t)dt + 10\int_{0}^{0.1}\sin(10n\pi t)dt$$

$$= \frac{1}{n\pi}[\cos(n\pi) - \cos(0)]$$

$$= \begin{cases} -\dfrac{2}{n\pi} & \text{if } n = 1, 3, 5, \ldots \\[2mm] 0 & \text{if } n = 2, 4, 6, \ldots \end{cases}$$

Collecting these results gives the Fourier series for $f(t)$:

$$f(t) = 0.5 - \frac{2}{\pi}\sin(10\pi t) - \frac{2}{3\pi}\sin(30\pi t) - \frac{2}{5\pi}\sin(50\pi t) - \ldots \quad \blacktriangleleft$$

The property of orthogonality permits the decomposition of a periodic function in terms of the functions in a basis set, which in the case of Fourier series consists of a constant term and the sine-cosine functions. Because of the property of orthogonality:

- No function of the basis set can be expressed as a linear combination (a subseries) of the other functions in the basis set.
- Each component of the series can be calculated independently, and the calculations do not depend on the order in which the components are found.
- If the function is approximated by truncating the series by a finite number of terms, then the approximation is best in that the remaining residue is minimal using a least-squares criteria (this result has not been shown).

FOURIER SERIES OF COSINE TERMS

Using the trigonometric identity

$$A \cos \theta + B \sin \theta = \sqrt{A^2 + B^2} \cos(\theta + \phi) \tag{A.4}$$

where $\phi = \tan^{-1}(-B/A)$, the Fourier series given by equation A.1 can be converted into an equivalent series consisting of the dc component and only cosine terms, as shown by the following equation:

$$f(t) = a_o + \sum_{k=1}^{\infty} \sqrt{a_k^2 + b_k^2} \cos\left(k\frac{2\pi}{\tau}t + \phi_k\right) \tag{A.5}$$

where $\phi_k = \tan^{-1}(-b_k/a_k)$. The Fourier series expressed by equation A.5 has the advantage over the previous form of the series (equation A.1) in that each frequency component is given by a single term. Taken together, these terms represent a view of the function in the frequency domain, as shown by two plots. One plot shows the amplitude value of each component at its frequency (the dc component is shown at 0 frequency), and the other plot shows the phase value of each component, although the phase plot will not generally be shown. Example A.2 illustrates the representation of a signal in both the time and frequency domains.

Example A.2
Express the Fourier series

$$f(t) = 1 + 3 \sin(2\pi t) + 4 \cos(2\pi t) + 2 \sin(6\pi t) + 2 \cos(6\pi t)$$

as an equivalent series of cosine terms, and plot the result in both the time and frequency domains.

$$3 \sin(2\pi t) + 4 \cos(2\pi t) = \sqrt{3^2 + 4^2} \cos(2\pi t + \phi_1)$$
$$= 5 \cos(2\pi t - 0.6435)$$

where $\tan^{-1}(-3/4) = -0.6435$ radians.

$$2 \sin(6\pi t) + 2 \cos(6\pi t) = 2\sqrt{2} \cos(6\pi t - 0.7854)$$

where $\tan^{-1}(-2/2) = -0.7854$ radians. Together, these terms express the given series as an equivalent series of cosine terms:

$$f(t) = 1 + 5 \cos(2\pi t - 0.6435) + 2\sqrt{2} \cos(6\pi t - 0.7854)$$

Values of this function can be computed and plotted, giving the curve as a function of time.

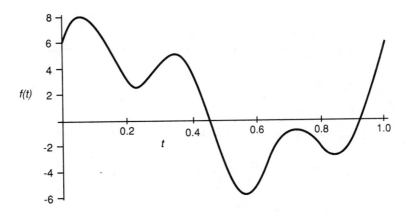

In the frequency domain, the function is given by the following two point plots, one showing the amplitudes and the other showing the phases.

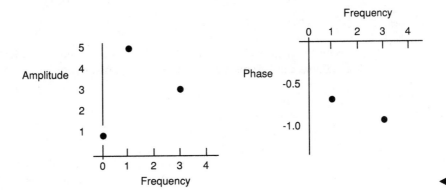

EXPONENTIAL SERIES

The formulation in the frequency domain that has been adopted in much of the presentation in this book is to express the function as a series of exponential terms with imaginary exponents. Before demonstrating the equivalence of this Fourier series to

Fourier sine-cosine series, we will review some basic properties of a complex variable.

A complex number can be represented as a point on the coordinate plane. Two systems typically employed for the coordinate plane are the Cartesian, or rectangular, system (x, y) and the polar system (r, θ). These coordinate systems are related to each other by the equations

$$r = \sqrt{x^2 + y^2}, \quad \theta = \tan^{-1}(y/x) \tag{A.6}$$
$$x = r \cos \theta, \quad\quad y = r \sin \theta \tag{A.7}$$

An ingenious representation of a complex variable can be derived from the formal expansion of the exponential function as a power series. In particular, when the exponent is an imaginary variable, then its power series is given by

$$e^{i\theta} = 1 + \frac{(i\theta)}{1!} + \frac{(i\theta)^2}{2!} + \frac{(i\theta)^3}{3!} + \frac{(i\theta)^4}{4!} + \cdots \tag{A.8}$$

Expanding this series and separating the real and imaginary parts result in

$$e^{i\theta} = \left(1 - \frac{\theta^2}{2!} + \frac{\theta^4}{4!} - \cdots\right) + i\left(\theta - \frac{\theta^3}{3!} + \frac{\theta^5}{5!} - \cdots\right) \tag{A.9}$$

By observing that the separate series for the real and imaginary parts are the series for the cosine and sine functions, respectively, we can rewrite equation A.9 more concisely as

$$e^{i\theta} = \cos \theta + i \sin \theta \tag{A.10}$$

With the help of this mathematical definition, called the **Euler identity,** a complex variable can be conveniently expressed in polar coordinates:

$$\begin{aligned} z &= x + iy \\ &= r(\cos \theta + i \sin \theta) \\ &= re^{i\theta} \end{aligned} \tag{A.11}$$

where $r = \sqrt{x^2 + y^2}$ and $\theta = \tan^{-1}(y/x)$. The sine and cosine terms can also be rewritten in terms of exponentials with imaginary exponents:

$$\cos \theta = \frac{e^{i\theta} + e^{-i\theta}}{2} \tag{A.12a}$$

$$\sin \theta = \frac{e^{i\theta} - e^{-i\theta}}{2i} \tag{A.12b}$$

Following these arguments and substituting equation A.12a into equation A.5 give the equivalent form for the Fourier series as an exponential series:

$$f(t) = a_o + \sum_{k=1}^{\infty} \left(\frac{\sqrt{a_k^2 + b_k^2}}{2} \right) \left[e^{i(k\frac{2\pi}{\tau}t + \theta_k)} + e^{-i(k\frac{2\pi}{\tau}t + \theta_k)} \right] \tag{A.13}$$

The absolute value $|z|$ of the complex number $z = x + iy$ is defined as

$$|z| = \sqrt{z\bar{z}} = \sqrt{x^2 + y^2} \tag{A.14}$$

where $\bar{z} = x - iy$, the complex conjugate of the number. Note that $|z|$ is the same as ρ in the polar coordinate system.

It can now be noted that $e^{i\theta}$ represents the points on the unit circle:

$$|e^{i\theta}| = \sqrt{\cos^2 \theta + \sin^2 \theta} = 1 \tag{A.15}$$

Stated otherwise, the exponential raised to an imaginary power exhibits periodic properties similar to the sinusoidal function:

$$e^{i\theta} = e^{i(\theta + 2\pi)} = e^{i(\theta + 4\pi)} = \cdots \tag{A.16}$$

With some minor changes, equation A.13 can be plotted in the frequency domain, using the imaginary exponent to give the frequency and phase and using the coefficient to give the amplitude of each component. Specifically, the plots of the exponential series and the trigonometric series in the frequency domain resemble each other except that:

- The phase and amplitude plots of the exponential series have components for both positive and negative frequencies.
- The amplitude values for the exponential series are one-half the values displayed for the trigonometric series except for the dc component shown at zero frequency, where the values are the same.

The following example illustrates the relationship between these two forms of representation in the frequency domain.

Example A.3

Rewrite the following sine-cosine series as an exponential series whose terms have imaginary exponents, and plot the amplitude and phase of both the trigonometric and exponential series as a function of frequency.

$$F(t) = 3 + 6\sqrt{3}\ \sin(2\pi ft) + 6\ \cos(2\pi ft)$$

$$F(t) = 3 + 12\ \cos(2\pi ft - \pi/3)$$

$$= 3 + 6(e^{i(2\pi ft - \pi/3)} + e^{-i(2\pi ft - \pi/3)})$$

$F(t) = 3 + 12\ \cos(2\pi ft - \pi/3)$ gives the following frequency plot.

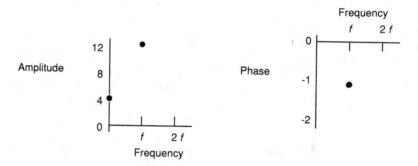

And $F(t) = 3 + 6(e^{i(2\pi ft - \pi/3)} + e^{-i(2\pi ft - \pi/3)})$ gives the following frequency plot.

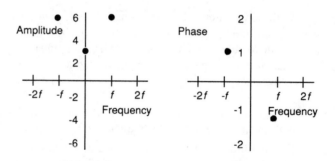

A more concise form of equation A.13 can be given as

$$f(t) = \sum_{k=-\infty}^{\infty} c_k e^{ik\omega t} \tag{A.17}$$

where ω is the fundamental frequency and the coefficients are complex constants. With this formulation, the coefficients in equation A.17 can be derived directly by the equation.

$$c_k = \frac{1}{\tau} \int_{-\tau/2}^{\tau/2} f(t)e^{-ik\omega t}\ dt \tag{A.18}$$

Equation A.18 can be justified by observing that the exponential terms also display the property of orthogonality, which can be expressed by

$$\frac{1}{\tau} \int_{-\tau/2}^{\tau/2} e^{in\omega t} e^{-im\omega t} \, dt = \begin{array}{ll} 1 & \text{if } m = n \\ 0 & \text{if } m \neq n \end{array} \qquad (A.19)$$

where ω is the fundamental frequency equal to $2\pi f$. ◀

Example A.4

Expand the rectangular wave as defined below directly as an exponential series, and express this series as a trigonometric series.

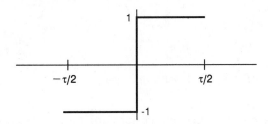

$$c_k = \frac{1}{\tau} \int_{-\tau/2}^{\tau/2} f(t) e^{ik\omega t} \, dt \qquad \text{where } \omega = 2\pi/\tau$$

$$f(t) = \frac{2}{i\pi} \left(e^{i\omega t} + \frac{1}{3} e^{i3\omega t} + \frac{1}{5} e^{i5\omega t} + \dots \right) - \frac{2}{i\pi} \left(e^{-i\omega t} + \frac{1}{3} e^{-i3\omega t} + \frac{1}{5} e^{-i5\omega t} + \dots \right)$$

$$= \frac{4}{\pi} \left(\sin \omega t + \frac{1}{3} \sin 3\omega t + \frac{1}{5} \sin 5\omega t + \dots \right) \qquad ◀$$

FOURIER TRANSFORM OF APERIODIC SIGNALS

To derive the analogous equations for an aperiodic signal, let the fundamental period in equation A.18 be arbitrarily large, and divide the equation by the fundamental frequency, giving an equation for the average amplitude per cycle. As the fundamental period is increased, the fundamental frequency approaches 0, and the spacing between harmonics becomes smaller until ultimately the frequency spectrum becomes continuous. Formally, this can be expressed by

$$\lim_{\substack{\omega \to 0 \\ \tau \to \infty}} 2\pi \frac{c_k}{\omega} = \lim_{\substack{\omega \to 0 \\ \tau \to \infty}} \int_{-\tau/2}^{\tau/2} f(t) e^{-ik\omega t} \, dt \qquad (A.20)$$

TABLE A.1

COMPARISON OF EQUATIONS FOR PERIODIC AND APERIODIC SIGNALS

PERIODIC SIGNALS	APERIODIC SIGNALS
$c_k = \dfrac{2}{\tau} \displaystyle\int_{-\tau/2}^{\tau/2} f(t)e^{-ik\omega t}\, dt$	$F(\omega) = \displaystyle\int_{-\infty}^{\infty} f(t)e^{-i\omega t}\, dt$
$f(t) = \displaystyle\sum_{k=-\infty}^{\infty} c_k e^{ik\omega t}$	$f(t) = \dfrac{1}{2\pi} \displaystyle\int_{-\infty}^{\infty} F(\omega)e^{i\omega t}\, d\omega$

The companion equation for describing the signal back to the time domain, equation A.17, can also be appropriately modified by replacing the discrete summation with the continuous summation of the components (i.e., by integration). A rigorous treatment of this intuitive argument results in the following Fourier transform equations:

$$F(\omega) = \int_{-\infty}^{\infty} f(t)e^{-i\omega t}\, dt$$

$$f(t) = \frac{1}{2\pi} \int_{-\infty}^{\infty} F(\omega)e^{i\omega t}\, d\omega$$

(A.21)

where $F(\omega)$ is the Fourier transform (also sometimes called the **spectral density**) of the aperiodic function $f(t)$. Unlike a periodic signal, an aperiodic signal is interpreted as a continuous sum of exponential terms whose coefficients are $F(\omega)$, rather than as a series of discrete sinusoidal components.

A side-by-side comparison of the equations for periodic and aperiodic signals, shown in Table A.1, accentuates the differences and similarities between the terms for these two types of signals. The continuous variable ω in the equations for aperiodic signals serves a role similar to $k\omega$ in the equations for periodic signals (where ω denotes the fundamental frequency). The Fourier transform, $F(\omega)$, and c_k (sometimes referred to as the **discrete Fourier transform**) both describe the amplitudes of the exponential terms, using integration in one case and summation in the other. The dimensions, however, of c_k and $F(\omega)$ are different; but for all intents and purposes, this presents only a minor problem in interpreting these values during analysis.

Exercises

A.1 Verify the orthogonality identities given by
(a) equations A.3
(b) equation A.19

A.2 Evaluate $e^{ik\pi/2}$ for $k = 0, 1, 2, \ldots$.

A.3 Show the details in the derivation of equations A.2, using equation A.1 and the orthogonality identities.

A.4 Prove the following, using Euler's identity:

Exercises *(continued)*

(a) equation A.12

(b) $\sin(a + b) = \sin a \cos b + \cos a \sin b$

(c) $\sin 3x = 3 \sin x - 4 \sin^3 x$

(d) $\sin x = -i \sinh ix$, where
$\sinh x = \frac{1}{2} (e^x - e^{-x})$

A.5 Express the following, using exponentials to an imaginary power:

(a) $5 \sin 2\pi t$

(b) $2 \sin t + 3 \cos t$

(c) $3 \sin t + 4 \sin 3t$

(d) $A \sin \omega t + B \cos \omega t$

(e) $A \cos (\omega t + \emptyset)$

A.6 Find the Fourier series for each of the following functions, whose amplitude and period equal 1 and 0.2, respectively:

$|\sin 10 \pi t|$

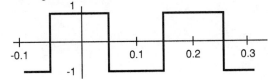

Rectangular wave

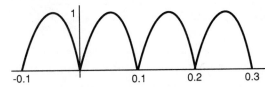

Sawtooth signal

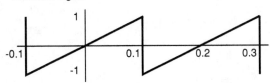

A.7 Using equation A.18, find the exponential series for each of the signals shown in exercise A.6.

A.8 Calculate and plot the spectral density for each of the following signals:

(a) $\sin \omega t$ defined for $-\pi \leq \omega t \leq \pi$

(b) unit rectangular pulse
$f(t) = 1 \qquad$ for $-\frac{1}{2} \leq t \leq \frac{1}{2}$
$\quad\ = 0 \qquad$ otherwise

(c) $e^{-|t|}$

(d) Unit triangular pulse
$f(t) = 1 + t \qquad$ for $-1 \leq t \leq 0$
$\quad\ = 1 - t \qquad$ for $\ \ 0 \leq t \leq 1$
$\quad\ = 0 \qquad\quad$ otherwise

A.9 Show that $\sin \omega t = \frac{1}{2} e^{i(\omega t - \pi/2)} + \frac{1}{2} e^{-i(\omega t - \pi/2)}$.

A.10 Express equation A.5 as a series consisting of the dc component and only sine terms.

KEY TERMS

Orthogonality   Spectral density

Euler identity   Discrete Fourier transform

SUGGESTED READINGS

Stanley, W. D. *Electronic Communication Systems*. Reston, Va., 1982.

Stremler, Ferrel G. *Introduction to Communication Systems*. Reading, Mass.: Addison-Wesley, 1977.

CODE ALPHABETS

Codes cannot be treated only as an abstract combination of 0's and 1's, neglecting the morphological aspects needed for exchanging information between devices. Consider, for example, the different ways of representing information; on the input media, as physical signals over a transmission line, in the computer's memory, and for human recognition. The format on input media might consist of patterns of holes on punched cards or tape, magnetic spots on tapes or discs, or printed bar code stripes. For transmission, the physical codes depend on the devices supporting the exchange of information and may include synchronization and device controls. The internal machine code structures attempt to facilitate the intended operations of the machine's mechanisms. Most important for human recognition, the code requires a visual representation meaningful to the application.

Over the years, code alphabets have emerged that have evolved into standards. Notwithstanding the variety of code alphabets that have been adopted, the attention here will focus exclusively on code alphabets whose code words are of a fixed length. Although fixed-length codes have an obvious convenience, a criticism lodged against them is that they are limited in the number of possible code words that can be assigned to represent the distinct symbols of the alphabet. For example, the prevalent codes of 5, 6, 7, or 8 bits limit the number of code words to 2^5, 2^6, 2^7, and 2^8, respectively. This apparent restriction on a code, however, can be removed by assigning code words as control characters to allow an expanded alphabet.

Because of the large number of available code alphabets and their variations, it is futile to attempt to present many examples and treat their individual nuances uniformly. A few examples will suffice that have been referred to in the text. In particular, the 5-bit Baudot code, the 6-bit Transcode, the 7-bit ASCII code, and the 8-bit EBCDIC code will be presented, which have been selected for variety and the principles involved.

ASCII

ASCII, the acronym for the **American Standard Code for Information Interchange,** was developed by the American National Standards Institute to give structure to a 7-bit code consisting of 128 defined characters. This code often includes an eighth bit to make it compatible with devices that have been organized into byte-sized units. When the eighth bit is included, it is set uniformly to 1 or to the parity of the remaining bits.

The ASCII code structure (Figure B.1) divides the code word into graphic characters represented by pictorial symbols and another class of characters that serve as control functions for the exchange of information and the support of devices. The control characters are assigned an acronym given by the mnemonic that reflects their intended use. Two of the graphic characters, SP and DEL, have no pictorial symbol and appear to be anomalies to the classification of characters into control and graphic characters. SP (space) depicts an empty space devoid of a pictorial symbol, such as the space character on the typewriter. The DEL (delete) character occupies the posi-

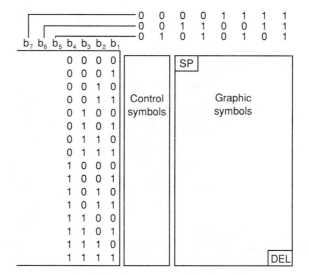

FIGURE B.1 Structure of the ASCII code.

tion in the code whose bit pattern consists of all 1's and can be interpreted as a filler having no graphic or control function, serving to replace a previously used character.

The particular code shown in Figure B.2 is the ANSI X3.4-77 (the last two digits gives the date the code was issued). The graphic character set includes the upper- and lowercase alphabet, the numerical digits, punctuation marks, mathematical operators, and other special symbols. The monetary characters may be changed to conform to other national standards. An important feature of the ASCII code is that it has many possibilities for creating compatible subsets of shortened codes that can be used in specialized applications.

Referring again to Figure B.2, note that the control characters are divided into six categories of characters according to their intended use:

- Communication controls, 10 characters
- Format effectors, 6 characters
- Device controls, 4 characters
- Information separators, 4 characters
- Code expanders, 3 characters
- Special codes, 5 characters

The communication control characters facilitate the transmission of data over the communication lines. The 10 characters are: SYN (synchronize), EOT (end of transmission), SOH (start of header), STX (start of text), ETX (end of text), ETB (end

b7 b6 b5 b4	b3 b2 b1	0 0 0	0 0 1	0 1 0	0 1 1	1 0 0	1 0 1	1 1 0	1 1 1
0 0 0 0		NUL	DLE	SP	0	@	P	`	p
0 0 0 1		SOB	DC1	!	1	A	Q	a	q
0 0 1 0		STX	DC2	''	2	B	R	b	r
0 0 1 1		ETX	DC3	#	3	C	S	c	s
0 1 0 0		EOT	DC4	$	4	D	T	d	t
0 1 0 1		ENQ	NAK	%	5	E	U	e	u
0 1 1 0		ACK	SYN	&	6	F	V	f	v
0 1 1 1		BEL	ETB	'	7	G	W	g	w
1 0 0 0		BS	CAN	(	8	H	X	h	x
1 0 0 1		BT	EM	)	9	I	Y	i	y
1 0 1 0		LF	SUB	*	:	J	Z	j	z
1 0 1 1		VT	ESC	+	;	K	[	k	{
1 1 0 0		FF	FS	,	<	L	\	l	|
1 1 0 1		CR	GS	-	=	M	]	m	}
1 1 1 0		SO	RS	.	>	N	^	n	~
1 1 1 1		SI	US	/	?	O	_	o	DEL

FIGURE B.2   The ASCII code set.

of block), ENQ (inquiry), ACK (acknowledge), NAK (negative acknowledge), and DLE (data link escape). The role that each of these characters plays in establishing communication standards has been covered in the text.

The format effectors—three horizontal and three vertical effectors—are used to control layout or positioning of information in printing or displaying devices. The horizontal format effectors are BS (backspace), HT (horizontal tab), and CR (carriage return). The vertical format effectors are LF (line feed), VT (vertical tab), and FF (form feed). As clear as these characters appear to be, when applied to different devices, they are often a source of problems in information exchange.

The device control characters are used to control ancillary devices associated with data processing equipment and telecommunication systems. In particular, they are used to turn the devices on or off. The four characters are simply designated DC1, DC2, DC3, and DC4 (device controls 1, 2, 3, and 4) to give specialized equipment manufacturers the option of how to use them for control. In any case, when used with keyboard terminals, DC1 and DC2 are designated to turn the devices on, and DC3 and DC4 to turn the devices off.

The information separators group information in a hierarchical manner. Four levels of separation are defined: FS (file separator), GS (group separator), RS (record separator), and US (unit separator).

ASCII permits extensions to the code to include other graphic or control characters. Three code expanders—SI (shift in), SO (shift out), and ESC (escape)—can be used to expand the code while maintaining the 7-bit environment. SI and SO affect only the set of graphic symbols, shifting a designated set of graphic symbols in or out. This allows other graphic sets to be included within the standard (e.g., sets of graphic symbols in different fonts). The ESC character is used under restricted conditions to change the specific character immediately following the ESC character. DLE, the other code expander, permits the control characters to have their prescribed meaning, even when transmitting codes whose lengths may be longer or shorter than the ASCII set. An important use of this character has been described in the text with the BISYNC protocol.

The remaining five characters are used for special purposes and cannot be functionally categorized together by a common use. NUL (null) can be used to mark time during transmission. The CAN (cancel) character alerts the receiver that the data are being transmitted with errors. SUB (substitute) is used as a substitute character for a character that is in error, so that transmission can be continued. EM (end of media) is used to indicate the physical end of media. And BEL (bell) is used to actuate an attention alarm available on some devices.

BAUDOT

The forerunner of the ASCII code is the **Baudot code,** shown in Figure B.3. More properly, this code should be called the Murray code after the American who developed this code to supersede the code developed by Baudot. There are 6 special characters in this code: ƀ (blank), LF (line feed), SP (space), CR (carriage return), FIG (figure shift), and LTS (letter shift).

CR, ƀ, LF, and SP are specialized control functions whose meanings are clearly defined. With the exception of these special characters, the other two control char-

$b_5\ b_4\ b_3$	$b_2\ b_1$	0 0	0 1	1 0	1 1
0 0 0		ƀ	CR	T/5	O/9
0 0 1		E/3	D/*	Z/*	B/*
0 1 0		LF	R/4	L/*	G/*
0 1 1		A/*	J/*	W/2	FIG
1 0 0		SP	N/*	H/*	M/*
1 0 1		S/*	F/*	Y/6	X/*
1 1 0		I/8	C/*	P/0	V/*
1 1 1		U/7	K/*	Q/1	LTS

FIGURE B.3 The Baudot code set (* marks the position of 16 characters that can be arbitrarily defined).

acters, LTS and FIG, change the interpretation of the characters that follow in sequence. LTS establishes the transmission mode so that each following character is interpreted as a letter. FIG establishes the transmission mode so that each of the following characters is interpreted as a digit or as a character that has a specialized meaning in a particular discipline (e.g., weather, stock). This code is fairly efficient for low-speed transmission of a material language. With 5 bits, 58 different characters can be defined (26 + 26 + 6) and transmitted with only a small overhead.

THE 6-BIT TRANSCODE

For a long time, the computer's structure was based on some multiple of 6, such as 12 bits, 24 bits, 36 bits, or 60 bits for memory devices or 7 tracks (6 information bits plus parity) for magnetic tapes. As a result, many 6-bit codes have been defined, giving a character set of up to 64 characters. For the most part, these codes have

b_6 b_5	b_4 b_3 b_2 b_1	0 0	0 1	1 0	1 1
	0 0 0 0	SOH	&	-	0
	0 0 0 1	A	J	/	1
	0 0 1 0	B	K	S	2
	0 0 1 1	C	L	T	3
	0 1 0 0	D	M	U	4
	0 1 0 1	E	N	V	5
	0 1 1 0	F	O	W	6
	0 1 1 1	G	P	X	7
	1 0 0 0	H	Q	Y	8
	1 0 0 1	I	R	Z	9
	1 0 1 0	STX	SP	ESC	SYN
	1 0 1 1	.	$	,	#
	1 1 0 0	<	*	%	@
	1 1 0 1	BEL	US	ENQ	NAK
	1 1 1 0	SUB	EOT	ETX	EM
	1 1 1 1	ETB	DLE	HT	DEL

FIGURE B.4 The 6-bit Transcode.

been based on punched-card technology, and every vendor has defined at least one 6-bit code (often called binary coded decimal codes, or BCD). Figure B.4 illustrates one such code, the **6-bit Transcode.**

EBCDIC

A motivation for changing the structure of the computer from 6 bits to 8 bits (i.e., byte-structured machines) was to allow a larger character set. Other than the ASCII code augmented with an extra bit, the most important 8-bit code was introduced by IBM when they introduced their byte-structured machines; it is the **Extended Binary Coded Decimal Interchange Code (EBCDIC).** While potentially capable of defining 256 characters, not all bit patterns have been assigned a symbol (Figure B.5). In addition to the standard shown in the figure, a national standard has been adopted for this code on punched cards and 9-track tape (8 information bits plus parity).

b_8				$b_4 b_3 b_2 b_1$	0000	0001	0010	0011	0100	0101	0110	0111	1000	1001	1010	1011	1100	1101	1110	1111
				0000	NUL	DLE	DS		SP	&	-						{	}	\	0
				0001	SOH	DC1	SOS				/		a	j			A	J		1
				0010	STX	DC2	FS	SYN					b	k	s		B	K	S	2
				0011	ETX	DC3							c	l	t		C	L	T	3
				0100	PF	RES	BYP	PN					d	m	u		D	M	U	4
				0101	HT	NL	LF	RS					e	n	v		E	N	V	5
				0110	LC	BS	ETB	UC					f	o	w		F	O	W	6
				0111	DEL	IL	ESC	EOT					g	p	x		G	P	X	7
				1000		CAN							h	q	y		H	Q	Y	8
				1001		EM							i	r	z		I	R	Z	9
				1010	SMM	CC	SM		¢	!		:								
				1011	VT				.	$	,	#								
				1100	FF	IFS		DC4	<	*	%	@								
				1101	CR	IGS	ENQ	NAK	(	)	_	`								
				1110	SO	IRS	ACK		+	;	>	=								
				1111	SI	IUS	BEL	SUB	|	-	?	"								

FIGURE B.5 The EBCDIC code set.

Exercises

B.1 Define a 16 character subset suitable for some application and find the position of these characters in the ASCII code set.

B.2 Write a computer program in FORTRAN to translate a FORTRAN program from EBCDIC to AS-CII. Repeat for Pascal.

B.3 Define the 16 special characters of the Baudot code for some application.

B.4 Refer to the vendor's literature to find the punched card format for the EBCDIC code. Write an algorithm to convert the hole punches representing the symbols into their numerical representation.*

B.5 Write an algorithm for conversion of the graphic symbol form EBCDIC code set to the ASCII code set. Explain the anomalies in the two sets.

*See footnote, page 7.

KEY TERMS

American Standard Code for
Information Interchange (ASCII)
Baudot code

6-bit Transcode
Extended Binary Coded Decimal
Interchange Code (EBCDIC)

SUGGESTED READINGS

ANSI X3.4-77. "American National Standards Code for Information Interchange." American National Standards Institute.

Green, Paul E. Jr. (ed.) *Computer Network Architectures and Protocols.* New York: Plenum, 1982.

Housley, Trevor. *Data Communications and Teleprocessing Systems.* 2nd ed. Englewood Cliffs, N.J.: Prentice-Hall, 1987.

McNamara, John E. *Technical Aspects of Data Communication.* 2nd ed. Bedford, Mass.: Digitial Press, 1982.

Rowe, Stanford H., II. *Business Telecommunications.* Chicago, Ill.: Science Research Associates, 1988.

THE HUFFMAN CODE

In the course of discussion, the question was posed, Can the reliability of transmission be improved without changing the physical characteristics of the channel by encoding the information, and if so, how? To answer the question, code redundancy was added, which increased the length of the bit sequence transmitted for a fixed amount of information. The question will now be answered again, but this time by encoding the information into a minimum-bit sequence and thereby decreasing the likelihood of an error.

This discussion on code compression will be limited to the Huffman procedure, which gives an elegant solution to the following well-defined problem:

Given n messages, $m_1, m_2, \ldots m_n$, together with their probabilities of occurrence, $p_1, p_2, \ldots p_n$, respectively, and an alphabet of d symbols, encode these messages such that the code is uniquely decodable and optimal.

A code is optimal if any average sequence of encoded messages requires a minimum number of symbols. Consider the number of symbols assigned to the code words representing the individual messages in an average sequence of M messages (Table C.1). By definition, an average sequence of M messages has Mp_i occurrences of message m_i. If l_i equals the length of the code word assigned to message m_i, then Mp_il_i gives the number of symbols used to encode the occurrences of message m_i in the M messages. The total number of symbols, T, used to encode all the messages in an average sequence is

$$T = \sum_{i=1}^{n} Mp_il_i \tag{C.1}$$

The total number of symbols used to encode the M messages can also be expressed by ML, where L represents the average word length assigned to the individual

TABLE C.1
DISTRIBUTION IN THE NUMBER OF SYMBOLS USED TO REPRESENT THE n INDIVIDUAL MESSAGES IN AN AVERAGE SEQUENCE OF M MESSAGES.

MESSAGE	PROBABILITY OF OCCURRENCE	LENGTH OF CODE WORD	NUMBER OF SYMBOLS IN AN AVERAGE SEQUENCE OF M MESSAGES
m_1	p_1	l_1	Mp_1l_i
m_2	p_2	l_2	Mp_2l_2
m_3	p_3	l_3	Mp_3l_3
m_4	p_4	l_4	Mp_4l_4
.	.	.	.
.	.	.	.
.	.	.	.
m_n	p_n	l_n	Mp_nl_n

messages. The value of L can be formulated by equating this expression to T in equation C.1 and eliminating M, giving

$$L = \sum_{i=1}^{n} p_i l_i \qquad (C.2)$$

Clearly for an optimal code, the value of L must be a minimum.

BASIC CONCEPTS

If there is only one way to decode all possible sequences of code words from a given code set, then the code set is said to be **uniquely decodable.** The decoding process normally inspects the symbols in a sequence of code words one at a time in the order of their appearance. The convention will be adopted of scanning the sequence from left to right. If each code word in all possible sequences of code words can be unambiguously identified when encountered without inspecting further symbols in the sequence, then the code is said to be **instantaneously decodable.** Obviously, an instantaneously decodable code has advantages in implementation.

If the code words of a code are all the same length, then the code is instantaneously decodable. However, the code words of a code need not be the same length to be instantaneously decodable. When a code word matches the front end of another code word, symbol by symbol, it is called the **prefix** of the other code word. A code can be shown to be instantaneously decodable if and only if no code word in the code is the prefix of any other code word in the code. The simplicity of this theorem makes it a viable criterion for developing instantaneously decodable codes.

Example C.1

Determine whether the following binary code sets are instantaneously decodable:

Code set 1:	00, 01, 10, 001
Code set 2:	00, 10, 001
Code set 3:	01, 11, 001

Code set 1 does not satisfy the prefix criterion, since 00 is the prefix of 001; consequently, the code set is not instantaneously decodable. In fact, this code is not uniquely decodable. Consider the sequence 001001. This sequence can be decoded in two ways: 00, 10, 01 or 001, 001.

Code set 2 also does not satisfy the prefix criterion and so is not instantaneously decodable. Consider, as an example, the code sequence 0010. After receiving 00, it cannot be determined if the first code word is 00 or 001. Even after receiving 001, it still is not clear if the first code word should be 00 or 001. After the complete code sequence has been received, it can be uniquely decoded into 00 and 10. Of course, this example does not prove that this code can be uniquely decoded, since there might be another code sequence that can be decoded in more than one way. In this particular case, however, the code is uniquely decodable. Note that the code satisfies the prefix criterion when scanned from right to left, perhaps better called the suffix criterion. If the total sequence is scanned from right to left after it has been received, then each code word would be unambiguously identified without having to inspect additional symbols in the sequence.

Code set 3 is instantaneously decodable, since it satisfies the prefix criterion. As an example, consider the code sequence 00111001. This sequence can be decoded into 001, 11, 001, and no other way. Note that after the last symbol of each code word in the code sequence has been scanned, the code word can be unambiguously identified without the need to inspect any additional symbol. ◄

CODE COMPRESSION

Huffman's coding procedure solves the problem by producing a compressed code that also satisfies the prefix criterion to give an instantaneously decodable code. This procedure creates an optimal code by assigning code words to the messages according to their probability of occurrence, using shorter code words for messages that have the higher probabilities, and longer code words for messages that have lower probabilities. The logic of this strategy can be demonstrated by observing the assignment of any two messages whose probabilities are $p_i \geq p_j$ and code word lengths are $l_i \leq l_j$. Suppose that the code length assignments are just reversed. The partial sum of their combined contribution to the average word length is changed from $p_i l_i + p_j l_j$ to $p_i l_j + p_j l_i$. Subtracting these two partial sums gives

$$(p_i l_i + p_j l_j) - (p_i l_j + p_j l_i) = (p_i - p_j)(l_i - l_j) \leq 0$$

It can be concluded from this result that the assignment producing the partial sum $p_i l_i + p_j l_j$ results in an average word length that is no longer than that produced by the reverse assignment.

While Huffman's procedure assigns an optimum code, other codes may be equally optimal. For example, the symbols in a Huffman code may be uniformly substituted for each other, or the code words may be exchanged between equally probable messages. The following example illustrates these options.

Example C.2

Consider a binary code set consisting of the code words 0, 10, and 11, which are assigned to the messages m_1, m_2, and m_3, respectively. The probabilities of occurrence for these messages are 1/2, 1/4, and 1/4, respectively. Develop three other code sets that are equally optimal.

which can be rewritten as

$$r = n - k(d - 1)$$

To solve for r, it is necessary to find an integer value of k (an integer, since k is the number of steps) such that the value of r is constrained by $1 < r \leq d$. This can be computed as follows:

For $d = 2$, $r = 2$
For $d > 2$, $r = d - 1$ when $n \bmod(d - 1) = 0$ (C.3)
         $= d$ when $n \bmod(d - 1) = 1$
         $= n \bmod(d - 1)$ when $n \bmod(d - 1) > 1$

Example C.3

Find the Huffman code for nine equally probable messages using an alphabet of four symbols: A, B, C, and D.

For nine messages, 9 mod(3) = 0, and therefore $r = 3$.

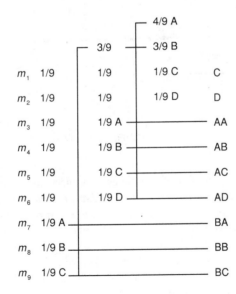

When the alphabet consists of two symbols, 0 and 1, $r = 2$ independent of the number of messages. An example can best illustrate the features of a binary Huffman code.

	CODE 1	CODE 2	CODE 3	CODE 4
m_1	0	0	1	1
m_2	10	11	01	00
m_3	11	10	00	01

The given code, code 1, which had been produced by Huffman's procedure, can be taken as the point of reference. Code 2 is identical to code 1, except that the code words assigned to messages m_2 and m_3 are exchanged. This exchange should have no effect on the average word length, since the probability of message m_2 equals the probability of message m_3. By simply replacing 0 for 1 and 1 for 0, codes 3 and 4 can be constructed from codes 1 and 2, respectively. By equation C.2, the average word length for all these code sets is the same:

$$L = (1/2)1 + (1/4)2 + (1/4)2 = 3/2$$

Before giving the general procedure developed by Huffman for assigning messages to an optimal code, we will demonstrate the steps of the procedure with a specific example. Figure C.1a gives five messages and their respective probability of occurrence to be encoded by an alphabet of four symbols. We start by putting the messages in the order of their probability (Figure C.1b). Huffman's procedure assigns the least probable messages the longer code words. Unfortunately, there are not enough symbols to give each message a separate symbol, so we combine the two least probable messages into a supermessage whose probability is the sum of the probabilities of the two individual messages, and we place the supermessage in its relative position with the remaining sorted messages (Figure C.1c). The reason why two messages were selected to be combined into one supermessage will be left open for the time being. The number of messages has now been reduced to four, which corresponds to the number of symbols in the alphabet. Each of these messages (the three most probable messages and the supermessage) can be assigned a unique symbol from the alphabet (Figure C.1d). The supermessage, in particular, has been assigned the letter B. Each of the subordinate messages of this supermessage can now be assigned a letter of the alphabet prefixed by the letter B. This gives each message a distinct code word that satisfies the prefix criterion (Figure C.1e).

HUFFMAN'S ALGORITHM

Following Figure C.2, the general procedure for deriving the Huffman optimal code for a group of messages from their probabilities of occurrence can now be outlined. After arranging the messages in the order of their probabilities of occurrence, r messages with the lowest probabilities are replaced by one supermessage whose probability is equal to the sum of the probabilities of the r messages, where $r < d$ (recall that d equals the number of symbols in the alphabet). For the moment, assume that the value of r is known. Each of the r messages is assigned one of the symbols of

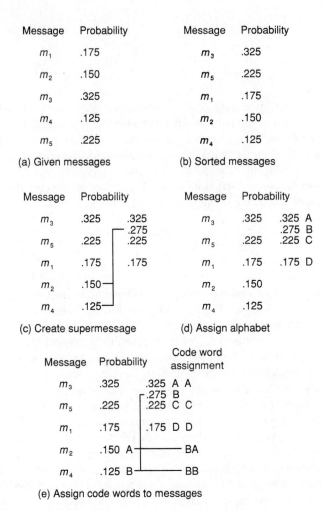

Message	Probability
m_1	.175
m_2	.150
m_3	.325
m_4	.125
m_5	.225

(a) Given messages

Message	Probability
m_3	.325
m_5	.225
m_1	.175
m_2	.150
m_4	.125

(b) Sorted messages

(c) Create supermessage

(d) Assign alphabet

(e) Assign code words to messages

FIGURE C.1 Illustration of the Huffman coding procedure.

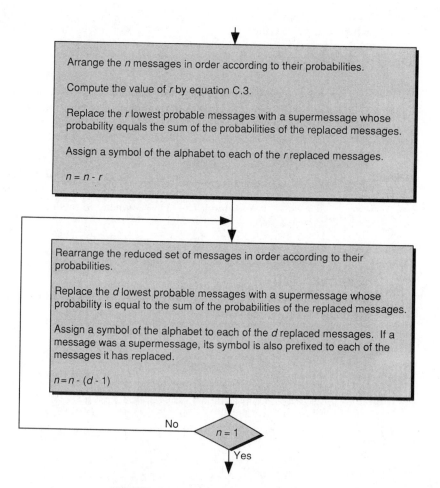

Arrange the n messages in order according to their probabilities.

Compute the value of r by equation C.3.

Replace the r lowest probable messages with a supermessage whose probability equals the sum of the probabilities of the replaced messages.

Assign a symbol of the alphabet to each of the r replaced messages.

$n = n - r$

Rearrange the reduced set of messages in order according to their probabilities.

Replace the d lowest probable messages with a supermessage whose probability is equal to the sum of the probabilities of the replaced messages.

Assign a symbol of the alphabet to each of the d replaced messages. If a message was a supermessage, its symbol is also prefixed to each of the messages it has replaced.

$n = n - (d - 1)$

No $n = 1$

Yes

FIGURE C.2 Huffman's coding algorithm.

the alphabet. Ultimately, these messages whose probabilities are the lowest will be assigned the longest code words.

In the body of the iterative loop, the reduced set of messages are again ordered according to their probabilities of occurrence. For the remaining part of the algorithm, d messages with the lowest probabilities are replaced by one supermessage whose probability is the sum of their probabilities, and each of the replaced messages is assigned a symbol of the alphabet. If any of the messages which had been replaced was itself a supermessage, then the symbol to which it had been assigned is also prefixed to each of its subordinate messages. This process is continued until ulti-

mately the number of messages is reduced to one supermessage whose probability is 1. *The value of* r *is chosen such that at each step, except for the first step, exactly* d *messages can be combined to produce a supermessage.*

Observe that each step of the procedure except the first step reduces the number of messages by d and adds one new supermessage, which results in reducing the number of messages by $d - 1$. The initial step reduces the number of messages by r and adds one new supermessage. The value of r must be greater than 1 to reduce the set and less than or equal to the number of available symbols, d (i.e., $1 < r \leq d$). The process is carried out in k steps until one supermessage remains. For n messages, this process can be expressed by the equation

$$1 = n - k(d - 1) - (r - 1)$$

Example C.4
Encode seven equally probable messages using a binary Huffman code.

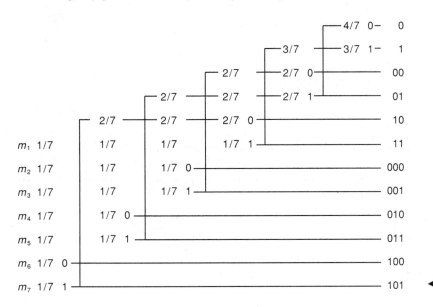

Exercises

C.1 Construct the Huffman code for 15 equally probable messages using an alphabet of six symbols. Repeat the exercise using an alphabet of five, four, three, and two symbols.

C.2 Given nine messages whose probabilities are .2, .3, .07, .08, .05, .12, .06, .03, and .09, construct the Huffman code using five symbols. Repeat the exercise using an alphabet of four, three, and two symbols.

C.3 Construct the binary Huffman code for 64 equally probable messages. Repeat the exercise for 32 and 16 equally probable messages.

C.4 Construct the Huffman code using an alphabet of three symbols, and compute the average word length for each of the following sets of eight messages whose probabilities are as given:

	SET 1	SET 2	SET 3	SET 4
m_1	.125	.35	.65	.93
m_2	.125	.35	.05	.01
m_3	.125	.05	.05	.01
m_4	.125	.05	.05	.01
m_5	.125	.05	.05	.01
m_6	.125	.05	.05	.01
m_7	.125	.05	.05	.01
m_8	.125	.05	.05	.01

C.5 Verify that equation C.3 satisfies the conditions for selecting the value of r.

C.6 Write a computer program for encoding n messages with d symbols by the Huffman algorithm.

C.7 Plot the values of r versus n for values of d in the range from 2 to 8.

KEY TERMS

Uniquely decodable
Instantaneously decodable
Prefix

SUGGESTED READINGS

Hamming, R. W. *Coding and Information Theory*. Englewood Cliffs, N.J.: Prentice-Hall, 1980.

Huffman, D. A. "A Method for the Construction of Minimum Redundancy Codes." *Proceedings of the IRE,* vol. 40, no. 10, September 1952, pp. 1098–1101.

Peebles, Peyton Z., Jr. *Digital Communication Systems*. Englewood Cliffs, N.J.: Prentice-Hall, 1987.

NETWORK CAPACITY

The capacity of a line has been shown to depend on its bandwidth and quality. While it is unlikely that any line in a network will be utilized to its capacity, all lines contribute to the total capacity of the network and also to the robustness of the network to stay operational when lines fail. In this section, the total capacity of a network will be examined in terms of the capacity of the individual lines.

For an analogous situation to line traffic, consider the traffic flow through a tunnel that can pass C vehicles per hour. If the vehicles arrive at the tunnel at a uniform, steady rate, say R, then so long as $R \leq C$, the vehicles can pass through the tunnel at a rate equal to R with a maximum rate of $R = C$. If $R > C$, then some vehicles will have to form a queue and wait to pass. Consequently, C represents the maximum uniform, steady flow through the system. The rate that traffic passes through the tunnel does not improve when vehicles arrive at a nonuniform rate. The loss of time when the tunnel traffic is idle during nonuniform flow cannot be recaptured, and therefore not only does nonuniform flow reduce the effective processing rate, but it can also cause a queue to form even though the average flow rate is less than the capacity. Such flow patterns can be treated statistically (see Appendix E). However, to establish an upper bound of the flow rate through a network, only uniform flow through the channels needs to be considered.

MAXIMUM NETWORK FLOW PROBLEM

Viewed from a global viewpoint, the problem of maximum network flow can be phrased as follows:

> For a network with a given capacity of each line in the network, what is the capacity of the network?

To understand this problem, the term *capacity* must be redefined as it applies to a network. Identifying some node as the source and another node as the sink, the **capacity of a network** can be defined as the maximum rate of end-to-end communications in bits per second or fixed blocks per second that can pass from source to sink.

Consider the network shown in Figure D.1 with node A identifying the source and node G identifying the sink. Each link is labeled by its capacity. With the ex-

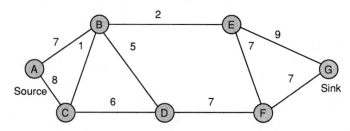

FIGURE D.1 Network.

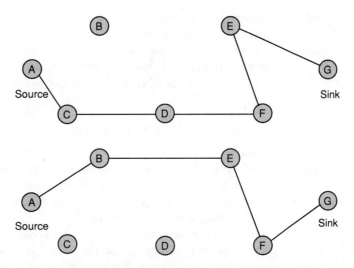

FIGURE D.2 Examples of routes for the network shown in Figure D.1.

ception of the links connected to the source or sink, flow may occur in either direction. Obviously, many different paths may provide the end-to-end connection between the source and sink. Figure D.2 shows a few of the possible paths.

From the paths shown in Figure D.2, it becomes evident that the maximum rate of flow in any route from source to sink depends on the link in the route with the lowest capacity. Table D.1 lists all routes from source to sink for the network shown in Figure D.1 together with the maximum flow possible in each route (routes are

TABLE D.1
ALL ROUTES FOR THE
NETWORK IN FIGURE D.1

ROUTE	MAXIMUM FLOW
ABCDFEG	1
ABCDFG	6
ABDFEG	5
ABDFG	2
ABEFG	5
ABEG	2
ACBDFEG	1
ACBDFG	1
ACBEFG	1
ACBEG	1
ACDBEFG	2
ACDFEG	6
ACDFG	6

excluded where any node is revisited). But such an enumeration does not solve the problem of determining network capacity. The flow to or from a node depends on the capacities of all the links connected to the node. For example, the flow occurring simultaneously in links BD and CD can both contribute to the flow in link DF. To determine network capacity, all parallel links providing end-to-end communications must be considered.

MINIMUM CUT–MAXIMUM FLOW THEOREM

The problem of network capacity can be solved with a theorem with a most descriptive name, the **minimum cut–maximum flow theorem.** It is noted in passing that while the theorem can be simply stated and gives an excellent insight into network flow, the practical computation of capacity for a large and complex network is far from trivial and is best delegated for machine solution.

If links are removed from the network such that the nodes are separated into two disjoint sets, one set containing the source and the other containing the sink, then all end-to-end communications are severed. The links removed, called a cut, are essential in maintaining the connectivity of the network; that is, restoring any link removed by the cut produces at least one path from source to sink. A capacity can be assigned to each cut equal to the sum of the capacities of all links removed by the cut.

Figure D.3a illustrates a cut in a network together with its capacity. Items normally flowing from the source to the sink must pass through one of the links removed

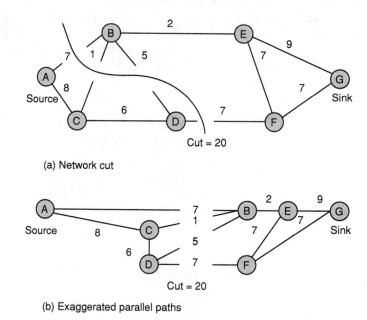

(a) Network cut

(b) Exaggerated parallel paths

FIGURE D.3 Illustration of cut capacity.

by the cut. The cut capacity represents the maximum possible end-to-end flow through the severed links independent of the route the flow takes through the network. By exaggerating the configuration shown in Figure D.3a but leaving the topology of the nodes unaltered, Figure D.3b makes obvious that the cut capacity is the amount of maximum possible flow through the severed links.

Considering all possible cuts, the cut with the minimum capacity determines the maximum possible flow in the network. From this argument, the minimum cut–maximum flow theorem can be stated explicitly as follows:

> The maximum flow from source to sink is equal to the minimum capacity of all the cuts between them.

Example D.1
Calculate the network capacity for the network shown in Figure D.1.

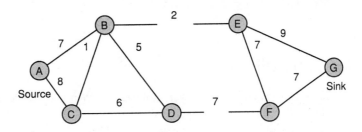

The maximum flow is the minimum capacity of all cuts, which is 9.   ◀

Exercises

D.1

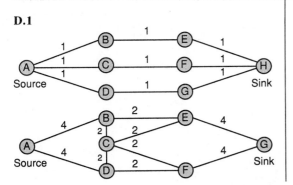

(a) Determine the network capacity for each of the networks shown above.

(b) Enumerate the paths for each of the above networks, and determine the maximum flow through each path.

(c) Calculate the capacity of the above networks if node F becomes inoperative.

(d) Calculate the capacity of the above networks if node B is given as the source node.

Exercises *(continued)*

D.2

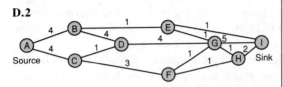

(a) Calculate the capacity of the above network.

(b) Assume that the given individual link capacities are in units of blocks per second and that the delay that a block suffers in passing through a node

is equal for all nodes. What route would give the minimum delay through the network?

(c) What would be the minimum-delay route (using the assumptions of part b) and network capacity if node E fails?

D.3 Write a computer program to calculate the network capacity from the individual line capacities. Use the program to study how line failures affect the network capacity.

KEY TERMS

Capacity of a network
Minimum cut-maximum flow theorem

SUGGESTED READINGS

Bertsekas, Dimitri, and Gallager, Robert. *Data Networks*. Englewood Cliffs, N.J.: Prentice-Hall, 1987.

Taha, Handy A. *Operations Research*. New York: Macmillan, 1971.

Tanenbaum, Andrew S. *Computer Networks*. Englewood Cliffs, N.J.: Prentice-Hall, 1981.

QUEUING MODELS

Intuitively, one expects that so long as the input rate does not exceed the maximum rate that the incoming items can be serviced by a processor, then the items can be serviced as soon as they arrive and need not wait for the processor to become free. Indeed, this is the situation when the items arrive serially at a uniform rate. When the pattern of arrivals and service is not uniform, however, then a queue will form even though the average arrival rate is less than the processor's capacity to service the arrivals. Queuing theory is the study of modeling the performance parameters that describe the congestion formed by multiple customers, events, transactions, calls, packets, and so on, at a service facility.

Consider the familiar example of a checkout counter at a self-service grocery or department store. Customers arrive and mill around the store selecting goods for purchase. When the time comes for them to depart, they must pass through the checkout counter. When no one else is waiting for service at the counter, the only delay a customer suffers is the time the clerk takes to process the purchases. Often, however, the clerk is busy, and the customer must stand in a **waiting line.** So the amount of delay a customer suffers depends on the amount of congestion that has developed by chance before the customer arrived at the checkout station.

Figure E.1 depicts the general **queuing** situation. Shown at the left is the population of potential customers. When ready to be serviced, the customer moves to the processing station. If the processor is already busy, then the customers form a waiting line and wait their turn. A customer may choose to balk in joining the waiting line and depart before being serviced to await for a more opportune time to reenter the queue. Even after servicing has started, the processor may postpone completing the service and send the customer back to rejoin the queue. When the service has been completed, the customer departs the system and the processor proceeds with the next scheduled customer in the waiting line. Obviously, an enormous number of parameters enter this complex situation, many of which have been extensively studied. Here, two models will be presented, notated in queuing theory by M/M/1 and

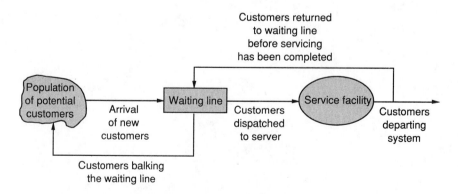

FIGURE E.1 General queuing model.

M/M/m (the notation for models follows that developed by David Kendell), from which first approximations for the performance of a node can be evaluated.

The M/M/1 and M/M/m queuing models, while similar, differ in the number of independent servers participating in the servicing facilities. The 1 and m in the last parameter simply indictate the number of processors in the service facilities, with 1 designating a **single-server model** and m designating a **multiserver model.** Both models assume that the source consists of an unlimited population from which items join the queue and are dispatched to service facilities in a first-in first-out (FIFO) order. Once an item joins the system, it does not depart until it has been serviced.

ARRIVAL AND SERVICE TIME DISTRIBUTION PATTERNS

The first letter in the Kendell notation, M, specifies the statistics of the arrival pattern as having a **Poisson distribution,** and the second letter, again M, specifies the service time needed to process the items in the service facilities as being statistically **exponentially distributed.** Two parameters describe these distributions, λ and μ, where

λ = the average arrival rate

μ = the average rate each processor in the service facility can service the items

The Poisson arrival process describes the arrival pattern that approximates the behavior of the queues found in practical systems. Mathematically, the distribution of arrivals is given by the formula

$$p(k) = \frac{(\lambda T)^k e^{-\lambda T}}{k!} \qquad \text{(E.1)}$$

where $p(k)$ gives the probability of k arrivals over the time interval T. The mean number of arrivals over this time interval and the variance σ^2 of this distribution both equal λT; that is

$$\bar{k} = \lambda T \qquad \text{(E.2)}$$

and

$$\sigma^2 = \lambda T \qquad \text{(E.3)}$$

Throughout this discussion, the overscored variable will be used to indicate the mean (i.e., average) value of the variable, and $p(\quad)$ will be used to indicate the probability of the variable's value.

It is instructive to compare the Poisson distribution with the more familiar **bi-**

TABLE E.1
PROBABILITY OF A PARTICULAR
COMBINATION OF OUTCOMES OF 3
TRIALS

OUTCOME OF 3 TRIALS	PROBABILITY OF OCCURRENCE
s s s	P^3
s s f	$P^2(1 - P)$
s f s	$P^2(1 - P)$
s f f	$P(1 - P)^2$
f s s	$P^2(1 - P)$
f s f	$P(1 - P)^2$
f f s	$P(1 - P)^2$
f f f	$(1 - P)^3$

nomial distribution. The binomial distribution expresses the probability of exactly k successes occurring out of n attempts of a discrete event. Suppose a discrete event can succeed with a probability of P and fail with a probability of Q, which numerically equals $1 - P$. Table E.1 lists all the possible outcomes of three attempts, with s and f indicating whether the event succeeded or failed, respectively. The probability of the particular combination occurring out of the three trials is also given in the table. Out of this enumeration, it can be computed that the probability of three successes is P^3, the probability of two successes is $3P^2(1 - P)$, the probability of one success is $3P(1 - P)^2$, and the probability of zero successes is $(1 - P)^3$.

Extending the analysis of Table E.1, the number of ways and probabilities that exactly k successes can occur in n trials follows the terms of the binomial expansion of $(P + Q)^n$, where $Q = 1 - P$, giving

$$p(k,n) = \binom{n}{k} P^k (1 - P)^{n-k} \tag{E.4}$$

It can be shown that for a rare event and a large number of trials, say for $nP < 5$ and $n > 50$, the Poisson distribution and the binomial distribution approximate each other. The following example illustrates this relationship.

An important characteristic of the Poisson arrival pattern is that the time interval between two successive arrivals, called the **interarrival time,** is independent of the interarrival times between any previous or successive arrivals and that the interarrival time has an exponential distribution. The following equation expresses this relationship, where λ and t_a represent the mean arrival rate and mean interarrival time, respectively, and $p(t_a \leq t)$ represents the probability of the mean interarrival time being less than or equal to time t. Figure E.2 shows this distribution graphically.

$$p(t_a \leq t) = 1 - e^{-\lambda t} \tag{E.5}$$

Example E.1

Compare the Poisson distribution with a value $\lambda T = 2$ and the binomial distribution with a value $nP = 2$ that result from 60, 30, and 15 trials.

Using equation E.1 for the Poisson distribution and equation E.4 for the binomial distribution, we get the values given in the following chart.

k	POISSON DISTRIBUTION $p(k)$	BINOMIAL DISTRIBUTION $p(k,\ 60)$	BINOMIAL DISTRIBUTION $p(k,\ 30)$	BINOMIAL DISTRIBUTION $p(k,\ 15)$
0	.1353	.1308	.1262	.1169
1	.2707	.2706	.2705	.2697
2	.2707	.2753	.2801	.2905
3	.1804	.1835	.1867	.1937
4	.0902	.0902	.0900	.0894
5	.0361	.0348	.0334	.0303
6	.0120	.0110	.0100	.0078 ◀

SINGLE-SERVER QUEUING MODEL

For the single-server queuing model (Figure E.3), items will arrive to join the queue at random times and depart the system at random times, so that the arrival times and departure times are uncorrelated. The probability of an arrival and the probability of a departure are $\lambda \delta t$ and $\mu \delta t$, respectively, where δt represents a time interval sufficiently small such that the probability of an arrival and departure occurring simulta-

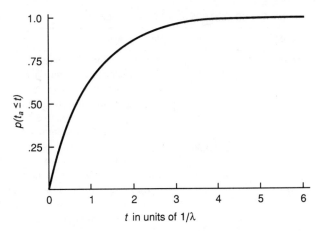

FIGURE E.2 Exponential distribution of inter-arrival time.

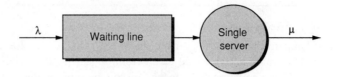

FIGURE E.3   Single-server queuing system.

neously is negligible (i.e., $\lambda\delta t\mu\delta t = 0$). After the system achieves a steady-state condition, the probability of there being exactly N items in the queuing system that are either waiting in line or being serviced by the processor can be expressed by the equations

$$p(N) = \lambda\delta t p(N - 1) + \mu\delta t p(N + 1) + (1 - \lambda\delta t)(1 - \mu\delta t)p(N) \tag{E.6a}$$

and

$$p(0) = \mu\delta t p(1) + (1 - \lambda\delta t)p(0) \tag{E.6b}$$

Table E.2 gives the significance of each of the terms in these equations.

Equations E.6a and b can be rewritten to give the difference equations:

$$p(N + 1) - (1 + \rho)p(N) + \rho p(N - 1) = 0 \tag{E.7a}$$

$$p(1) - \rho p(0) = 0 \tag{E.7b}$$

where $\rho = \lambda/\mu$, called the **utilization factor.**

TABLE E.2

SIGNIFICANCE OF TERMS IN EQUATION E.6

TERM	SIGNIFICANCE
$\lambda\delta t p(N - 1)$	Represents the probability of a change in the number of items in the system when there are $N - 1$ items and there is an arrival in the time interval δt
$\mu\delta t p(N + 1)$	Represents the probability of a change in the number of items in the system when there are $N + 1$ items and there is a departure from the system in the time interval δt
$(1 - \lambda\delta t)(1 - \mu\delta t)p(N)$	Represents the probability of no change in the number of items in the system when there are N items and there is neither an arrival nor a departure in the time interval δt
$\mu\delta t p(1)$	Represents the probability of a change in the number of items in the system when there is 1 item and there is a departure from the system in the time interval δt
$(1 - \lambda\delta t)p(0)$	Represents the probability of no change in the number of items in the system when there is no item and there is no new arrival in the time interval δt

For $\rho < 1$, the solution of these difference equations with the added constraint that the sum of all the probabilities [i.e., all the $p(N)$'s] equals 1, given by the equation

$$\sum_{N=0}^{\infty} p(N) = 1 \qquad (E.8)$$

results in an explicit formula for the values of $p(N)$:

$$p(N) = (1 - \rho)\rho^N \qquad (E.9)$$

Example E.2

Compute the probability of exactly 0, 1, 2, 3, 4, or 5 items waiting in the queue when 300 packets per second arrive at a node that can service 400 packets per second.

The utilization factor for the node is $\rho = 3/4$, which gives the following probabilities by equation E.9:

N	$p(N)$
0	.2500
1	.1875
2	.1406
3	.1055
4	.0791
5	.0593

◄

The mean value of the queue size can be computed by

$$\overline{N} = \sum_{N=0}^{\infty} Np(N) = \sum_{N=0}^{\infty} N(1 - \rho)\rho^N \qquad (E.10)$$

Noting that the series $\rho + 2\rho^2 + 3\rho^3 + \ldots$ equals $\rho/(1 - \rho)^2$, equation E.10 can be rewritten as:

$$\overline{N} = \rho/(1 - \rho) \qquad (E.11)$$

The probability of the queue size being less than or equal to some value n, $p(N \le n)$, can be derived in a similar fashion, giving the formula

$$p(N \le n) = 1 - \rho^{n+1} \qquad (E.12)$$

MULTISERVER QUEUING MODEL

Clearly, when the incoming rate of arrivals is greater than the processing rate of the processor in the service facility (i.e., $\lambda/\mu \geq 1$), the service facility requires more than one processor to handle the traffic. One way of handling the traffic is to form a separate waiting line for each processor (Figure E.4a). The analysis of this configuration is similar to that of the single server with an input rate of λ/m. Another way of configuring the system is to form a common waiting line for all the processors and to dispatch the items waiting in the queue to the next available processor on a FIFO basis (Figure E.4b). The queue formed in this way leads to more efficient operations.

Under the assumption that the m processors in the service facility are identical, the quantity $m\mu$ gives the total capacity of the service facility for handling the incoming items. The utilization factor of the system, ρ, is given by

$$\rho = \lambda/(m\mu) \tag{E.13}$$

The mean number of items in the system, which includes the items being processed and those waiting in the queue, is

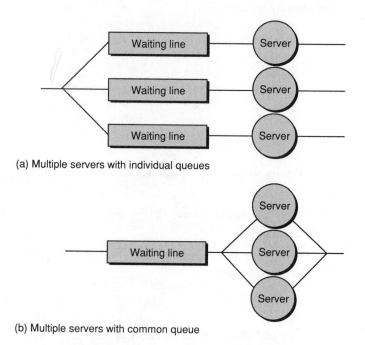

(a) Multiple servers with individual queues

(b) Multiple servers with common queue

FIGURE E.4 Service facility configured with multiple servers.

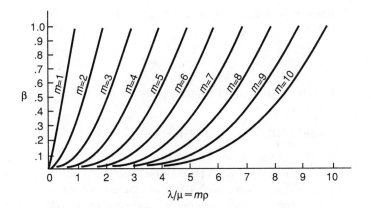

FIGURE E.5 Probability that all servers in a multiserver queuing system are busy.

$$\overline{N} = \frac{\beta\rho}{1 - \rho} + m\rho \tag{E.14}$$

where β is the probability that all the servers are busy. Figure E.5 gives the value of β as a function of the load divided by the processing rate of each processor (i.e., λ/μ). The explicit formulation for this formula is beyond the scope of this presentation. Nevertheless, it can be observed that the formula for the single-server queue conforms to this formula by noting that for a single-server system, ρ is the probability the server is busy.

Example E.3

Four nodes are used to process packets whose arrival rate at each node is 300 packets per second. Each node can process the packets at a average rate of 400 packets per second. It has been decided to centralize these processors and process the packets through a common queue. Compare the mean number of packets in these two systems.

In the first case, $\rho = 300/400 = 3/4$. Equation E.11 gives $\overline{N} = .75/.25 = 3$ for each single-server system. For the four separate queuing systems, the total number of packets awaiting service and being serviced equals 12.

When the processors are assembled into a centralized service facility, the mean arrival rate is 4×300, and the processing rate is 4×400, again giving a utilization factor of $\rho = 1200/1600 = 3/4$. Using a load factor of $\lambda/\mu = 1200/400 = 3$, Figure E.5 gives the probability of all processors being busy as $\beta = .55$. The total number of packets awaiting service and being served can be computed by equation E.14:

$$\overline{N} = (.55)(.75/.25) + 3 = 4.65$$

showing a considerable improvement in performance.   ◄

BASIC QUEUING PERFORMANCE PARAMETERS

Besides giving the amount of delay that items suffer in passing through the system, queuing theory helps determine the amount of storage needed in the system. In the grocery store example cited earlier, the amount of storage represents the floor space needed for customers waiting in line. Analogous to this, the amount of storage for a communication node is the amount of buffer space needed for the transactions that have arrived and are waiting for a processor to become free. Figure E.6 repeats the diagram of the queuing model together with various parameters used to determine the amount of storage and delays. Table E.3 defines these variables.

The relationship of these parameters follows directly from their definitions:

$$t_n = t_q + t_s \tag{E.15}$$

and

$$N = N_q + N_s \tag{E.16}$$

The companion equations for the mean values of these quantities are

$$\bar{t}_n = \bar{t}_q + \bar{t}_s \tag{E.17}$$

and

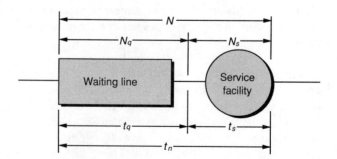

FIGURE E.6 Basic queuing system performance parameters.

TABLE E.3
BASIC QUEUING PARAMETERS

PARAMETER	DEFINITION
N	Number of items in the queuing system, which includes the items being serviced and the items waiting in line to be serviced
N_q	Number of items waiting in line to be serviced
N_s	Number of items receiving service
t_n	The total time an item spends in the queuing system, which includes the time spent while being serviced and the time spent waiting in line before being serviced
t_q	The time an item spends waiting in line before it is serviced
t_s	The time an item spends being serviced

$$\overline{N} = \overline{N}_q + \overline{N}_s \tag{E.18}$$

For a steady-state queuing system, J.D.C. Little has formulated that under very general conditions, the average number of items in a system component is equal to the average amount of time the items spend in the component multiplied by the average arrival rate. This formulation, known as **Little's law,** is expressed by the following formulas:

$$\overline{N} = \lambda \overline{t}_n \tag{E.19}$$

$$\overline{N}_q = \lambda \overline{t}_q \tag{E.20}$$

and

$$\overline{N}_s = \lambda \overline{t}_s \tag{E.21}$$

For the single-server queue, $t_s = 1/\mu$, and therefore

$$\overline{N}_s = \rho \tag{E.22}$$

It has also been shown that

$$\overline{N} = \frac{\rho}{1 - \rho} \tag{E.23}$$

and therefore, by equation E.18,

$$\overline{N}_q = \frac{\rho^2}{1 - \rho} \tag{E.24}$$

Example E.4

During the peak hour, 10 customers following a Poisson distribution call a reservation desk and are kept waiting at the switchboard until the clerk is free. If the clerk can handle 12 customers per hour on the average, how long must a customer wait on the average before being served by the clerk?

The utilization factor is $\rho = 5/6$. The average number of customers in the system is $\overline{N} = \rho/(1 - \rho) = 5$, of which $\overline{N}_q = \rho^2/(1 - \rho) = 4\ 1/6$ are waiting in the queue and $\overline{N}_s = 5/6$ are being served. Since one customer arrives on the average every 6 minutes (i.e., $\lambda = 1/6$ customer per minute, the customer spends $\bar{t}_n = \overline{N}/\lambda = 30$ minutes in the system from the time of arrival to the time of departure, of which $\bar{t}_q = \overline{N}_q/\lambda = 25$ minutes are spent waiting for service and $\bar{t}_s = \overline{N}_s/\lambda = 5$ minutes are spent being served. ◄

For the multiserver queue, $\bar{t}_s = 1/\mu$ (since the processors are assumed to be identical and μ is the processing rate of a single processor). Therefore, by equation E.21,

$$\overline{N}_s = \lambda/\mu = m\rho \tag{E.25}$$

Equation E.14 gives the average number of items in a multiserver queuing system (those being processed and those waiting in the queue):

$$\overline{N} = \frac{\beta\rho}{1 - \rho} + m\rho \tag{E.26}$$

and therefore, by equation E.16

$$\overline{N}_q = \frac{\beta\rho}{1 - \rho} \tag{E.27}$$

Example E.5

During peak hours, 27 long-distance calls are expected to be made through a switchboard, with each call taking an average of 10 minutes. If all lines are busy, the caller is put in a queue and given the first line that becomes free. Calculate the number of OutWATS lines that can service the callers so that a caller's average waiting time before being assigned a line is less than 3 minutes.

Calls arrive at the switchboard at a rate of $\lambda = 27$ calls per hour (or 0.45 call per minute), and a line services calls at a rate of $\mu = 6$ calls per hour (or 0.1 call

per minute), giving $\lambda/\mu = 4.5$. For this traffic, the following table gives the probability that all lines are busy (β from Figure E.5) for various numbers of lines (m), the utilization factor (ρ from $m\rho = \lambda/\mu = 4.5$), the average number of callers waiting in the queue [$\overline{N}_q = \beta\rho/(1 - \rho)$], and the average time a caller will spend in the queue ($\overline{t}_q = \overline{N}_q/\lambda = \overline{N}_q/0.45$ minute).

m	β	ρ	$\overline{N}_q$	$\overline{t}_q$
9	.04	.5	0.05	0.1
8	.10	.56	0.14	0.3
7	.22	.64	0.39	0.9
6	.42	.75	1.27	2.8
5	.76	.9	6.86	15.2

From these data, it can be seen that six lines will provide the needed service. However, services start to degrade quickly with added traffic at this level of utilization, so it might be advisable to install seven lines. ◀

Exercises

E.1 Show that $\overline{k} = \lambda T$ is the mean number of arrivals for the Poisson distribution.

E.2 Plot the average number of customers waiting in the system, including those being processed, as a function of the utilization factor for one, two, and four processors.

E.3 Plot the probability of k arrivals in a time interval of 1 second for items whose arrival pattern follows a Poisson distribution with at a mean arrival rate of 2.5 arrivals per second.

E.4 Compare the Poisson distribution with a value of $\lambda T = 2$ and the binomial distribution with a value of $nP = 2$ that result from 50 and 25 trials.

E.5 Show that arrivals from two independent sources that follow a Poisson distribution with parameters λ_a and λ_b follow a Poisson distribution with a parameter of $\lambda_a + \lambda_b$.

E.6 Prove that $\overline{N} = \rho/(1 - \rho)$ for a single-server queue.

E.7 Expand the binomial expression $(P + Q)^n$ and identify the terms of the resulting series.

E.8 The probability that all servers are busy in a multiserver queue is given by the formula

$$\beta = \frac{1 - a}{1 - a\rho}$$

where

$$a = \frac{\sum_{i=0}^{m-1} \frac{(m\rho)^i}{i!}}{\sum_{i=0}^{m} \frac{(m\rho)^i}{i!}}$$

Write a computer program to compute the average number of items waiting in the system for a range of m and ρ, and plot the results as a function of ρ.

E.9 Packets arrive at a multiprocessor composed of three computers at a rate of 100 packets per second. Each computer can process 40 packets per second. How many packets will be in the multiprocessor on the average at any time?

E.10 If messages arrive at an average rate of two per second, what is the probability that there will be five or less messages in the system both waiting and being transmitted?

Exercises *(continued)*

E.11 Verify that the formula for the average number of items in a single-server queuing system conforms to equation E.14.

E.12 Calculate the amount of increase in traffic that would degrade the system in example E.5 past its acceptable level of performance if six lines had been installed.

E.13 Another way of deriving the queuing model difference equations is by a state transition diagram. In the diagram below the circle represents the system state labled by the probability of there being *n* items in the system and the arcs represent the flow into and out of the state labeled by the flow rates. Use the principle that the flow rate in = flow rate out, derive the difference equations E.7a and E.7b.

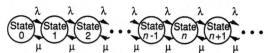

E.14 A communication device contains buffer space for *N* items which include the items in the queue and those being processed. The formula:

$$P_N = (1 - \rho)\, \rho^N / (1 - \rho^{N+1})$$

gives the probability that an incoming item will find the buffer full and will be blocked from entering the system. Derive this formula from the difference equations.

E.15 It has been found by observation that the probability of a message being blocked in a node with a buffer for one message is 0.20. What would be the probability of a message being blocked if the buffer space is doubled (see exercise E.14)? How much would the workload have to increase before the system degrades to its previous blocking level?

KEY TERMS

Waiting line

Queuing

Singl-server model

Multiserver model

Poisson distribution

Exponentially distributed

Binomial distribution

Interarrival time

Utilization factor

Little's law

SUGGESTED READINGS

Allen, Arnold O. *Probability, Statistics, and Queuing Theory*. New York: Academic Press, 1978.

Hammond, Joseph L., and O'Reilly, Peter J. P. *Performance Analysis of Local Area Networks*. Reading, Mass.: Addison-Wesley, 1986.

Hayes, Jeremiah F. *Modeling and Analysis of Computer Communications Networks*. New York: Plenum, 1984.

Kleinrock, Leonard. *Queueing Systems*. Vol. 2: *Computer Applications*. New York: Wiley, 1976.

Martin, James. *Systems Analysis for Data Transmission*. Englewood Cliffs, N.J.: Prentice-Hall, 1972.

Schwartz, Mischa. *Telecommunication Networks*. Reading, Mass.: Addison-Wesley, 1987.

GLOSSARY

Å. Abbreviation for the Ångstrom unit; equals 10^{-8} cm.

access control machine. An abstract machine defined by the IEEE token-passing bus access standards that resolves the nodes right to transmit and organizes the modes into a ring structure.

ACK. Positive acknowledgment control character in an alphabet.

A/D. See *analog-to-digital conversion*.

ADCCP. Advanced Data Communication Control Procedures, a bit-oriented protocol developed by ANSI.

address. The field in a data unit identifying a service access point; also, the identification of the source or destination node.

alias. A frequency component of a signal whose frequency has been displaced by sampling to lie in the frequency spectrum of a replica of the signal.

alphabet. The collection of basic symbols and their representation used to encode information.

AM. See *amplitude modulation*.

amplitude. The maximum magnitude of a sinusoidal function.

amplitude modulation. A form of sinusoidal modulation using the amplitude of the carrier to shift the frequency spectrum of the signals.

amplitude response curve. The ratio of the output amplitude to the input amplitude of a sinusoidal as a function of frequency.

amplitude-shift keying. A way of representing digital values by a finite number of levels in the amplitude of a sinusoidal; abbreviated ASK.

analog line. A line used to transmit signals in an analog format; refers especially to such lines available from common carriers.

analog-to-digital conversion. The process of converting the value of an analog signal into a digital format; abbreviated A/D.

angle of incidence. The angle that a ray of light strikes an optical boundary, such as the core-cladding boundary in an optical fiber.

angle of reflection. The angle that a light ray striking an optical boundary reflects back from the optical boundary, equal to the angle of incidence.

angle of refraction. The angle that a light ray striking an optical boundary is bent as it passes through the boundary, determined by Snell's law.

ANSI. American National Standards Institute.

answer node. The called node; also, the node assigned the answer node's frequencies for transmitting and receiving signals during full-duplex operations.

aperiodic signal. A signal that is not periodic.

application. The functions and facilities serviced by the communication substructure at an end node.

application layer. Layer 7 of the ISO OSI model, which functions as the interface to the actual application and provides the services that are tailored to the specific application.

application management. The management functions assigned to the application layer for the control and monitoring of the activities associated with the semantics that the data share with the application.

application node. An end node in a network where the application resides.

architecture. Defines the harmonious relationships among the elements of a structure.

ASCII. American Standard Code for Information Interchange.

ASK. See *amplitude-shift keying*.

asynchronous transmission. A mode of data transmission using a start signal and stop signal to frame the bits of a character for serial transmission; also refers to serial transmission whereby timing information is not embedded with the transmitted signals, but uses identical and independent clocks at the transmitter and receiver to time the bits.

auto answer. A modem option that allows a node to automatically answer a call placed by another node and establish communications without human intervention.

auto call. A modem option that allows a node to automatically dial and establish communications with a remote node without human intervention.

AWG. American Wire Gauge, the voluntary standard for wire sizes such that the wire resistance increases and the wire weight decreases for a given length by an approximate factor of 10 for each 10 gauges.

balanced circuit. The electrical connection between the DTE and DCE for making the forward and return paths that uses two separate conductors that have been especially conditioned to avoid anomalies in the transmitted signals.

bandlimited signal. A signal whose frequency components lie within a finite frequency range.

bandpass system. A system whose response attenuates all sinusoidals to a zero value except those in a finite band of frequencies.

bandwidth. The frequency range producing a positive response in a bandpass system.

baseband transmission. The transmission of bandlimited signals whose frequencies lie within the bandpass of the channel.

basis set. A collection of orthogonal functions such as the sine and cosine functions used to decompose a periodic signal into a Fourier series.

baud. The unit of signaling speed measured by the rate the line signals change state electrically.

BCD. Binary coded decimal, a code that expresses the decimal digits by their binary equivalence.

beam radio. A form of radio transmission that circumvents omnidirectional transmission for data transmission by directing the signal through a narrow, directed beam.

Bell 103. A Bell modem designed to support low-speed, duplex communications over a switched voice-grade line, supporting asynchronous transmission operating by FSK and used as a prototype for other modems.

Bell 202. A Bell modem designed to support medium-speed, half- or full-duplex communications over dial-up or leased lines, supporting either synchronous or asynchronous transmission operating by FSK and used as a prototype for other modems.

Bell 212. A Bell modem designed for medium-speed, duplex communications over a switched voice-grade line, supporting both synchronous and asynchronous transmission operating by PSK and used as a prototype for other modems.

Binary Synchronous Communications. A character-oriented protocol that uses the DLE character to identify control characters in any arbitrary data sequence.

binomial distribution. Distribution that expresses the probability of exactly k successes occurring out of n attempts of a discrete event; for a large number of rare events, this distribution approximates the Poisson distribution.

BISYNC. See *Binary Synchronous Communications*.

bit-oriented. Refers to a protocol that permits arbitrary patterns of bits to be transmitted by framing the information between two flags whose bit pattern cannot occur elsewhere in the frame.

block code. A code that disburses the parity bits among the checked information bits.

blocking. Combining several protocol data units so they can be transported as a single protocol data unit.

bps. Bits per second.

bridge. A protocol converter that converts the protocols of two networks that differ at the data link layer.

broadband transmission. The transmission of bandlimited signals over a portion of a channel by moving the spectrum of the signal (e.g., by AM, FM, or PM techniques) to conform to the bandpass of the subchannel assigned for transmission.

broadcasting. Signal transmission whereby a signal can be potentially received by many stations.

bus network. A network topology in which a collection of nodes are interconnected to a common line.

byte count. A character-oriented protocol that frames the control information and data into separate fields and identified the data characters by a count in one of the fields.

CATV. See *Community Antenna Television*.

CBX. Computerized branch exchange.

CCITT. Comité Consultatif Internationale de Télégraphique et Téléphonique.

centralized information system. A computer configuration in which a central node provides the computing services.

channel. The path connecting two or more nodes, through which the nodes can exchange data.

channel capacity. The theoretical maximum rate that information can be transmitted through a channel and be recovered; for analog transmission, it is given in pulses per second, and for digital transmission, it is given in bits per second.

character-oriented. Refers to a protocol such as BISYNC, where the data are framed into characters; See also *byte count*.

CIB. Computer-integrated business.

CIM. Computer-integrated manufacturing.

circuit switching. A form of sharing line resources whereby lines are assigned from a bank of available lines to establish a path through the network.

cladding. Optical material surrounding the core of an optical fiber that reflects the light rays through the core.

clear phase. The communication phase used to disconnect the links acquired during the connection phase at the termination of communications between stations.

coaxial cables. A form of metallic media for wire-line construction using a copper core separated by dielectric insulation from an outer, tubular or braided conductor to complete the electric circuit.

code efficiency. The number of information bits divided by the code's length, or the number of information bits in a bit sequence divided by the total number of bits in the sequence.

code length. The number of symbols in a code word.

code polynomial. A code whose code words are expressed in a polynomial format.

code redundancy. The check bits added to a code to improve the reliability of transmission.

code set. A collection of code words selected from all possible sequences of an alphabet.

code word. A finite sequence of symbols from an alphabet that is used to represent a fragment of information.

Community Antenna Television. A coaxial cable system that is used with commercial cable television and that is also used in the implementation of CSMA/ CD LAN's; abbreviated CATV.

common carrier. A government-regulated supplier of communication services offered to the public.

concatenation. Packaging together several service data units so they can be transported as a single protocol data unit.

concentrator. Commonly refers to a statistical multiplexer that also selects and controls the transmission lines.

confirm. One of the four primitive commands associated with each service performed by a communication layer; it acts to inform the user making a request the status of the request.

connection-oriented services. Data link control services that permits nodes to exchange information after they have preestablished a logical or physical data link connection.

connection phase. The communication phase used to acquire the links connecting the stations before they can start to exchange information.

contention. The procedure a node uses to acquire the right to transmit when it finds the line free of other traffic.

control characters. The characters of a standard code set that are assigned a control function (see also *graphic characters*).

convolution code. A code that disburses the parity bits of one block among the information bits of a block transmitted later.

core. In optical fibers, it refers to the optical material through which light is transmitted; in coaxial cables, it refers to the inner conductor, which together with the outer conductor forms the electrical circuit.

core-cladding boundary. The boundary between two substances in an optical fiber whose indices of refraction are approximately equal.

cosine series. Fourier series whose terms include the dc component, but only the cosine functions of the fundamental frequency and harmonics of the periodic signal that it represents.

CRC. Cyclic redundancy code, a code whose error-checking information is formed by the modulo arithmetic with a polynomial.

crossover cable. A cable for making the physical connections between communication nodes that are normally made by a modem.

crosstalk. Interference in a channel caused by the signals in an adjacent channel.

CSMA/CD. Carrier Sense Multiple Access with Collision Detection, a LAN protocol that gives the right to transmit to a node when it finds the line free of traffic.

cut. A partitioning of the nodes of a network such that one set contains the source node and the other contains the sink node.

cut capacity. The sum of the individual line capacities of all the lines removed by a cut.

cyclic code. A code such that every rotation of a code word is also a code word of the code.

cyclic code theorem. A theorem that states that every cyclic (n, k) code is generated by a factor of $x^n + 1$ of degree $n - k$, and conversely, that every factor of $x^n + 1$ of degree $n - k$ generates a cyclic (n, k) code.

data circuit-terminating equipment. The interface equipment used with digital technology between the line and the data terminal equipment that generates the digital signals transmitted over the line; abbreviated DCE.

data communication equipment. The interface equipment used with analog technology between the line and the data terminal equipment that generates the digital signals transmitted over a line; abbreviated DCE.

data communications. The process of transferring information from where it is generated or stored to where it is used in a reliable and efficient manner.

data communications network. A collection of computers and computing devices that operate autonomously, are remotely separated from each other, and are interconnected to cooperate in providing computing services.

data complete. A parameter sent from the MAC sublayer to the PLS sublayer to mark the end of the encapsulated data.

datagram. A type of packet used in packet switching that can be routed through a network independent of the route taken by other packets. Datagrams need not take the same route through the networks.

data link. The communication line interconnecting two or more nodes through which communication signals are exchanged; also refers to the packaged data and control units passed between nodes by the data link layer of the communication structure.

data link layer. Layer 2 of the ISO OSI model; which frames the bits for reliable data transfer between adjacent nodes.

data terminal equipment. The portion of equipment located at a node that interfaces the DCE where the data are generated or used; the equipment can range in complexity from a dumb terminal to a sophisticated computer.

data transfer phase. The communication phase used to exchange information between cooperating partners.

data unit header. The control information a layer appends in front of the data it transmits on behalf of the layer above.

data unit trailer. The error-checking and framing information a layer appends at the end of the data it transmits on behalf of the layer above.

db. See *decibel*.

dc component. The constant term in a Fourier series.

DCE. Acronym for either data circuit-terminating equipment or data communication equipment, depending on whether digital or analog technology is used, respectively.

DDCMP. Digital data communication protocol, a byte count protocol developed by the Digital Equipment Corporation.

DDD. Direct Distance Dialing, the telephone service that enables a user to call a subscriber outside a local area without operator intervention.

deblocking. The separation of a protocol data unit into individual protocol data units.

decentralized information system. A collection of computer configurations that are distributed over several nodes to provide independent computing services.

decibel. The unit used to compare two power values as a ratio on a logarithmic scale that has been divided into decades; $10 \log_{10} P_o/P_i$; abbreviated db.

decoding matrix. The matrix that in standard format consists of the parity bit submatrix on top and an identity matrix on the bottom and which is used for checking the bits received at a node.

demodulation. The process of recovering signals that had been previously modulated.

dial-up line. A commercial line obtained from a common carrier for making an end-to-end connection between subscribers on a demand basis.

dibit. Digital format where each pulse represents 2 bits of data.

dielectric insulator. A nonconductor of electricity.

differential Manchester encoding. A scheme for encoding four symbols with embedded timing information by signals that can have no transition, a transition in the beginning, a transition in the middle, or a transition both in the beginning and in the middle.

digital line. A line transmitting signals representing the digital information in an electrical form and/or format that has been dictated by the network; refers especially to such lines available from common carriers.

Direct Distant Dialing. Public long-distance dial-up tariff.

dish antenna. A paraboloidal reflector used for microwave transmission.

distributed system. An arrangement of remotely dispersed processing facilities that are interconnected to cooperate with each other.

DLE. Data link escape control character in an alphabet, used to identify the control characters transmitted among the text characters in the BISYNC protocol.

DTE. Data terminal equipment.

duplex line. A communication line that can transmit in both directions simultaneously.

EAI. Electronic Industries Association.

EBCDIC. Extended Binary Coded Decimal Interchange Code.

echos. Line disturbances on a signal due to the reflection of a previously transmitted signal.

echoplexing. The selection of the keyboard, modem, or remote site, as the source of characters displayed on the screen.

echo suppression. Installation of equipment on a leased line to block echoes.

ECMA. European Computer Manufacturers Association.

end node. A terminal node in a network.

end-to-end connection. The interconnected path from a data source to a data sink, formed from one or more line segments.

end-to-end protocol. The protocol or suite of protocols used to exchange information between terminal nodes in a network.

ENQ. Inquiry control character in an alphabet.

enterprise. An entity or collection of entities organized to accomplish certain goals and objectives in its environment.

error-correcting code. A code designed to detect and correct selected errors without retransmission.

error-detecting code. A code designed to detect selected errors.

establishment phase. The communication phase used to set the control for communicating with a partner at a previously connected station.

ETB. End-of-block control character in an alphabet, used in place of ETX when more related data follow in successive frames.

ETX. End-of-text control character in an alphabet.

Euler indentity. $e^{i\theta} = \cos\theta + i\sin\theta$.

even parity. A scheme whereby the total number of 1's in a selected group of information bits and an associated parity bit are made an even number.

exchange. Refers to a switching station that selects the path and directs the communications between tributaries.

exponential distribution. Statistical distribution describing the interarrival time between successive items as an exponential curve.

exponential series. Fourier series expressed as a linear sum of exponentials raised to an imaginary power.

FCC. Federal Communications Commission.

FM. See *frequency modulation*.

foreign device. A network device provided by a vendor other than the one supplying the communication line facilities.

foreign exchange. A trunk line to a remote common carrier exchange that permits local access to all subscribers connected to that exchange; abbreviated FX.

Fourier series. A mathematical series representing a periodic signal as a finite or infinite sum consisting of a constant term and sinusoidal terms given at integer multiplies of the periodic signal's frequency.

Fourier transform. The transformation of an aperiodic signal from the time domain to the frequency domain.

Fourier transform pair. A pair of integral equations for transforming an aperiodic signal from the time domain to the frequency domain, and vice versa.

frequency. The number of repetitions a periodic function makes per unit of time.

frequency-division multiplexing. A scheme for sharing a channel by dividing its bandwidth into subchannels.

frequency domain. The response of a system given as a function of frequency; see also *time domain*.

frequency modulation. A form of sinusoidal modulation using the frequency of the carrier to shift the frequency spectrum of the signals; abbreviated FM.

frequency-shift keying. A way to represent digital values by a finite number of tones; abbreviated FSK.

FSK. See *frequency-shift keying*.

fundamental frequency. The frequency of a periodic signal.

FX. See *foreign exchange*.

G. Abbreviation for the prefix giga, used to indicate 10^9 units.

gateway. A protocol converter that converts the protocols of two networks that differ at any of the upper four layers; also used to indicate any protocol converter, including repeaters, bridges, and routers.

Gaussian noise. A form of random noise.

generator matrix. The matrix used for encoding, which in standard format consists of an identity matrix followed by the parity bit submatrix.

generator polynomial. A polynomial factor of $x^n + 1$ used to encode and decode a cyclic redundancy code.

graphic characters. The characters of a standard code set that represent the pictorial symbols but also includes the DEL and blank characters.

GSA. General Services Administration.

guard band. An unassigned gap between the subchannels in frequency division multiplexing that serves to shield the subchannels from interference from adjacent subchannels.

guard time. An unassigned time slice or other overhead loss in time-division multiplexing that serves to separate and coordinate the users sharing the channel.

half-duplex line. A communication line that can transmit in both directions, but only one direction at a time.

Hamming code. Refers to single-error-detecting and -correcting codes produced by Hamming's encoding method.

hamming distance. The number of bit positions two n-tuples disagree.

harmonics. Integer multiples of the fundamental frequency of a periodic signal.

Hartley-Shannon theorem. A theorem that gives the capacity of a noisy digital channel by the formula $C = W \log_2 (1 + S/N)$.

head-end modulator. A device used with the token-passing bus access method when a two-channel configuration is used that retransmits the signals which it receives on the receiving channel over the transmitting channel.

hertz. A unit of frequency equal to 1 cycle per second; abbreviated Hz.

holding circuit. A circuit that retains the value of a sample while a pulse modulator embeds the value into a pulse for transmission.

host node. An end node in a network that services the applications accessed by the tributary stations.

Huffman code. Any of the instantaneously decodable, optimal codes developed by Huffman's coding procedure.

Hz. See *hertz*.

identity matrix. A square matrix with 1's along the diagonal and 0's elsewhere.

IEEE. Institute of Electrical and Electronics Engineers.

impulse noise. Temporary spikes occurring in a channel as a result of some outside disturbance.

incident ray. A ray of light striking an optical boundary.

index of refraction. A property of optical material given by the ratio of the velocity of light in a vacuum to the velocity of light in the material.

indication. One of the four primitive commands associated with each service performed by a communication layer that alerts the remote service access point that a request for service has arrived.

information flow. The collection of data exchanged between cooperating processors.

instantaneously decodable. Refers to a code in which the code words in all possible sequences can be unambiguously identified when encountered, without having to inspect further symbols in the sequence.

interarrival time. The time interval between successive arrivals.

interface. A boundary shared between separate units of a system.

interface machine. An abstract machine defined by the IEEE token-passing bus access standard that serves to interface the LLC sublayer with the MAC sublayer.

intermediate node. A node in the network that relays information through the interconnecting paths of the network.

internetworking device. A protocol converter placed between two homogeneous networks (i.e., networks whose nodes conform to a common suite of protocols) so that the end nodes in either network can exchange information with the end nodes of the other.

interoffice line. A trunk line connecting two common carrier exchange stations.

ISO. International Organization for Standardization.

J symbol. One of two symbols (K is the other); besides the 0 and 1 data symbols, used by the token ring access method to format the starting delimiter and ending delimiter of the frame.

k. An abbreviation for the prefix kilo, used to indicate 10^3 units.

K symbol. One of two symbols (J is the other), besides the 0 and 1 data symbols, used by the token ring access method to format the starting delimiter and ending delimiter of the frame.

lambda (λ). Notation for the wavelength of a sinusoidal wave such as that of light; in queuing theory; it represents the average arrival rate.

layer architecture. Defines the harmonious relationships of the functions of the communication substructure and organizes them into layers.

layer management. The management functions assigned to the individual communication layers for handling exceptional conditions.

layer model. The division of the communication functions into modular layers, where the entities at a layer provide communication services to the layer above or may request the services available from the layer below; also refers to the arrangement of functions into seven layers by ISO.

leased line. A dedicated line leased from a common carrier for private use.

line. The physical circuit through which signals are transferred between nodes.

linear system. A system whose mathematical formulation states that if the system responds by θ_1 and θ_2 to the individual system inputs I_1 and I_2, respectively, then the system's response to a linear combination of the input signal $a_1I_1 + a_2I_2$ will be $a_1\theta_1 + a_2\theta_2$, where a_1 and a_2 are arbitrary constants.

line balancing. Electrically modifying a line to provide better circuit characteristics for data reception.

line conditioning. The enhancement of a private line to improve its characteristics against noise or distortions due to phase delays in the signal.

line driver. A device that serves to reamplify the signals on a line before they degenerate.

line-of-sight transmission. The requirement that the transmitter and receiver be in direct view of each other, indigenous of wireless transmission.

line splitter. A component that divides the signal power into two equal parts for branching which may be used for branching with the token-passing bus access method.

line turnaround time. The delay a station incurs when its role changes from that of a transmitter to that of a receiver, and vice versa.

LLC classes. Two data link control services defined by the IEEE LAN standards, with class I permitting only unacknowledged connectionless services and class II permitting both unacknowledged connections and connection-oriented services.

local area network. A network that directs the communications between devices over a confined geographical area and which does not extend outside a company's premises; abbreviated LAN.

local loop. The wire-line connection connecting an individual telephone subscriber to the nearest telephone exchange.

logical link control. The common upper sublayer of the Data Link Layer defined by the IEEE LAN standards that serves to generate and interpret the link control commands.

logical ring. The arrangement of the nodes attached to a common bus that assigns the order for circulating the token.

m. An abbreviation for the prefix milli, used to indicate 10^{-3} unit.

M. An abbreviation for the prefix mega, used to indicate 10^6 units.

Manchester encoding. A form of encoding the bits for transmission that embeds a timing transition in the middle of the signals representing 0 or a 1.

MAP. Manufacturing Automation Protocol, a suite of protocol standards selected by agreement by commercial users for implementing communications between shop floor devices that require real-time response.

mark state. The name of the physical signal used in asynchronous transmission to represent a 1 or to indicate no traffic.

material flow. The material or goods transferred between processors.

matrix coding. A scheme using a generator matrix to encode the information bits into a parity check code.

matrix decoding. A scheme using a matrix to compute the syndrome of the received bits that had been encoded using matrix coding.

medium. The substance or technology used for the propagation of the physical signals.

medium access control. The lower sublayer of the data link layer defined by the

IEEE LAN standards that serves to frame the data units and acquire the right to access the medium.

medium access unit. A sublayer of the physical layer defined by IEEE for CSMA/CD LAN that is connected to the medium to allow the physical separation of the equipment at a node.

mesh network. A network configuration that provides alternate paths between the connected nodes.

message switching. A form of sharing line resources whereby preconnected lines are used to move messages from station to station toward their destination.

microwave. A form of wireless transmission using electromagnetic waves with very short wavelengths that are transmitted by a narrow beam between stations.

minimum cut–maximum flow theorem. The theorem used to determine the network capacity; it states that the maximum flow from source to sink equals the minimum capacity of all the cuts between them.

minimum distance. The minimum hamming distance needed to detect or detect and correct a fixed number of errors.

modem. A line-interfacing device whose name is derived from the terms *modulator/demodulator* and which forms the digital signals to conform to the network's transmission facilities and restores these signals into their original form on reception.

modem emulator. A device replacing a modem that allows the physical connections with the DCE to be made but does not perform the other modem functions.

modem sharing. A modem option that allows the modem to be shared by multiple devices, but only one at a time.

modulation. The process of changing the frequency content of a signal.

modulo arithmetic. The remainder after integer division.

mu (μ). A symbol for the prefix micro, used used to indicate 10^{-6} unit; in queuing theory, it represents the average rate each processor in the service facility can service the incoming items from the queue.

multidrop. See *multipoint*.

multilevel AM/PSK. One of the signaling techniques that may be used with the IEEE standard for the token-passing bus access method, in which three distinct amplitude levels are used and the PSK component of the modulation is used to reduce the signal bandwidth rather than carry additional data.

multimode graded-index fiber. A type of optical fiber whose relatively large core has a gradual change in the index of refraction and a smooth transition at its core-cladding boundary.

multimode step-index fiber. A type of optical fiber whose relatively large core has a step jump in the index of refraction at its core-cladding boundary.

multipin connector. A connector for making the physical connection between the DTE and DCE.

multipoint. A common line interconnecting many stations.

multipoint tariff. The charges and services specified for commercial lines that allow a station to be added in between the stations located farthest from each other or allow many to one or one to many stations to communicate, such as WATS line services.

multiserver queue. A queuing model whose service facility contains more than one identical processor to service the incoming items from a common queue.

n. An abbreviation for the prefix nano, used to indicate 10^{-9} unit.

NAK. Negative Acknowledge, a response returned from a station that has not received the communications sent.

narrow-band line. A commercial line whose bandwidth is less than that of a voice line.

NBS. National Bureau of Standards.

network capacity. The maximum possible flow from a source to a sink node.

network layer. Layer 3 of the ISO OSI model, which routes the data between adjacent points.

(n, k) code. A parity check code of length n used to encode k information bits.

node. The collection of functions and facilities located at a site and connected to a network; a node may serve as an intermediate node or as an end node.

nondata IDL signal. A special signal used to mark the end of the information encoded by Manchester encoding that does not have a transition in the middle of the signal.

nondata symbol. A symbol used to format the start delimiter and end-of-transmission delimiter in the token-passing bus frame.

n-tuple. Any of the possible bit patterns of length n.

Nyquist frequency. The minimum theoretical sampling frequency needed to recover a signal from its samples (twice the highest frequency in the signal spectrum).

odd parity. A scheme whereby the total number of 1's in a selected group of information bits and an associated parity bit are made an odd number.

office facilities. The monitoring, control, and reporting facilities organized to manage and administer an enterprise.

open wire. A form of metallic media for wire-line construction using pairs of unsheathed copper wires, now obsolete.

optical fiber. Cable constructed from two nearly similar light-transmitting materials used to guide light signals for wire-line construction.

originate node. The node initiating communications; also; the node assigned the originate node frequencies for transmitting and receiving signals during full-duplex operations.

orthogonality. A property exhibited by functions such as the dc, sine, and cosine terms of a Fourier series that permits the components to be computed independent of each other in any order.

OSI. Open Systems Interconnection.

p. An abbreviation for the prefix pico, used to indicate 10^{-12} unit.

PABX. Private automatic branch exchange.

packet assembler/disassembler. A devise needed to interface an X.25 packet-switching network.

packet switching. A form of sharing line resources by organizing the data into manageable fixed-size frames for transmission over the network.

pad-idle symbol. A symbol sent from the MAC sublayer in the IEEE LAN standard for the token-passing bus access method to format the frame preamble.

PAM. See *pulse-amplitude modulation*.

parallel mode. The transmission of a group of bits simultaneously on separate lines, indigenous of the operations internal to a computer system.

parity bit. A bit used to record whether a group of selected bits in a code word contains an even or odd number of 1's.

parity bit submatrix. The submatrix used to encode the parity bits of a parity check code that forms an integral part of the generator matrix and decoding matrix.

PBX. Private branch exchange.

PCM. See *pulse-code modulation*.

PDM. See *pulse-duration modulation*.

peer entitites. The entities that reside at the same layer level.

period. The time interval between repetitions of a periodic function's pattern.

periodic signal. A signal whose pattern continuously repeats at fixed intervals of time.

permanent virtual circuit. A form of packet switching that uses special packets to assign the physical path so that packets can be exchanged without requiring the stations to make further call connections or call terminations.

phase. The delay in the start of a sinusoidal function given as an angular value.

phase-coherent FSK. One of the signaling techniques that may be used with the IEEE token-passing bus access method in which the transitions between signaling frequencies occur only when the sinusoidal waveform makes a zero crossing so as to prevent any sudden signal jumps.

phase-continuous FSK. One of the signaling techniques that may be used with the IEEE token-passing bus access method in which the transition between signaling frequencies occurs as smooth changes as opposed to the sudden changes occurring by discrete switching.

phase modulation. A form of sinusoidal modulation using the phase of the carrier to shift the frequency spectrum of the signals; abbreviated PM.

phase response curve. The phase difference between the output and the input of a sinusoidal as a function of frequency.

phase-shift keying. A form of representing digital values by a finite number of sinusoidal phases; abbreviated PSK.

physical layer. Layer 1 of the ISO OSI model, which physically encodes the bits and provides the mechanical connections to the medium for transferring the bits between nodes.

physical ring. The network structure used with the token ring access method that physically links a station to two neighbors such that the token and other information pass from station to station in sequence.

physical signaling. The sublayer of the physical layer defined by the IEEE standard for CSMA/CD LAN that serves to generate the physical signals and to monitor the signal activities on the line to sense when the line is free or when a collision has occurred.

PM. See *phase modulation.*

point-to-point connection. The direct interconnection of two nodes by a link.

point-to-point mileage. The distance between switching stations measured in air miles, computed by a specified tariff formula.

point-to-point protocol. The set of rules that govern the exchange of data between nodes that are directly connected to each other.

Poisson distribution. Distribution that describes the statistical pattern of arrivals and that follows the formula $p(k) = (\lambda T)^k e^{-\lambda T}/k!$, where $p(k)$ equals the probability of k arrivals over the time interval T; the mean number of arrivals and variance for this distribution both equal λT.

polling. The scheme of controlling the right to transmit, in which one station invites each station in sequence to transmit when ready, or each station passes the right to transmit to the next station in sequence, in contrast with the contention method.

polynomial decoding. A method using a polynomial to compute the syndrome of the received bits that had been encoded using polynomial encoding.

polynomial encoding. A method using a generator polynomial to encode the information bits for transmission with redundant parity check bits.

PPM. See *pulse-position modulation.*

prefix criteria. The rule used to develop instantaneously decodabe codes, which is based on the theorem that a code is instantaneously decodable if and only if no code word of the code set is the prefix of any other code word in the code.

presentation layer. Layer 6 of the ISO OSI model, which ensures data compatibility by transforming the data to the format needed by the application layer.

primitive factor. A factor, say, of the polynomial $x^n + 1$, that is irreducible to factors of lower degree.

priority token. Token used by a station in a token-passing network to request the right to transmit data that it has ready for transmission before other stations in the network transmit data of lower priority.

private line. See *leased line.*

protocol. The rules and conventions used by peer entities to exchange information.

protocol control information. Information transferred between peer entities to co-ordinate their joint activities.

protocol converter. An intermediate node used to receive data using one protocol and transmit it with another up to the level where the two protocols differ.

protocol data unit. The data unit transferred between entities at a layer that contains the control information used by the layer and the data the layer transmits on behalf of the user.

PSK. See *phase-shift keying*.

public line. See *dial-up line*.

pulse-amplitude modulation. A form of pulse modulation that embeds the value of the sample into the amplitude of the pulse; abbreviated PAM.

pulse-code modulation. A form of modulation for encoding the analog value of a sample into a digital format; abbreviated PCM.

pulse-duration modulation. A form of pulse modulation that embeds the value of the sample proportional to maximum duration or width of the pulse; abbreviated PDM.

pulse-position modulation. A form of pulse modulation that embeds the value of the sample into the time the pulse occurs from the start of the sampling time; abbreviated PPM.

pulse spreading. The amount of delay an optical pulse suffers in passing through the optical-fiber cable; given by the difference in time between rays that take the longest path and those that take the direct path.

quadbit. Digital format where each pulse represents 4 bits of data.

quantizer. A unit that formats the value of a sample into one of a finite number of values.

queuing model. The framework used to study the performance parameters that describe the congestion formed by multiple customers, events, transactions, calls, packets, etc., at a service facility.

radio. A form of wireless transmission used for omnidirectional transmission, primarily used by AM and FM radio.

radio noise. Interference in a channel caused by electronic disturbances in the equipment or in the atmosphere.

random noise. Extraneous, uncorrelated interference in a channel.

real-time process. A process that must complete its response within a critical dead-line or else the results of its operations become moot.

reassembling. Recombining the data that had been previously segmented into several individual protocol data units.

receive machine. An abstract machine defined by the IEEE token-passing bus access standards to accept symbols from the physical layer and reconstruct the frames.

Reference Model for Open Systems Interconnection. A layer communication model formulated by ISO to expedite the development of implementation standards by independent teams of experts.

reflected ray. A ray of light reflected from an optical boundary.

refracted ray. A ray of light bent as it propagates through an optical boundary.

regenerative repeater machine. An optional machine defined by the IEEE token-passing bus access standards that serves to extend the distance covered by the LAN without having to implement the complete MAC sublayer at the intermediate nodes.

repeater. A protocol converter that converts the protocols of two subnetworks that differ at the physical layer.

request. One of the four primitive commands associated with each service performed by a communication layer; it initiates the service.

response. One of the four primitive commands associated with each service performed by a communication layer; it allows the remote station to respond after it has reacted to a request for services.

ring network. A network topology where the right to transmit passes from node to node in a circular fashion; the interconnected nodes may be organized into a virtual ring or a physical ring; in a virtual ring, nodes are interconnected to a common bus, and the right to transmit passes from a node to a designated node regardless of its placement on the bus; in a physical ring, each node is physically connected to its nearest neighbor, to whom the right to transmit and all communication pass.

route. The collection of interconnected point-to-point lines establishing the path for an end-to-end connection.

router. A protocol converter that converts the protocols of two networks that differ from each other at the network layer.

sampled data theorem. The theorem that states that a bandlimited input signal can be recovered from a periodic sampled sequence of the signal if the sampling frequency is at least twice the highest frequency in the signal's spectrum.

sampler. A real or abstract device for generating a sequence of pulses representing discrete values of a continuous signal.

satellite. A radio repeater station placed in a controlled orbit, such as a geostationary orbit, which serves to circumvent the inherent problem of line-of-sight transmission between antennas on the earth's surface.

segmentation. The separation of a large service data unit into several protocol data units that are individually transported between peer entities.

self-test. A modem option that allows the modem to automatically test possible points of trouble in the devices servicing the communication path.

separation. The reconstruction of the individual service data units that had previously been concatenated into a single protocol data unit.

serial mode. The sequential transmission of a group of bits one after the other over a single line.

service access point. A point where the services requested or provided to a layer are accessible.

service data unit. The data transferred between peer entities on behalf of the user.

service provider. A model depicting all the entities supplying services at a layer level as a single functional unit that shows the interfaces with the layer above.

session layer. Layer 5 of the ISO OSI model, which serves to synchronize and manage the dialogue between cooperating end nodes.

Shannon's second theorem. The theorem that states that if the rate of transmission is less than the theoretical capacity of a noisy channel, then the reliability of transmission can be arbitrarily improved by coding.

shop floor. The production functions and facilities of an enterprise.

signal distortion. The deformation of a signal occurring during transmission.

signal-to-noise ratio. The relative power of the signal to the power of the extraneous noise in a line, usually given in decibels.

silent signal. A signal transmitted repeatedly by the head-end remodulator in the token-passing bus access method to report that it is not receiving a signal.

simplex line. A communication line that can transmit in only one direction.

sine-cosine series. Fourier series whose terms are the dc component and the sine and cosine functions of the fundamental frequency and harmonics of the periodic signal that it represents.

single-cable mid-split. A particular designation of 6 MHz channels that has been assigned to the bandpass available on a CATV cable.

single-mode step-index fiber. A type of optical fiber whose very small diameter core allows only rays that take a straight path to pass through the fiber.

single-server queue. A queuing model whose service facility contains one processor.

sink (data). An end node that serves as the destination node for the transferred data.

sinusoidal function. A sine or cosine function.

sinusoidal modulation. The shifting of the frequency spectrum of a bandlimited signal by a sinusoidal carrier to another frequency range in the bandpass of the transmission channel.

SME. Society for Manufacturing Engineering.

Snell's law. $\sin \theta_r / \sin \theta_i = n_2/n_1$; where θ_r is the angle of refraction and θ_i is the angle of incidence of a ray as it passes from a material whose index of refraction is n_2 to a material whose index of refraction is n_1.

SOH. Start-of-header control character in an alphabet.

source (data). An end node where data transfer is initiated.

space state. The name of the physical signal used in asynchronous transmission to represent a 0.

spectral density. The frequency content of a signal; also; the curve produced by the Fourier transform.

star network. A network configuration connecting all tributary nodes directly to a central node through which all communications pass.

start-stop transmission. Asynchronous transmission.

state transition diagram. A diagrammatic method used by programmers and logic designers to specify the actions a machine must perform when it is stimulated by an input.

state transition table. A tabular method for displaying the specifications given in a state transition diagram.

static. See *radio noise*.

statistical multiplexer. A time-division multiplexer that assigns time slots to the active users dynamically on a demand basis.

steady-state response. That portion of the total response of a system remaining after the system is given enough time for the transient portion to die out.

store and forward. The technique of storing a message and later retransmitting it, used to automate message switching.

STX. Start-of-text control character in an alphabet.

suite of standards. A collection of implementation standards specified for the communication layers that are organized to work together.

supermessage. A message used to systematically reduce the number of messages in the Huffman coding procedure and whose probability is the sum of the probabilities of the messages it replaces.

suppressed-carrier double-sideband modulation. The process of transmitting and recovering a signal from both sidebands of an amplitude-modulated signal.

suppressed-carrier single-sideband modulation. The process of transmitting and recovering a signal from one sideband of an amplitude-modulated signal.

suppressed-carrier vestigial-sideband modulation. The process of transmitting and recovering a signal from one sideband and a part of the other sideband of an amplitude-modulated signal.

switched virtual circuit. A form of packet switching that uses special packets to temporarily assign the physical path.

switching station. An intermediate node that serves as a central point for selecting lines connecting the tributary stations of a network.

synchronous satellite. A communications satellite that rotate the earth once every 24 hours so that it appears stationary to fixed points on the earth's surface.

synchronous transmission. Serial transmission using SYN characters at the start of an incoming block to alert the receiver and embed the timing information with the data bits.

syndrome. A pattern of $n-k$ bits calculated from the received bits of an (n, k) parity check code that characterizes the error or indicates that no error of the type expected has occurred.

system management. The management functions assigned to the application layer for the control and monitoring of the resources of the system.

tariff. A document filed by a common carrier for approval by a regulatory agency, defining the services and the charges for the services offered to the public.

termination phase. The communication phase used to notify a communicating partner that transmission has ended and allow either partner to establish communications with another partner at the connected station.

thermal noise. Noise due to the random variations inherent in the thermal properties of materials.

time delay. The delay in the start of a sinusoidal function given in units of time.

time-division multiplexing. A scheme for sharing a channel by dividing the available time into time slices.

time domain. The response of a system described as a function of time; see also *frequency domain*.

time sequence diagram. A working diagram showing the temporal order of commands issued to or from the service provider.

token. A specific control frame circulated sequentially from station to station, giving each station the exclusive right to transmit.

token-passing bus. The scheme of broadcasting communications to all stations connected to a common bus whereby each station accepts frames addressed to itself, bypasses all others, and passes the right to transmit by a token.

token-passing ring. The scheme of passing all communications and the right to transmit by a token from station to station in a physical ring.

tone. A sinusoidal frequency; usually designates a frequency in the audio range.

TOP. Technical and Office Protocols, a suite of protocol standards selected by agreement by commercial users for communications between office facility devices.

Transcode. A standard 6-bit code set that has evolved from punch card technology.

transient response. That portion of the total response of a system that reflects the dynamic change occurring in the output when the system goes from one steady state to another.

transmit machine. An abstract machine defined by the IEEE token-passing bus access standards that acts to pass symbols from the MAC sublayer to the physical layer.

transport layer. Layer 4 of the ISO OSI model, whose role is to ensure reliable data transfer between end nodes.

tree network. A network configuration whereby the interconnected nodes are organized into a hierarchical structure that directs the communications through branches toward their destination.

trunk. A communication channel between two central offices or between a private branch exchange and a central office.

twisted pairs. A form of wire-line medium using pairs of sheathed electrical conductors whose strands are twisted together by various amounts so as to reduce the amount of electrical interference among circuits.

unacknowledged connectionless. Data link control service that permits nodes to exchange information without first establishing a data link connection.

unbalanced circuit. The electrical connection between DTE and DCE that shares a common return line with other interface circuits for completing the circuit.

uniquely decodable. A code in which there is only one way for decoding all possible sequences of code words.

universe of discourse. Semantics shared by the application and the application layer.

utilization factor. The ratio of the mean rate that items arrive at a queue to the mean rate that the service facility can process the items.

value-added carrier. A vendor that has enhanced the communication services offered by common carriers and offers these services to the public.

virtual circuit. Packet switching that uses special control packets to establish the path through the network.

voice channel. A bandpass system in the range of 300 to 3300 Hz, normally used to transmit voice.

voice-grade line. A commercial line whose bandwidth and quality is that of a voice line.

voluntary standards. Recommendations established by consensus and published by a standards group for public use.

WATS. See *Wide Area Telephone Services*.

wavelength. The linear distance of one cycle of a periodic function.

white noise. A form of random noise whose spectrum is uniformly distributed.

Wide area network. Network facilities made available to the public by a commercial vendor for long-haul, external communications.

Wide Area Telephone Services. Bulk-line tariff offered to permit a subscriber to call and/or receive calls from any other subscriber in a zone.

wide-band line. A commercial line whose bandwidth is greater than a voice line, normally formed by a group of consecutive voice-grade lines.

wireless. Referring to a communication path that uses electromagnetic waves through open space as the medium.

wire-line. Referring to a communication path created by using metallic conductors or optical fibers as the medium.

words per minutes. A unit of transmission speed that is numerically equal to the line speed in bps when 10 bits are used to encode each character; abbreviated wpm.

workstation. An end node in a network where a user can perform local services on the data.

wpm. See *words per minute*.

SOLUTIONS TO SELECTED EXERCISES

1.2

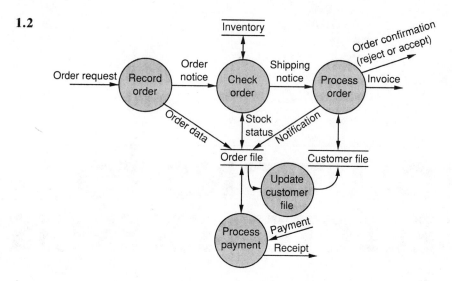

Note that the 'order confirmation' should have been included in the context diagram. This planned response mechanism covers only the information flow associated with the mission of the enterprise. To complete the picture many other external communications and response mechanisms need to be included (e.g., the material handling operations, the purchase and payment of new stock, the handling of returned goods, the correspondence dealing with complaints, the payment of taxes and compliance with government regulations, labor relations, and many others).

1.3   A letter has been confirmed to have been sent when it is put into a mailbox or has been picked up by a postal employee.

A letter has been confirmed to have been delivered when it is deposited into the mail box identified by the destination address on the letter.

A registered letter has been confirmed to have been received and accepted by the receiver when the sender receives the receipt of delivery.

1.7   The number of lines needed to interconnect n nodes to each other is $1 + 2 + 3 + \ldots + (n - 1) = n(n - 1)/2$. The formula can be demonstrated by constructing some of the configurations.

1.10

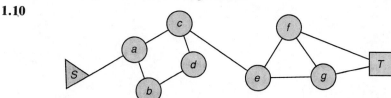

One approach is to transform the network into the directed graph shown in the following figure by combining nodes when there is only one path connecting two nodes.

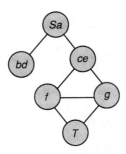

From this equivalent graph the possible paths can be seen to be:

SacefT   SacefgT   SacegT   SacegfT
SabdcefT SabdcefgT SabdcegT SabdcegfT

As a follow-up exercise, write an algorithm that will enumerate all the paths between two nodes in an arbitrary network.

2.1 The figure below identifies each of the parameters of the sinusoidal $F(t) = A \sin [(2\pi/\tau) (t - t_0)]$:

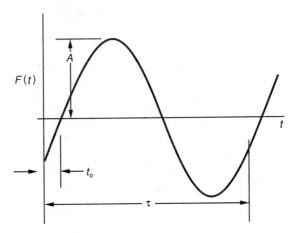

2.2 The output responses are
(a) $\sin (t - .1) + \frac{1}{2} \sin (2t - .2)$
(b) $\sin (t - .1) + \frac{1}{2} \sin (2t - .2) + \frac{1}{3}\sin (3t - .3)$

After the response curves have been plotted, it can be seen that the curves replicate the input curves except that they are displaced in time.

2.5

Function	A	f	ω	τ	φ	t_o
$5 \sin 6 (t - 1)$	5	.955	6	1.047	−.167	1
$5 \sin (120t + 0.75)$	5	19.099	120	.052	.75	.006
$6 \sin (2\pi/5) (t - 3)$	6	.2	1.257	5	−3.770	−3
$6 \cos (10\pi t - 0.1)$	6	5	31.416	.2	1.471	.047

2.6 $(1 + 0.1 \cos 5t) \cos 100t = \cos 100t + .1 \cos 5t \cos 100t$ From the trigonometric identity $\cos a \cos b = \frac{1}{2} \cos (a + b) + (\frac{1}{2}) \cos (a - b)$, the above equation can be rewritten by the linear combination of three sinusoidals: $\cos 100 \, t + 0.05 \cos 105t + 0.05 \cos 95t$

2.7

Note		C	D	E	F	G	A	B	C
Frequency		264	297	330	352	396	440	495	528
Frequency difference			33	33	22	44	44	55	33
Wave length (inches)		15	13	12	11	10	9	8	7

2.8 $R_{db} = 10 \log_{10} (Po/Pi) = 10 \log_{10} (Eo/Ei)^2 = 20 \log_{10} (Eo/Ei)$

2.9 The frequency response curves are:

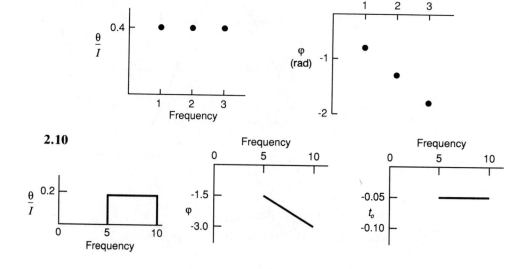

2.11 The approximate values are:

(a) $R_{db} = 10 \log_{10} (2P_i/P_i) = 3$ db.

(b) $R_{db} = 10 \log_{10} (.5P_i/P_i) = -3$ db.

2.12
$$P_3/P_1 = (P_3/P_2) (P_2/P_1)$$
$$10 \log_{10} (P_3/P_1) = 10 \log_{10} (P_3/P_2) + 10 \log_{10} (P_2/P_1)$$
$$(P_3/P_1)_{db} = (P_3/P_2)_{db} + (P_2/P_1)_{db}$$
$$P_3/P_1 = 10^{[(P_3/P_2)_{db} + (P_2/P_1)_{db}]/10}$$

2.13 The phase delay for an ideal linear system is cf where f is the frequency and c is a constant. Also the attenuation or amplification of the amplitude $\theta/I = k$ where k is a constant. For any arbitrary sinusoidal input $A \sin 2\pi ft$ that lies within the bandpass of the system the output response is

$$kA \sin (2\pi ft + cf) = kA \sin 2\pi f(t + t_o)$$

where $t_o = c/2\pi$ which is a constant independent of the frequency.

2.14 If $F(t)$ is a linear combination of sinusoidals that pass through the bandpass of a linear system, then each sinusoidal is amplified or attenuated by a constant factor k and is delayed by a constant time t_o; therefore the output is $kF (t - t_o)$.

2.17
$$F_1 (\omega) = \int_{-\infty}^{\infty} f_1 (t)e^{-i\omega t}dt$$

$$F_1 (\omega) = \int_{-\infty}^{\infty} f_1(t)e^{-i\omega t}dt$$

$$a_1F_1 (\omega) + a_2F_2 (\omega) = a_1 \int_{-\infty}^{\infty} f_1(t)e^{-i\omega t}dt + a_2 \int_{-\infty}^{\infty} f_2(t)e^{-i\omega t}dt$$

$$= \int_{-\infty}^{\infty} [a_1f_1(t) + a_2f_2 (t)]e^{-i\omega t}dt$$

which is the Fourier transform of $a_1f_1 (t) + a_2f_2 (t)$. The theorem shows that the Fourier transform satisfies the properties of a linear system.

2.18
$$e^{-i\omega\tau}F(w) = e^{-i\omega\tau} \int_{-\infty}^{\infty} f(t)e^{-i\omega t}dt$$

$$= \int_{-\infty}^{\infty} f(t)e^{-i\omega(t+\tau)}dt$$

Using a change in variable $T = t + \tau$, then

$$= \int_{-\infty}^{\infty} f(T - \tau)e^{-i\omega T}dT$$

which is the Fourier transform for $f(t - \tau)$.

2.19 Using a change of variable $W = \omega - \omega_o$ in the equation:

$$\frac{1}{2\pi} \int_{-\infty}^{\infty} F(\omega - \omega_o)^{i\omega t}d\omega = \frac{1}{2\pi} \int_{-\infty}^{\infty} F(W)e^{i(W + \omega_o)t}dW$$

$$= \frac{1}{2\pi} \int_{-\infty}^{\infty} F(W)e^{i\omega_o t}e^{iWt}dW$$

$$= e^{i\omega_o t}\left[\frac{1}{2\pi} \int_{-\infty}^{\infty} F(W)e^{iWt}dW\right]$$

where $\dfrac{1}{2\pi} \displaystyle\int_{-\infty}^{\infty} F(W)e^{iWt}dW$ is the function $f(t)$.

2.22
$$F(t) = \left(\frac{1}{\pi} + \frac{1}{2}\right) + \left(\frac{2}{\pi} + \frac{1}{2}\right) \cos \omega t + \frac{2}{3\pi} \cos 2\omega t$$

$$- \frac{2}{3\pi} \cos 3\omega t - \frac{2}{15\pi} \cos 4\omega t + \frac{2}{5\pi} \cos 5\omega t + \ldots$$

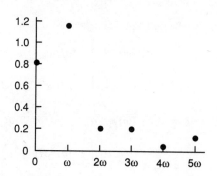

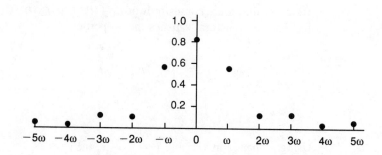

2.25 (a) 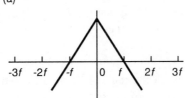   (b)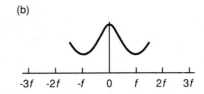

3.1 $(S/N)_{W_1} - (S/N)_{W_2} = 10 \log_{10}(S/N_1) - 10 \log_{10}(S/N_2)$

$= 10 \log_{10}(N_2/N_1)$

For thermal noise $N = kW$, therefore:

$= 10 \log_{10}(W_2/W_1)$

$= (W_2/W_1)_{db}$

3.2 $T = A(1 + m \sin 2\pi t) \sin 20\pi t$

$= A[\sin 20\pi t + .5m \sin (18\pi t + \pi/2) + .5m \sin (22\pi t - \pi/2)]$

Arbitrarily set the value of A to 1 and plot the curve for various values of m.

3.3 $T = A \sin[(20\pi \sin 2\pi t)t]$

Write a computer program to calculate values of this function and plot the results.

3.4 $T = A \sin [20\pi t + (\pi/2)\sin 2\pi t]$

Write a computer program to calculate values of this function and plot the results.

3.5   Wave length for the 100 Hz signal is:
$\lambda = 3 \times 10^5/100 = 3000$ km
Wave length of the 100 kHz signal is:
$\lambda = 3 \times 10^5/10^5 = 3$ km

3.6

Original signal	2	5
1st multiple of sampling frequency	5, 9	2, 12
2nd multiple of sampling frequency	12, 16	9, 19
3rd multiple of sampling frequency	19, 23	16, 26

The replicas about other multiples of the sampling frequency can be computed in a similar fashion. Note that the frequency components from the two sampled signals overlap each other.

3.9   The theorem is based on an infinite number of samples.

3.10 The frequency components of the replicas of the sampled noise may create an alias in the frequency spectrum of the bandlimited signal.

3.15 Several PCM pulses are used to represent the value of each PAM pulse. For example, if the value of the PAM pulse is quantized to 8 bits and each PCM pulse represents a dibit, then the bandwidth for transmitting the PCM pulses is 4 times the bandwidth for transmitting the PAM pulses.

3.16 A couple of ways might be considered:

- Use several consecutive voice grade lines.
- Digitize the symphony and play it back after it has been transmitted.

3.20 For ASK: $T = S_A \sin 2\pi ft$

where S_A is a switch that selects different amplitude values.

For FSK: $T = A \sin 2\pi s_f t$

where S_f is a switch that selects different frequency values.

For PSK: $T = A \sin (2\pi ft + S_\phi)$

where S_ϕ is a switch that selects different phase values.

3.21 Compute $100\ (C_1 - C_2)/C_1$ where $C_1 = \log_{10} (1 + S/N)/\log_{10} 2$ and $C_2 = (S/N)_{db}/3$ (note that the bandwidth W cancels out of the equation and

$$\frac{S}{N} = \frac{10^{(S/N)db}}{10}.$$

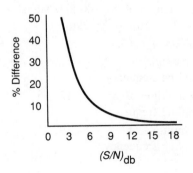

2.25 (a)   (b)

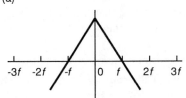   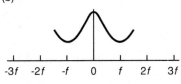

3.1 $(S/N)_{W_1} - (S/N)_{W_2} = 10 \log_{10}(S/N_1) - 10 \log_{10}(S/N_2)$
$$= 10 \log_{10}(N_2/N_1)$$

For thermal noise $N = kW$, therefore:

$$= 10 \log_{10}(W_2/W_1)$$
$$= (W_2/W_1)_{db}$$

3.2 $T = A(1 + m \sin 2\pi t) \sin 20\pi t$
$= A[\sin 20\pi t + .5m \sin (18\pi t + \pi/2) + .5m \sin (22\pi t - \pi/2)]$

Arbitrarily set the value of A to 1 and plot the curve for various values of m.

3.3 $T = A \sin[(20\pi \sin 2\pi t)t]$

Write a computer program to calculate values of this function and plot the results.

3.4 $T = A \sin [20\pi t + (\pi/2)\sin 2\pi t]$

Write a computer program to calculate values of this function and plot the results.

3.5   Wave length for the 100 Hz signal is:
$\lambda = 3 \times 10^5/100 = 3000$ km
Wave length of the 100 kHz signal is:
$\lambda = 3 \times 10^5/10^5 = 3$km

3.6

Original signal	2	5
1st multiple of sampling frequency	5, 9	2, 12
2nd multiple of sampling frequency	12, 16	9, 19
3rd multiple of sampling frequency	19, 23	16, 26

The replicas about other multiples of the sampling frequency can be computed in a similar fashion. Note that the frequency components from the two sampled signals overlap each other.

3.9 The theorem is based on an infinite number of samples.

3.10 The frequency components of the replicas of the sampled noise may create an alias in the frequency spectrum of the bandlimited signal.

3.15 Several PCM pulses are used to represent the value of each PAM pulse. For example, if the value of the PAM pulse is quantized to 8 bits and each PCM pulse represents a dibit, then the bandwidth for transmitting the PCM pulses is 4 times the bandwidth for transmitting the PAM pulses.

3.16 A couple of ways might be considered:

- Use several consecutive voice grade lines.
- Digitize the symphony and play it back after it has been transmitted.

3.20 For ASK: $T = S_A \sin 2\pi ft$

where S_A is a switch that selects different amplitude values.

For FSK: $T = A \sin 2\pi s_f t$

where S_f is a switch that selects different frequency values.

For PSK: $T = A \sin (2\pi ft + S_\phi)$

where S_ϕ is a switch that selects different phase values.

3.21 Compute $100 (C_1 - C_2)/C_1$ where $C_1 = \log_{10} (1 + S/N)/\log_{10}2$ and $C_2 = (S/N)_{db}/3$ (note that the bandwidth W cancels out of the equation and

$$\frac{S}{N} = \frac{10^{(S/N)db}}{10}.$$

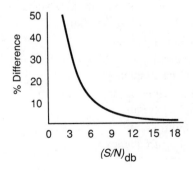

3.22 $C_{rw} = rW \log_2 (1 + S/N)$

For large signal to noise ratio and thermal noise (i.e., $N = kW$) the above equation can be rewritten by:

$$C_{rw} = rW \log_2 \frac{S}{rkW}$$
$$= rW \log_2 \frac{S}{kW} - rW \log_2 r$$
$$= rC_W - rW \log_2 r$$

3.24 (a) For ASCII characters $S_{bps} = 1.1 S_{wpm}$

(b) For Baudot characters $S_{bps} = .742 S_{wpm}$ to $.75 S_{wpm}$.

4.3 $\Delta t = (L/v_{core}) (c/c) (n_{core}/n_{cladding} - 1)$
$$= (L/c) (n_{core}/n_{cladding}) (n_{core} - n_{cladding})$$

where $c = 3 \times 10^5$ km/sec.

For $L = 1$ km and for n_{core} approximately equal to $n_{cladding}$, then the theoretical limit for the transmission rate:

$(1/\Delta t) = c/(n_{core} - n_{cladding})$ bits per second

4.4 Approximating the index of refraction in air by the value 1, gives:

$$\theta_{glass} = \sin^{-1} (1/1.65) = 37.3°$$
$$\theta_{diamond} = \sin^{-1} (1/2.417) = 24.4°$$

4.5
$$NA = \sqrt{(n_{core} + n_{cladding}) (n_{core} - n_{cladding})}$$
$$\sqrt{2(n_{core} + n_{cladding}) (n_{core} - n_{cladding})/2}$$
$$\sqrt{2n\delta}$$

where $n = (n_{core} + n_{cladding})/2$ and $\delta = n_{core} - n_{cladding}$.
From exercise 4.3, it has been shown that:
$(c\Delta t/L) = n_{core} - n_{cladding}$, therefore:
$$NA = \sqrt{2nc\Delta t/L}$$

4.7

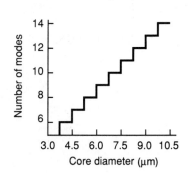

Number of modes vs Core diameter (μm)

The angular spacing between modes is λ/D. For single mode fibers, the rays from one mode are allowed to propagate and the remaining rays are absorbed in the cladding after they are refracted. To satisfy this condition, the maximum angle of incident must be approximately equal to $(\pi/2 - \lambda/D)$ where λ/D is the angle of the first mode (i.e., $n_{cladding}/n_{core}$ must be approximately equal to $\sin(\pi/2 - \lambda/D)$. Since λ/D is a small value, a working approximation for single mode fiber material is:

$$n_{cladding}/n_{core} = 1 - .5(\lambda/D)^2$$

and therefore

$$D = \lambda/\sqrt{2(1 - n_{cladding}/n_{core})}$$

4.8   For rays that take a straight path through the fiber:

$$\Delta t = L/v_1 - L/v_2$$
$$= (c/c)\,(L/v_1) - (c/c)\,(L/v_2) \text{ where } c = 3 \times 10^5 \text{ km/sec}$$
$$= (L/c)\,(n_1 - n_2)$$

This formula is seen to be similar to that for a step index fiber as developed in exercise 4.3. For $L = 1$ km, the theoretical limit for the transmission rate:

$$1/\Delta t = c/(n_1 - n_2) \text{ bits per second}$$

4.9   Microwaves in the range of 1 to 300 GHz have a wave length of .1 to 30 cm. For visible light the spectrum runs from about from $.49 \times 10^{-4}$ to $.79 \times 10^{-4}$ cm.

4.10   Assuming the transmitter and receiver are at the same height, then (see figure):

$$d = 3959\theta \text{ and } \cos(\theta/2) = 3959/(3959 + h)$$

Therefore:

$$h = 3959[1/\cos(d/7918) - 1]$$

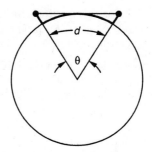

For small angles $1/\cos x$ can be approximated by $1 + x^2/2$, giving the approximation:

$$h = d^2/6$$

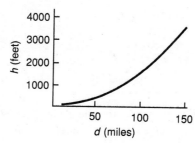

4.11

$$P_r = \left(\frac{4\pi df}{c}\right)^2 P_t$$

Doubling the distance between transmitting antenna and receiving antenna or doubling the transmission frequency gives:

$$P_{r2} = \left(\frac{8\pi df}{c}\right)^2 P_t$$

Therefore:

$$10 \log_{10} (P_{r2}/P_r) = 10 \log_{10} 2^2$$
$$= 6 \text{ db}$$

4.13 Assuming the earth stations are equally space on the circumference of the earth (see figure), then the distance from a station to the satellite and back to a station on the earth's surface is $d = 49040$ miles.

The delay a signal suffers in traversing this distance is 0.26 seconds. With such a delay, it would be prohibitive to require the receiver to acknowledge each message separately.

4.14 Hint: see solution for exercise 4.10.

5.1 The number of ways of selecting two or more words of N possible code words is:

$$S = \sum_{t=2}^{N} \binom{N}{i}$$

A closed form expression for the right hand side of this equation can be formed from the binary expansion of $(x + y)^N$ with $x = y = 1$, that is:

$$2^N = (1 + 1)^N$$

$$= \sum_{i=0}^{N} \binom{N}{i}$$

$$= 1 + N + S$$

For an n bit code there are 2^n possible code words. Substituting $N = 2^n$ into the above equation and solving for S gives:

$$S = 2^{2^n} - 2^n - 1$$

For an alphabet of k symbols, k^n possible code words can be formed (i.e., $N = k^n$), giving the possible number of sets with two or more words as:

$$S = 2^{k^n} - k^n - 1$$

5.2

	Weights 5 1 1 1 1		Weights 4 2 2 1
0	0 0 0 0 0	0	0 0 0 0
1	0 0 0 0 1	1	0 0 0 1
2	0 0 0 1 1	2	0 0 1 0
3	0 0 1 1 1	3	0 0 1 1
4	0 1 1 1 1	4	0 1 1 0
5	1 0 0 0 0	5	1 0 0 1
6	1 1 0 0 0	6	1 1 0 0
7	1 1 1 0 0	7	1 1 0 1
8	1 1 1 1 0	8	1 1 1 0
9	1 1 1 1 1	9	1 1 1 1

5.3 None of the suggested weights can be used to construct a k-out-of-*n* code that can encode the decimal numbers in 9's complement. A necessary condition for such a code is that must be an even number of weights whose sum equals nine. The following is an example of a 9's complement, 3-out-of-6 code:

	Weights
	4 3 2 1 0 -1
0	0 0 0 1 1 1
1	0 0 1 0 1 1
2	0 1 0 0 1 1
3	1 0 0 0 1 1
4	1 0 0 1 0 1
5	0 1 1 0 1 0
6	0 1 1 1 0 0
7	1 0 1 1 0 0
8	1 1 0 1 0 0
9	1 1 1 0 0 0

5.4 (a)
```
 0 0000
 1 0001
 2 0011
 3 0010
 4 0110
 5 0111
 6 0101
 7 0100
 8 1100
 9 1101
10 1111
11 1110
12 1010
13 1011
14 1001
15 1000
```
An important feature of this code for real time applications is the various symmetries exhibited by the counting sequence.

(b) The gray code, 10110101, has the value of 217.

(d) Illustration of the conversion formula, $g_i = b_i \oplus b_{i+1}$:

```
1 1 0 1 1 0 0 1     Binary code
  1 1 0 1 1 0 0     Binary code shifted one position
─────────────────
1 0 1 1 0 1 0 1     Gray code
```

(e) Illustration of the conversion formula, $b_i = b_{i+1} \oplus g_i$:

1 0 1 1 0 1 0 1	Gray code
0 1 1 0 1 1 0 0	Binary code shifted one position
0 1 1 0 1 1 0 0 1	Binary code

5.5 (a)

	00000	10101	01010
00000	0	3	2
10101	3	0	5
01010	2	5	0

(b)

	000000	010101	101010	110110
000000	0	3	3	4
010101	3	0	6	3
101010	3	6	0	3
110110	4	3	3	0

5.6 $d(010, 011) + d(101, 011) \geqslant d(010, 101)$

$\qquad 1 \quad + \quad 2 \quad = \quad 3$

5.7 $d(100101, 011010) = 6$

5.8

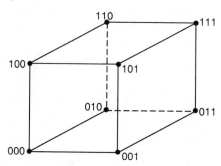

The hamming distance between any two code words is the number of edges traversed.

5.9 To correct for 2 errors, the minimum hamming distance between any two code words must be at least 5.

To detect 3 errors, the minimum hamming distance between any two code words must be at least 4.

To correct for 2 errors and detect an additional 3 errors, the minimum hamming distance must be at least 8.

5.10 $m \leqslant 128/(1 + 7) = 16$

The Hamming code for encoding four information bits, discussed in section 5.2, is an instance of such a code.

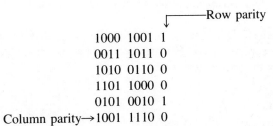

5.11 For even parity the appended parity bit is:

  (a) 1

  (b) 0

  (c) 0

5.13

                                    ┌────────Row parity
                                    ↓
              1000 1001 1
              0011 1011 0
              1010 0110 0
              1101 1000 0
              0101 0010 1
  Column parity→1001 1110 0

The rectangular code can correct for any single error.

5.15 (a) 0 000 111

  (b) 110 000 110

  (c) 100 011 010 010 100

5.16 (a) An error is indicated in bit position 4.

  (b) An error is indicated in bit position 12, but since there are only 11 bits there must have been multiple errors.

  (c) An error is indicated in bit position 2.

5.18

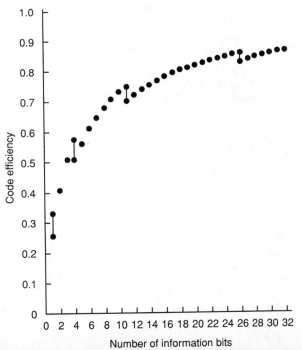

Code efficiency vs. Number of information bits

5.19 After the first encoding of the information bits into a Hamming code, the code word is 1 010 010. The second encoding gives the code word 10 100 011 011. This scheme can correct for two errors.

5.20 The value of c_1 is zero when there is no error or an even number of errors in bit positions p_1, i_3, i_5, or i_7. For c_2 to equal zero there must be no errors or an even number of errors in bit positions p_2, i_3, i_6, or i_7; and similarly for c_4 to equal zero there must be no errors or an even number of errors in bit positions p_4, i_5, i_6, or i_7. Only particular combinations can results in a 000 in the three check bits; for example, an error in bit positions i_3, i_5, i_6 and i_7.

5.21 In each of these examples, the identity submatrix forms the front submatix of the generator matrix. For the decoding matrix, the identity matrix would appear below the parity submatrix.

(a) (1 11)

(b) 100 110
010 101
001 011

(c) 10000 1001
01000 0111
00100 0110
00010 0101
00001 0011

(d) 10000000000 1111
01000000000 1110
00100000000 1101
00010000000 1100
00001000000 1011
00000100000 1010
00000010000 1001
00000001000 0111
00000000100 0110
00000000010 0101
00000000001 0011

5.22 (a) $x^2 + 1$

(b) $x^3 + x + 1$

(c) $x^7 + x^5 + x^4 + x^3 + x + 1$

5.25 If $x^3 + x + 1$ or $x^3 + x^2 + 1$ were not primitive factors than they would be exactly divisible by $x + 1$.

5.26 $x^{30} + 1 = (x^{15} + 1)^2$

which is equivalent to

$$(x + 1)^2(x^2 + x + 1)^2(x^4 + x + 1)^2(x^4 + x^3 + 1)^2(x^4 + x^3 + x^2 + x + 1)^2$$

5.27 It is simpler to use the polynomial operations directly on the polynomial coefficients rather than express the polynomials explicitly.

(a)
```
            1 110
  1101)1000 000
       1101
        101 0
        110 1
         11 10
         11 01
            110   Parity bits
```

The resultant code word is 1000 110.

5.29 It is simpler to use the polynomial operations directly on the polynomial coefficients rather than express the polynomials explicitly.

(a)
```
            1 110
  1101)1011 101
       1101
        110 1
        110 1
            001   Syndrome
```

The syndrome indicates an error in the received code word.

(b) The operations result in a syndrome of 0011.

5.30 There are 30 possible polynomials. Besides the 5 primitive polynomials; there are 10 polynomials which can be found by multiplying the primitives two at a time, 10 polynomials which can be found by multiplying the primitives three at a time, and 5 polynomials which can be found by multiplying the primitives four at a time.

5.31

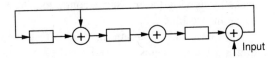

The exclusive-or component effectively acts as a straight-through line when one of its input lines is open.

5.32

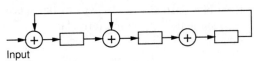

The exclusive-or component effectively acts as a straight-through line when one of its input lines is open.

6.2   The overhead penalty for transmitting a typical 8 bit character by asynchronous transmission consists of 3 bits, the START and STOP bit for framing and a parity bit for checking. This gives an overhead to block size ratio of 3/11.

For synchronous transmission the situation is more complex. The 2 SYN characters and the 4 CRC characters in a typical block of 512 characters only give an overhead penalty ratio of 6/512. Besides these overhead characters the block contains other control characters for framing which serve to identify the type of frame being transmitted.

6.3   An echo suppression circuit effectively turns a full duplex line into a half duplex line.

6.4   All eight bits must exactly correspond to the SYN character to give a false synchronization.

6.5   All stations may listen on channel A for communications from any station that wants to initiate the exchange of data. The receiving station can respond on channel B.

Another scheme serves when a host station controls all communications from a number of tributaries in the network. The host station may be arbitrarily assigned channel A for transmission and all the tributary stations transmit on channel B. This scheme allows all stations to use fixed frequencies for transmission and reception.

6.6   Two well-known strategies for assigning variable blocks of memory to independent users are by first-fit and best fit. The first-fit strategy assigns the first unused area of memory from the top of memory's address space that fits the message. The best fit strategy keeps a record of all blocks of unused contiguous space and assigns the block that would leave the least amount of unused space for each message. Both of these strategies will fragment the memory into smaller blocks with each incomming message and will coalesce blocks into larger blocks when a message departs the system and produces two contiguous blocks of unused space. A possible cure is to "garbage collect" the unused space by moving the messages contiguous to each other and leaving the unused space in one block.

Another, less dramatic method is to fragment the memory into blocks and transmit the messages by fixed sized pieces that will fit into any unused block. This method, however, introduces new complications in exchanging data between stations (discussed in later sections of the text).

6.7 $t = 1/S$ where S is given in units of $k$bps and t is the time for transmitting 1000 bits. Using 3×10^5 $k$ps as the speed of propagation gives the distance between nodes, d, by the formula:

$$d = (3 \times 10^5)/S \ km$$

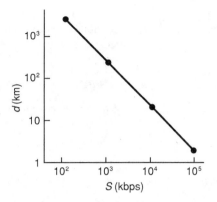

6.10 A triangular array of switching points (shown below) can connect any input line to any output line that is not already in service. For n stations, a triangular array requires $n(n - 1)/2$ semiconductor or metallic contacts.

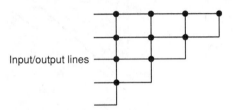

Input/output lines

6.11 (a) In the figure below the lines from stage 1_A to stage 2_A and 2_B are blocked, and the lines from stage 2_C and stage 2_D to stage 3_C are blocked. Although input line 1 and output line 9 are available in this configuration, any path that might be constructed is already blocked. However, this situation would be changed if there were another crossbar switch at stage 2, say stage 2_E, that would offer an unblocked line from stage 1_A to stage 2_E, and an unblocked line from stage 2_E to stage 3_C.

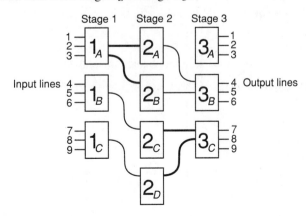

(b) $C = (2n - 1) [2N + (N/n)^2]$

For a large number of input lines to each crossbar switch, the factor $2n - 1$ can be approximated by $2n$, so that the above equation can be rewritten as:

$$C = 2n [2N + (N/n)^2]$$

The optimal value of C can be computed from:

$$\frac{dC}{dn} = 0$$

giving $n = \sqrt{N/2}$ and $C_{opt} = 4N\sqrt{2N}$.

(c)

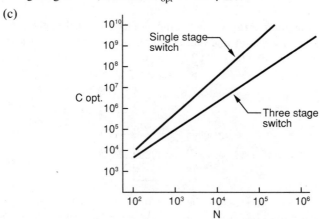

6.12 For two subchannels the guard band of 600 Hz is placed between the channels. For three subchannels, a guard band of 300 Hz is placed inbetween any two subchannels. This not only changes the size of the guard band but also relocates the carrier frequency used to transmit the signals. Since the transmitter and receiver must agree on the modulation technique used, the receiver must be equally agile to track any change in frequency.

6.19

Local echo	Modem loopback	Remote loopback	Characters displayed
off	no	no	0
off	no	yes	1
off	yes	no	1
off	yes	yes	2
on	no	no	1
on	no	yes	2
on	yes	no	2
on	yes	yes	3

7.1 The guests effectively place the order with the cook. The host communicates this order to the clerk who in turn places it with the cook. The phone system with all of its nuances provides the physical means for the order to be transported from one place to the other. The envelope for delivering the services can now be physically identified; the cook gives the pizza to the clerk with the order form, the clerk boxes the pizza with it's delivery address, and the delivery van encloses all of the orders to be delivered. The road taken to deliver the order is immaterial, other than the fact that some path must pre-exist.

7.7 It is assumed that translators cannot be found that can render a translation into a common language and a translator can be found that can act as an intermediary between the two translators. In this communications situation (see diagram), another node needs to be added. Note, however, that the intermediate node handles the message only up to the second level and that a minister's level would serve no purpose.

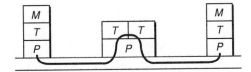

7.12 Peer-to-peer communications occurs between entities at the same level. The physical level does not have a lower layer from where it can request services, but entities at this layer can provide services to each other through their service access points.

7.17

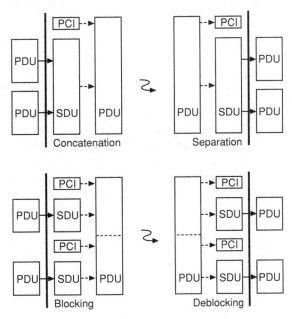

7.18

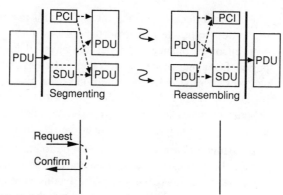

Segmenting ≳ Reassembling

Request

Confirm

(a) Confirms that message has been sent.

Request

Indication

Confirm

(b) Confirms that message has arrived.

Request

Indication

Response

Confirm

(c) Confirms that message has been received.

8.1 For connectionless services, the path between end nodes must be pre-connected so that only the data transfer primitives need be included in the set of commands (see diagram a). This service is exemplified by the message switching technology where messages are transferred among the switching offices towards their destination without explicit connect and disconnect commands. Circuit switching requires the connection-oriented services to connect the point-to-point links before the end nodes start to exchange data and to disconnect them during the clear phase (see diagram b).

(a)

Data transfer

Data.request

Data.indication

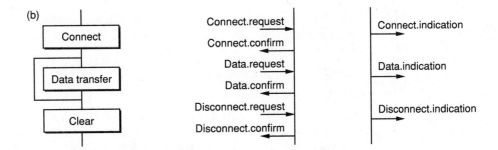

Packet switching has been designed to permit either of these services. Virtual circuit switching provides a dedicated connection between end stations analogous to the connection-oriented service used by circuit switching. Datagrams, on the other hand, use connectionless services to pass the data frames unacknowledged from station to station towards their destination by different paths.

8.2 The line storage for a cable length of 2.5 km would be approximately 216 bits. However, an added delay ensues as the data frames pass through the relay stations connecting the cable segments which accounts for the larger minimum frame size.

8.3 The line storage acts as a buffer for the data frame being communicated. If the line is already busy, then each station will hold any data frame it has ready for transmission until the line is free of other transmissions. The buffers at the individual stations can be looked upon as forming a queue for the communication line. This queueing situation is depicted by two formulas derived in Appendix E; one giving the probability, P_1, that a data frame will be rejected from entering the line if the line is already busy, and the other giving the number of data frames waiting in the waiting line, N_q. The chance of a collision increases when data frames are waiting in the waiting line. A collision effectively decreases μ and therefore increases ρ. This forms a potentially unstable condition. A decrease in ρ increases P_1, which increases N_q, which further decreases P_1 and so on, until ultimately multiple collisions occur that decrease μ even further (see exercise 8.4).

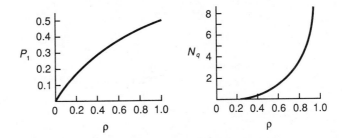

8.4   The worst case scenario occurs when a station backs-off the maximum number of time slots each time an attempt to transmit fails up to 10 attempts, giving a maximum delay of:

$$(2^n - 1)t_{\text{slot time}} = .102 \text{ seconds}$$

for 2036 time slots.

8.8   (a) When station 40 attempts to send the token to station 30, it would listen to hear the line signal that would normally emanate from station 30. After station 40 tries again to pass the token and continues to hear silence, it sends a "who follows 30" control frame. Station 20 would respond to this control frame and reestablish the ring.

(b) When station 30 wants to leave the ring, it waits until it has the token and sends station 40 a "set successor to 20" control frame and passes the token to station 20 before leaving the ring.

8.13   In the token ring access method the active stations are responsible for maintaining the continuity of the line. When a station is removed from the ring the line must be automatically reconnected to preserve its continuity while at the same time it bypasses the station removed from the ring.

9.5   By crossing the circuit wires in a crossover cable, both DTE's are given the impression that they are receiving their signals from a DCE (i.e., modem). The primary wires that must be connected are:

- Ring indicator (CE) with data terminal ready (CD)
- Received line signal detector (CF) with clear to send (CB)
- Transmitted data (BA) with received data (BB)
- Transmitter signal element timing (DA) with receiver signal Element timing (DD)

9.6

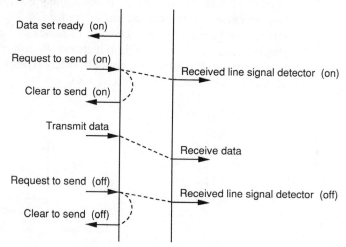

9.8 In the diagram shown, states 16 and 19 can be entered from any state except the ready state (state 1).

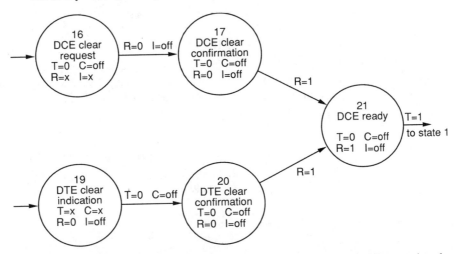

9.9 Refer to Table 9.4. From the ready state (state 1), the DCE can signal an incoming call (state 8) at the same time the DTE is signaling a call request (state 2). In such an event, state 2 and state 8 both make a transition to call collision (state 15) which decides the conflict by abandoning the incoming call and signaling the transition to the proceed-to-select state (state 3). This is the normal transition from the call request state.

9.10

$b_6\ b_5\ b_4$ / $b_3\ b_2\ b_1$	0 0 0	0 0 1	0 1 0	0 1 1	1 0 0	1 0 1	1 1 0	1 1 1
0 0 0	NUL NUL	 BS	DLE DLE	CAN CAN				
0 0 1	SOH SOH	 HT	DC1 DC1	EM EM			SYN 	
0 1 0	STX STX	 LF	DC2 DC2	 SUB			SYN 	
0 1 1	ETX ETX	VT VT	DC3 DC3	 ESC				
1 0 0	 EOT	FF FF	 DC4	IFS FS				DC4
1 0 1	HT ENQ	CR CR	 NAK	IGS GS	LF 	ENQ 		NAK
1 1 0	 ACK	SO SO	BS SYN	IRS RS	ETB 	ACK 		
1 1 1	 BEL	SI SI	 ETB	IUS US	ESC 	BEL 	EOT 	SUB

9.16 Data: 2, 5, 7, 8, 9, 11

Control: 4, 13, 15

Throw-away: 1, 3, 6, 10, 12, 14

9.17 The transmitting machine will insert a 0 after detecting five consecutive 1's. The underlined 0's shown in the following bit sequence simply indicates the inserted 0's in the example. 01110011 1110̲10000 00111100 1111̲10011 1110̲11111 0̲1111110̲100

A.2 $e^{ik\pi/2} = 1$ for $k = 0, 4, 8, \ldots$
$\qquad\qquad\quad i \qquad\quad 1, 5, 9, \ldots$
$\qquad\qquad\; -1 \qquad\quad 2, 6, 10, \ldots$
$\qquad\qquad\; -i \qquad\quad 3, 7, 11, \ldots$

A.4 (a) $e^{i\theta} = \cos\theta + i\,\sin\theta$
$\qquad\; e^{-i\theta} = \cos\theta - i\,\sin\theta$

Adding these equations gives equation A.12a and subtracting them gives equation A.12b.

(b) $e^{i(a+b)} = e^{ia}e^{ib}$
$\cos (a + b) + i \sin (a + b) = (\cos a + i \sin a)(\cos b + i \sin b) =$
$(\cos a \cos b - \sin a \sin b) + i (\sin a \cos b + \cos a \sin b)$

Therefore

$\sin (a + b) = \sin a \cos b + \cos a \sin b$

A.5 (a) $5 \sin 2\pi t = -5i\,(e^{i2\pi t} - e^{-i2\pi t})/2$
$\qquad\qquad -i = e^{-i\pi/2}$
Therefore

$5 \sin 2\pi t = (5/2)\,[e^{i(2\pi t - \pi/2)} - e^{-i(2\pi t + \pi/2)}]$

(b) $2 \sin t + 3 \cos t = \sqrt{13} \cos^{\,i(t - .588)}$
$\qquad\qquad\qquad\quad = (\sqrt{13}/2)\,[e^{i(t - .588)} + e^{-i(t - .588)}]$

A.8 (b)
$$F(\omega) = \int_{-\infty}^{\infty} f(t)e^{-i\omega t}dt$$
$$= \int_{-1/2}^{0} e^{-i\omega t}dt + \int_{0}^{1/2} e^{-i\omega t}dt$$
$$= (e^{i\omega/2} - e^{-i\omega/2})/i\omega)$$
$$= \sin (\omega/2)/(\omega/2)$$

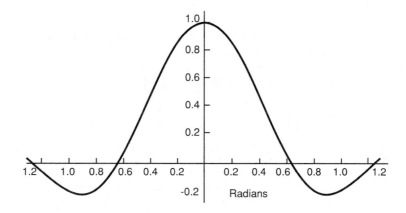

A.9 $\sin \omega t = -i\,(e^{i\omega t} - e^{-i\omega t})/2$
$= (-ie^{i\omega t} + ie^{-i\omega t})/2$
$i = e^{i\pi/2}$
$-i = e^{-i\pi/2}$

Therefore

$$\sin wt = [e^{i(\omega t - \pi/2)} + e^{-i(\omega t - \pi/2)}]/2$$

B.1 The following character set is selected for implementing the four rules of arithmetic.

b_7 b_6 b_5	b_4	b_3	b_2	b_1		
						0 / 0
						1 / 1
						0 / 1
	0	0	0	0		0
	0	0	0	1		1
	0	0	1	0		2
	0	0	1	1		3
	0	1	0	0		4
	0	1	0	1		5
	0	1	1	0		6
	0	1	1	1		7
	1	0	0	0		8
	1	0	0	1		9
	1	0	1	0	*	
	1	0	1	1	+	
	1	1	0	0		
	1	1	0	1	-	=
	1	1	1	0	.	
	1	1	1	1	/	

B.4 Several sets are defined in:

McNamara, John E. *Technical Aspects of Data Communication*. 2nd ed. Bedford, Mass: Digital Press, 1982.

C.1 Using the digits as the symbols of the alphabet gives:

Message	$d=6,$ $r=5$	$d=5,$ $r=3$	$d=4,$ $r=3$	$d=3,$ $r=3$	$d=2,$ $r=2$
m_1	2	3	00	10	111
m_2	3	4	01	11	0000
m_3	4	00	02	12	0001
m_4	5	01	03	20	0010
m_5	00	02	10	21	0011
m_6	01	03	11	22	0100
m_7	02	04	12	000	0101
m_8	03	10	13	001	0110
m_9	04	11	20	002	0111
m_{10}	05	12	21	010	1000
m_{11}	10	13	22	011	1001
m_{12}	11	14	23	012	1010
m_{13}	12	20	30	020	1011
m_{14}	13	21	31	021	1100
m_{15}	14	22	32	022	1101

C.4 $d = 3$, 8 mod 2 = 0, $r = 2$

Using the alphabet A, B and C gives the following code sets:

Message	Set 1	Set 2	Set 3	Set 4
m_1	AA	A	A	A
m_2	AB	B	BB	BB
m_3	AC	CC	BC	BC
m_4	BA	CAA	CA	CA
m_5	BB	CAB	CB	CB
m_6	BC	CAC	CC	CC
m_7	CA	CBA	BAA	BAA
m_8	CB	CBB	BAB	BAB

C.5 The value of n can be expressed by the equation:

$$n = m(d - 1) + n \bmod (d - 1)$$

where m is an integer. Substituting this expression for n into equation C.3; i.e., $r = n - k(d - 1)$, gives:

$$r = (m - k)(d - 1) + n \bmod (d - 1)$$

where $m - k$ is an integer which must satisfy the constraint:

$1 < r \leq d$
   For $n \bmod (d - 1) = 0$ and $m - k = 1$ then $r = d - 1$.
   For $n \bmod (d - 1) = 1$ and $m - k = 1$ then $r = d$.
   For $n \bmod (d - 1) > 1$ and $m - k = 0$ then $r = n \bmod (d - 1)$.

D.1 (a) Network capacity = 3

   (b)

Path	Number of delays
ABEH	3
ACFH	3
ADGH	3

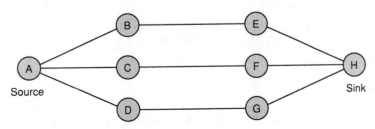

(c) Network capacity = 2

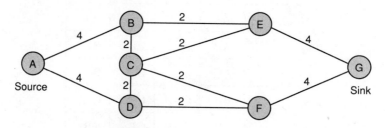

(a) Network capacity = 8

(b)

Path	Number of delays
ABEG	10
ABCEG	12
ABCFG	12
ABCDFG	14
ADFG	10
ADCEG	12
ADCFG	12
ADCBEG	14
ABECFG	14
ABECDFG	16
ADFCEG	14
ADFCBEG	16

(c) Network capacity = 4

D.2 (a) Network capacity = 7

(b) Path ABEI with 2 delays

(c)

Path	Number of delays
ABDGI	3
ACFHI	3
ACDGI	3
ACFGI	3

E.1 From the Poisson distribution:

$$p(k) = \frac{(\lambda T)^k e^{-\lambda T}}{k!}$$

the mean number of arrivals is given by the formula:

$$\sum_{k=0}^{\infty} kp(k) = \lambda Te^{-\lambda T}[1 + (\lambda T)/1! + (\lambda T)^2/2! + (\lambda T)^3/3! + \ldots]$$

The series in the square brackets is equal to $e^{\lambda T}$, therefore:

$$\text{mean number of arrivals} = \lambda Te^{-\lambda T}e^{\lambda T}$$
$$= \lambda T$$

E.2

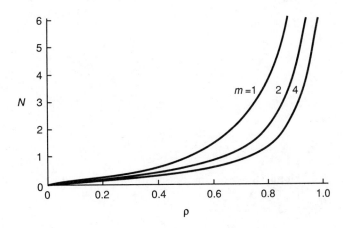

E.3

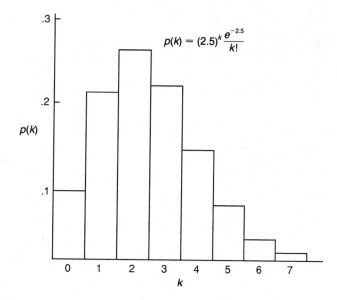

$$p(k) = (2.5)^k \frac{e^{-2.5}}{k!}$$

E.5 The probability of k arrivals from the two independent sources a and b is given by:

$$P(k) = \sum_{i=0}^{k} p_a (i) p_b (k - i)$$

where $p_a(k) = \dfrac{(\lambda_a T)^k e^{-\lambda_a T}}{k!}$ and $p_b(k) = \dfrac{(\lambda_b T)^k e^{-\lambda_b T}}{k!}$

Therefore:

$$p(k) = e^{-\lambda_a T} e^{-\lambda_b T} \left[\frac{(\lambda_b T)^k}{k!} + \frac{(\lambda_a T)(\lambda_b T)^{k-1}}{(k-1)!} + \frac{(\lambda_a T)^2 (\lambda_b T)^{k-2}}{2! (k - 2)!} \right.$$
$$\left. + \frac{(\lambda_a T)^3 (\lambda_b T)^{k-3}}{3! (k-3)!} + \dots + \frac{(\lambda_b T)^k}{k!} \right]$$

Noting the series in the square brackets is the binomial expansion for $[\lambda_a T + \lambda_b T]^k$, then:

$$p(k) = \frac{[(\lambda_a + \lambda_b)T]^k e^{-(\lambda_a + \lambda_b)T}}{k!}$$

E.6

$$p(N + 2) = (1 - \rho)p(N + 1) - \rho p(N)$$
$$p(1) = \rho p(0)$$
$$p(2) = (1 - \rho)p(1) - \rho p(0) = \rho^2 p(0)$$
$$p(3) = (1 - \rho)p(2) - \rho p(1) = \rho^3 p(0)$$

.

.

.

$$p(n) = (1 - \rho)p(n - 1) - \rho p(n) = \rho^n p(0)$$
$$\sum_{N=0}^{\infty} p(N) = 1$$
$$p(0) (1 + \rho + \rho^2 + \rho^3 + \dots) = 1$$
$$p(0)/(1 - \rho) = 1 \text{ and therefore } p(0) = 1 - \rho$$
$$p(N) = (1 - \rho)\rho^N$$
$$\overline{N} = \sum_{N=0}^{\infty} Np (N)$$
$$= (1 - \rho) (\rho + 2\rho^2 + 3\rho^3 + \dots)$$
$$= (1 - \rho)\rho/(1 - \rho)^2$$
$$= \rho/(1 - \rho)$$

E.9 $\lambda = 100$

$\mu = 40$

$\overline{N}_s = m\rho = \dfrac{100}{40} = 2.5$ (number of packets being served)

$\overline{N} = \beta\rho/(1 - \rho) + m\rho$

$\rho = 2.5/3$ and $\beta = .75$ (from figure E.5)

$\overline{N} = 6.25$ (number of packets waiting and being served)

E.10 $\lambda = 2$

$\mu = 3$

$\rho = 2/3$

$p(N \leq 5) = 1 - \rho^6 = .9122$

E.11 $\overline{N} = \dfrac{\beta\rho}{(1 - \rho)} + m\rho$

For single server queue, $m = 1$ and $\beta = \rho$ (i.e., ρ is the probability that the server is busy), then:

$\overline{N} = \dfrac{\rho^2}{(1 - \rho)} + \rho = \dfrac{\rho}{(1 - \rho)}$

E.13

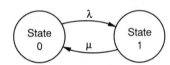

$\mu p(1) = \lambda p(0)$

$p(1) = \rho p(0)$

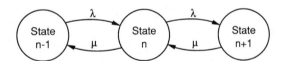

$\mu p(n + 1) + \lambda p(n - 1) = (\mu + \lambda)p(n)$

$p(n + 1) - (1 + \rho)p(n) + \rho p(n - 1) = 0$

E.14 Following the derivation in exercise E.6:

$$p(n) = \rho^n p(0)$$

$$\sum_{i=0}^{N} p(i) = 1$$

$$p(0)(1 + \rho + \rho^2 + \rho^3 + \ldots + \rho^N) = 1$$

$$(1 + \rho + \rho^2 + \rho^3 + \ldots + \rho^N) = (1 - \rho^{N+1})/(1 - \rho)$$

$$p(0) = (1 - \rho)/(1 - \rho^{N+1})$$

$$p(N) = (1 - \rho)\rho^N/(1 - \rho^{N+1})$$

E.15 $\rho/(1 + \rho) = 1/5$
$$\rho = 1/4$$

If the buffer space is doubled then the probability of a message being blocked from the system is:

$$\rho^2/(1 + \rho + \rho^2) = 1/21$$

The increase in workload for the system to degrade to its previous blocking level is:

$$\rho^2/(1 + \rho + \rho^2) = 1/5$$
$$4\rho^2 - \rho - 1 = 0$$
$$\rho = .64$$

INDEX

INDEX